PROTEST, POLITICS, AND PROSPERITY

Black Americans and
White Institutions, 1940–75

PROTEST, POLITICS, AND PROSPERITY

Black Americans and White Institutions, 1940-75

by Dorothy K. Newman, Nancy J. Amidei,
Barbara L. Carter, Dawn Day,
William J. Kruvant, Jack S. Russell

PANTHEON BOOKS
New York

Library of Congress Cataloging in Publication Data

Main entry under title:

Protest, Politics, and Prosperity.

   Includes bibliographical references and index.
   1. Afro-Americans—Economics conditions. 2. Afro-Americans—Employment. 3. Afro-Americans—Housing.
4. Afro-Americans—Health and hygiene. I. Newman, Dorothy Krall.
II. Title.
E185.8.P7   301.45′19′6073   77–5191
ISBN 0–394–41202–8
ISBN 0–394–73448–3 pbk.

Manufactured in the United States of America

First Edition

Grateful acknowledgment is made to Chappell & Co., Inc., for permission to reprint the excerpt from "I Got Plenty o' Nothin'" by George Gershwin on page 236. Copyright 1935 by Gershwin Publishing Corporation. Copyright Renewed, assigned to Chappell & Co., Inc. International Copyright Secured. All rights reserved. Used by permission.

Preface

We set out to write a book that would be of interest to the general public and would use selected examples from this country's social and economic institutions to analyze how black Americans make progress or are thwarted in achieving it. We chose the historical perspective from 1940 both because the seminal work, Gunnar Myrdal's *An American Dilemma,* stopped about that time, and because we thought that three and a half decades provided a necessary perspective for understanding the course of social change.

We have been a closely knit team, with differing disciplines and expertise. Every chapter is the work of all or several of us. None is the work solely of one author. All of the book has benefited from insights and suggestions from each of us. Our contributions are more in substantive areas than by chapter.

For instance, Barbara L. Carter undertook the extensive historical research on black protest and wrote all the sections in each chapter concerning it. We could not have managed without her insights and her experience in the civil rights movement. William J. Kruvant was our statistical and economics consultant throughout the course of our work and, as such, made substantial contributions to all the chapters. He did the intensive research required for and wrote "But Not Next Door" (Chapter 5). He also wrote most of "Making Do" (Chapter 7). Dawn Day contributed to the methodology in two of the chapters on employment, "Unequal Employment Opportunity" (Chapter 2) and "Learning Without Earning" (Chapter 3), assisted in the analytical phases of the chapter about "Uncle Sam As Employer" (Chapter 4), and in the welfare sections of "Making Do" (Chapter 7), besides preparing a large proportion of the material used in the chapter on "Second-Class Medicine" (Chapter 6). Jack S.

Russell did all of the research for "Uncle Sam As Employer" (Chapter 4) and much of the analysis and writing. He also contributed to the research and analysis for "Second-Class Medicine."

I directed the study as a whole, with the assistance of Barbara Carter, whose wisdom in administration and competence in sociology benefited us all throughout our work together. I am responsible chiefly for "Unequal Employment Opportunity" (Chapter 2) and "Learning Without Earning" (Chapter 3), and the part in "Making A Difference" (Chapter 1) that discusses the significance of the economy in the struggle for equality.

Nancy J. Amidei performed in two significant roles. As an expert in health, welfare, and social security programs, she wrote most of the chapter on "Second-Class Medicine" (Chapter 6) and those parts of "Making Do" (Chapter 7) dealing with social and welfare programs. And, if the book has any merit as being interesting reading and well written, Ms. Amidei is responsible. Her broad understanding of all of the materials gave a special dimension to her ability to translate sometimes dull prose into an absorbing story. This is not to depreciate the quality of the content or the writing style of the other authors, but to praise especially the creativity of the one who made it all fit together.

Whatever my contribution may have been, it was made better and direction of the work easier because of the teamwork, scholarship, and integrity of my coauthors. As one of us so often likes to say, "The whole is greater than the parts," and that was the case. I am deeply grateful for their assistance in all ways, and especially for that wellspring of generosity and good fellowship that is rare in so many, working so hard together, for so long.

We could not have survived without a quality support staff. Most important of all was our librarian, Carl R. Kessler, who contributed immeasurably to the breadth and depth of the research we could do within our limited time frame. He could come up magically with just the right sources at the right time. We owe the comprehensiveness and accuracy of our documentation to him. William R. Beachy and Deborah C. Vincent undertook a wide variety of research tasks using substantial initiative. Ms. Vincent was responsible for the important task of checking the text for substantive accuracy. Ms. Vincent, Kathryn S. Bardsley, Joanne C. Bullard, Stephen H. Cornwell, Sheila A. Edwards, G. Regina Nixon, and Lillian Silverberg performed the statistical work required to produce our quantitative results that are summarized in the tables and text. Back of these summaries are stacks of work tables, checked and rechecked, and more stacks of computer printouts. We depended on Lillian Silverberg for the many administrative tasks so important for efficient performance.

Among those outside of our immediate group who helped us to think more clearly and improve our product were Bernard E. Anderson, Leslie W. Dunbar, James C. Evans, Robert B. Hill, Anthony W. Hudson, Alfred McClung Lee, Richard J. Margolis, Ann R. Miller, Bradley R. Schiller, Alvin L. Schorr, Conrad E. Snowden, and Lloyd Street. Any mistakes or errors in judgment are solely our responsibility.

We owe a great deal to those many unnamed "bureaucrats," so often maligned, but except for whom we would have had few facts and fewer figures. Economists, social scientists, statisticians, and librarians in the federal government answered our numerous questions and requests for data promptly, efficiently, graciously, and with the kind of judgment that exhibits a high quality of expertise.

We are especially indebted to Alan Pifer, President of Carnegie Corporation of New York, and to the Carnegie staff who encouraged us in our work, gave us generous support, and assisted us administratively in many helpful ways.

We are most deeply grateful to James Dyer, of Carnegie Corporation of New York, who was our mentor throughout, always honestly critical, never praising if it was not due, but always encouraging and supportive. His special insights and knowledgeable comments during these past two years have made our product better and our task lighter.

DOROTHY K. NEWMAN

With the consent of:
NANCY J. AMIDEI
BARBARA L. CARTER
DAWN DAY
WILLIAM J. KRUVANT
JACK S. RUSSELL

Contents

6 Second-Class Medicine   **187**

7 Making Do   **236**

Figures

Tables

PROTEST, POLITICS, AND PROSPERITY

Black Americans and
White Institutions, 1940–75

1

Making a Difference

ON A WARM DAY in 1946, a black soldier named Isaac Woodard began making his way from an army camp in Georgia to his home in North Carolina. He had served three years—fifteen months in the jungles of the South Pacific—and he was very glad to be going home. During the long bus ride, he asked to use the restroom at one stop, only to be cursed out by the driver for having taken too long. Later, at a stop somewhere in South Carolina, the driver asked the chief of police to arrest Woodard for being drunk and disorderly. When Woodard protested—he'd been neither—he was cruelly beaten by the police chief, first with a blackjack, and then with a nightstick used so viciously that he was blinded in both eyes. After a night in jail without food or medical care, he was fined fifty dollars and costs, more money than he had, and seen by a doctor only when the condition of his eyes became so bad that the officers of the court became alarmed. The army doctors who examined him found the corneas of both eyes injured beyond repair.

The brutal police chief was eventually found, indicted, tried, and acquitted—to the cheers of a crowded courtroom. A local jury absolved the bus company from any responsibility. And the army in which he'd served, though holding a discharged veteran subject to army discipline until midnight of the day of discharge, refused Woodard a pension on the ground that his disability was not incurred while in service.[1]

Isaac Woodard's story is in some sense the story of all black Americans in the forties, for although not everyone met with the same debilitating brutality as Woodard, the possibility was there for all. No matter how well-mannered or respectable, no matter that he wore the uniform of one who had fought to protect his country, no matter that he had done nothing wrong, Isaac Woodard's only crime was being black. And that was something he shared with them all.

In those days three out of four black Americans still lived in the South, but North or South virtually the only jobs open to them were the most menial: over half of all black workers were employed in agriculture or personal service.[2] How much education a black man or woman might have meant little; skilled jobs involving contact with white workers were simply not available. Such jobs as blacks could get paid scarcely human wages: long days at stoop labor sometimes brought $3 or less a week, sunup to sundown; domestic work little more.[3] Black children went to schools that were open fewer days each year (to free them for field work during picking seasons), and black adults could still expect to be beaten or fired from their jobs for attempting to register to vote.[4] Ordinary life was conditioned by discrimination: separate parks, separate water fountains, separate lines and waiting rooms, separate sections of the bus or train. One wartime munitions factory in St. Louis went so far as to build a separate factory for black workers; elsewhere, places that did hire black secretaries or clerks hid them behind partitions.

"No colored need apply." "Whites only." "Negroes served in back." America had its own version of apartheid. In the South the signs were everywhere and a matter of law; in the North they were not common except in want ads, and a matter of custom rather than law, but the effect was similar. Black and white everywhere shared the same geographical space while living in different worlds. Black accident victims would bleed to death before white hospitals would treat them. White restaurants would serve German prisoners-of-war inside, while black American soldiers were made to stay, unfed, outside.[5] Municipal services were skimped in black neighborhoods which, if patrolled at all, were patrolled by white police. To be black was tantamount to being marked for victimization. It is little wonder that black people were more often disabled, more often sick, more often dead in what should have been the prime of life.

Much has changed in the intervening years, and most of the change has been for the better. Isaac Woodard's story would almost certainly have a different ending today, and the old indignities of separate lines and separate drinking fountains are now the exception rather than the rule. That is clear evidence, to be sure, that the old social system, based on the degradation of one race by another, has collapsed. In the daily lives of ordinary black Americans, that alone is a powerful and important change.

If the recital of change could end at this point, with an acknowledgment of the passing of the old social order, we might all retire, content. Unfortunately, any recounting of the changes that have taken place must be followed by the single word "but." Having recognized how important it is that we can eat at the same lunch counter, ride in the same buses, work in the same factories, get the same kinds of education, and be treated in the same hospitals, we still must go on to say, "but discrimination remains." Americans continue to notice the color of a person's skin and in a variety of ways adapt the things that are said and done to that one fact. What has happened to reduce the force of discrimination, and how much of it remains, is the story of this book.

Because ours is a majority white society, this is by implication a book about white people and the institutions they have built. White Americans, by sheer force of numbers, determine how things will be for others as long as they act *as white people* who are somehow different from others who are not. We will know that color is no longer relevant only when the good and bad that this country has to offer fall on black and white with equally random abandon, when white is as likely as black to be unemployed, be in charge of the unemployment office, or be the owner of the company.

Until then we must be concerned with what has happened to black people in good times and bad, and the workings of discrimination in many of its forms. And so this is also a book about black people: black people's rights in white institutional arrangements; black people's lives as the workings of white society determine them; black people as they have struggled to win their rights and shape their destinies.

The Economy

Among the most important forces for greater equality is one over which blacks have little control: the economy. Yet how the economy fares—whether it is healthy and expanding or troubled and constricted—has been critical for black jobs and opportunities. A growing economy means that more jobs will be available for everyone, including black workers; that if a household head is steadily employed the family's teenage sons and daughters will not need to leave school in order to work; that women will have a better chance of finding work; and that more money will be collected in tax revenues

for meeting public needs. Yet, the usual indices of a healthy economy
—more housing starts, new car sales, increased consumer-goods
sales—only tell us that someone is buying houses and cars and
dishwashers, not that black families are able to. The new cars in the
garages of white households don't automatically lead to new jobs for
black workers on the assembly lines of Detroit or in the gas stations
of Milwaukee. In fact, national prosperity has not meant as many
jobs or as high income for black workers as for white workers.

The big events in the life of our national economy are the recessions and booms. Between 1940 and 1975, those periods have tended
to be closely though not exclusively related to peace or war. Prosperity has special properties during wartime, for then production soars
to unusual heights and workers on the home front are in especially
short supply. Black workers gain significantly then because they are
given a better chance at the kinds of jobs that had previously been
closed to them—but not an equal chance. In only four years since
1948 have even the lowest unemployment rates among blacks been
lower than the highest unemployment rates among whites. In nineteen of those years black unemployment was over 8 percent, a rate
never reached by white workers. Just relying on the workings of the
economy, even when it is performing at its height, has only brought
black unemployment down to the worst rates tolerated for whites in
the worst of economic conditions.

As charted by the Gross National Product (GNP) alone, our
recessions during the thirty-five years from 1940 to 1975 appear
short and relatively mild. The American economy was moving on a
generally upward course. For all that the occasional dips have been
real and felt on Madison Avenue as surely as in Bedford-Stuyvesant
or Hough or Watts, for most white Americans it was a largely
prosperous time. Average white family incomes scarcely faltered in
a virtually steady climb upward. Black family incomes increased too,
but on a more zig-zag course. The ratio of black to white income rose
only for short periods, dropping frequently, so that from 1947 to
1975 it gained only a sparse 11 points, going from 51 percent of the
white average, to a mere 62 percent. Incomes remain lower for black
families than for white families who are otherwise like each other.
Earnings still tend to be less for blacks of similar age and background
holding similar kinds of jobs. Higher education, particularly post-
graduate education, goes a long way to bridge the gap, but even that
does not always close it.

Employment is at the root of the gap in incomes between the races, because black people, even more than white, derive almost all their income from earnings, and most other income from sources whose amounts are pegged to how much the earnings were—that is, Social Security and unemployment insurance. Few get much if any income from property. But employment equality remains elusive, even at the height of prosperity. A fast rate of economic growth has been what is often called a "necessary but not a sufficient condition" for gains in employment equality. That is because economic growth by itself does not eliminate the one condition most basic to black employment prospects: discrimination in the job market.

Employment discrimination is clearly demonstrated when we see that black workers are far less likely than white to be employed in jobs that require no prior training and special skills; when they are last to be put on even when labor is desperately needed; and when they must agitate for work even in wartime. Then when the job market eases, they are the first to be let go, whatever their age or education, and whatever the line of work. Discrimination is demonstrated further when black workers who have achieved the specified qualifications for particular jobs are less likely than whites, qualified or not, to get the positions or to move up the occupational ladder. Discrimination has been the creator of Fair Employment Practices Commissions and laws by making them necessary in the first place. The puny powers of those agencies or laws, either in the states or the federal government, reveal the ambivalence of a society that would protect equal rights while withholding the means for accomplishing them.

It is significant that the Congressional Black Caucus is one of the main supports of full employment legislation and other measures designed to ensure blacks their share of jobs whatever the state of the economy. They know the power of discrimination in the job market. For blacks, public policies whose goal is full employment are crucial. Such policies would deal directly with carefully measured and regularly acknowledged differences in unemployment between the races —differences which have never seemed to count for much at the economic conference table.

Public Policy and Black Employment

Public policymakers have long been aware of the importance of jobs, but jobs have not been the first priority of public economic policy since the forties. Presidents Roosevelt and Truman had good reason to be mindful of the Great Depression of the thirties and the economic dislocation expected with the end of the war, and they were at least willing to adopt full employment as a goal. During the wartime boom, it seemed a reasonable one. The initial draft of the 1946 Employment Act[6] asserted: "All Americans able to work and seeking work have the *right* to useful, remunerative, regular, and *full-time employment*"[7] (italics added). As finally passed in 1946,[8] the law committed the federal government only to act

> consistent with its needs and obligations . . . to coordinate and utilize all its . . . resources . . . *in a manner calculated to foster and promote free competitive enterprise and the general welfare,* conditions under which there will be afforded useful employment . . . for those able, willing, and seeking work, *and to promote maximum employment, production, and purchasing power.*[9] (Italics added)

It is not hard to see how these words can be as easily interpreted to support a policy of decreased spending to induce lower prices, as one of increased spending to provide jobs. Every administration since then has taken the position "that the Government should conduct its economic affairs in a manner which would promote both reasonably full employment and relatively stable prices."[10] If anything, government policy since 1946 has leaned heavily in favor of protecting purchasing power or the value of dollars that people already had, rather than providing the opportunity to earn them.

In spite of the hardships faced by black workers, especially during the late fifties, economic policy until the sixties was highly restrictive. By 1958 black unemployment was a staggering 12.6 percent, while the administration in office busily pursued a goal of balancing the budget. The more stimulative policies of the early sixties—government spending, budget deficits, decreased taxes—helped revive the economy in general.[11] Nevertheless black unemployment remained "double digit" until the Vietnam War spending and the cumulative effect of earlier policies could take hold.

The mid-sixties were in many respects the best of economic times. The growth rate of the GNP was well above average, prices were rising only modestly, corporate profits were increasing by leaps and bounds, and family incomes were going up. Yet under those favorable economic conditions the gap between black and white incomes only decreased; it never disappeared. The black unemployment rate fell only to 6.4 percent in 1968, when white unemployment was well below 4 percent, and black incomes did not rise to even two-thirds of the incomes of whites.

That period brought better times for many but not good times for all. To a large degree economic policy was organized around the idea that if unemployment declined "too much" prices would rise "too much." There was even supposed to be a mathematical relationship between the two, incorporated in a theory called the Phillips Curve,[12] which has held American economic policymakers in thrall ever since.[13] As a result, our policy has kept the unemployment rate from falling as much as it could have to avoid a projected or estimated rise in prices.

From the mid-sixties into the seventies, the Phillips Curve theory encouraged policymakers to keep redefining full employment, instead of fighting on both fronts: against unemployment as well as inflation within a coordinated economic policy.[14] The full-employment goal crept up from 3 percent to an interim target of 4 percent in the Kennedy and Johnson years and went up to 5 percent in 1974 under President Nixon. The 1974 Annual Report of the Council of Economic Advisers reads:

> Last year we described "maximum employment," which is the goal specified in the Employment Act, as a "condition in which persons who want work and seek it realistically on reasonable terms can find employment." We believe that condition was approximately met in 1973, even though the average unemployment rate was 4.9 percent rather than 4.0 percent which conventionally defines full employment.[15]

Since blacks' unemployment rate is typically about twice as high as that of whites, redefinition of full employment for the whole economy from 3 to 5 percent means that "full employment" unemployment for blacks will rise from 6 to 10 percent—depression levels.

Thus, black workers have never received the full benefits of prosperity. Their employment opportunities routinely gave way to the perennial fight against inflation before being caught up in the still more devastating recession of the middle seventies.

In the face of a 14 percent black unemployment rate, and even higher rates in central cities, President Ford could say, "We may have to suffer for a short period of time higher unemployment than we like."[16] His black listeners knew all too well who was meant by "we."

Had official economic policies since 1946 defined a healthy economy as one of full employment, the job of combatting discrimination would have been far easier. If official policy had embraced both a commitment to full employment and the eradication of discrimination, the gap between black and white might have closed. But since these actions do not occur spontaneously, black struggle for full employment and equal opportunity must continue.

The Black Struggle

Because black people have not been in a position to control American economic policy, they have had to use whatever leverage they could to bend policy decisions to their advantage: demonstrations, lobbying, group pressure, court action, electoral politics, and any other weapon at their command. What has redounded to the benefit of blacks in good times has not been eagerly handed over; it had to be wrested from an unwilling white majority. What has been retained during downturns has been fiercely contested. That has been central to much of the struggle in every area of life.

When black votes were clearly of value to presidents and other politicians, blacks used that fact to win concessions. When none of the traditional mechanisms of politics or law were possible or equitably applied, less traditional forms of pressure would be brought—at lunch counters, on picketlines, in the streets—singly or in groups, even when jail would be the outcome. Blacks have been willing to go the nontraditional route from necessity more than choice.

If there were no discrimination, no resistance to fulfilling the American ideal of equality, there would be no need for protest. Instead, every step in civil rights progress has been preceded by negotiation, exhortation, and often tortuous controversy. The unrelenting efforts from 1940 to the present have been necessary just to realize at last the promises of Reconstruction. Protest and the struggle within the polity and economy have not always been successful, but they account for much of the progress that has been made.

Politics and economic policies do not spontaneously favor minorities nor do they operate from altruistic motives.

The Struggle in the 1940s

In 1940 separation of the races was written into law or was a matter of strict etiquette. Either way, it was almost total in the South and practiced extensively in the North. The United States military establishment and federal government offices were segregated, as were churches, theaters, buses, railroad stations, hotels, restrooms, public libraries, parks, playgrounds, museums, soda fountains, restaurants, taxicabs, laundromats, funeral homes and hearses, beauty parlors, barbershops, golf courses, retail stores, public beaches, cemeteries, and countless other places. Even by September 1949,[17] only eighteen states had outlawed discrimination in places of public accommodation, and those laws were limited in application, usually to fewer than five kinds of public places where segregation might be found.[18] On the other hand, most states in 1949 specifically authorized or required one or more various forms of segregation relating to intermarriage, transportation, public accommodations, public schools, colleges, or universities. The specific requirements for segregated facilities were numerous, including separate textbooks, libraries, places of work, toilets, homes for the aged or for orphans, sports contests, voting booths, fraternal orders, and even telephone booths.

The most prominent action against discrimination in the 1940s was the threatened march on Washington for equal employment opportunity which A. Philip Randolph[19] organized at the start of World War II. When the mobilization for the war began and blacks were excluded both from the war-related jobs, and from full participation in the armed services, jobs became the focus of the black press, the NAACP, and the National Urban League, plus a host of organizations and individual black people in virtually every town and city.[20]

"Appeal after appeal," wrote Walter White of the NAACP, "was made to Washington with little tangible result. Conference after conference was held, and nothing happened. . . . Discontent and bitterness were growing like wildfire among Negroes all over the country."[21] So Randolph put out a call across the country, urging aroused and bitter black Americans to march on Washington and demand their right to wartime jobs. The major black organizations all joined in. Not just an isolated action but a March on Washington

Movement was born, to demand nothing less than a presidential order ending discrimination in employment.

Franklin Roosevelt was not easily bent. It was only when his wife, his emissaries, and his own considerable personal charm had failed to dissuade the black leaders, and the possibility of 100,000 blacks marching on Washington loomed large, that he gave in.[22] So many angry black Americans was no small threat in still-segregated Washington, D.C. The marchers would have few drinking fountains or washrooms near the White House to use, few restaurants that would serve them food, and virtually no hotels where they might stay the night. Mr. Roosevelt had good reason to want the march called off, and so he issued Executive Order 8802,[23] creating the first Committee on Fair Employment Practice (FEPC). Under that order all money let in federal contracts would be awarded only to those who would hire black and white workers on an equal basis.

Executive Order 8802 marked the first positive presidential action taken in direct response to organized black protest, but it proved only a beginning. As had happened before and would happen again, getting the words on paper was almost the easy part; the hard part came in trying to give life to the paper promises.[24] During the five-year span of the FEPC, blacks filed nearly 14,000 complaints against continued discrimination.[25]

The FEPC was not always successful in settling complaints and enforcement was weak. Twenty-six of the thirty-five nondiscrimination compliance orders issued to employers in a single year simply went unheeded, and nine of the ten unions cited for discrimination refused to comply with FEPC directives.[26] Some things were too big for the "toothless tiger" that was the FEPC. Between March 1 and May 31, 1943, white workers cost the country nearly 2.5 million man-hours, representing 102,000 man-days of war production time, through hate strikes directed against the employment or upgrading of black workers.[27]

Early in the war, blacks in the North organized local demonstrations and pickets to dramatize the irony of their exclusion from a war against Nazi racism. As labor shortages increased and FEPC hearings and investigations persisted alongside picketlines and demonstrations, companies and unions gradually began to relax their exclusionary and discriminatory policies. Typical was the case of J. H. Kindelberger, president of North American Aviation, who said in 1941 that it was against company policy to hire blacks as aircraft mechanics and workers. After a year of sustained demonstrations by

Kansas City blacks, North American Aviation gave in. Other employers were soon following suit, though not enthusiastically.[28] Black workers lodged complaints against railroad companies and railway unions; against Washington-based government agencies that refused to recruit or promote black workers; against munitions factories and tractor plants that produced war weapons and machinery but excluded blacks; against northern foundries and southern steel mills, western aircraft industries and southern shipyards, and countless other industries that discriminated against blacks.[29]

The executive order, the persuasion powers of the FEPC, the continuing struggle of black organizations and individuals, and above all, the urgent need for workers converged to promote expansion in the range and quality of jobs for which blacks were hired. Blacks gained significantly relative to whites during the war, but again, lost relative to whites after the war, when white workers were not laid off or demoted as much as blacks. It took the Korean conflict to push the relative black occupational position up another few notches.

At the same time that the jobs struggle was taking place, events in the political arena took on significance, first to get the ballot itself, and then, using it, to advance black progress on various fronts.

In a democracy voting is a key to the political process, and having the good will of a handful of sympathetic whites in 1940 —however committed or courageous they may have been—in no way compared to having black hands on the levers of electoral power and local politics. That fact was not lost on either civil rights workers or their opponents. Black activists and their white allies brought the issue of southern white primaries into the courts long before the early forties, and the white political structure used ever more ingenious ways to circumvent blacks who wished to exercise the right to vote.[30] An important victory came in 1944 when the Supreme Court ruled in *Smith v. Allwright*[31] that excluding blacks from voting in the Democratic primaries of the solid Democratic South was unconstitutional because it infringed on their fundamental right to vote.

Both *Smith v. Allwright* and growing attention paid to black voters inspired recalcitrant southerners to new heights of resistance; violence and the intimidation of black voters increased. Arkansas barred blacks from state elections altogether; Alabama required potential voters to explain the Constitution; some states adopted "qua-

lification" standards used to bar blacks from voting; and Mississippi's Senator Theodore Bilbo, a "virulent racist," "urged whites to
employ any means to bar Negroes from voting."[32] Despite these
actions, by 1952 black voter registration campaigns were having an
effect; nearly 1.2 million blacks were registered to vote in the South,
close to double the number (750,000) just four years before.[33]

Black voting power was being felt for the first time since Reconstruction. Even before the white primary fight was won in 1944, both
Roosevelt and Willkie directed their 1944 campaigns at black wards
in the North and made promises related to black issues;[34] both parties
actively wooed the black vote again in 1948.[35] But the events surrounding the election of 1948 proved far more significant, and heavily underscored the rising influence of black voting power.

During the closely contested 1948 campaign, President Truman
made what was then a strong civil rights stand. Threatened with
organized black resistance to continued service in a Jim Crow army,[36]
and recognizing the political implications of the force that might be
unleashed, Truman signed Executive Order 9981,[37] ordering the
desegregation of the armed forces, just three months before the
election. This was a landmark. But, in addition, Truman ran his 1948
campaign with an open and calculated appeal for black votes. In the
two years before the election alone: he delivered a special civil rights
message to Congress around a set of strong civil rights proposals; he
insisted on a strong civil rights plank in the Democratic platform (the
actual precipitating cause for the Dixiecrat walkout); he agreed to
the first Department of Justice involvement on the side of black
plaintiffs in a Supreme Court case;[38] he ordered creation of a Fair
Employment Board; and he asked Congress for a permanent Civil
Rights Commission. Concentrating his last days of campaigning on
the key industrial states of the North, Truman gave a series of
impassioned pro–civil rights speeches. Winding up in Harlem—the
first president to talk there—he pledged himself to the fight for equal
rights. On election day, two-thirds of the blacks voting voted for
Truman, giving him the victory.[39] Presidential power had responded
to black power.

The Struggle in the 1950s

The struggle in the 1950s was dominated by two powerful civil rights
strategies. One was very old; the other was new and had a dramatic
form. The first is exemplified by a series of lawsuits begun in 1938

that finally resulted in outlawing racial segregation in education in 1954. The second, mass nonviolent protest began with the Montgomery, Alabama, bus boycott led by Martin Luther King, Jr., in 1955. That boycott was the most important precursor of the mass protests of the sixties, and tested both the tactics and some of the leaders of those later events.

The legal strategy was primarily southern in its focus and directed by the NAACP against the legally couched but blatantly discriminatory practices and policies that resulted in denial of the vote, of equal education, of equal access to public transportation and a host of other public accommodations. In case after case over the years, the NAACP waged the struggle before the state and federal courts to establish the legal rights of black Americans.

The most important legal battle, the one that was to mark the end of Jim Crow segregation in the South, arose in the field of education. The historic 1954 Supreme Court decision in *Brown v. Board of Education*[40] was itself no lucky accident, but the product of a systematic and carefully orchestrated legal assault carried out over twenty years by the NAACP.[41]

Between 1938 and 1954, the NAACP argued five higher education cases before the Supreme Court.[42] Part of a strategy that was first articulated in 1934, all of them systematically whittled away at "separate but equal" until little remained of that once-powerful tenet.[43] By the time that the NAACP came before the Supreme Court to argue the cases that combined as *Brown v. Board of Education,*[44] there was nothing left for the Court to do but rule as it did. It had conceded too many other points in all of the cases that had come before.[45]

The May 17, 1954 Supreme Court ruling that state-instituted "separate but equal" public educational facilities are "inherently unequal" was a dramatic blow not only to the dual school system but to the whole of the legally structured system of Jim Crow segregation in the South. It was immediately recognized as such by black and white Americans alike. With it the "separate but equal" doctrine that had governed the lives of black Americans in the South for almost sixty years was struck down. That doctrine had provided legal justification, in a nation ruled by law, for keeping black Americans in the worst schools, at the back of the bus, away from lunch counters, and out of the mainstream of American society.

However, it soon became clear to black Americans in the South that the legal battles won by the NAACP would become living realities only when blacks took a more direct hand in exercising the legal rights they had won. The first thrust toward direct action needed to make the accumulated legal rights of black Americans meaningful came in 1955–56 when the black population of Montgomery, Alabama, were successful in a boycott to end segregation on the city's buses under the direction of the youthful Dr. Martin Luther King, Jr. The boycott to protest against the indignities suffered on Montgomery's buses was intended for one day, and began when Rosa Parks, former state secretary of the Alabama chapter of the NAACP, was arrested for refusing to give her seat to a white rider who boarded after she had. The boycott lasted for an entire year, and became a full-fledged movement that integrated the racially segregated bus company of Montgomery. More significantly, it foreshadowed a new era.[46]

In the North, where "separate but equal" had never had the force of a legal doctrine, the struggle for jobs remained a central issue throughout the postwar period. It was spearheaded by a mixed coalition of civil rights, labor, religious, and civic groups, today known as the Leadership Conference on Civil Rights, that had come into being to fight for FEPC legislation.[47] In 1950 the NAACP organized a minimarch on Washington with the support of some sixty organizations making up the new civil rights coalition. The march was a sign of the growing black organizing power. More than 4,000 delegates from thirty-three states came to Washington to lobby Congress on behalf of the civil rights issues of the North and South. For the South, the coalition sought antilynching laws and voting rights legislation. For the North, it sought permanent fair employment practices legislation.[48]

FEPC legislation passed the House in 1950 but failed to make it through the Senate. Local chapters organized to press the issue in state legislatures. Between 1945 and 1958, sixteen states passed fair employment practices legislation with enforcement provisions, and several others enacted FEPCs that relied on voluntary compliance.[49] Using symbolic action as well, in 1951 the civil rights forces held a tenth anniversary service for the wartime FEPC at the grave of President Roosevelt. This public event, some think, helped convince President Truman to establish a Committee on Government Contract Compliance, which would oversee fair employment practices in federally supported production contracts.[50]

The struggle for jobs enlisted almost all the civil rights forces.

Randolph, the NAACP, the Urban League, and various local black labor groups all called for an end to discrimination by employers and unions. The NAACP went to court against both employers and organized labor, while both the NAACP and the Urban League issued periodic reports on the status of blacks in industry and labor unions. Within labor itself, A. Philip Randolph and black labor caucuses waged battle against discriminatory union practices and policies.[51]

The fifties were years of more lip service than action on the part of politicians. Yet the language of the political platforms in that decade suggests that black voters had become an important part of the political reality. By the fifties it was estimated that the northern black voting concentration

> holds the potential balance of power in seventeen states with 281 votes in the electoral college—fifteen more than the 266 necessary to elect a President.[52]

In 1952 a worried Democratic party needing black votes spelled out fifteen pages of platform pledges along with a summary of their record. They even promised to support legislation "to perfect existing federal civil rights statutes and to strengthen the administrative machinery for the protection of civil rights."[53] The Republicans, for their part, condemned attempts to mislead, exploit, or confuse minority groups for political purposes and expressed the opinion that the federal government ought to oppose discrimination.[54] Dwight D. Eisenhower, Republican, swept into office. Despite his party's pronouncements, no civil rights legislation was able to get past the Congress elected that year.

The 1952 election and the Supreme Court decision in the *Brown* case had brought about some shift of black votes into the Republican column. The 1956 election campaign found the Democrats preoccupied with downplaying the Republicans' part in the *Brown* decision, which had come during a Republican administration. The Republicans reiterated their civil rights record while expressing reservations about their responsibility for implementing school desegregation.[55] Eisenhower was re-elected, again by a landslide. The black vote clearly was not a deciding influence one way or the other.

With the 1956 election over, voting rights legislation that had been actively sought for more than two years was brought up once again.

Lobbying on the issue was intensified within the Congress, while plans were being made for a mass march in Washington in support of it. By summer's end a bill had passed both House and Senate and been signed into law. To win passage, the Civil Rights Act of 1957 —the first civil rights legislation since the nineteenth century—had been stripped of most of its effectiveness, but civil rights advocates recognized the importance of even a symbolic victory.[56] A decade later Roy Wilkins, by then a veteran of all the major civil rights battles, and close observer of all of the administrations since the war, described the Eisenhower years as adversary times, times for dealing with enemies.[57]

The Struggle in the 1960s

The 1960s became a whirlwind of activity in the worlds of ordinary politics and more extraordinary protest. When the 1960 election came around, the Republicans were credited with having sent federal troops into Little Rock, Arkansas, to ensure desegregation of the schools there, in addition to the 1957 Civil Rights Act. Nixon was able to capitalize on the Eisenhower years, and Kennedy was largely unknown to black voters. From the first the election was expected to be a close race, with no clear answers as to how the black vote might go. Nixon lost to Kennedy by fewer than 113,000 votes. The margins in key electoral college states left no mistake about what had put Kennedy in the White House:

Illinois,	a 9,000 vote margin,	a 250,000 black vote;
Michigan,	a 67,000 vote margin,	a 250,000 black vote;
South Carolina,	a 10,000 vote margin,	a 40,000 black vote.[58]

What is widely accepted as decisive to the outcome of the 1960 campaign is John Kennedy's actions when informed that Martin Luther King, Jr., had been jailed on a technical charge and sentenced to four months in a Georgia state prison. After first calling Mrs. King to express his concern, both Kennedy and his brother Robert intervened to get King released from prison. Martin Luther King, Sr., retracted his earlier endorsement of Nixon (who had done nothing upon hearing of the jailing), and other black religious leaders soon followed his lead. Aided by Kennedy's publicists and word of mouth (one million copies of a pamphlet describing Kennedy's role were distributed), black voters everywhere had heard the story by election day.

As one political commentator noted:

> In 1960, Kennedy, his advisers, and most political observers knew the black vote had been responsible for his election to the Presidency. The immediate civil-rights thrust of his administration, with its historic Negro appointments, established this fact.[59]

The new era of massive direct action came to maturity with the outbreak of student-led sit-ins in the South that began in the early spring of 1960. Soon protest touched the lives of virtually every city and town of any size with a black population. Armed only with the technique of nonviolent civil disobedience, the tactics of direct-action protest, and the determination to prevail, black America was on the march. For the rest of the decade they sat-in, boycotted, went on freedom rides and picketlines, and staged massive voter registration campaigns. The struggle was long and bloody. The demonstrators were threatened, hosed, beaten, and maimed; harassed, chased, spied upon, and hunted by dogs; fired from their jobs, driven from their homes, evicted from their land. Above all, they were terrorized for trying to exercise the most fundamental American right, the right to vote like any other citizen.

Black strategists recognized the importance of the voting issue and made it a central thrust of the 1960s struggle. It involved the heroic efforts of many young workers in the Student Nonviolent Coordinating Committee (SNCC), but it depended for its existence, and for the protection of those young workers, on poor, rural, frequently elderly and uneducated southern blacks. These rural blacks protested by giving shelter, by driving the young SNCC workers over back roads late at night, by showing up in countless little churches all across the South to listen to the exhortations of those youngsters that experience told them only could mean trouble. Most of them didn't carry placards or join marches, but they came, and they listened, and they made the protest of the young workers possible. They took risks, sang hymns, and offered prayers. They believed, and supported, and in their own quiet ways protested too. The measure of how much they cared and how deeply the struggle mattered to them can be seen in their homes. Walk into any of them, perhaps especially the poorest of them, and there on the wall, or pasted to the door of a cupboard, beside the high school graduation picture of a daughter or a nephew, is a picture of Martin Luther King, Jr., and in some houses also of John Kennedy and Robert Kennedy. They believed with Reverend

King that it was right for them to feel pride, and dignity, and indignation.

Equally important was the struggle to use public facilities. The wave of protest beginning with the Greensboro lunch-counter sit-in in 1960 dramatized the public accommodations issue. It swept into the black colleges of Atlanta and then spread widely. Black youth especially, with the support of black adults, tried entry into every kind of public place to which blacks had been denied. During 1960, over 50,000 people, mostly black, participated in some kind of demonstration in a hundred cities, and over 3,600 of those demonstrators were put in jail. Sit-ins, freedom rides, wade-ins, and even pray-ins in churches continued through the early sixties. Rising public sympathy for the activists grew not so much in support of what the protestors were demanding as in revulsion against the violent white reaction to peaceful demonstrations that was witnessed on the evening news. Brutal assaults and mass jailings offended the public sense of justice.[60]

In 1963 a massive civil rights March on Washington that included large numbers of white sympathizers capped three years of mass protest. Just a few short years before, such a march would not have been possible, but much had happened in the intervening time. Reverend King's Southern Christian Leadership Conference (SCLC) had moved onto the national stage. The Student Nonviolent Coordinating Committee (SNCC) had built a grassroots movement in the South of local people in small towns and rural areas. The Congress of Racial Equality (CORE), previously based in the North, had gone South to organize freedom rides to desegregate buses and bus terminals. Above all, black people had revealed a wellspring of personal courage which would not easily be overcome. Bayard Rustin, one of the organizers of the 1963 March, wrote that year in *Liberation:*

> . . . children as young as six paraded calmly when dogs, fire hoses and police billies were used against them. Women were knocked to the ground and beaten mercilessly. Thousands of teen-agers stood by at churches throughout the whole country, waiting their turn. . . . Day after day the brutality and arrests went on. And always, in the churches, hundreds of well-disciplined children awaited their turns.[61]

When President Johnson told the Congress that the finest legacy to the assassinated President Kennedy would be passage of civil rights legislation, a new national milestone had been passed. It would be hard to know what counted most in winning the historic Civil

Rights Act that finally passed in 1964—the demonstrations, public reaction to the senseless brutality unleashed on peaceful protestors,[62] the March on Washington, or the presence of sympathetic individuals in high office. But the vote was a solid affirmation that the country might finally be ready to move.

The most visible activity was taking place in the South in the first half of the decade, but the North was by no means quiescent. In the summer of 1962 a Commission on Civil Rights report noted that "agitation against segregation and discrimination Northern style is actively being pursued in 43 cities in 14 Northern and Western states," and that "it is doubtful that any single 18-month period has seen as much intensive activity even in the South." By the fall of 1963 the NAACP reported significant activity was under way in 75 cities in 18 states.[63]

Northern demonstrations focused on housing, employment, and education and peaked before any of the urban riots that first brought national attention to the civil rights struggle outside the South.[64]

It was in Harlem that northern black frustration first boiled over. In July 1964, blacks took to the streets to protest the shooting of a black teenager by an off-duty white policeman. Theirs was not the carefully organized and skillfully articulated protest of the nonviolent movement in the South. This was spontaneous. Harlem was followed by Bedford-Stuyvesant and before the summer was over, by Rochester, New York; Jersey City, Paterson, and Elizabeth, New Jersey; Philadelphia; and a suburb of Chicago. Then, in the summer of 1965, came Watts, the seven-day Los Angeles rebellion that left hundreds of millions of dollars worth of damage, 34 dead, and 856 injured. Street rebellions continued through the summers of 1966, 1967, and most poignantly in the spring of 1968 after the Reverend Martin Luther King, Jr., was assassinated. In 1967, between June and August, street rebellions occurred in sixty-seven cities, among them Detroit, where over 1,000 people were injured and 41 killed. These urban rebellions, and the commissions appointed to consider them, broadened the issue to embrace the whole of what came to be known as the "urban crisis."[65]

As the urban riots subsided, many argued that new directions in the struggle to equalize black life chances were needed. This became a time of intense and fiery ideological ferment, particularly among black intellectuals and young militants, many of whom had been involved in the earlier struggles in the South. They increasingly questioned the continued value of the philosophy and practice of nonviolent direct action that had dominated the struggle in the South; focused on the continuing plight of the black urban and ghettoized poor; raised the issue of greater pride in blackness and stronger identification with Africa and the "Third World"; questioned the significance of the changes that had occurred in the South; and discussed whether violent revolution was necessary for fundamental changes to occur in the lives of black Americans throughout the nation.

The Black Panthers came out of the North and the West with their cry of "revolution" and their strong commitment to action against economic insecurity and police brutality in the ghetto. New heroes, symbols, slogans, and groups emerged. In death Malcolm X became the symbol of militant black nationalism, a hero to Eldridge Cleaver, "Rap" Brown, and countless unnamed young blacks. "Black is Beautiful," "I'm Black and I'm Proud," and African-style dress became the slogans and symbols of a burgeoning black pride. The "Black Muslims" became the respectable symbol of black separatism and self-help, while the Black Panthers stood as the symbol of revolutionary struggle, and "Black Liberation" the object of the struggle. The writings of Frantz Fanon became the revolutionary's handbook. And central to it all seemed to be the theme, power for black people, popularized in the slogan "Black Power."[66]

The cry "Black Power" first became prominent on a 1966 Mississippi civil rights march against fear initiated by James Meredith, the first black to be enrolled at the University of Mississippi. When Meredith was wounded by a sniper's bullet his march was taken up by representatives from all of the major civil rights organizations of that time. Among them was the youthful Stokely Carmichael of SNCC, a veteran of numerous civil rights campaigns in the Deep South. When he called out for "Black Power," coverage by the national press made the slogan an instant success among the young and militant wing of the civil rights movement. It seemed to articulate the new feeling of indomitable strength gained by earlier victories. At the same time, it provided what seemed to be "an appropriate reply to the intransigence and hostility of whites symbolized by the shooting of Meredith."[67] For blacks, at any rate. White reaction was quite another matter. What was little enough understood, and variously interpreted by blacks themselves, was quickly translated by many whites into a threat of physical force—something few blacks were calling for. Whites in urban areas spoke of being afraid to be in cities at night, some seemed convinced that "Black Power" could only mean senseless violence against whites, and not a few white liberals reacted in hurt and anger.[68]

"Black Power" meant something far more pragmatic to most blacks. It soon became an integral part of the greater struggle for power, North and South, through increased participation in formal electoral politics. Caucuses within organizations and a mounting interest in developing programs and economic policies became the central elements of an operational black power. The caucus movement spread throughout the country during the last several years of the 1960s and the first years of the 1970s. Black trade unionists, schoolteachers, librarians, and blacks in other professional associations formed caucuses or separate organizations to press for their fair share of opportunities. In the North black students in "white" colleges and universities were demanding that black professors be hired, that more black students be enrolled, and that "black studies" programs be instituted.[69] These new directions reflected a definition of Black Power articulated in 1967:

> The goal of black self-determination and black self-identity—Black Power—is full participation in the decision-making processes affecting the lives of black people, and recognition of the virtues in themselves as black people.[70]

The spread of the Black Power theme, the urban riots, and the rise of the Vietnam War as an issue changed the political climate and the reactions of white Americans. Some lost interest in civil rights issues, while others became more openly hostile to all radical protest action. Armed with the change in public attitudes, the FBI, CIA, and special units in many local police departments broadened the extent of the spying and surveillance activities they had long conducted against black activists of all persuasions.[71]

Nevertheless, the decade started with legal segregation in the South and ended with free access to public accommodations and the end of legally supported dual school systems. The decade had begun with widespread disenfranchisement and ended with the right to vote a legally protected reality. The beginning of the sixties had seen blacks legally denied jobs and housing; 1970 saw the strict outlawing of both practices. These gains were won through relentless struggle. But too much was still only on paper.

The 1970s

By the early seventies, the long hot summers of urban rioting, the Black Panthers, the calls for separatism, and cries of Black Power and Black Liberation had largely receded. Quieter efforts by traditional groups like the NAACP and the Urban League persisted as they had for much of this century, and blacks continued to act in caucuses or form ad hoc groups around specific issues. But increasingly, the dominant focus of black activity was reliance on a strategy for change that could capitalize both on the voter registration gains won by the movement in the South and on the concentration of black voters in key urban centers of the North.

The deceptively simple route to meeting black objectives, as Bayard Rustin maintains, is "through political power."[72] And protest in the mid-seventies has been largely subsumed by electoral politics. Today, for every professional organization and institution, for every school board election, for every city council or mayoral race where black people live, there are black candidates. The civil rights activists from the sixties are now running for and holding office. SNCC activist Julian Bond sits in the Georgia legislature. Andrew Young of SCLC is ambassador to the United Nations and was formerly the first black congressman elected from Georgia since Reconstruction. Mel King, civil rights activist in Boston, holds a seat in the state legislature. Marion Barry, first chairperson of the Student Nonviolent Coordinating Committee, was elected first to the District of Columbia school board, and then as a member of the elected City Council. Sterling Tucker, another civil rights activist and former head of the Washington Urban League, chaired the District City Council. Former Black Panther activist Bobby Seale ran for mayor of Oakland, California, in a vote that was so close it required a run-off election. Detroit's Mayor Coleman Young was a founder of the National Negro Labor Council in the fifties and a long-time civil rights activist. The struggle for jobs continues in the Full Employment Bill introduced into the Ninety-fourth Congress by Congressman Augustus Hawkins, a black representative, and Senator Hubert Humphrey, a long-time civil rights advocate. Among the bill's most active supporters are the Congressional Black Caucus and the Joint Center for Political Studies, an important resource organization for black elected officials. Now, as Atlanta's first black mayor, Maynard Jackson, has said, the last great hurrah of the civil rights movement won't be found in the streets because it's in office.[73] Elective office has become the new frontier for black leaders. In the words of Andrew Young, "You don't have to demonstrate when you can pick up a phone and call someone."[74]

Few blacks were elected (or appointed) to any public office be-

tween Reconstruction and the late sixties. By the mid-seventies, 13
of Cleveland's 33 city council members and its president, the head
of its school board, one Ohio member of the U.S. House of Representatives, and two Ohio state legislators are black; and until recently, Cleveland had a black mayor as well.[75] Across the country
over 300 state legislators, 557 members of county governing boards,
and the mayors of 127 American cities, including Detroit, Atlanta,
Los Angeles, and Washington, D.C., were black. Sixteen members
of the U.S. House of Representatives, one member of the U.S. Senate,
and the lieutenant governors of two states were black. Across the
country nearly 4,000 elected officials were black.[76] In some ways
more heartening is the fact that Charles Evers, a black former state
NAACP leader and the brother of a slain civil rights worker, could
be one of Mississippi's most important political forces. He served
along with black civil rights activists Aaron Henry and the late
Fannie Lou Hamer, who once incurred the wrath of traditional
Mississippi politicians by forming a rival political party and taking
it to the 1964 National Democratic Convention. In some of the very
counties that once beat, chased, and harassed civil rights workers
and the local black residents who worked with them, there are now
black sheriffs and mayors and police and county board members.

But for all the glamour and symbolic importance that attaches to
the sight of a black member of Congress dining at the White House,
or a black mayor leading the U.S. Conference of Mayors, the Joint
Center for Political Studies estimates that at the rate blacks are
currently being elected, they will still hold only 3 percent of elective
offices by the year 2000. Even in areas where blacks are a majority
of the population, their representation on elective bodies is still small,
and of 103 counties with majority black populations, two-thirds still
have no elected black officials.[77] The full realization of black political
power continues to be hampered by low registration of black voters
(half of the nearly 14 million blacks who could have voted in 1972
were not registered)[78] and inadequate enforcement of the Voting
Rights Act of 1965.[79] But new political realities now hold sway. The
days when just a presidential order or mention in a major party
platform was the most that black voters could expect are over; the
era when black voting blocs can influence state and local elections
as well as presidential races is under way.

To the extent that voters can influence the actions of those elected,
the power of the vote is the most powerful right of a free citizen. In
a few places where black voters are the majority, they have been able

to erase "most of the existing mechanisms of discrimination."[80] That power also helps to explain the actions of Congress with respect to black rights. The relationship between black voters and the Congress is straightforward enough. As the movement North increased, so did the number of congressional districts with large, if not majority, black constituencies. By 1970, blacks were more than 25 percent of the population in one-fifth of the congressional districts of 20 states. Blacks are now estimated to be nearly one-third of the voters in 60 congressional districts and a majority in about 13.[81] But their presence was being felt for some years. Those who followed the actions of Congress with respect to U.S. involvement in Vietnam have a tendency to think of the House of Representatives as conservative and the Senate as liberal. But on civil rights issues the record is quite different. Though neither house has been eager to concede black rights, and members have routinely sought to avoid what they regard as politically damaging votes in favor of civil rights, more representatives seem to have needed black votes. The House has been far quicker to vote in favor of civil rights than the Senate, where the larger, statewide constituencies have always been predominantly white. These realities have long been reflected in the votes of the two houses. There were many House victories for anti–poll tax legislation in the forties (five, in seven years); in 1950 the House passed a bill to create a permanent Fair Employment Practices Commission, and in 1956, the Voting Rights Act when it was first introduced. None of these bills was even brought to a vote in the Senate. More than once the House of Representatives has passed major civil rights legislation only to have it filibustered to death by a handful of senators who still did not need black votes for re-election.[82] But even in the Senate small changes gradually became visible. As one illustration, Senator Strom Thurmond of South Carolina, who was candidate for president for the States' Rights party in 1948, was always known to refer to blacks in his state as "them Nigras." Always, until the Voting Rights Act was passed—and then he began to talk more circumspectly of his "colored constituents."[83] In 1975 he supported a black South Carolina lawyer, Matthew Perry, for the U.S. Court of Military Appeals. In recommending Mr. Perry, the senator said: "I do not necessarily place credence on whether a member should be black or white, but we do have a lot of men in service who are black, and I think it might inspire some confidence on their part."[84]

The issues haven't changed, although the tactics have. That reality is both evidence of the virulence and resilience of race prejudice remaining in America, and a credit to those whose persistence has won such progress as there has been and kept the struggle alive. Over a century ago a former slave, abolitionist, and adviser to presidents. said: *"Power concedes nothing without a demand.* It never did and it never will" (Frederick Douglass, August 4, 1857).[85]

Making a Difference

Black Americans continue to meet strong opposition and at the same time have made tremendous strides since 1940 toward achieving the goal of equality with whites in each of the basic conditions this book is about: getting a chance at making a living and improving it; having and keeping a family healthy; and living in a good home of one's choice. The opposition has taken on changing forms with time and has been more successful in thwarting progress in some areas than in others. As in a tug of war, improvements are greater or less depending on the relative intensity of the opposing force.

Black Americans achieved most when they themselves took up the fight, and also when economic advances were being made in the society at large, so that everyone was gaining and no one group was losing. Under these conditions, many whites joined blacks to help them. Relatively few whites have made black Americans' fight their own during an entire lifetime.

The black struggle, therefore, has been paramount as a driving force for achievement in every field we cover. It has had least success in desegregating housing. This is the most personal situation, reaching into the core of latent prejudice that rejects blacks—any black family next door—as a stepping stone to an intimacy still not in general practice in American society. In housing we see the last bastion of archetypical racism that ignites into ugly confrontation and violent behavior, including brutal assault. Fair housing, Title VIII of the Civil Rights Act of 1968, was the last right to be specifically "granted" and remains the least enforced and most evaded. And blacks' struggle simply for fair housing alone could not have achieved passage of this law. It took the combination of a stormy year of ghetto frustration and revolt, the assassination of Martin Luther King, and a confused and frightened white establishment to produce the end result.

That the physical structures themselves in which black Americans live are much better than they were in 1940 is almost beside the point. Housing has become better for everyone as a growing economy has brought ever higher standards of living. The problem for blacks lies not so much in the characteristics of their housing, although major improvements are necessary. The most intractable part of the housing struggle has been lack of choice of the housing and the neighborhoods that blacks may live in.

Health care has become more readily a matter of ability to pay rather than who is the client. It is an economic matter in the sense that blacks still are more likely to be sick and disabled, and less likely to benefit under quasi-universal public health programs such as Medicare and Medicaid. The rising level of living since 1940 has made it possible for all Americans to live longer and healthier lives. But the American health-care system, even when it nominally includes everyone, leaves out too many who must trade off making an out-of-pocket initial expenditure of $50, $80, or more for the doctor or the hospital stay against paying the rent or sending a child to school well fed and with a warm winter coat. This becomes the choice for blacks much more often than for whites.

Besides this, we have reaped a legacy of a whole generation of blacks who are more susceptible to illness and chronic disabilities. They are those over forty, who as infants and children went without care, only sometimes because of cost, but often because of white doctors' and hospitals' reluctance or refusal to treat blacks or to admit black practitioners into the health-care system.

Protest, assisted in time by the law, has given black medical students, nurses, and doctors more entry into training, universities and hospitals, but not everywhere. Collective action, the law, and litigation have freed hospital beds for black patients in most places, and Medicare and Medicaid have made care more accessible. But black and white still do not enjoy equal health care and longevity.

The right to work at jobs for which one is qualified is a straightforward bread-and-butter issue. Yet even when jobs have been plentiful and the unemployment rate so low that it seemed that anyone, at any age, could get a job, blacks were denied jobs because they were black; even in the labor-short war years. As with the other essentials of life, a generally growing economy has made more and better jobs available, and has helped blacks to move closer to whites in occupational achievement. Persistent organized struggle by blacks to pry loose their fair share of jobs continued, however, to be essential, whether in the worst or the best of times.

Several important conditions illustrate the resistances that remain and the need for pressure, regardless of the times. In the first place, blacks' occupational position relative to whites' falls in slack employment years. The black unemployment rate, with congruent loss of time on the job and therefore of seniority and experience, soars during recessions irrespective of the workers' age, sex, location, education, marital status, industry, or occupation in which employed. The force of discrimination is irrefutable.

Second, it is not just a matter of last in, first out, or some neutral rule of thumb. A powerfully convincing and elaborate rationalization persists that permeates all levels of society, that blacks are, under all circumstances, somehow less qualified than whites. The proposition appears never to have been challenged that even educated black Americans are not qualified when most jobs are learned by doing and require only a modest amount of schooling; or when expanding technology is reducing the amount of learning required for increasing numbers of jobs; or when Americans gladly buy consumer products made by untaught migrant workers in Western Europe's industries. The ebb and flow in and out of specific jobs that occurs with swings in the state of the economy illustrates the hypocrisy or self-deception involved. When times are good, blacks are qualified. In slack times, whites, whatever their credentials, are kept on.

Third, legal machinery to improve employment practices, just as in the case of voting rights, has had to be introduced over and over. The strongest instrument yet, lodged in the EEOC, remains weak, with a huge backlog of complaints. It reflects both large-scale discrimination in the job market and a weak national will to enforce the law that forbids it. Blacks have had to fight tirelessly for employment. Without that effort much of the ground that was gained either would not have been won in the first place, or more of it would have been lost in hard times.

The open struggle for jobs has been mostly in the private economy. Blacks won improvements in federal employment when the publicity was good for votes in election years or in times of open demonstrations. Otherwise the progress in the federal establishment was much the same as in private industry. Equal opportunity orders came, were lost, and were reissued; enforcement was weak and manipulation of the guidelines was easy. The Civil Service was still exempt even in the seventies from the broader and stronger conditions under which private industry operated. Black high officials are in policymaking positions mostly in agencies that administer programs for the "disadvantaged." In other agencies, they work outside their department's main mission, in charge of "equal opportunity" programs.

Just as in private employment, greatest access to the better jobs was achieved during periods of mass protest and the good times of the sixties. And so, during the Johnson years commitment to recruit and promote was strong. The momentum that builds under positive leadership and a relatively stable system of rewards and promotion has brought gains in the federal establishment that compare more than favorably with private industry. The fact remains, however, that Uncle Sam has not been a clear leader, way ahead of all others.

A job, whether in the private or the public sector, provides one's daily bread, but under the social and economic security institutions that were introduced with FDR's New Deal, a job determines future income too. The social insurance schemes are related to earnings and not to need. Discrimination that has led to low and intermittent earnings and work in industries or firms that were not covered under the New Deal insurances in earlier years have left many stranded without unemployment insurance during their working lives or without a pension on retirement. Even if insured, a disproportionate number of black workers get so little in benefits that they remain poor and must resort to public assistance.

Protest has been necessary to achieve more fair and lawful treatment under the welfare system especially. Within all the income security programs, expansions in coverage and benefits were generous only when prosperous times coincided with forceful civil rights initiatives.

Taxes have had a generally rising course too, and they bite off more dollars from those with less-than-average incomes (including most blacks) than from others. The combination of income, sales, real estate, and Social Security payroll taxes leaves everyone taxed in about the same proportion. Yet the wealthiest get most in government subsidies and tax deductions for income from assets. Few blacks have such assets. Yet such wealth is the quintessence of economic security. It conveys power and influence of a kind that could move administrations to enforce the civil rights laws on the books or improve them.

Some significant implications can be drawn from all of these facts. Our government, like our laws, reflects the society and does not move much beyond the majority electorate. This, in turn, prevents blacks (the largest minority in America) from achieving full representation in the government's major decisions in the conduct of domestic commerce, international relations, the control and distribution of natural resources, and, especially pertinent, attention to human needs. The result is that 25 million Americans remain almost wholly at the mercy of political policies and strategies designed by and for the remaining 200 million. Their most influential weaponry has been constant vigilance and protest.

Ironically, the greatest power blacks have over public policy is in their numbers in places where, from lack of choice in housing or neighborhoods, they make up a majority or an important swing vote in the electorate. Blacks have the power of the ballot more than ever before, and this makes a difference. Only time will tell how much of a difference it can make when the white majority has not yet over-come the inner feelings and outer manifestations of race prejudice.

Unequal Employment Opportunity

"**A**MERICA'S COMPETITIVE SPIRIT,** the work ethic of this people, is alive and well on Labor Day, 1971," the president said.[1]

It isn't easy to measure the work ethic of one's fellow Americans, but one group stands out as most committed to the notion—black Americans. No award for motivation is needed for the graduates of Ivy League business schools whose hard decisions involve which five- to six-figure-a-year career job they will choose, or professionals who know they'll always be in demand for good incomes under good conditions: doctors, lawyers, professors, and scientists. The place where motivation really counts, where neither glamour nor prestige turns the trick, is those vast middle and lower reaches of the occupational ladder where most black people could expect to be employed. Even a cursory observation would have told any black man or woman in the forties and the fifties, and many of the years since then, that getting a job meant hard work at low pay for an uncertain period of time. For too many blacks, the jobs at the end of the struggle would be the jobs with the least security, the lowest wages, the highest risks, and the worst conditions. People who still fight to work when experience tells them it will be for such jobs must be rated most imbued with the work ethic. Jobs have always been at the core of what black Americans have struggled for.

Jobs in the 1940s

In 1940, almost 1 million blacks were on emergency work[2] or unemployed.[3] Nearly two-thirds of those who did have jobs worked in one of two industries—agriculture or personal services (household and janitorial jobs). When black leaders pressed the White House in 1941 for a share in the jobs being generated by the war in Europe, their first task was simply to get black workers into industries from which they had been traditionally excluded. Black people had to defy a president and threaten to march, 100,000 strong, into a segregated southern city, which just happened to be their nation's capital, for the right to work on assembly lines in munitions factories, to operate machines in aircraft plants, to serve on the loading docks of naval yards, and to drive the trucks transporting war materials across the country.[4] All they wanted was the right to earn a living, to support a family in return for the energy and skill and muscle they could bring to the jobs they felt they would be lucky enough to do. It couldn't have been more solidly in the American tradition.

In the forties, jobs and the job market were highly segregated. Black workers were usually separated by function or location wherever they happened to find jobs. They frequently worked in completely black establishments, as black teachers in black schools, or in services that catered to the black community, like barbershops and funeral parlors. But more usually they worked in black shops or departments or sections within factories and businesses, or on the black maintenance crews that worked the night shifts when the white staff weren't around. There were segregated hiring halls, and the official placement service of the government, the U.S. Employment Service (USES), maintained segregated employment offices.[5] Discrimination was further maintained by the kinds of jobs available to blacks, who were virtually excluded from all the better-paying jobs. Unbreachable rules of thumb governed what progress black employees could make: they could not supervise whites, expect to work immediately alongside whites, or work in any setting that was considered "refined," like an office or a sales counter.[6] Those unwritten rules eliminated a wide range of employment opportunities, effectively prescreening blacks from any jobs that involved selling or dealing directly with whites. In a society which was 90 percent white, that covered a lot of ground. Since the unwritten rules also embraced such nonprofessional concerns as washrooms, drinking fountains, and lunchrooms, blacks could not even compete fairly for the jobs that did not require personal contact with whites unless the establishments had separate "facilities." In hotels and restaurants, blacks could work in the kitchens preparing the food, but often not out front serving it. Two surveys of New York City hotels conducted in the fifties still found that all thirty-three hotels in the survey, including those that employed blacks, "excluded Negroes from their bar service and front service departments."[7] Some procedures for maintaining segregation were unusually humiliating. In 1941, the Philadelphia Navy Yard instituted a new system of badges when black workers joined the staff. White workers' badges had a big "W" in front of the employee number, and black workers' badges had an equally prominent "N"—so that no one would be confused.[8]

The outcome of such a system is predictable, and was always recognized. An assistant secretary of President Roosevelt's wartime Fair Employment Practices Committee (FEPC)—the body responsible for ensuring nondiscrimination in private industries getting government contracts—acknowledged:

> It is indeed difficult to imagine a situation where a worker is segregated because of his race and yet is not restricted in his employment opportunities because of that segregation.[9]

The statistics available from those years reveal what happens under such a system of discrimination. Overwhelming numbers of blacks were concentrated in agriculture and personal services and in the lowest-paying industries in 1940 (Table 2–1).

The Uphill Climb

There have been some changes in thirty-five years. By 1974 only about 15 percent of black men and women with jobs were working in agriculture or personal services, as compared with almost 65 percent in 1940 (Table 2–1). Some of that change reflects real progress—blacks had moved into the same wide range of industries that whites have always worked in. But some of it is just because fewer workers of any kind (black or white, skilled or not) are in agriculture, and because many of the old cleaning tasks have become more mechanized and require fewer workers. If getting into the same industries as whites were the only criterion, then blacks with jobs would be very nearly on a par with whites today. But there is more to employment equality than access to the same industries. Black men and women continue to be brought in disproportionately at the lowest occupational levels (Table 2–2).

The Occupational Ladder

Getting a job is only the first step. Moving up the occupational ladder is next. This translates into higher pay and improved job benefits; longer vacation time and sick leave; life, health, and pension insurance; a chance for further job advancement, some prestige, and better working conditions. Although more jobs have been opening for blacks, blacks are still far from the position occupied by white workers in the kinds of work they get (Figure 2–1 and Table 2–3).

Tracing the occupational progress of black workers requires the use of some measure that can be applied from year to year to show losses or gains in standing. This is frequently done just by checking the gross number of black and white workers in different types of jobs each year, without taking into account the degree to which some jobs pay more than others, or the degree to which black workers are in the low- or high-paying jobs (Table 2–4). The "occupational position index"[10] used here shows, with a single number for each group, the degree to which black and white workers have moved into the higher-paying occupational groups, and how they compare with one another in this respect (Figure 2–2 and Table 2–3).

The ratio of the occupational position of blacks to the occupational position of whites, that is, the *relative* position of black workers, shows even more strikingly how black workers fare with changes in the economy when earnings in addition to holding a job are taken into account.[11] After gains in good times (as during the forties and through much of the sixties), the relative position of black workers slips back in times of recession. And when all workers tend to lose ground, black workers as a group lose more. This occurred at the end of the economic boom of the forties, and with the recessions of 1958, 1961, and 1971. The deep recession of 1974–75 was so severe that both whites and blacks lost substantially and blacks remained in the same relative occupational position to whites in both years (Figure 2–2 and Table 2–5). A return to more prosperous conditions has never been enough by itself to win equal standing. There is no year for which it might be said that occupational equality was reached.

FIGURE 2–1

Black Workers' Occupational Position Has Risen More than White
Workers' Since 1940, but by 1975 Had Not Even Reached the Whites'
1940 Level

Occupational Position by Race, 1940–75

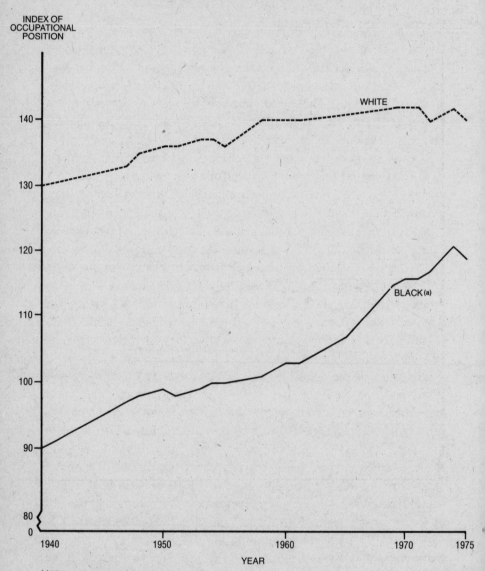

(a) Negro and other nonwhite races.

Source: See Table 2–3.

36

FIGURE 2-2

Black Workers' Occupational Position Relative to White Workers'
Stagnates or Falls During Recessions

Relative Occupational Position, Black[a] to White, 1940–75

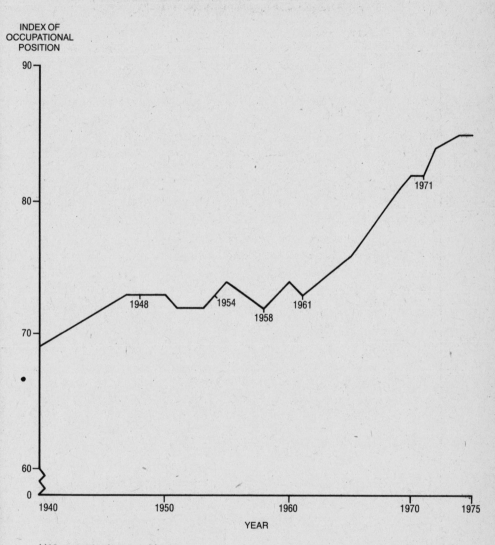

Source: See Table 2-5.

In 1940 the score was only 69, meaning that blacks were only 69 percent as likely as whites to get the better jobs. By 1975 the score was only 85, showing that the position of black workers nationally was still well below that of whites and, more important, had improved only 16 percentage points during thirty-five years of generally rising prosperity and levels of living.

In every region of the country prosperity alone proved unable to remove the differences between black and white workers. In regions where discriminatory practices were more actively tolerated, the differences were greatest. Thus within the same industries and occupations, over the same period of time the differences between black and white were markedly greater in the South. In that sense regional conditions play an important part in relative achievement. Even by 1970 blacks were still lagging well behind whites in getting work in the expanding range of southern industries.[12] They were almost on a par with whites in their industrial position in regions outside the South (Figure 2–3).

The gap in occupational position between black and white workers in 1970 was much greater than the gap in industrial position, and much greater in southern places of employment than elsewhere. This was true even after marked progress in the stormy sixties. In the South, where discrimination was greatest in the first place, the gap in occupational achievement by 1970 was as large as it had been among workers in the North twenty years earlier (Figure 2–4).

A major study of black employment in the South explains:

> The South's traditional institutions, including institutionalized discrimination, are being eroded by forces associated with industrialization and urbanization. . . . However, the erosion of racism is a slow process. . . . Indeed, at present rates of change black employment in the higher income . . . categories will not equal that of whites for many years.[13]

The author of that study attributes the uptrend after 1960 to both civil rights laws "establishing a moral climate proclaiming official opposition to racial discrimination," and "increasing black militancy." Southern business groups found that "demonstrations and race conflicts were bad for business and disrupted economic development."[14]

Explanations and Rationalizations

Explanations are legion for such advances as blacks have made or for the persistent and fluctuating differences between blacks and whites in employment and unemployment. Some explanations have been more popular or have had more influence at different times. But conditions that bring about black employment gains are always inter-related. A discussion of a few prominent explanations and rationalizations follow.

Having the Economy Shoulder It All

A popular notion, and one with remarkable staying power, is the idea that employment and pay rates for black workers are a simple matter of the health of the economy. According to this popular belief, the answer to black employment problems is a healthy, growing economy which will enable blacks to keep and increase whatever gains they are able to make in the labor force.[15]

An expanding economy is indeed good for all workers, but it has never been enough for black workers in the absence of strong measures to eliminate discrimination. There is no question that the position of black workers improves during good times, and that black workers lose more than whites during times of recession. In that sense it is, of course, true that good economic times are good for black progress. But, good times or bad, black workers have never found themselves on a par with white workers. In the years since the Employment Act of 1946 was passed, there have been six recessions.[16] In the worst of times, the black unemployment rate soared to levels that would have been labeled depressions or disasters if the same rates had applied to the white labor force or represented the average for the nation. Even in the best of times, the unemployment rate of black workers has usually been greater than the white rate in the depths of a recession (Figure 2–5 and Table 2–6), and never as low as the rates regarded as "acceptable" for the labor force as a whole (9 in 10 of whom are white).

Employment shifts for black workers are aptly described by the acronym LIFO—Last In, First Out. Even when times are good, it takes a while before jobs open up and black workers are hired in sizable numbers. That is one reason why the black unemployment

FIGURE 2–3

Black Workers' Industrial Position Has Become Almost the Same as for Whites in All Regions Except the South

Industrial Position Indices by Race and Region, 1940–70, Nonfarm

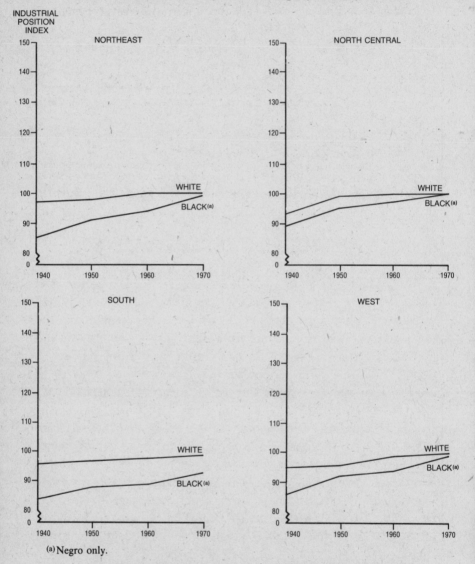

(a) Negro only.

Source: Derived from 1940 Census of Population, *Labor Force, Vol. 3, Pt. 1, U.S. Summary,* Table 76, pp. 188–9; 1950 Census of Population, *Characteristics of the Population, Vol. 1, Pt. 1, U.S. Summary,* Table 128, pp. 276–8; 1960 Census of Population, *Characteristics of the Population, Vol. 1, Pt. 1, U.S. Summary,* Table 213, p. 569; 1970 Census of Population, *Characteristics of the Population, Vol. 1, Pt. 1, Sec. 2, U.S. Summary,* Table 236, pp. 801–3.

FIGURE 2–4

Black Workers' Occupational Position Has Remained Well Below White Workers', Especially in the South Where Progress Occurred Only After 1960

Occupational Position Indices by Race and Region, 1940–70, Nonfarm

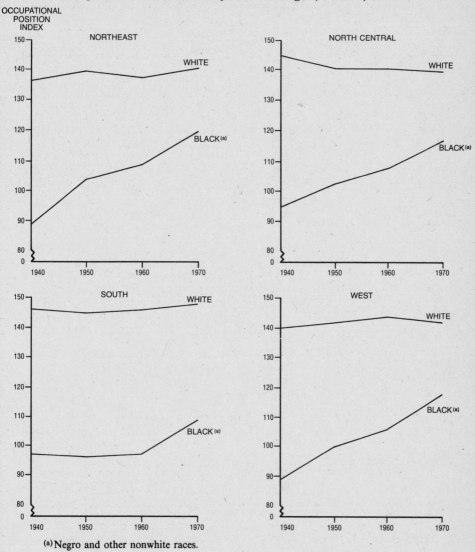

(a) Negro and other nonwhite races.

Source: Derived from 1940 Census of Population, *Labor Force, Vol. 3, Pt. 1, U.S. Summary,* Table 63, p. 93–4, 96; 1950 Census of Population, *Characteristics of the Population, Vol. 1, Pt. 1, U.S. Summary,* Table 159, pp. 400–2; 1960 Census of Population, *Characteristics of the Population, Vol. 1, Pt. 1, U.S. Summary,* Table 257, pp. 717–9; 1970 Census of Population, *Characteristics of the Population, Vol. 1, Pt. 1, Sec. 2, U.S. Summary,* Table 294, pp. 1273–9.

rate falls dramatically only well after a prosperous period has begun
and the white unemployment rate has reached a new low. Throughout a boom, the black unemployment rate, of course, remains substantially higher than the white—usually twice as high. At the end
of the boom, the black unemployment rate rises faster in the down-
turn than it does for whites (Figure 2–5 and Table 2–6).

One way of evaluating the LIFO phenomenon is to consider
whether it is possible that all of the black workers hired in times of
prosperity were poor risks, "bottom of the barrel" workers, of little
use to the economy except in good times. Because one-fourth or
fewer of all workers had ever been in unions before the 1970s and
subject to collectively bargained seniority rules, it is unlikely that
union contracts would explain LIFO practices.[17] In fact, since the
white labor force is normally more fully employed than the black,
their exceptionally full employment in prosperous times is more
likely to result in more "marginal" white than "marginal" black
workers on the job. And when business is slow and white workers
are kept on in preference to blacks, it is logical that more "marginal"
white than "marginal" blacks are retained.

What is operating is the combined effect of discrimination that
both favors white workers over black under virtually all circumstances and disproportionately confines the employment of those
who are black, young, or inexperienced to the jobs most vulnerable
to unemployment. Skilled and administrative staff, who are usually
white, are kept on in hope of better times, while the production
workers, cleaners, and sweepers, large numbers of whom are black,
are let go as soon as activity declines.[18]

Even this is not the whole explanation, because blacks—skilled or
unskilled—have consistently had higher unemployment rates than
whites. White workers outnumber blacks in all kinds of work (Table
2–7), and it is unlikely that all of them are better trained, since
training for both groups is likely to have been on the job.[19] Yet even
among the least desirable jobs in our economy and those most vulnerable to unemployment, white and black unemployment rates
show clearly over a period of twenty years that, whether it is the best
of times or the worst, employers keep proportionately more white
than black workers on their payrolls (Table 2–8).

If black employment prospects were decided merely by the state
of the economy, the combination of the economic upsurge and the
labor shortages during World War II should have resulted in ample

FIGURE 2–5

Black Workers' Unemployment Rates Rise and Fall at Far Higher Levels than White Workers', and Much More Sharply

Unemployment Rates by Race, 1948–75

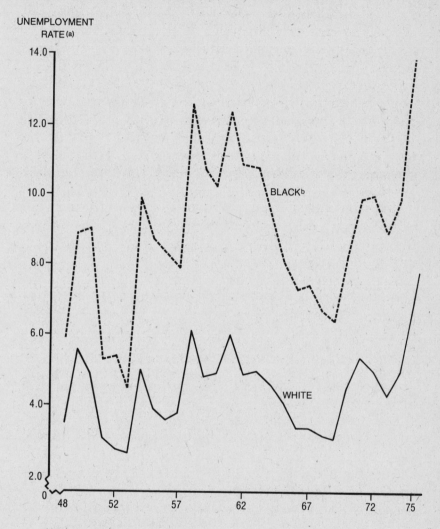

(a) Percentage of the civilian labor force.
(b) Negro and other nonwhite races.

Source: See Table 2–6.

black progress. Those years were special in another sense as well, for if ever Americans were in a mood to practice the American creed, the time was at hand. Patriotism was high, times were good, labor was desperately needed, and blacks were active in demanding their share. Yet even though sustained, effective black protest in the forties led employers to hire black workers for jobs from which they were previously barred, resistance to this remained widespread throughout the war period.

Presidential promises to stimulate economic growth, and public policies recognizing the responsibility of government to maximize conditions of employment, important as they are, are not enough. The heart of the problem lies, not in the size of the GNP or the Dow Jones average, but in discriminatory practices and the lack of effective machinery to deal with them.

Is It the Changing Composition of the Labor Force?

More and more frequently the higher unemployment rate of blacks has been explained away by pointing out that the black labor force tends to include larger proportions of the groups with the highest unemployment rates—women and teenagers. This explanation was especially prevalent in the seventies recession. One bizarre illustration of the thinking of public policymakers appeared in a statistical exercise that derived the unemployment rates as they would be if only men in the prime working years were included.[20] The president's economic advisers calculated in 1975 that if only twenty-five- to sixty-four-year-old men who had worked the previous year were counted, the black unemployment rate would be considerably less than the average for all black workers, and only one point more than the white rate.[21] But the presidential advisers hadn't managed to get the black rate down to the white rate even by eliminating nearly 6 out of 10 black workers from the labor force (and about half the white workers). Those excluded were all of the working women, all of the young people just out of school and starting their families, and all of the older black men and women who must continue to work because when young they were denied jobs that might have given them enough in pensions or Social Security benefits to let them retire. The nation's businesses, to say nothing of individual families, could hardly survive without those workers. Women especially have become an increasingly essential and steadily growing part of the labor force for decades. What such analyses prove is that discounting workers with high unemployment rates makes the unemployment rate seem lower; it does nothing to point the way to a solution of their economic plight, nor does it recognize their significance to the economy.

Whatever their number or proportion, the vulnerable groups, women and youth, closely mirror the general pattern of each business cycle, with the blacks among them always reflecting the swings at substantially higher levels than whites (Table 2–9). Their presence does not account for the higher rates of unemployment among blacks. Neither the total unemployment rate nor the black or white rates separately have risen consistently with the increasing labor-force participation of groups like women and young people who are particularly vulnerable to unemployment.

The deep recessions of 1957–58 and 1974–75 were not the product of some sudden rush of women into the marketplace, or the graduation of some previously ignored cohort of baby-boom teenagers (Table 2–10). Certainly this was not true of blacks. Through it all—the booms, the busts, and the minor swings in the business cycle—black Americans have continued to make up 11 percent of the nation's total labor force. And women and teenagers have become an ever so slowly increasing proportion of that 11 percent (Table 2–11).

Was It Migration?

Black migration out of the South has been a vast economic and social movement. The net migration from the South totaled over 4 million black people in the thirty years from 1940 to 1970—the largest migration stream of any single group in the United States. One demographer describes it as possibly the most rapid and extensive shift by any large population group in modern history.[22] It ran about 125,000 annually during the 1940s, 146,000 each year in the 1950s, and 138,000 in the 1960s.[23] The proportion of blacks living in the South fell from over three-fourths in 1940 to a little over half by 1970.[24]

Black migrants have not been dissimilar from other migrants. They were usually young, in their twenties, and better educated than those whom they left behind. Many southern blacks who migrated were already city dwellers even by 1940. In fact, among all adult black immigrants to urban areas of the North and West in 1967, close to 60 percent had come from urban places.[23] Also, most southern migrants since 1940 had not been employed in agriculture. Only about 40 percent of southern blacks altogether were in farming in 1940, their numbers declining rapidly by halves—to 20 percent in 1950, 10 percent in 1960, and 5 percent in 1970.[26]

Those who had been in agriculture experienced (along with white farmers) rapid farm mechanization, abandonment of the share-tenant system, the loss of southern cotton markets to other fibers and to other regions, and increasingly large holdings and fewer farms.[27] In general, wages were lower in the South, in or out of agriculture, and the diverse jobs in northern industry were attractive.[26] Assessing motives for migration is difficult—the push versus the pull.

Black farm workers and tenants were the most likely to be displaced as southern agriculture changed, and the relatively few black farm owners or part-owners dropped sharply too.[29] Just between 1954 and 1969, black landowners lost about 5 million acres in fourteen southern states. The number of black landowners in those states fell by 62 percent in that period, from 175,000 to 67,000.[30]

Migration from farms in the South did not reduce or improve the *relative* occupational position of blacks to whites. Blacks' relative occupational standing is the same whether farm workers are included in or excluded from the calculations (Table 2–5). One reason is that whites as well as blacks left agriculture in large numbers. Urbanization since 1940 was not an important influence on blacks' relative achievement either, because by then blacks were chiefly urban anyhow; most black migrants moved from one city to another after 1955.[31]

> . . . the description of the average black migrant to the city as an ill-trained person of rural background and low socio-economic status . . . will not hold. He or she is in fact well educated by current standards and judging from the occupational position of those employed, relatively successful at utilizing this education.[32]

Black migrants like white migrants moved to better themselves, and they did, but they did not catch up to their white fellow workers.

Did Jobs Programs Help?

Public programs specifically designed to provide work or work training have been of a fair scale only during the Great Depression and
its immediate aftermath, and since 1962, after the 1960–61 recession.
This ushered in the 1962 Manpower Development and Training Act
(MDTA), which was succeeded by about ten other job programs of
varying size and for differing target groups.[33]

In 1940, just before our entry into World War II, the WPA and
CCC (Works Progress Administration and Civilian Conservation
Corps) were still producing a sizable number of jobs. When added
to student and out-of-school part-time work under the National
Youth Administration, these programs siphoned off almost 2 million
persons who might otherwise have been added to the eight million
who were unemployed in 1940.[34]

In April 1941, blacks were an estimated 16 percent of the workers
on WPA, a slightly larger share than their proportion of the unemployed. Their representation was much greater in the North than the
South. In the South, WPA jobs paid substantially more than blacks
would receive in private employment, especially agriculture, so
blacks were kept off the rolls.[35]

WPA jobs varied widely, from ballet dancing to digging ditches.
Although construction jobs were paramount throughout the WPA
years from the thirties on, work in education, research, and the arts
was significant. Monuments of the WPA and CCC are New York's
Central Park Zoo, San Francisco's Aquatic Park, Chicago's water-
front, the Philadelphia Art Museum, the restoration of Indepen-
dence Hall in Philadelphia and Faneuil Hall in Boston, and thousands of miles of woodland trails. WPA orchestras played before
millions. WPA educational projects cut the illiteracy rate in Arkansas by an estimated 40 percent. Artists and writers, blacks among
them, received their first professional training under the program.
Richard Wright's first job in WPA was as a manual laborer, but on
the basis of a sample of his literary work, he was transferred to a
writer's project in 1936 for which he wrote *Uncle Tom's Children;*
four years later, he published *Native Son.*[36]

But the kinds of activities supported under WPA are not the stuff
of which modern manpower programs are made. One conclusion
about the jobs programs introduced since the 1960s is:

Only a very small number of those who need assistance participate.
. . . Those who do . . . learn little or nothing that prepares them for
entering into expanding sectors of the economy. Negro participation
is concentrated in those programs that lead to low paid, unskilled
jobs.[37]

Later evaluations come to the same conclusion, including one based
on a review of 250 evaluation studies prepared between 1964 and
1972.[38] Modern jobs programs may have had less success because
they were not so much intended to perform useful tasks and assure
that workers would be well employed as was true under WPA. And
in the case of the Neighborhood Youth Corps, the program for
in-school and out-of-school youth and with a large summer component, "annual congressional debates indicate that the legislators view
the summer program as 'riot insurance'."[39] Blacks accounted for half
or more of all enrollees in some of the major programs, whose scope
was much too limited to affect the problem of relative deprivation.
Evaluations of the program with the greatest longevity—MDTA—
show "no *definitive* evidence one way or the other about MDTA
outcomes."[40]

The Public Employment Program, under the Emergency Employment Act of 1971, was the first to establish varied employment
opportunities in state and local governments, as part of a federal
revenue-sharing effort. But it skimmed the cream of the unemployed,
who would not have had much trouble getting unsubsidized work,
even though it included a proportionately large share of blacks.[41]
American jobs policy, it has been said, "had a supplementary, remedial, mopping-up" role "operating on the fringes of the labor market."[42] When the 1974–75 recession descended, the worst since WPA
days, the American work policies proved much too limited to deal
with the employment problems among whites, much less among
blacks.

Possibly the most that can be said for the work programs of the
1960s and 1970s is that some of the fragments could have spreading
and cumulative effects in the years to come. Blacks were represented
on the staffs of jobs programs in twice their proportion in the total
population,[43] and some 200,000 young black students a year received
part-time work stipends to help them stay in school.[44] This presented
an opportunity for leadership and eventual entrepreneurship that
was not generally available elsewhere. Putting blacks in those positions could have ripple effects through the social networks operating
in the black community, particularly by helping to locate good jobs

for black applicants, and helping to lay the groundwork for future
dividends.

Are Rising Educational Levels the Answer?

The educational level of all Americans has risen sharply in the years
since World War II, and by 1975 the black labor force was almost
on a par with the white labor force in the extent of its schooling[45]
(Table 2–12). Blacks had achieved 94 percent of whites' educational
position by 1974 and 1975, compared with 79 percent in 1940. But
whatever the year, blacks' occupational position did not match their
educational position. Even the young and most highly educated
segment of the black labor force (twenty-five to thirty-four years old)
did not escape differences in hiring and promotion.[46]

If education were in fact the key to success in the labor market,
then blacks' standing in the job world should have become more
nearly equal as they acquired more nearly equal educations. Instead,
something besides education seems to have made the critical difference. In the booming sixties when jobs were plentiful and workers
were in demand, the job position of blacks improved more than their
educational levels. Yet in the economically uncertain seventies, when
jobs were scarce but blacks were catching up to whites in education
levels, their position in the labor force did not rise as fast.

Of all the ways by which blacks are said to have gained access to
better jobs and more stable employment—economic growth, migration, and advances in schooling being among the most important—
not one has placed them on an equal footing with whites in three and
a half decades. In the recitation of reasons for black Americans'
progress, the influence most overlooked and yet the most pervasive,
persistent, and important of all has been black protest. Without their
battles on their own behalf, all the measures of economic success
would have been far less impressive than they were.

Protest

Quiet Struggle—the Postwar Years

After the tumult of the war years, when they had wrested jobs from
an economy that desperately needed their labor, blacks began a long
struggle to maintain their gains. Among the earliest postwar actions
were those of the National Urban League (NUL) and the NAACP.
By the mid-forties, the NUL, long dedicated to getting better jobs for
blacks, was quietly at work to break down barriers in such major

corporations as General Electric, Western Electric, RCA, Safeway, NBC, CBS, and Time. Its strategy, meek as it may seem today, was then considered a new frontier. Through persuasion it sought to place blacks, often a single highly trained black, in what it called "entrance" jobs. The technique was to approach someone like a university-trained chemist who had sought help from the Urban League. With that person's consent the league's industrial secretary checked background and references and then got in touch with a nearby plant, part of a large corporation. A place was found on the payroll, usually as a laborer—the "entrance" job. When all agreed, the new employee began work, and the league's industrial secretary began the next task: convincing management to upgrade the new employee, level by level, and finally into the target, the laboratory. This carefully negotiated approach was time-consuming, agonizing, and humiliating, but that was the way it had to be done to persuade employers then to accept blacks who were qualified in every respect except race.[47] The Urban League formalized this approach in 1947 as the "Pilot Placement Project." Its modest goal, as the economy was slowing down, was to place a mere fifty blacks a year in fields in which few or no blacks had been hired. Advances in this program, with increasing emphasis on the construction and building trades, remain part of the continuing efforts of the Urban League.[48]

The league also developed a program beginning in 1949 to persuade corporate executives to send recruiters to black schools. The considerable time, energy, and legwork required for this have amounted to thousands of visits to management offices and union headquarters.

On other occasions the Urban League concerned itself with the discriminatory hiring practices of large government contractors. In 1950, for example, it focused on and sought to change the hiring practices of corporations contracting with the U.S. Atomic Energy Commission (AEC). After repeated negotiations with the AEC, its contractors, and labor unions, thousands of jobs, many of them skilled, were opened to black workers.[49]

The NAACP, while in the forefront of the legal struggle to win fair employment practices, has waged still other battles on behalf of black workers. In the late forties, as the job market was tightening, it established a labor department to investigate and expose discriminatory employment practices in private business. Simultaneously, it brought together and worked with influential union officials to eliminate instances of discrimination in the unions of the AFL and the CIO. Beginning in 1952, when blacks had moved again into wartime jobs, it attacked provisions in union contracts that maintained separate seniority lines for black and white workers. By working with unions to eliminate these provisions it opened jobs for black workers in the southern oil and chemical industries.[50] In some instances when negotiations failed, the NAACP resorted to direct-action picketing. In 1952, for example, hundreds of job opportunities were opened to blacks at the Philco Company plant in Philadelphia after NAACP picketing. Throughout the Truman, Eisenhower, and Kennedy years, the NAACP continued to lodge complaints to ensure enforcement by government contract compliance committees.[51]

FEPC to EEOC

The issue of permanent fair employment practices legislation became the prime focus of the civil rights fight at the end of World War II when Congress killed the wartime FEPC. In 1945–46 the National Council for a Permanent FEPC, a coalition of civil rights, liberal, labor, religious, and civil groups organized by A. Philip Randolph in 1943, lodged a vigorous but unsuccessful lobbying campaign to get the Seventy-ninth Congress to pass permanent FEPC legislation. The civil rights coalition again failed to get the Eightieth Congress to pass FEPC legislation. But the climate of civil rights pressure for a permanent FEPC, the election-year politics of 1948, and the bold decision of A. Philip Randolph to call for a civil disobedience campaign directed at the draft, successfully combined to push President Truman to issue two important executive orders on July 26, 1948. Executive Order 9980 established a Fair Employment Board in the Civil Service Commission to eliminate bias in federal employment.[52] Executive Order 9981 established the President's Committee on Equality of Treatment and Opportunity in the Armed Services to end discrimination in the military. For Randolph, and for others, the issues of discrimination in government employment and segregation in the military were closely related. At a congressional hearing on the draft, Randolph asked a Senate committee:

. . . how could any permanent Fair Employment Practices Commission dare to criticize job discrimination in private industry if the Federal Government itself were simultaneously discriminating against Negro youth in military installations all over the world?[53]

At the beginning of 1950 the NAACP called together a National Emergency Civil Rights Mobilization that brought more than 4,000 delegates to Washington to lobby Congress for FEPC and other civil rights legislation.[54] But the coalition of southern Democrats and conservative Republicans successfully foiled efforts in Congress to pass FEPC or any other civil rights legislation.

Just as they had done during World War II, advocates of more equal job opportunities seized on the Korean War mobilization and the need for labor to launch a vigorous campaign for FEPC. They hoped to convince President Truman to issue an executive order in 1950, similar to Roosevelt's Executive Order 8802 of 1941. The result was two executive orders between February and December of 1951. The first, Executive Order 10210, authorized the secretaries of defense and commerce to require and enforce nondiscrimination clauses in government contracts.[55] The second, Executive Order 10308, created the President's Committee on Government Contract Compliance. This was an advisory body with no enforcement powers.[56] (Similar committees were reconstituted under executive orders issued by Presidents Eisenhower and Kennedy.)[57]

Congress continually failed to pass equal employment rights legislation until the wave of direct-action mass participation protest of the early 1960s produced the Civil Rights Act of 1964. Title VII of that act established the Equal Employment Opportunity Commission (EEOC) to investigate charges of employment discrimination. The commission's enforcement powers, however, were limited to informal methods of persuasion and conciliation. In 1972 Congress amended Title VII by empowering the EEOC to take its cases directly to the courts when conciliation failed.

With passage of the first permanent federal fair employment practices legislation, much of the fight for equal job opportunity became institutionalized in filing complaints with the EEOC. Between July 1, 1971, and June 31, 1972, 32,840 individuals filed employment discrimination complaints with EEOC. Two years later, 56,953 individuals filed discrimination complaints, and the number escalated in later years.[58] The majority of the complaints were by blacks, even though the EEOC has jurisdiction over any infringement of equal opportunity.

The rush of complaints exceeded EEOC's financial and organizational capabilities, and almost from its inception it has been plagued with a growing backlog of unsettled cases. To make it more effective, the U.S. Commission on Civil Rights recommended that more of the agency's limited energy and resources should attack "broad patterns of systemic discrimination, rather than the hopeless task of eliminating the backlog of individual charges."[59] The 1972 amendments to Title VII permitting the EEOC to sue directly made this type of action more possible and protest activities much more effective. Settlements in the 1970s affecting hundreds of thousands of workers grew out of litigation initiated by blacks and deriving their legal basis from Title VII of the Civil Rights Act of 1964.

As early as the mid-sixties the NAACP was focusing its attention on developing complaints that documented broad patterns of discrimination in major industries and by organized labor.[60] Among the most publicized of these, and a landmark case, was the 1971 ruling by the Supreme Court in *Griggs v. Duke Power Company*,[61] which struck down the use of aptitude tests that operate to exclude minorities from employment or promotion, unless the tests proved directly related to performance on the job. Another, brought by the black caucus of the steel industry with NAACP assistance, was *U.S. v. Bethlehem Steel* in 1971, which cited discriminatory company and union seniority and transfer provisions.[62] Another notable case of the seventies involved Detroit Edison (the city's light and power company). It was brought by the Association for the Betterment of Black Edison Employees, a black labor caucus, with NAACP help. A federal district court ruled that the company and two union affiliates of the AFL-CIO had engaged in a practice of discrimination against black workers. Detroit Edison, with the Utility Workers Union and the International Brotherhood of Electrical Workers, were instructed to pay $4 million in compensatory and punitive damages to the black workers designated. Still other cases were pending in the courts in the mid-seventies.[63]

Direct Action and the 1960s

The pre-eminent strategy of protest in the 1960s was direct action. Then jobs became more plentiful, and the task was to see that blacks got their share. In the summer of 1963 hundreds of demonstrators in New York were arrested while lying on muddy streets and locking arms to block supply trucks and cement mixers on a $23.5 million Harlem Hospital project. They were protesting the freeze-out of blacks in the building and construction trades. Thousands picketed at the construction site of the Downstate Medical Center in Brooklyn, the Rutgers housing project in Lower Manhattan, and the Rochdale apartments in Queens. At the Rochdale construction site four of the demonstrators chained themselves to a crane sixty feet above the ground. Sit-ins lasting more than six weeks were conducted in the mayor's office and in the governor's New York office. Similar dramatic and highly publicized demonstrations took place in Philadelphia, Washington, D.C., Cleveland, Newark, and other places.[64]

These demonstrations at sites where public facilities were under construction were specifically aimed at discriminatory practices in the building and construction trades. And while the immediate gains for blacks were small, the demonstrations highlighted the problem as a national issue and provided a wedge for other groups like the Urban League, and for union organizations themselves to develop continuing programs to promote change.

Sponsored by CORE chapters, NAACP branches, and various local groups, construction-site demonstrations of 1963–64 were themselves part of a larger pattern of direct action against job discrimination that emerged after the 1961 freedom rides in the South. The two years following the freedom rides to desegregate public accommodations in the South saw an increasing stream of direct-action protest—mass picketing, work-site blockages, grocery shop-ins, street demonstrations, and rallies aimed at job discrimination around the country, but especially in the North. From New York to California, in Boston and Philadelphia, Cleveland, Chicago, and Seattle, black activists and interracial civil rights organizations were highly visible protesting the discriminatory hiring practices of department and retail stores, food chains and restaurants, banks, public transport companies, dairies, and craft unions.[65]

In 1964 the NAACP undertook a nationwide campaign to open new job opportunities in automobile manufacturing. The push was for supervisory, professional, technical, and managerial jobs, and for admitting blacks to specialized company training programs. Public demonstrations focusing on the auto industry occurred in forty-two cities from San Francisco to Buffalo, New York, and culminated in a one-day mass demonstration at the General Motors Building in Detroit.[66]

The impact of these demonstrations was far greater than their immediate objectives. Sustained demonstrations against a single employer or industry was often sufficient to prompt other employers and industries to accept applications from blacks and to hire them. Around the nation, in city after city, in establishments where they had never before worked, blacks were hired as bank tellers and store clerks, supermarket managers and company sales representatives, and for a host of other jobs from which they had been traditionally excluded.[67] Routinely, the more vigorous direct-action protest demonstrations were accompanied by quieter and longer-term efforts to equalize job opportunities for black workers, and the double-barreled approach worked.

In 1964 an independent black group made its own approach to getting jobs for unemployed blacks. The Reverend Leon Sullivan of Philadelphia organized Opportunities Industrialization Centers (OIC), a job training and job placement program that in six years spread to eighteen cities, trained some 66,000 persons, mostly blacks, and placed 41,000 in jobs as carpenters, draftsmen, secretaries, chefs, and some two hundred other occupations.[68]

Passage of Title VII of the Civil Rights Act of 1964 changed the context in which all job-related protest took place. The NAACP sponsored area and regional conferences in a number of major cities to familiarize employers, unions, public and private employment agencies, and local NAACP leaders with provisions of the act and procedures for making it work.[69] In its efforts to realize the full potential of Title VII, the NAACP filed more than 2,000 complaints from thirty-seven states with EEOC in 1966 alone.[68] In 1970 the NAACP expanded further a comprehensive legal attack to improve the effectiveness of the law as an instrument for combatting discrimination in employment.[70]

Blacks in Organized Labor

No account of the long and continuing fight against discrimination in job opportunities is complete without recognizing the sustained efforts that were carried on inside the labor movement. Central to so many of these efforts was A. Philip Randolph. A staunch trade unionist and firm supporter of the labor movement, Randolph took the floor year after year at AFL conventions, and later at executive board meetings of the AFL-CIO, to lead the fight against racial

discrimination within the ranks of organized labor. In 1955 he was
a leader among black trade unionists who sought to ensure that the
constitution of the soon-to-be-merged AFL and CIO would take
strong stands and impose sanctions against racial discrimination in
its affiliates. In May 1960, as the sit-in movement was spreading
across the South, Randolph pushed the struggle ahead by joining
with other black trade unionists to form the Negro American Labor
Council (NALC). The NALC, with Randolph as its president, was
the first to call for the historic 1963 "March on Washington for Jobs
and Freedom."[71]

One of the lesser-known groups of black labor activists in the fifties
was the militant National Negro Labor Council (NNLC), of which
a founding member was Coleman Young, then on the staff of the
Amalgamated Clothing Workers union,[72] and later the first black
mayor of Detroit.

Between 1951 and 1956 the NNLC waged an active campaign
against discrimination. Around the country its affiliates organized
write-in campaigns, formed picketlines, negotiated with employers,
and otherwise sought to establish the right of black workers to their
fair share of jobs. In some instances, local groups of black ministers
and educators, together with sympathetic whites, local unions, and
branches of the NAACP and the NUL, joined with the NNLC.
Together they pushed to get jobs for blacks as office workers at the
Ford Motor Company; at the front counters of hotels and banks in
San Francisco; as baseball players on the Detroit Tigers; as produc-
tion-line workers in Brooklyn breweries; as dairy-truck drivers in
New York; and as administrative and clerical workers in the Sears,
Roebuck chain. In Louisville, Kentucky, the NNLC spearheaded a
highly organized and successful "Let Freedom Crash the Gateway
to the South" campaign to win jobs for blacks at General Electric,
Westinghouse, and Reynolds Aluminum.

As an organization of black trade unionists, the NNLC sought to
represent the interest of black workers in union-employer conflicts.
And in those unions with a long and active history of accepting
blacks in their ranks, the NNLC campaigned to get blacks into the
highest decisionmaking bodies of the organizations.

But the NNLC functioned in a climate of red-baiting and anticommunist hysteria, and like other vocal activists of that period was
subjected to unsubstantiated charges of being Communist. In 1956,
when faced with the possible expense of $100,000 to defend NNLC
against the charge of being a Communist-front organization, its

members voted to dissolve the organization, thus bringing to an end
one of the best-organized protest efforts on behalf of black workers.
But this did not bring an end to the concern of militant black trade
unionists with the status and problems of black workers.[73]

With the birth of the Black Power movement in the late sixties, the black trade unionist movement gained new momentum.
Black labor caucuses emerged and demanded an end to industry
and labor-union discrimination: company hiring practices, union
seniority policies, and policies that perpetuated the practice of
blacks as the last hired and first fired. Between 1968 and the
early 1970s, black union caucuses, as well as interest in an independent black union movement, spread throughout the country.
In Chicago, black trade unionists organized work stoppages on
the city bus system to protest union and company bias, and to
demand that blacks be included in the higher ranks of union
leadership. Steelworkers picketed at the national meeting of the
steelworkers' unions to demand black representation in the ranks
of leadership. The almost wholly black and Puerto Rican International Ladies Garment Workers Union (ILGWU) formed caucuses to protest the absence of minorities in higher-level jobs and
in the ranks of union leadership.

Detroit has always been one of the centers of the labor movement,
and the United Auto Workers (UAW) has had black caucuses for
almost as long as the union has existed. The auto workers' black
caucus movement accelerated in the late sixties. New militant groups
protested bias in union seniority systems, general working conditions, the pace of automated work, company promotion policies, and
lack of black representation in the higher echelons of union leadership. Among the most active were the Dodge Revolutionary Union
Movement (DRUM), the federated League of Revolutionary Black
Workers, the Ad Hoc Committee of Concerned UAW Members, and
the United Brothers.[74]

Union black caucuses were formed in Philadelphia, New York,
San Francisco, Cleveland, and other cities—in almost all unions
where blacks were concentrated. Steelworkers, teachers, auto workers, garment workers, construction workers, and bus drivers were
only among the most visible of black workers in the forefront of the
caucus movement of the sixties.[75]

By the seventies there were over 2 million black American trade
unionists, accounting for about a fifth of all black workers—the same
proportion as among whites.[76] In September 1972, more than 1,200

of them from some thirty-seven national labor unions came together in Chicago to form the Coalition of Black Trade Unionists (CBTU). Initially gathered to endorse George McGovern's campaign for president, the organization soon expanded its concerns to the general problems of black workers in the trade union movement. At its third annual meeting in 1974, CBTU reflected the expanded interests of black workers by articulating dissatisfaction with their limited role in the policymaking activities of local and national unions.[77]

The more subtle forms of discrimination common to the seventies put the effectiveness of black union activity to a difficult test. By using the mechanism of the labor movement itself, black unionists had won themselves a privileged position, expanded job opportunities for all black workers, and a standard by which to judge the employment opportunities available to blacks. Simply by securing union-standard wages, benefits and rights for 2 million black workers, the position of all black workers has been raised.

Perception and Reality

These struggles for employment, so often overlooked in reviews of black economic progress, are nevertheless at the heart of it. They are a potent force and a necessary ingredient.

The black struggle for jobs continues because inequality still prevails. Racial discrimination and acceptance of the resulting inequality remain embedded in the white-dominated job market, buttressed by many rationalizations. One of the most appealing rationales is that good economic conditions will remove or at least mitigate inequality. When everyone is progressing, with blacks better off than before but still almost as far behind whites, the remaining gap is easily ignored, at least by the majority.

Another rationalization points to how much blacks have gained since 1940, and especially since 1960, thus projecting the occurrence of equal status in the future as an automatic consequence. That vague future leaves room for an underlying assumption that permeates American private and public thought, that blacks will never be equal in the job market because whatever a person's qualifications or a job's requirements, white is likely to be better.

This convoluted thinking fails to see that many more inexperienced and untaught white workers are employed than there are blacks seeking jobs. It fails to perceive why blacks have had to fight to work even in times of severe labor shortage. It typically regards the black migrant from the South, usually a city dweller already or an experienced farmer, as an oaf who cannot get along in an urban setting. It establishes training programs that teach black workers skills for which there is little demand. And it creates equal employment opportunity committees and commissions to stamp out or punish discrimination without providing sufficiently for either administration or enforcement.

Self-deception has gone hand in hand with race prejudice. In spite of all the evidence to the contrary, the blame for blacks' inequality with whites in the job market is too often placed on them, as being less enterprising, less intelligent, less qualified, and without enough education to do the work.

TABLE 2–1

Black Workers Have Advanced into All Types of Industries Since 1940

Percentage Distribution of Employed Workers in Key *Industry* Groups, by Wage Level and by Race, 1940 and 1974

Industry group	Black[a]		White	
	1940	1974	1940	1974
Total	100	100	100	100
Agriculture, forestry, fishing	34	3	18	4
Personal service	29	10	7	4
Other	37	87	75	92
Total	100	100	100	100
Low wage[b]	86	65	67	63
High wage	14	35	33	37

[a] Negro and other nonwhite races.
[b] Low-wage occupations are those in which median earnings of men in 1969 were less than $8,000.

Source: Derived from 1940 Census of Population, *The Labor Force, Vol. 3, Pt. 1, U.S. Summary,* Table 76, pp. 188–9, and unpublished data from the Bureau of the Census.

TABLE 2–2

*Black Workers Made Large Occupational Gains 1940–75, but Remained
More Likely than White Workers to Be in Low-Wage and Service Jobs*

**Percentage Distribution of Employed Workers in Key *Occupation* Groups, by
Wage Level and by Race, 1940 and 1975**

Occupation group	Black[a]			White	
	1940	*1975*		*1940*	*1975*
Total	100		100	100	100
Farm	33	3		17	4
Service (excl. protective)	33	26		8	12
All other	34	71		75	84
Total	100		100	100	100
Low wage[b]	93	76		69	60
High wage	7	24		31	40

[a] Negro and other nonwhite races.

[b] Low-wage occupations are those with median earnings in 1969 of less than $8,000.

Source: Derived from 1940 Census of Population, *The Labor Force, Vol. 3, Pt. 1, U.S.
Summary,* Table 62, pp. 88–90; U.S. President, *Employment and Training
Report of the President, 1976* (Washington, D.C.: Government Printing Office,
1976), Table A–16, p. 236.

TABLE 2–3

*Black Workers' Occupational Position Increased Dramatically After 1940,
but by 1975 Had Not Even Reached the Position White Workers Held in
1940*

Occupational Position Indices[a] by Race, Selected Years, 1940–75

Year	Black[b]	White
1940	90	130
1947	97	133
1948	98	135
1950	99	136
1951	98	136
1953	99	137
1954	100	137
1955	100	136
1958	101	140
1960	103	140
1961	103	140
1965	107	141
1969	115	142
1970	116	142
1971	116	142
1972	117	140
1974	121	142
1975	119	140

[a] The index for each racial group for each year is the result of multiplying the relative
earnings of each of nine occupation groups in 1969 (nonfarm laborers = 100) times
the percentage of workers in each of the occupation groups and then adding the
resulting scores of each occupation group together. This final score is then multiplied
by 100 so that the index is in whole numbers.

[b] Negro and other nonwhite races.

Source: Derived from 1940 Census of Population, *The Labor Force, Vol. 3, Pt. 1, U.S.
Summary*, Table 62, pp. 88–90; 1950 Census of Population, *Characteristics of
the Population, Vol. 2, Pt. 1, U.S. Summary*, Table 128, pp. 276–8; BLS,
Handbook of Labor Statistics 1972, Bulletin 1735 (Washington, D.C.: Government Printing Office, 1972), Tables 3, 16, pp. 29, 56; U.S. President, *Manpower
Report of the President, March 1964* (Washington, D.C.: Government Printing
Office, 1964), Table 147, p. 199; U.S. Congress, Senate Committee on Labor
and Public Welfare, Subcommittee on Civil Rights, *Employment and Economic Status of Negroes in the United States: A Staff Report*, 83rd Cong., 2nd
sess. 1954, Table 18, p. 16; CPR, Series P–50, No. 66, *Employment of White
and Non-white Persons: 1955*, Table 3, p. 8; BLS, *Handbook of Labor Statistics
1974*, Bulletin 1825 (Washington, D.C.: Government Printing Office, 1974),
Table 19, pp. 69–73; BLS, *Handbook of Labor Statistics 1975—Reference
Edition*, Bulletin 1865 (Washington, D.C.: Government Printing Office, 1975),
Table 19, p. 72; CPR, Series P–60, No. 75; *Income in 1969 of Families and
Persons in the United States*, Table 50, p. 113; U.S. President, *Employment and
Training Report of the President, 1976* (Washington, D.C.: Government Print-
ing Office, 1976), Table A–16, p. 236.

TABLE 2–4

In Spite of Some Shift to Higher-Paying Jobs Since 1940, About Two-Thirds of Black Workers Remained in Low-Paying Occupations While Two-Thirds of White Workers Stayed in the Higher-Paying Jobs

Percentage Distribution of Employed Workers by Occupation Group and by Race, 1940, 1975, and 1969 White Median Earnings

Occupation group (ranked by median income)	1940 Black[a]	1940 White	1975 Black[a]	1975 White	Median 1969 earnings (white)[b]
All occupations	100	100	100	100	
Managerial and admin.	1	9	4	11	$10,123
Professional and technical	3	8	11	16	8,553
Craft (incl. protective)	3	14	9	13	8,196
Operatives	11	19	20	15	5,628
Sales	1	7	3	7	5,473
Clerical	1	11	16	18	4,751
Labor (excl. farm and mine)	1	6	9	4	4,557
Farm	33	17	3	4	3,810
Service (excl. protective)	33	8	26	12	2,554

[a] Negro and other nonwhite races.
[b] Median earnings of all persons other than blacks.

Source: Derived from 1940 Census of Population, *The Labor Force, Vol. 3, Pt. 1, U.S. Summary,* Table 62, pp. 88–96; U.S. President, *Employment and Training Report of the President, 1976* (Washington, D.C.: Government Printing Office, 1976), Table A–16, p. 236. Median estimated from CPR, Series P–60, No. 75, *Income in 1969 of Families and Persons in the United States,* Table 50, p. 113.

TABLE 2–5

The Occupational Position of Black Workers Relative to Whites Has Shown Its Greatest Improvement Since 1960

Relative Occupational Position (Black to White)[a] for Total and Nonfarm Occupations, Selected Years, 1940–75

Year	Occupations covered	
	Total	Nonfarm
1940	69	66
1947	73	71
1948	73	72
1950	73	72
1951	72	71
1953	72	71
1954	73	72
1955	74	72
1958	72	71
1960	74	74
1961	73	73
1965	76	75
1969	81	81
1970	82	82
1971	82	81
1972	84	83
1974	85	84
1975	85	84

[a] Relative occupational position (black to white) is calculated by dividing the occupational position of blacks by the occupational position of whites for each year. The final score is multiplied by 100 so that the relative position figure is a whole number.

Source: Derived from 1940 Census of Population, *The Labor Force, Vol. 3, Pt. 1, U.S. Summary,* Table 62, pp. 88–90; 1950 Census of Population, *Characteristics of the Population, Vol. 2, Pt. 1, U.S. Summary,* Table 128, pp. 276–8; BLS, *Handbook of Labor Statistics 1972,* Bulletin 1735 (Washington, D.C.: Government Printing Office, 1972), Tables 3, 16, pp. 29, 56; U.S. President, *Manpower Report of the President, March 1964* (Washington, D.C.: Government Printing Office, 1964), Table 147, p. 199; U.S. Congress, Senate Committee on Labor and Public Welfare, Subcommittee on Civil Rights, *Employment and Economic Status of Negroes in the United States; A Staff Report,* 83rd Cong., 2nd sess., 1954, Table 18, p. 16; CPR, Series P–50, No. 66, *Employment of White and Non-white Persons: 1955,* Table 3, p. 8; BLS, *Handbook of Labor Statistics 1974,* Bulletin 1825 (Washington, D.C.: Government Printing Office, 1974), Table 19, pp. 69–73; BLS, *Handbook of Labor Statistics 1975: Reference Edition,* Bulletin 1865 (Washington, D.C.: Government Printing Office, 1975), Table 19, p. 72; CPR, Series P–60, No. 75, *Income in 1969 of Families and Persons in the United States,* Table 50, p. 113.

TABLE 2–6

*Black Workers' Unemployment Rates Usually Far Exceed 5 Percent—the
1975 National Target—Whereas White Workers' Rates Have Seldom
Been That High Except in the Recession 1970s.*

Unemployment Rates by Race, 1948–75 and January–August 1976

Period		Total	Black[a]	White
1948		3.8	5.9	3.5
1949		5.9	8.9	5.6
1950		5.3	9.0	4.9
1951		3.3	5.3	3.1
1952		3.0	5.4	2.8
1953		2.9	4.5	2.7
1954		5.5	9.9	5.0
1955		4.4	8.7	3.9
1956		4.1	8.3	3.6
1957		4.3	7.9	3.8
1958		6.8	12.6	6.1
1959		5.5	10.7	4.8
1960		5.5	10.2	4.9
1961		6.7	12.4	6.0
1962		5.5	10.9	4.9
1963		5.7	10.8	5.0
1964		5.2	9.6	4.6
1965		4.5	8.1	4.1
1966		3.8	7.3	3.4
1967		3.8	7.4	3.4
1968		3.6	6.7	3.2
1969		3.5	6.4	3.1
1970		4.9	8.2	4.5
1971		5.9	9.9	5.4
1972		5.6	10.0	5.0
1973		4.9	8.9	4.3
1974		5.6	9.9	5.0
1975		8.5	13.9	7.8
1976[b]	January	7.8	13.2	7.1
	February	7.6	13.7	6.8
	March	7.5	12.5	6.8
	April	7.5	13.0	6.7
	May	7.3	12.2	6.6
	June	7.5	13.3	6.8
	July	7.8	12.9	7.1
	August	7.9	13.6	7.1

(Table 2–6, continued)

[a] Negro and other nonwhite races.
[b] Seasonally adjusted.

Source: Derived from U.S. President, *Economic Report of the President, 1976* (Washington, D.C.: Government Printing Office, 1976), Table B–24, p. 199; BLS, *Employment and Earnings* 22 (September 1976): Table A–36, p. 44.

TABLE 2–7

The Number of White Workers Is Many Times That of Blacks in Jobs at All Skill Levels

Percentage of Whites in Selected Occupations, 1950, 1960, and 1970

Occupation group	1950	Percent 1960	1970
All occupations	90	89	90
Professional and technical	96	95	95
Accountants and auditors	99	98	98
Drafting	99	98	97
Teachers, elem. and sec.	92	91	92
Clerical	97	95	92
Bank tellers	100	99	96
Secretaries	[a]	98	97
Telephone operators	99	97	89
Sales	98	98	97
Retail	98	97	96
Crafts	96	95	94
Compositors and typesetters	98	97	95
Electricians	99	98	97
Airplane mechanics	98	96	95
Tool and die makers	100	99	98
Operatives	90	89	87
Bus drivers	96	90	86
Service (excl. protective and pvt. hsehold)	77	77	81
Police	98	96	93

[a] Not available.

Source: Derived from 1950 Census of Population, *Special Reports, Vol. 4, Pt. 1, Chap. B, Occupational Characteristics,* Tables 10–11, pp. 107–22; 1960 Census of Population, *Subject Reports, PC (2)–7A, Occupational Characteristics,* Table 9, pp. 116–29; 1970 Census of Population, *Subject Reports, PC (2)–7A, Occupational Characteristics,* Table 5, pp. 59–86.

TABLE 2–8

In All Types of Jobs Black Workers' Unemployment Rates Fluctuate with the Business.
Cycle Just as Whites' Rates Do, but at a Much Higher Level

Unemployment Rates[a] by Selected Occupation Group and by Race,
1955, 1965, 1971, and 1975

	Prosperity				Recession			
Occupation group	1955		1965		1971		1975	
	Black[b]	White	Black[b]	White	Black[c]	White	Black[c]	Whit
All occupations	7.9	3.6	8.3	4.1	9.9	5.4	13.9	7.8
Operatives	8.2	5.5	7.4	5.2	10.9	7.9	17.3	12.5
Nonfarm laborers	12.0	9.8	9.7	7.9	12.0	10.5	18.4	14.9
Service	7.2	4.8	7.1	4.5	8.5	5.7	11.3	7.9
Private hsehold	5.6	3.0	5.9	2.8	5.8	3.5	6.4	4.8
Other	8.7	5.2	7.8	4.8	9.4	5.9	12.3	8.1

[a] Data are for the total experienced civilian labor force.
[b] Negro and other nonwhite races.
[c] Negro only.

Source: Derived from BLS, *The Negroes in the United States: Their Economic and Social Situation,* by
Dorothy K. Newman, Bulletin 1511 (Washington, D.C.: Government Printing Office, 1966),
Table II A–9, p. 88; CPR, Series P–23, No. 42, *The Social and Economic Status of the Black
Population in the United States, 1971,* Table 43, p. 59; unpublished BLS data.

TABLE 2–9

The Unemployment Rates of the Groups Most Vulnerable to Unemployment—Women and Youth—Mirror the Business Cycle, with the Black Workers Among Them Following the Up- and Downswings at Much Higher Unemployment Levels than the White

Unemployment Rates in Business Cycle Periods, by Sex, Age, and Race, 1957–75

Business cycle period	Women Black[a]	White	Teenagers Black[a]	White	20–24 year olds Black[a]	White
1957	7.3	4.3	19.2	10.5	12.5	6.3
1958	10.8	6.2	27.4	14.4	19.3	10.0
1960	9.4	5.3	24.4	13.5	14.0	7.9
1961	11.8	6.5	27.7	15.3	16.9	9.4
1969	7.8	4.2	24.1	10.7	10.1	5.1
1970	9.3	5.4	29.0	13.5	13.8	7.4
1971	10.8	6.3	31.6	15.1	16.7	9.0
1973	10.5	5.3	30.2	12.5	14.9	6.7
1974	10.7	6.1	33.0	13.9	16.6	8.0
1975	14.0	8.6	36.9	17.9	22.8	12.3

[a] Negro and other nonwhite races.

Source: Derived from BLS, *Handbook of Labor Statistics 1975—Reference Edition,* Bulletin 1865 (Washington, D.C.: Government Printing Office, 1975), Tables 3, 60, 63, pp. 31–4, 146, 153–5; *Monthly Labor Review* 99 (March 1976): Table 4, p. 70; U.S. President, *Employment and Training Report of the President, 1976* (Washington, D.C.: Government Printing Office, 1976), Table A–18, p. 239.

TABLE 2–10

The Proportion of Adult Women in the Labor Force Rose Very Gradually in the 29 Years from 1947 to 1976; Teenagers' Proportion Edged Up Slightly

Adult Women and Teenagers as a Percentage of the Civilian Labor Force, 1947–75 and January–August 1976

Period		Adult women[a]	Teenagers
1947		25	7
1948		26	7
1949		26	7
1950		27	7
1951		28	7
1952		28	7
1953		28	6
1954		28	6
1955		29	6
1956		29	6
1957		30	6
1958		30	6
1959		30	7
1960		30	7
1961		31	7
1962		31	7
1963		31	7
1964		32	7
1965		32	8
1966		32	9
1967		33	8
1968		33	8
1969		34	9
1970		34	9
1971		34	9
1972		34	9
1973		35	10
1974		35	10
1975		36	9
1976[b]	January	36	10
	February	36	9
	March	36	10
	April	36	10
	May	36	10
	June	36	9
	July	36	9
	August	36	10

(Table 2–10, continued)
(a) 20 years old and over.
(b) Seasonally adjusted.

Source: Derived from BLS, *Handbook of Labor Statistics, 1975—Reference Edition*,
Bulletin 1865 (Washington, D.C.: Government Printing Office, 1975), Table
3, p. 31; BLS, *Employment and Earnings* 23 (September 1976), Table A–33,
p. 42.

TABLE 2–11

*Black Workers Have Remained a Constant 11 Percent of the Total
Labor Force Since 1954. Black Women and Teenagers Rose Only
Slightly and Very Gradually as a Percentage of the Black Labor Force
During the 22 Years from 1954 to 1976*

**Black Workers as a Percentage of the Total Civilian Labor Force, and Black
Women and Teenagers as a Percentage of the Black Labor Force, 1954–75 and
January–August 1976**

Period	All black[a] workers as percent of total civilian labor force	Black[a] workers as percent of black labor force	
		Adult women[b]	Teenagers
1954	11	36	7
1955	11	36	7
1956	11	36	7
1957	11	36	7
1958	11	37	7
1959	11	37	7
1960	11	37	7
1961	11	37	7
1962	11	38	7
1963	11	38	7
1964	11	38	7
1965	11	39	8
1966	11	39	9
1967	11	39	9
1968	11	39	9
1969	11	40	9
1970	11	40	9
1971	11	40	8
1972	11	41	8
1973	11	41	9
1974	11	41	9
1975	11	42	8
1976[c] January	11	42	9
February	12	42	9
March	11	43	9
April	12	42	9
May	12	42	9
June	11	42	8
July	11	42	8
August	12	42	9

(Table 2–11, continued)

[a] Negro and other nonwhite races.

[b] 20 years old and over.

[c] Seasonally adjusted.

Source: Derived from BLS, *Handbook of Labor Statistics–Reference Edition,* Bulletin 1865 (Washington, D.C.: Government Printing Office, 1975), Table 3, pp. 31–4; BLS, *Employment and Earnings,* 22 (January 1976, September 1976), Tables A–3, pp. 26–7, and A–33, 35, pp. 42–3.

TABLE 2–12

Blacks' Educational Position Relative to That of Whites Remains Well Above Their Occupational Position; the Gap of Around 10 Points Has Been Almost Constant Since 1940

Relative Black[a] to White Educational and Occupational Position Compared, Decennial Years 1940–70, and 1974–75

Year	Relative black to white	
	Educational position	Occupational position
1940	79	69
1950	84	73
1960	85	74
1970	89	82
1974	94	85
1975	94	85

[a] Negro and other nonwhite races.

Source: See note on page 297 for derivation of the educational position index and Table 2–11 for the occupational position index derivation and sources. Sources used for the educational position index are as follows:
1940 Census of Population, *Occupational Statistics (Sample Statistics),* Table 3, pp. 59–112; 1950 Census of Population, *Special Reports, Vol. 4, Pt. 5, Chap. B, Education,* Table 9, pp. 5B–73–82; 1960 Census of Population, *Subject Reports, PC(2)–7A, Occupational Characteristics,* Table 9, pp. 116–29; 1970 Census of Population, *Subject Reports, PC(2)–7A, Occupational Characteristics,* Table 5, pp. 59–86; unpublished data from the Bureau of Labor Statistics.

Learning Without Earning

OVER TIME, the idea that education through high school was necessary to achieve the qualifications for getting and holding a job became one that few in official circles were willing to challenge. And being a nation of immigrants who needed something other than wealth or established position as a route to success, we have been receptive to that argument. We have heard the education argument repeated a good deal over the years, but somehow it is always more frequently heard in the years when the economy is slowing down and jobs of any kind are scarce, in times when it seems it would be just as well if young people stayed in school.

And the argument has always had another side. It has provided a handy rationale for denying jobs to people who were not likely to have stayed in school after the mid-teens and whom employers were not particularly eager to hire. In this connection, one especially stubborn and widespread notion has persisted into the seventies and is as ill-founded for the present as for the past. This is the firm belief that blacks are more likely to be unemployed because they are not "qualified" for jobs in the American economy and, in particular, not "qualified" for those jobs resulting from changing technology.

Job Requirements and Education

It is curious that Americans should have been so taken with the notion that workers must have many years of formal education in order to do a good job, because until recently few adult Americans had much schooling. In addition to the millions of immigrants whose only formal education in this country occurred in night schools where they learned enough to pass their citizenship exams, there were other millions whose plans for formal education were ruled out by the Depression, or who did not seek an education by choice and custom. Nor were people without high school diplomas only in the least desirable jobs. Police, salespeople, and office workers were well respected in American communities of the forties and fifties, and many of them did their jobs and raised their families very much according to the middle-class standards of the day, without having finished high school. The people actually doing the jobs neither had nor needed what the labor-market experts urged was so essential.

In 1950, a prosperous year when America entered the Korean conflict and the economy was picking up steam, white dropouts made up half the total experienced civilian labor force (Table 3–1). That year, white workers who had not finished high school were:

65 to 70 percent of all the skilled and semi-skilled workers in industry (in crafts or production jobs);

50 percent of police;

40 percent or more of all sales workers;

30 percent of all clerical workers.

In 1960, which saw the end of 1959 prosperity and the beginning of a recession, whites without a high school diploma were still nearly half of the labor force (46 percent), including:

60 to 65 percent of all industrial workers;

50 percent of all private service workers (excluding domestic workers);

40 percent of police and of sales workers;

25 percent of all clerical workers;

10 percent of workers in accounting and drafting, and in professional and technical jobs.

By 1970, the schooling level of all workers had increased substantially, the economy was on the decline, and employers could hire anyone they might choose. Even then, one-third of the total labor force consisted of white workers who had not finished high school, including:

50 percent (approximately) of all production workers;

30 percent of sales workers;

30 percent of airplane mechanics;

20 percent of clerical workers;

20 percent of police.

Defining Job Requirements—the Government's Role

Employers, supervisors, and personnel officers are the usual managers of each firm's work force, but the federal government plays an important role by introducing policies to help industry meet its labor requirements and by helping workers find jobs. The U.S. Employment Service (USES) was set up in the Labor Department[1] in the early 1930s to fulfill this role. To improve and speed screening and hiring under World War II emergency conditions, the USES introduced a relatively untried method for personnel selection: job analysis in terms of the worker traits required for successful performance.[2] A key objective was to reduce the use of arbitrary criteria as much as possible, since such criteria screened out people who were able to do the work, and slowed down recruitment and production.

Armed with its new approach, the USES produced a job-analysis manual to accompany a *Dictionary of Occupational Titles*. The manual provided specifications for several thousand occupations. The *Training and Reference Manual for Job Analysis* was first published in 1944, and then updated in 1956 and 1965.[3] The Bureau of Labor Statistics published less technical and detailed information than the USES over the same period of time in its *Occupational Outlook Handbook*.[4] The *Dictionary*'s manual tends to be used by labor specialists and scholars, while the *Handbook* is a standard reference for high school counseling. These reference works have continued to be in substantial agreement that the overwhelming majority of the American work force has had as much schooling, in the formal sense, as their jobs demanded, or more. This has been as true for black workers as for white[5] (Table 3–2). The few occupations in which schooling tended to be less than the amount recommended are jobs for which learning the skill on the job is paramount (e.g., carpenters, machinists, coppersmiths, plumbers, electricians, and tool and die makers).[6]

Both the *Dictionary* and the *Handbook* still make the important point that most jobs in the labor force can be learned on the job, in a short time, and without a high school diploma—jobs the white labor force has long managed to hold without a diploma, while the black labor force has been labeled "disadvantaged" for lack of it.[7] Other authorities on the subject, in and out of government, failed to notice.

The Mythology of Increasing Job Complexity

White Collar—Blue Collar

It is not surprising that white workers without high school diplomas had learned enough in their jobs to do them well. However, the remarkable constancy of labor-market reliance on dropouts seems to have been lost on those who are determined to prove the need for more education by upgrading the labor force with statistics. There is a circular sort of argument involved. It begins with the artificial division of workers into blue-collar and white-collar. Because the white-collar occupation group has always included professional, technical, and managerial positions, it is easily overlooked that all those in the group are not doctors and lawyers who make substantial salaries for highly skilled work requiring many years of training and preparation. In fact, most of today's "white-collar" workers get low pay for routine work that is far removed from the demands of a college or, in many cases, even a high school education.

There has been an increase in white-collar jobs from nearly one-third of the labor force in 1940 to one-half in 1975 (Table 3–3). And, without considering the kinds of jobs that are done or what they pay, it is then argued that if there are now more people in white-collar jobs, there must be a greater need for educated workers.

Looking at actual job requirements, rather than at blue-collar/white-collar labels, leads to very different conclusions. In those terms, the change is far less dramatic in thirty-five years. About one-sixth of the labor force may have needed a high school diploma or more in 1940, and only about one-fourth in 1975 (Table 3–3). Since 1960, the white-collar group of workers has expanded by roughly 15 million people, but about four-fifths of the increase was in sales and clerical jobs, for most of which completing high school is not necessary.[8]

The number of doctors, lawyers, and skilled technicians had increased, but they were only 9 percent of the work force in 1950 and had risen to only 11 percent by 1960—just the time when the campaign was being launched for a more educated work force (Table 3–4). The only one of the professional occupations that increased significantly and needs extensive education was elementary and secondary school teaching, which has traditionally paid less well and conferred less status than some other professions.[9] The largest increases in the conglomerate of white-collar occupations were among clerks for banks, computer processing, in stores, and in government. Growth in this group of workers is scarcely grounds for insisting that these and all the others, too—those processing or packing foods, producing and packaging industrial products, and monitoring or operating machines—need more education for the work they do.

Yet that has apparently happened, although for over twenty-five years the standard government references on worker qualifications have consistently maintained, "Most jobs in industrial production do not require a high school diploma."[10]

Technology

The changing nature of jobs makes the distinction between blue-collar and white-collar work increasingly misleading. Machine jobs in industry have become more clerical, while clerical and sales jobs have become more mechanical. Whatever the job sphere, technological advances have generally resulted in the need for less skill rather than more.

Studies prepared for the U.S. National Commission on Technology, Automation, and Economic Progress as early as 1966 show that, while technological change created many new types of jobs, most of the new jobs had low skill requirements. Only a few required substantial knowledge or technical training.[11] The industries studied varied widely, from some that included mostly clerical and administrative personnel—banking and insurance—to those with a large concentration in machine operations—manufacturing tires and tubes, meatpacking, and machine-shop trades. In all of these, technology introduced a few highly skilled jobs that required knowledge of a new mechanical system or new skills, and many unskilled monitoring jobs. Highly complex equipment does not usually need highly skilled operators. The "skills" are built into the machines.

This is as true in clerical and sales work as in industrial plants. Bookkeepers have been converted into machine operators. Bank tellers have become, in part, keypunch operators. The use of precomputed materials is increasing as well, making the jobs more routine and clerical. Machines take coded cards and transact any number of functions—deposits, withdrawals, transfers between accounts, and loan repayments. The revolution in banking technology has gone so far that automated tellers have replaced human tellers in increasing numbers. Processed cards are being used in parking facilities and subways. An ever-expanding amount of work is being done by programmers, coders, keypunch operators, and a host of clerical operatives who finally put it all in envelopes. Anyone who has carried on a correspondence with a department store computer to get a bill corrected knows how automated businesses have become.

In many large offices, secretarial work has also become more routine, while executive responsibilities are reserved for a chosen few. Dictating and copying machines make office detail less complicated, and file-finding systems cut down time as well as the need for special skills. As long ago as 1935, a typical large office was described as "nothing but a white-collar factory."[12] Jobs in retail sales (in which approximately half of all sales workers are employed)[13] require less personal service as the shift to self-service has become almost complete, and the next level of depersonalization, optical scanning of prices, is on the way. With the growth of rapid-food chains, cooks no longer cook but stack and serve food from warming ovens. Automatic gas pumps are becoming common, leaving station attendants to monitor screens from the office.

Yet employers have seized on "technological advances" as yet another excuse for not hiring black workers. Prominent writers, blacks themselves included,[14] were readily persuaded by the conventional wisdom. One writer echoed the prevailing view of technology's impact on black workers when he wrote:

> In some cases there was an actual demand for Negro personnel that could not be met. . . . At lower levels, new techniques and the rapid advance of automation were steadily reducing the number of jobs which could be filled without specialized skills.[15]

It would have been hard to describe the situation in terms more divorced from the truth.

The Stay-in-School Campaign

By the decade of the sixties, the idea that youth should complete high school to be employable had acquired official sanction, and it took its most elaborate form in the 1963 Dropout Campaign. The proponents of the stay-in-school position were powerful people. No less a figure than the secretary of labor wrote in 1961 (a year of increasing unemployment):

When you realize that only four out of every 100 jobs available today
do not require education, the need for a good education and hard
work becomes apparent.[16]

After another half-year of high unemployment and not much prospect that young people of any kind would be able to get jobs, he put
the matter even more strongly:

The minimum for useful employment, and the minimum for a rich
fruitful happy life, is a high school education. And that's the very
minimum.[17]

The arguments in favor of staying in school took many forms.
Some directly acknowledged that it was not so much the education
that was important as having the diploma when a prospective employer demanded it. One young victim of credentialism, a high
school dropout, presented his story in *Reader's Digest* in 1961. His
was a tragic first-person account. Others, he predicted, "will soon
find, as I did, that nearly all employers today demand employees
with a diploma."[18]

By 1962, *Science Digest* was calling the dropout problem the
"great American tragedy of our times."[19] They were joined by *Ebony*
and *School Life* magazines,[20] people like the president of Harvard,[21]
and groups like the National Urban League,[22] all of whom got on the
bandwagon to try to convince young people, particularly young
black people, that a high school diploma was the key to the future.
Even the *Monthly Labor Review* began to make its contribution in
the form of annual articles on how much better off a graduate is.[23]
All of them managed to stress the importance of staying in school,
without feeling the need to question why black high school graduates
had higher unemployment rates than white dropouts.[24] In 1968, the
Manpower Administration of the Department of Labor finally acknowledged that perhaps a diploma might not be all that it had
seemed.

The requirement of a high school diploma has in fact become a kind
of shibboleth in personnel practice, often applied without thought as
to its usefulness in selecting workers able to perform the jobs that are
to be filled.[25]

But by then the economy was booming, jobs were plentiful, and,
irrespective of whether credit is due to the stay-in-school campaign
or to the American faith in the value of learning, American youth
were among the longest-educated in the world. The group toward

whom the campaign was frequently directed, black youth, had made
the greatest strides. Schooling among blacks was skyrocketing, just
in time for the official tune to have changed.

In 1971 a study for the federal government's Office of Management and Budget concluded that

> it is hard to escape the conclusion that the reported high level of
> education of the American labor force reflects not occupational re-
> quirements but a broader set of social values.[26]

The new concern of that day was the frustrated, over-educated,
underutilized college graduates.[27] A careful analysis of longtime
trends in education and the requirements of the labor market noted
that

> the availability of jobs which, in earlier periods, were conventionally
> associated with higher levels of education has not kept pace with the
> growth in educational levels.[28]

All those years, the education campaign had been quixotically
waged within the context of an overqualified work force and too few
jobs, rather than in terms of realistic job requirements. Fact was
bound to catch up with rhetoric, and eventually it did. When there
are severe labor shortages, employers tend to reduce or eliminate the
unrealistic hiring standards that are imposed when workers are plentiful and jobs scarce. The government and business communities
finally recognized openly that credentials (particularly the requirement that all workers have a high school diploma) were being used
as a screening device irrelevant to job performance.[29] Among social
scientists, the idea of inappropriate credentialism fast became a fad.
Studies appeared, detailing the frustrations of workers hired with
more education than their jobs demanded, and the importance of
nonacademic qualities for getting a job done.[30]

When special studies were conducted to learn whether those who
left high school without a diploma were unemployed longer, earned
less, or had lower job status, research groups found to their surprise
that dropouts did as well or better than their high school graduate
counterparts.[31] Dropouts, it was learned, were at a disadvantage only
when employers demanded diplomas as a requisite for hiring, not
after they were on the job. Earlier attention to the need for more and
more schooling no doubt reflected the biases of the academic world
and senior management more than it did the realities of the work that
had to be done. Research is usually performed by academic people

with long years of education to their credit, who find it hard to conceive of work in terms of all those things that are not taught or measured by our schools—initiative, a keen artistic sense, mechanical dexterity—yet make a worker suited for the job. The jobs held by the vast majority of workers have little relation to their education. When it finally became obvious that the kind of education given to most workers was largely unrelated to the jobs available and needing to be done, the pendulum began to swing to the opposite extreme. At that point, the argument began to be heard that young people were staying in school too long.[32]

Blacks' Rising Education Levels

Black young men and women were strongly influenced by the social climate that blamed black unemployment on a lack of education and promised rewards for achieving it. In one important sense they were right. Higher education might not have been necessary for whites in search of good, steady jobs with a future, but for black men and women it was regarded as a minimum requirement for the higher-paying jobs. By 1975, black young men and women born after 1940 had completed high school in about the same proportion as whites, and many had gone on to college.[33]

While the stay-in-school and learn-for-earning campaign was a broadside one, intended for black and white alike, the influence on whites was much more modest than on blacks.[34] In terms of actual jobs available, whites' limited aspirations were realistic. There are just so many professional, technical, and managerial jobs to do, and whites from a variety of ethnic backgrounds already held them in very nearly equal proportions. The same was not true for black Americans (Figure 3–1).

Education, long regarded as their springboard to success, represents in a classic way the struggle of black Americans to achieve. In the 1940s, it was said:

> As self-improvement through business or social improvement through government appeared so much less possible for them, Negroes have come to affix an even stronger trust in the magic of education. . . . the masses of Negroes show even today a naive, almost religious faith in education.[35]

Walter White, then executive director of the NAACP, was fond of recounting that the first major black protest in Atlanta in

1916 was over education. From it, Atlanta's black community kept its seventh grade, and got its first high school, plus better grammar schools.[36]

In the late fifties and sixties, blacks were only willing to have their children confront the jeering anti-integration mobs because education was so important to them. The ability of the NAACP to wage the long legal battle for equal education opportunity was rooted in the value that blacks in communities around the nation assigned to education. This was clearly seen in the five very different cases that came together in the historic 1954 *Brown v. Board of Education* decision.[37] They did not grow out of grand egalitarian designs, but out of the simple desire of concerned parents for good schools. One of those cases had its beginnings in the dirt-farm countryside of Clarendon County, South Carolina, where black sharecroppers led by their schoolteacher-minister petitioned the school board for bus transportation to their children's school. Another grew out of the efforts of working-class parents to protest the overcrowded District of Columbia schools that their children were confined to while the city's white schools went half-filled. In Prince Edward County, Virginia, high school students watched their parents plead with little success for improved conditions and new construction at the local black high school, and then, led by a sixteen-year-old girl, took action into their own hands. The result was a two-week-long school walkout against inadequate facilities. In Topeka, Kansas, black parents rose up to protest against their children having to travel in cold and stormy weather well beyond white schools. Parents who resented the physically unequal schools in Wilmington, Delaware, turned to the NAACP and the courts when their children were turned away from the better-equipped white schools. In each of these five cases, and in hundreds of similar actions, black parents acted because they believed that education could shape their children's futures.[38]

Thus, the stay-in-school campaign of the sixties only reinforced the aspirations that blacks on all levels already held for themselves. When black high school seniors were surveyed in the sixties, it was learned that 9 out of 10 of their mothers wished them to go on to college, and two-thirds of the students saw a college education as the best way to get ahead.[39] In the late sixties, groups as disparate as black student activists and black college presidents pressed for better opportunities in higher education. Parents and children staked their

FIGURE 3–1

White Ethnic Groups,ᵃ as Workers, Are Roughly Distributed According to the Composition of the Total U.S. Labor Force. Blacks Are Not: Far Fewer Are in Skilled, Professional, Sales, or Office Jobs

Percentage Distribution of American Workers by Ethnic Group[a] and Occupation, March 1972

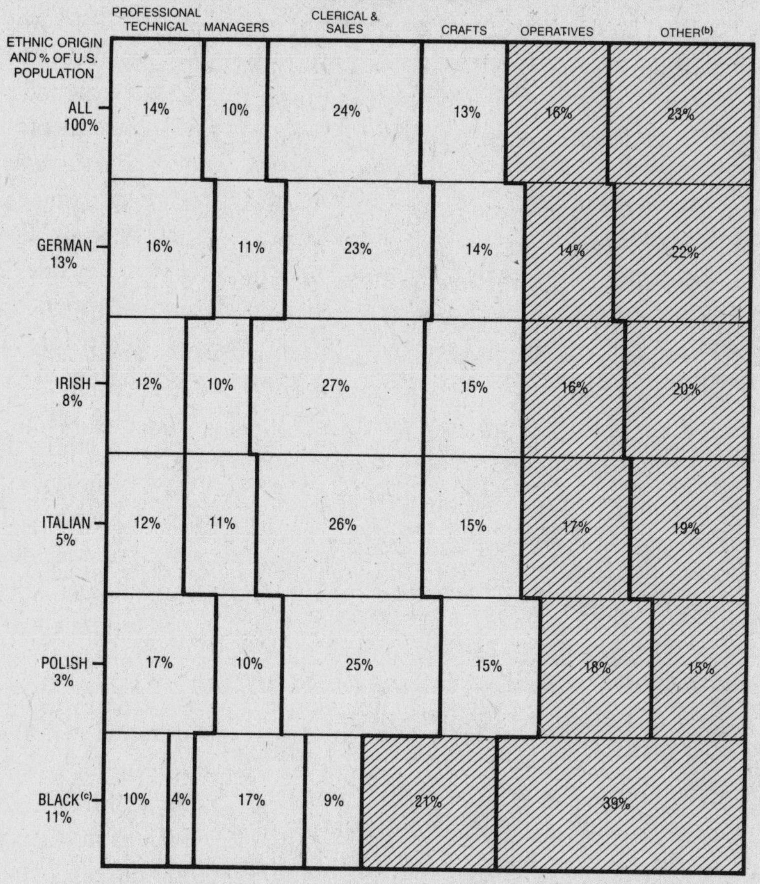

ETHNIC ORIGIN AND % OF U.S. POPULATION	PROFESSIONAL TECHNICAL	MANAGERS	CLERICAL & SALES	CRAFTS	OPERATIVES	OTHER[b]
ALL 100%	14%	10%	24%	13%	16%	23%
GERMAN 13%	16%	11%	23%	14%	14%	22%
IRISH 8%	12%	10%	27%	15%	16%	20%
ITALIAN 5%	12%	11%	26%	15%	17%	19%
POLISH 3%	17%	10%	25%	15%	18%	15%
BLACK[c] 11%	10%	4%	17%	9%	21%	39%

(a) Those in the specified ethnic groups identified themselves as such during a national sample survey, household interview. Persons reporting multiple ethnic origin are not included. The data refer to 25.5 million of German origin, 16.4 million Irish, 8.8 million Italian, and 5.1 million Polish.

(b) Includes laborers, farmers and farm managers, service workers, and private household workers.

(c) Negroes and other nonwhite races.

Source: Derived from CPR, Series P–20, No. 249, *Characteristics of the Population By Ethnic Origin, March 1972 and 1971,* Table 7, p. 24; CPR, Series P–23, No. 46, *The Social and Economic Status of the Black Population in the United States, 1972,* Table 37, p. 49.

futures on good schools and more schooling; black youth aspired to a good education. They were not, as some have argued, unwilling to pursue an education because the adults around them had poor jobs.[40]

The spurt in achievement in the sixties and early seventies was won with particular difficulty at the college level. It came after Autherine Lucy confronted the University of Alabama between 1952 and 1955, finally gaining entrance to the school of library science; after honor high school students Charlayne Hunter and Hamilton Holmes pressed for and finally won admission to the University of Georgia in 1961; after James Meredith confronted "Ole Miss" in 1961 and entered in 1962 under white rioting that brought federal troops and loss of life; and during and after a wave of demonstrations by blacks in predominantly white northern colleges and universities to push for more black student admissions.[41]

The upsurge in black educational achievement in the most expensive kind of schooling—college and university—is extraordinary because so much of the catching up took place in a few short years, and because it must have meant great sacrifice for the relatively lower-income black families. In 1974, for instance, almost two-thirds (63 percent) of all black families with young people eighteen to twenty-four years old attending college full-time had incomes below $10,-000, when the national median family income was almost $13,000. By contrast, over three-fourths of white families with college enrollees had incomes over $10,000 (Table 3–5). By 1975, 11 percent of blacks between the ages of twenty-five and twenty-nine were college graduates; for whites of the same age, 23 percent were college graduates.[42] This is not much of a difference considering public rhetoric that suggests blacks have felt frustrated in pursuing higher education, and the odds in favor of whites. Equal or not in the marketplace, the inherent value of education in itself is as dear to black Americans as it is to white.

Questioning the Quality of Blacks' Education

Just about the time that the gap in average school years was narrowing between black and white, emphasis shifted from staying in school (for everyone) to questioning the quality of the education received by black youth. The work of James Coleman made headlines in 1966 especially for its material concerning the educational "years" that black children were behind the average white child at various grade levels.[43] Blacks may receive the same quantity of schooling, it said, but not the same quality, as measured by objective test results in reading and math.[44] Coleman's influential work, on which many studies have since been based, is itself careful to point out what the averages mean: that some black children performed better than many white children and that, while proportionately more black children fell below the national median, half the white children did, too.[45] This means, in gross numbers, that many more white than black children scored lower than average, and the averages applying to the groups provide no clue to the merit of an individual worker applying for a job. Since there are nine times as many white workers as black, an employer is more likely to encounter a poorly qualified white than a poorly qualified black.

A fairer test would be to compare black and white students of similar characteristics in similar kinds of schools. Studies in which this was done show that black and white pupils of the same socioeconomic status do equally well.[46] A study in the seventies concluded that just putting black and white children together would prove to be no advantage to the black students when their new white classmates were equally poor: "There is little evidence that black test scores are any higher in schools where the whites are as poor as the blacks."[47] Poor black students do no better or worse than poor white students, and black and white students of similar backgrounds do equally well.

The quality of education in terms of scholastic achievement is almost beside the point. On the single issue of what is needed to perform well in most jobs, the more usual measures of "quality" are not especially critical. Requirements of the labor market aside, however, American parents believe that every child has the right to the same experiences in school: equally devoted and competent teachers, lab and library resources, and all those supporting services that can make American education exceptional. For too many black children that is not yet the case.

In training for the professions the traditional criteria for "quality" in educational institutions become especially important. But when two groups of college graduates, white and black, were carefully matched—for comparable social status, equal grade-point averages, and the same or comparable schools, basic resources, and years of experience in the job market, only two major differences emerged. The black graduates were found to have been more likely to have gone on to graduate school, and the black graduates earned less.[48]

The quality of black colleges may even be higher than that of similar white colleges as a general rule. When black and white colleges were carefully matched for features like enrollment, endowment, faculty, library, and other facilities, the black schools were more often found to be more fully accredited than the white[49] (Table 3–6). Only a few predominantly black colleges were not accredited, whereas nearly six times the number of matched white schools, with seven times as many students, were unaccredited. If all the students enrolled in 1967–68 in the unaccredited matched colleges were looking for jobs in 1971, the number of "unqualified" white applicants would have been more than seven times the number of "unqualified" blacks.

Black American Workers in International Perspective

If any more proof is needed that persistent, high black unemployment rates and lower-paying, less prestigious jobs are not a matter of poorer or less education, but of prejudice, it can be found as close at hand as the nearest shopping center. Americans have long been eager to buy the goods of Western Europe. Any highway in the United States will have Volkswagens alongside Chevrolets; any car fancier worth his salt will have coveted a German Porsche or an Italian Lamborghini. Americans serve Dutch and Danish beer, wear Liberty prints from London, sit on Scandinavian furniture, put their feet and hands in Spanish leather, and wear the fashions of Paris. For everything from scientific and precision instruments, through printing presses and other durable goods, to delicate laces and fine china, European products are in demand. While producing all of these goods, and handling all of the clerical, administrative, sales, and service functions associated with them, the Western European labor force has had markedly less schooling than that of American blacks (Table 3–7).

During the 1960s, when West Germany and France enjoyed a period of almost unprecedented prosperity, consuming abundantly at home and exporting so much abroad that their own labor force proved insufficient, they relied heavily on the labor of immigrants. Among the main emigration countries were Greece, Turkey, and Portugal.[50] The immigrants worked in the full range of construction

—from light building to heavy work on dams and hydro plants—and in the production of autos, refrigerators, television sets, and machinery of all kinds, in textile and apparel manufacture and in chemical industries.[51] Some of the foreign national groups were concentrated in a few areas within their host countries and became a significant part of the locality's labor force. Turks were 38 percent of all foreign nationals in Cologne in 1967, working chiefly for the Ford Motor Company, which has a large plant in that German city.[52] Yet, in the countries from which they came, a large proportion of the population was illiterate and few had gone beyond primary school (Table 3–8). This meant that many supposedly complex jobs were being performed by relatively uneducated workers. In Portugal, for instance,[53] only about half the professional and technical workers had any education beyond secondary school. Half the clerical workers and almost all the sales workers had not gone as far as secondary school. The production workers were either illiterate (20 percent) or had received only a primary school education (Table 3–9).

The distribution of the foreign men in the West German work force in 1960 illustrates that while many of these foreign workers were in the unskilled manual jobs of Western Europe (in construction or in industrial production), a sizable proportion held semiskilled and skilled jobs, the sort for which many American employers require a high school diploma.

Percentage Distribution of Foreign Male Workers in West Germany, by Occupation Type in 1960[54]

| Occupation type | All countries | Origin | | |
		Greece	Portugal	Turkey
All occupations	100	100	100	100
Nonmanual	(a)	(a)	(a)	(a)
Skilled manual	20	7	12	16
Semiskilled manual	36	53	43	38
Unskilled manual	34	37	43	43

(a) Precise data not available.

Immigrants in sections of each of the major receiving countries actually formed the majority of the labor force in some factories.[55] Several countries, notably France, West Germany, Sweden, and the United Kingdom, provided vocational training programs to assist foreigners in achieving upward mobility, even though the newcomers were not considered assimilable or long-term residents.[56] Thus, the Eastern and Southern European workers in modern industry who fashioned goods that sold worldwide did not know the host country's customs and language, were often illiterate in any language, and were without any industrial training whatever.[57] Black Americans know the language and culture, attend school almost until their majority, and beyond, yet are considered "disadvantaged" in the American job market.

Today, with black and white Americans having about the same number of years of schooling, credentialism—fairly applied—would mean that the unemployment rates of white and black high school graduates would be similar, and black graduates would have a lower unemployment rate than dropouts of either race. But the requirements have never been equally applied: young white dropouts have had consistently lower unemployment rates than young black graduates. Among employed male workers in the same age and education groups, having a high school diploma or better does not give black workers the same occupational status as whites (Table 3–10). Proportionately fewer blacks with post-high-school training got the professional and technical jobs that their educators prepared them for, and proportionately more blacks than whites were in low-paying, less prestigious jobs—despite having high school diplomas. What has made a difference in working or not, at high-status jobs or not, has not been possession of a high school diploma; it has been the color of the applicant's skin. It is difficult to review the evidence for every age and educational group since 1940, and come to any other conclusion (Table 3–10). The gap may be narrowing, but inexcusable differences remain.

If the results were not so serious, credentialism would be a comedy of errors. The notion that workers needed high and rising levels of education during the past several decades was energetically promoted to American people, both black and white. By not making a comparable effort to eliminate discrimination, we have produced the best-educated work force in the world and the best-educated unemployed—who are disproportionately black.

TABLE 3-1

White Workers Without a High School Diploma Were About Half the Total Labor Force in 1950 and 1960 and One-Third in 1970

White "Dropouts"* as a Percentage of the Labor Force in Selected Occupations, 1950, 1960, and 1970

Occupation	Percent of total experienced civilian labor force		
	1950	1960	1970
All occupations	52	46	33
Professional and technical	10	8	6
Accountants and auditors	11	9	5
Drafting	14	12	8
Teachers, elem. and sec.	3	1	1
Clerical	28	27	19
Bank tellers	16	15	11
Secretaries	13[a]	12	8
Telephone operators	40	39	22
Sales	44	43	30
Retail	49	51	37
Crafts	65	59	46
Compositors and typesetters	51	45	30
Electricians	57	51	35
Airplane mechanics	40	40	29
Tool and die makers	58	52	34
Operatives	68	65	52
Bus drivers	69	63	46
Service (excl. protective and pvt. household)	55	54	46
Protective service—police	50	38	19

* Less than 12 years of schooling.
[a] Includes stenographers and typists.

Source: Derived from 1950 Census of Population, *Special Reports, Vol. 4, Pt. 1, Chap. B, Occupational Characteristics,* Tables 10–11, pp. 107–22; 1960 Census of Population, *Subject Reports, PC (2)–7A, Occupational Characteristics,* Tables 9–10, pp. 116–43; 1970 Census of Population, *Subject Reports, PC (2)–7A Occupational Characteristics,* Tables 5–6, pp. 73–86, 87–114.

TABLE 3-2

Since 1950, Black as Well as White Workers in Jobs of All Kinds Have Tended to Have More Education than Their Jobs Required

Required General Education (Estimated for 1956 and 1966) and Median Years of School Completed, by Selected Detailed Occupations and by Race, 1950, 1960, and 1970

Occupation	General educational development required—years of school		Median years of school completed					
			1950		1960		1970	
	1956	1966	Black(a)	White	Black(a)	White	Black(b)	White
Professional and technical								
Accountants and auditors	13–14	13–14	15.1	14.0	15.1	14.8	14.3	15.2
Drafting	13–14	13–14	14.9	12.9	13.6	12.9	12.9	13.0
Engineer	15–16	15–16	16.0	16+	16.3	16.1	15.8	16.2
Lawyers and judges	15–16	15–16	16+	16+	17+	17+	17+	17+
Nurses, professional	9–12	13–14	13.2	13.5	12.8	13.3	12.7	13.4
Physicians and surgeons	15–16	15–16	16+	16+	17+	17+	17+	17+
Social welfare workers	(c)	13–14	16+	(c)	16.7	16.5	15.7	16.5
Teachers, elementary	13–14	13–14	16+	16+	16.6	16.3	16.6	16.5
Teachers, secondary	13–14	13–14	16+	16+	16.8	17+	16.7	17+
Clerical								
Bank tellers	7–8	9–12	15.5	12.6	12.8	12.5	12.7	12.6
Bookkeepers	9–12	9–12	12.8	12.7	12.7	12.5	12.7	12.5
Cashiers	7–8	7–8	12.1	12.2	12.1	12.0	12.2	12.2
Mail carriers	4–6	7–8	12.5	12.2	12.5	12.3	12.5	12.5
Secretaries	7–8	9–12	(c)	(c)	12.9	12.6	12.7	12.7
Stenographers	7–8	7–8	(c)	(c)	12.8	12.6	12.7	12.8
Telephone operators	7–8	7–8	12.2	12.2	12.4	12.2	12.5	12.4
Typists	7–8	7–8	12.8	12.6	12.7	12.5	12.6	12.7
Sales								
Insurance	9–12(d)	9–12	12.2	12.7	12.6	12.9	12.8	13.1
Real estate	9–12(d)	9–12	12.4	12.6	13.1	12.7	12.8	12.9

Retail trade	7–8	7–8	10.2	12.3	11.3	12.0	12.2	12.3

	7–8	7–8	10.2	12.3	11.3	12.0	12.2	12.3
Craftsmen and foremen								
Carpenters	9–12	9–12	6.6	8.8	8.1	9.4	9.3	10.9
Compositors and typesetters	9–12(d)	9–12	12.1	11.8	12.1	12.1	12.2	12.3
Crane, hoist and derrick	9–12(c)	7–8	7.5	8.8	8.6	9.0	9.9	10.5
Electricians	9–12	9–12	10.2	11.2	12.1	11.8	12.3	12.3
Machinists	9–12	9–12	9.6	10.1	10.2	10.8	12.0	12.1
Mechanics	(d)							
Airplane	9–12	9–12	12.2	12.1	9.2	10.4	12.3	12.0
Auto	9–12(d)	9–12	8.3	9.6	8.9	10.0	10.3	11.3
Radio and TV	9–12(c)	9–12	12.2	12.2	12.1	12.2	12.2	12.4
Painters and paperhangers	7–8	7–8	8.0	8.9	8.8	9.1	10.0	10.4
Plumbers and pipefitters	9–12	9–12	6.9	9.5	8.3	10.3	11.9	10.0
Stationary engineers	9–12	9–12	8.1	10.2	10.1	12.2	11.7	12.1
Tin, sheetmetal, coppersmiths	9–12	9–12	8.8	10.2	11.1	10.8	12.1	12.1
Tool and die makers	9–12	9–12	8.8	11.0	11.8	11.7	12.2	12.3
Operatives								
Bus drivers	9–12	7–8	10.3	9.8	10.3	10.0	12.0	11.6
Meat cutters (excl. pkghse.)	9–12	7–8	8.7	10.2	8.8	10.8	10.7	11.9
Packers and wrappers	4–6	4–6	(c)	(c)	9.5	9.7	10.8	10.8
Textile operatives	4–6	4–6	6.4	8.3	8.5	8.5	11.1	9.4
Taxi drivers and chauf.	7–8	7–8	8.6	9.2	9.2	9.3	10.3	11.2
T/T (trailer) drivers	7–8	7–8	6.6	8.9	8.1	9.3	9.6	10.6
Welders and flamecutters	7–8	7–8	8.8	9.5	9.7	9.7	11.1	11.0
Private household workers	4–6	4–6	7.1	8.6	8.2	8.8	8.5	9.9

| | General educational development required—years of school | | Median years of school completed | | | | | |
| | | | 1950 | | 1960 | | 1970 | |
	1956	1966	Black[a]	White	Black[a]	White	Black[b]	White
Service (excl. pvt. household and protective)								
Attendants (institutional)	(c)	7–8	10.4	10.2	11.3	10.5	11.9	12.0
Barbers	7–8	7–8	10.4	10.5	10.2	9.1	11.9	11.4
Cooks	9–12	9–12	8.0	8.8	8.7	9.3	10.2	10.7
Hairdressers and cosmetol.	9–12	9–12	(c)	(c)	11.7	12.5	12.1	12.3
Practical nurses	9–12	9–12[d]	10.5	10.8	11.9	10.9	12.4	12.4
Waiters	4–6	7–8	9.6	10.4	10.6	10.6	11.4	11.5
Protective service work								
Guards, watchers	7–8	7–8	7.7	8.6	9.0	8.9	11.4	11.7
Fire	7–8	7–8	11.4	11.3	12.3	12.1	12.4	12.4
Police	9–12	9–12[e]	12.2	11.8	12.4	12.2	12.6	12.5
Farm[f]	(c)	4–6	5.2	8.4	5.8	8.6	6.9	9.6
Laborers (excl. farm and mine)								
Construction	2–3	4–6	6.0	8.5	7.2	8.7	8.3	10.2
Warehousing	4–6	4–6[g]		(a)	9.9	10.8	11.1	12.1

(a) Negro and other nonwhite races.
(b) Negro only.
(c) Data not available.
(d) From 1957 edition of BLS *Occupational Outlook Handbook*, Bulletin No. 1215, pp. 403–4 (airplane mechanic); p. 309 (auto repair); p. 475 (radio and TV repair).
(e) From 1968–69 edition of BLS *Occupational Outlook Handbook*.
(f) Foremen and women excepted; could require more education.
(g) Stores laborer, any industry. DOT 922.887.

Source: Derived from U.S. Employment Service, *Estimates of Worker Traits Requirements For 4000 Jobs as Defined in the Dictionary of Occupational Titles*, (Washington, D.C.: Government Printing Office, 1956); U.S. Bureau of Employment Security, *Selected Characteristics of Occupations (Physical Demands, Working Conditions, Training Time): A Supplement to the Dictionary of Occupational Titles*, 3rd ed. (Washington, D.C.: Government Printing Office, 1966); 1950 Census of Population, *Special Reports, Vol. 4, Pt. 1, Chap. B, Occupational Characteristics*, Table 10–11, pp. 107–22 (5 percent sample); 1960 Census of Population, *Subject Reports, PC (2)–7A, Occupational Characteristics*, Tables 9 and 10, pp. 116–29, and 13–143

TABLE 3–3

*Jobs Requiring Higher Education Have Risen Only a Little Since 1940;
Those Classified as "White Collar" Have Risen a Lot*

**Percentage Distribution of the Labor Force, by Two Occupation Groupings,
Decennial Years 1940–70, and 1975**

Occupational grouping— traditional and by job requirement	1940	1950	1960	1970	1975
All occupations	100	100	100	100	100
Traditional grouping					
White collar	31	37	42	48	50
Blue collar and other[a]	69	63	58	52	50
Job requirement grouping[b]					
Higher (needing h.s. diploma or more)	15	18	20	23	26
Lower	85	82	80	77	74

[a] Includes service and farm.

[b] Higher are professional, technical, managerial, and administrative.

Source: Derived from 1940 Census of Population, *The Labor Force, Vol. 3, Pt. 1, U.S.
Summary,* Table 62, pp. 88–90; 1950 Census of Population, *Special Reports,
Vol. 4, Pt. 1, Chapter B, Occupational Characteristics,* Table 10, pp. 107–14;
1960 Census of Population, *Subject Reports, PC (2)–7A, Occupational Characteristics,* Table 9, pp. 116–29; 1970 Census of Population, *Subject Reports, PC
(2)–7A, Occupational Characteristics,* Table 5, pp. 73–86 and BLS, *Handbook
of Labor Statistics 1975—Reference Edition,* Bulletin 1865 (Washington, D.C.:
Government Printing Office, 1975), Table 6, p. 41; U.S. President, *Employment and Training Report of the President, 1976* (Washington, D.C.: Government Printing Office, 1976), Table A–16, p. 236.

TABLE 3–4

*Only Professional, Technical, and Managerial Jobs Might Require
Education Beyond High School; in 1975 They Were Only One-Fourth of
All Jobs*

**Distribution of the Labor Force by Occupation Group, Decennial Years
1940–70, and 1975 (Percentage of the Civilian Experienced Labor Force)**

Occupation group	1940	1950	1960	1970	1975
All occupations	100	100	100	100	100
Professional and technical	7	9	11	15	15
Managerial and administrative	8	9	9	8	11
Clerical	10	12	15	18	18
Sales	6	7	7	7	6
Crafts[a]	13	15	15	15	13
Operatives	19	20	20	18	15
Service[a]	11	9	11	13	14
Nonfarm laborers	8	6	5	5	5
Farm	18	12	6	3	4

[a] Protective service workers are included with the crafts and excluded from the service group. Protective service workers were 1 percent of the labor force throughout the period shown.

Source: Derived from 1940 Census of Population, *The Labor Force, Vol. 3, Pt. 1, U.S. Summary,* Table 62, pp. 88–90; 1950 Census of Population, *Special Reports, Vol. 4, Pt. 1, Chapter B, Occupational Characteristics,* Table 10, pp. 107–14; 1960 Census of Population, *Subject Reports, PC (2)–7A, Occupational Characteristics,* Table 9, pp. 116–29; 1970 Census of Population, *Subject Reports, PC (2)–7A, Occupational Characteristics,* Table 5, pp. 73–86; BLS, *Handbook of Labor Statistics 1975—Reference Edition,* Bulletin 1865 (Washington, D.C.: Government Printing Office, 1975), Table 6, p. 41.

TABLE 3–5

Black College Students Disproportionately Come from Lower-Income Families

Percentage of Families with 18–24-Year-Olds Enrolled in College Full Time, by Family Income and Race, 1971 and 1974

Family income	1971[b]		1974[b]	
	Black[a]	White	Black[a]	White
All families with full-time students	100	100	100	100
Under $10,000	75	30	63	21
$10,000 and over	25	70	37	79

[a] Negro only.
[b] Family income is for 1970 for 1971 students, and for 1973 in the case of 1974 students.

Source: Derived from CPR, Series P–20, No. 241, *Social and Economic Characteristics of Students, October 1971*, Table 13, pp. 38–9; CPR, Series P–20, No. 286, *School Enrollment—Social and Economic Characteristics of Students, October 1974*, Table 13, pp. 41–4.

TABLE 3–6

*Seven Times as Many White as Black Students Were Attending
Unaccredited Four-Year Colleges of Similar Size and Location in
1967–68; a Larger Proportion of Predominantly Black than Matched
White Colleges Were Accredited*

**Comparison of Accreditation of Matched Predominantly Black[a] and
Predominantly White Four-Year Colleges,[b] 1967–68**

Accreditation[c] of colleges and students enrolled	Black[a]		White	
	Number	Percent	Number	Percent
All matched colleges[d]	88	100	425	100
Accredited	72	82	324	76
Not accredited	16	18	101	24
Students attending all the matched colleges	143,735	100	657,924	100
Attending accredited colleges	134,797	94	592,930	90
Attending nonaccredited colleges	8,938	6	64,994	10

[a] Negro only.

[b] Predominantly white private four-year colleges were selected to match similar black colleges in the same states where the predominantly black institutions are located. The predominantly white private institutions are below university level and their enrollments are below 3,500. The predominantly white public institutions selected are below university level and their enrollments are below 8,000.

[c] Only regional accrediting associations recognized.

[d] All schools selected for the study.

Source: Derived from Carnegie Commission on Higher Education, *Between Two Worlds: A Profile of Negro Higher Education* (New York: McGraw-Hill Book Co., 1971), App. A-F, pp. 286–318; C. E. Burckel, *The College Blue Book,* 12th ed., Vol. 1 (Los Angeles: College Planning Program, LTC, 1968).

TABLE 3–7

Black American Workers Had Far More Schooling than their Western European Counterparts Around 1960

Percentage of Workers Who Completed Secondary School and Above, by Occupation Group, in the United States (by Race) and in Selected Developed Countries, Around 1960

| | Developed countries | | | | | |
| | United States | | France | Netherlands | Sweden | United Kingdom |
Occupation group	White	Black[a]				
All occupations	49	26	6	10	7	10
Professional	91	89	39	59	35	53
Administrative	65	43	36	37	35	30
Clerical	72	69	7	37	8	16
Sales	56	44	5	6	5	9
Crafts and other manual [b]	30	20	1	1	(c)	2
Farmers	26	6	(c)	1	1	7

[a] Negro and other nonwhite races.
[b] Includes skilled, semiskilled, service, and laboring jobs.
[c] Less than 0.5 percent.

Source: Derived from 1960 Census of Population, *Subject Reports, PC(2)–7A, Occupational Characteristics,* Table 9, pp. 116–29; Moshe Sicron, *Interrelationship Between the Educational Level and Occupational Structure of the Labor Force: An International and Inter-Temporal Comparison* (Ph.D. dissertation, University of Pennsylvania, 1968), Table 4.8, p. 117.

TABLE 3–8

Few Workers in Developing Countries Have Attended Secondary School

Educational Distribution of the Civilian Labor Force in Selected Developing Countries, Early 1960s

Education level	Greece	Portugal[a]	Turkey
Total labor force	100	100	100
Primary school or less	90	93	[b]
Secondary school or more	10	5	[b]

[a] Does not include that 1 percent of the labor force, whose educational attainment is unknown.

[b] No distribution available, but 62 percent of the population was illiterate in 1964. See U.S. Bureau of the Census, *1969 Statistical Abstract of the United States* (Washington, D.C.: Government Printing Office, 1969), Table 1268, p. 860.

Source: Derived from Organization for Economic Co-operation and Development, *Statistics of the Occupational and Education Structure of the Labour Force in 53 Countries* (Paris: Organization for Economic Co-operation and Development, 1969), Table IIA, p. 50, 83.

TABLE 3–9

*The Vast Majority of Portuguese Workers, Including Administrators, Had
Not Gone Beyond Primary School in 1960; Half the Professional and
Technical Workers Had Not Gone Beyond Secondary School*

Civilian Workers in Portugal by Occupation Group and Education, 1960

			Percent			
Occupation group	Total	Unable to read	Primary	Secondary	Higher Education (including normal school)	At school other
All occupations	100	31	62	4	2	1
Prof., technical, and related	100	1	21	22	53	3
Admin., exec., managerial	100	3	72	18	6	1
Clerical	100	—	53	39	2	6
Sales	100	13	80	6	(a)	1
Crafts, products, mining, transport, and communication	100	20	77	2	(a)	1
Service, sport, and recreation	100	29	68	1	(a)	1
Farm	100	49	50	(a)	(a)	1
Other	100	28	67	3	1	1

(a) Fewer than 0.5 percent.

Source: Derived from the Organization for Economic Co-operation and Development,
*Statistics of the Occupational and Educational Structure of the Labor Force in
53 Countries* (Paris: Organization for Economic Co-operation and Development, 1969), Table II-A, p. 83.

TABLE 3–10

At the Same Age and Education, Sizable Gaps Have Remained in Job Levels Between Black and White Men; the Gap is Smallest and Declines Most for Those With College Degrees

Index of Dissimilarity[a] Between Occupational Distributions of Black[b] and White Men, by Education Level and Age Group, Decennial Years 1940–70

Years of school completed and year	Age group of male workers[c][d]			
	25–34	35–44	45–54	55–64
All education levels				
1940	46	43	42	36
1950	36	39	39	36
1960	35	37	38	39
1970	30	34	37	39
12 years				
1940	43	46	43	39
1950	32	37	40	37
1960	32	32	34	40
1970	25	29	30	35
13–15 years				
1940	37	38	37	41
1950	30	34	37	29
1960	28	32	31	32
1970	21	24	28	29
16 years and over				
1940	21	23	24	20
1950	12	13	20	17
1960	15	14	14	16
1970	8	12	11	11

[a] The index of dissimilarity between blacks and whites is the sum of the differences in the percentage distributions of each group, by occupation, at each age level in each year. The higher the resulting figure, the greater the amount of redistribution required to reach occupational parity.

[b] Negroes only in 1940 and 1970 and Negroes and other nonwhite races in 1950 and 1960.

[c] Employed males for 1940, 1950 and 1970; males in the experienced labor force for 1960.

[d] Reading diagonally, the italicized figures are for an age cohort—the same age group, 10 years later.

Source: The 1940, 1950 and 1960 data are from Nathan Hare, "Recent Trends in the Occupational Mobility of Negroes, 1930–1960; an Intracohort Analysis," *Social Forces* 44 (December 1965): 166–72; 1970 data were derived, according to Hare's technique, from 1970 Census of Population, *Subject Reports, PC(2)–5B, Educational Attainment,* Table 11, pp. 213–28.

4

Uncle Sam as Employer

BEFORE WORLD WAR II, the Register of the Treasury, Auditor of the Navy, and Recorder of Deeds for the District of Columbia were the three jobs of any importance in the federal government which were thought of as Negro jobs.[1] That such jobs were set aside indicated a grudging recognition that some few black people might be able to handle responsible jobs. Beyond that, black people were employed in government, but almost exclusively as maintenance men or cleaning women, and only very rarely as junior-level clerks or other personnel.

While it is certainly true that things were worse in private industry, the government even then should have done better. Individual employers might act out their prejudices in terms of whom they hired and for what kinds of jobs. But the government could not argue, like private industry, that economic conditions might dictate whether few or many workers would be hired, or that only certain kinds of workers could be used. Government could not even make the case that customers would stop using the services, or stop "buying" because of fair employment practices; the work of government is very much a monopoly enterprise. And the business of government is a constant thing, growing in time of war (and to some extent in times of economic growth) or national crisis, but always having a job to do. Nor could the seat of government in Washington avail itself of the excuses made elsewhere, that the black population was poorly educated, or just made up of rural farmers with no experience to suit them for an office job. Washington in 1940 was known as a black intellectual center, the home of black academics. Howard University is located in Washington, and the city had long been the home of black physicians, professors, presidential counselors, and businessmen. When the government began to expand during World War II, there were many educated black men and women in the Washington area who could have stepped into government jobs. And when government employment rose by thousands in a single month (15,000 just in January 1942),[2] it was particularly galling to black residents who were denied all of the good new jobs. From the perspective of the seventies, it is difficult to appreciate just how pervasive discrimination was in government agencies.

In one sense, Washington was no different from anywhere else: the only times that black concerns were taken seriously were election years. And in the campaign year of 1940, other forces were at work as well. Blacks were aware of and demanding their share of the government and war-related jobs that were opening up, and wartime was no time to be fighting internal racial battles—particularly not when the war was being fought against a European form of racism. But more important, concentrations of black voters in the cities led one member of the Roosevelt cabinet to acknowledge that "in several Northern states the Negro vote is likely to be the decisive vote in 1940."[3] A nondiscriminatory civil service was one of the prices being asked for that black vote. Both major parties were indicted by the NAACP:

> . . . discrimination in the federal government in Washington . . . has been galling to Negro Americans under several Presidents, Republican and Democratic. . . . The civil service unfairness to Negroes is another sore spot. . . .[4]

Campaigning before a black audience in Chicago, Republican candidate Wendell Willkie had responded to that concern when he decried the "regular Jim Crow departments" that existed in the government, and promised to see "that colored citizens are appointed to any branch of the Federal civil service to which they are qualified."[5]

Roosevelt, "restive under Negro pressure,"[6] was more than ready for the challenge posed by Willkie. That fall, the Ramspeck Act, a bill to reform the Civil Service, came before the Congress. Senator Neely, Democrat from West Virginia, was lobbied "by a spokesman for the colored people . . . just before I entered the Senate Chamber."[7] From that conversation, Neely was moved to add language to the Ramspeck Act banning discrimination in the Civil Service. At that point, Carl Hatch, Democrat from New Mexico, took the floor, saying that he had already drafted such an amendment; it was ac-

cepted and inserted in the bill.[8] Determined to claim credit for the
provision, Roosevelt went a step further and, three weeks before the
final vote in Congress on the Ramspeck Act, issued Executive Order
8587, declaring an end to discrimination in the Civil Service.[9] Although the combination of the president's order and the Ramspeck Act made discrimination illegal in the Civil Service, little changed because both were critically flawed by their lack
of enforcement provisions.

As a result, efforts to place qualified black applicants in government jobs were feeble at best, and black protest over their treatment
in the system continued. By June of 1941 Roosevelt felt forced to
issue yet another Executive Order, 8802. The strongest impetus for
that presidential action was the threatened march on Washington to
protest black exclusion from war-related industries. But discriminatory hiring by government agencies was part of the issue as well.
Government employment was still a very sore point with black
groups, and the result was language in 8802 covering both: ". . . there
shall be no discrimination in employment of workers in defense
industry or Government because of race, creed, color or national
origin."[10]

Without effective enforcement machinery, even that proved inadequate to the job. Early in September 1941, yet another antidiscrimination directive was issued in the form of a presidential letter to the
heads of all departments and independent government bodies. It said
in part:

> It has come to my attention that there is in the Federal establishment
> a lack of uniformity and possibly some lack of sympathetic attitude
> toward the problems of minority groups, particularly those relating
> to the employment and assignment of Negroes in the Federal Civil
> Service. . . . I shall look for immediate steps to be taken by all
> departments, and independent establishments of the Government to
> facilitate and put into effect this policy of non-discrimination in Fed-
> eral employment.[11]

With the expanded activities generated by the war, the responsibilities of the Civil Service Commission (CSC) were expanded, and
it established 13 district offices, 5,000 local boards, and 150 special
rating boards at large government industrial plants.[12] A new training
program and a Division of Information were set up to assist the
general public. Placement became a kind of "assembly line process,"
and blacks were channeled automatically into lower-echelon jobs.[13]

Within CSC rules, there were handy routes around the antidis-crimination clause and one, the "rule of three," was especially popular. The Civil Service administered the competitive exams and maintained the lists of available job candidates, but for every job opening it sent employers three names. Under the "rule of three," agency heads only had to "consider" the top three applicants who happened to be next in line for a job; they could choose any one of the three. And if, as often happened, the choice was anyone but the qualified black applicant, at least the law had not been transgressed—except in those rare instances when the top three candidates all happened to be black.

Even then there was a way out. One particularly devious ruse was used by an agency in need of a typist at the time that two black women headed the CSC roster for such positions. The agency head

> phoned his colleague at another agency, who thereupon requisitioned a typist. While the Negroes' papers were held at the colleague's agency for a normal 10 working days, the personnel officer who originally needed the typist requisitioned CSC and got the whites lower on the Commission Register.[14]

Black professionals got no greater consideration than did black applicants for jobs as messengers or clerks. A chief personnel expert in the Office of the Secretary of War during 1942 recounted the typical way in which black professionals were treated:

> The War Department in Washington, D.C. alone, was hiring approximately 700 people a day and from the start I began to see cases of Negroes with excellent training. They thought they were getting a break when they shifted from teaching in the south to a clerical job here. On one particular day a Negro Counselor couldn't resist picking one man out of the crowd. He had been teaching economics at North Carolina College, had his M.A. from Columbia University, and had scored in the 90's on an exam for Economist. CSC had screened the man and referred him for a CPC-3 (messenger or laborer) position at the War Department. . . . I sent his papers back to CSC for reclassification and to get his name on the Economist-Sociologist register. It took two months before the man was reclassified into a professional job. . . .[15]

Intervention of this sort was rare. Most officials did not bother to review the credentials of black applicants, and they could deny jobs or inappropriately classify black applicants without any expectation of reprisal.

Nothing seemed capable of changing the CSC. Despite the various executive orders, and the antidiscrimination provisions in the law, the CSC still honored a Department of Commerce request for a "colored messenger" in 1942. The man they sent had a CAF–1 classification, identifying him as a lower-level clerk. When he filed a discrimination complaint, it was learned that he was a law school graduate and a member of the bar. He had already spent a year dusting a division chief's desk, sorting and filing reports, and carrying books from one office to another—tasks for which his performance had been rated excellent. The complaint process also revealed that all of those involved had known his superior qualifications when they classified, hired, and attempted to transfer him. The greatest irony of his case is that the person he was to replace had been *promoted* to CAF–2 in spite of unsatisfactory performance.[16]

With the need for rapid recruitment during the war, agencies were permitted to hire outside the normal CSC procedures.[17] Their new hiring authority and the increased need for workers were not enough to get the older, more traditional agencies to hire blacks. These old-line agencies continued to think in terms of "white men's jobs," for which blacks would not even be considered.[18] Occasionally, cabinet officials were willing to change, but could not get their employees to respond. One department head tried to get each of his divisions to hire at least one black professional, but he was greeted with, "A Negro—why? I would not have one on my staff,"[19] from a subordinate regarded as the in-house liberal of his department. In one of the independent agencies, the top official personally set a policy contrary to the president's directives: No blacks were to be hired above the messenger level.[20]

In those agencies that changed their more restrictive practices because of the labor shortage, most nonetheless kept blacks in the most menial positions.[21] Those blacks whose qualifications were outstanding or whose reputations were well known to others in their fields, were selectively recruited, but then frequently were placed outside their areas of expertise. One black MIT-trained engineer was recruited by the Navy and then assigned to the secretary of the navy as a race relations adviser.[22] The war required specialists of all kinds but for blacks from every discipline, the specialization most often was to be custodian, messenger, or race relations adviser.

Working against the odds represented by a recalcitrant government bureaucracy was a group of black intellectuals. Most had originally been given appointments in New Deal agencies and were known collectively as the "Black Cabinet." Pressing the demands of black organizations from the inside,

> the Black Cabinet has managed to make definite strides in advancing the Negro's cause—always with the formidable aid of the mass-organization leaders. . . .[23]

Unlike the blacks who had held the traditional "Negro jobs" in the past, the members of the Black Cabinet had not come to their jobs by political routes.[24] They had different objectives, were people of exceptional ability, and had the kind of sophistication needed to operate successfully in the byzantine world of politics and government. Many served as racial advisers in the various war agencies, including Theodore Poston, William Hastie, James Evans, Truman Gibson, J. W. Trent, Channing Tobias, Mary McCloud Bethune, and Crystal Fauset (the only politician in the group).[25] In positions that dealt only at times with race relations, but which were more in line with their respective agencies' missions, were: Robert Vann, special assistant to the attorney general; Frank Horne, chief of race relations, Office of the Federal Public Housing Authority; Robert Weaver, War Manpower Commission; Ralph Bunche, division chief in the Department of State and Office of Strategic Services; Ira De A. Reid of the Social Security Board; and R. W. Logan, Office of the Coordinator of Inter-American Affairs.[26] Robert Weaver was later to become the first black secretary of an executive department;[27] Tobias and Bunche received appointments to the United Nations; and William Hastie was named governor of the Virgin Islands.[28] Probably none would have been permitted to serve in government had it not been for the war.

These black officials were active in-fighters in the government arena and, in the opinion of the Michigan *Chronicle,* "It was clear that the government advisors put the welfare of their people above their jobs."[29]

The few places in which blacks were well represented were the Federal Works Administration (42 percent)—which in those days was responsible for all custodial and building maintenance services —and the Government Printing Office (GPO) (31 percent black)— which also had an abundance of hard, dirty, often hazardous, and low-paying jobs.[30] The War Department and the Treasury were about 12 percent black, but they also had more than the average number of lower-level jobs to fill[31] (Table 4–1). The more traditional departments—State,[32] Agriculture, Interior, Justice, and Labor—

accounted for only a handful of black workers.[33] In these older agencies and the various regulatory commissions (the Tariff, Maritime, and Federal Trade Commissions), even hiring blacks for clerical positions was considered too extreme, and they were the last to refuse to make such appointments altogether.[34]

Although clearly part of the government, the postal service has always had its own salary scale and hiring procedures.[35] In 1944, blacks were only 7 percent of all the postal workers, and they were found chiefly in the lower-level jobs (Table 4-1). But despite that poor numerical showing, among blacks the post office had a reputation as a place for good job opportunities.

That reputation did not come from the opportunity of blacks to rise in meaningful numbers in the postal service ranks (blacks were not permitted to); it was because the post office was one of the few agencies which was not segregated in most large cities in the 1940s[36] and so did not present the personal humiliations that were part of working elsewhere. More important, the unskilled post office jobs, which most blacks ordinarily got, were widely dispersed throughout the country and generally offered comparatively good pay and job security in those places. It was not uncommon for black elementary school teachers to give up their jobs when one became available in the post office. The more flexible and usually earlier work hours also made it possible for many black postal workers to attend college or law school in the afternoons and evenings.[37] All of this meant that educated blacks who were closed out of opportunities in private industry and other parts of the federal government could at least get work in the post office, even though they might be working at unskilled jobs. As one long-time postal worker expressed the sentiment of those days: "You were still at the bottom but you made more money at the post office."[38] Its reputation was further enhanced by sheer size: by itself, the post office system accounted for most of the blacks employed by the non-war federal agencies in 1944 (Table 4-2).

Because the postal system was relatively more flexible and better-paid than other jobs available to educated blacks, black postal workers tended to have more education than their white coworkers, and that made them a force to contend with, to a degree not true in other government agencies. When they were not allowed to join the white postal union, black postal workers organized their own[39] (the National Alliance of Postal Employees) and used it to work actively against discrimination.[40]

Segregation on the Job

For those who landed jobs elsewhere in the government, discrimination remained a serious problem. Black employees worked in separate offices or were well hidden behind filing cabinets or screens. They used separate washrooms and drank at separate water fountains; only occasionally were black and white assigned to the same typing pools and dining halls.[41] But one rule operated everywhere: black units were almost always supervised by whites, but whites—no matter what their rank or seniority—were not supervised by blacks.[42] The overall effect of discrimination could readily be counted in the kinds of jobs that black workers held near the end of the war. In 1944, they were only 1 percent of professionals and about 5 percent of subprofessionals and clerical workers. At the opposite end of the scale, blacks were 61 percent of the clerical-mechanical workers who ran the most routinized machines (Table 4–3).

Despite the almost exclusive assignment of black workers to menial jobs, there was still room for wide variation in the manner in which the many government agencies treated their black employees. The Office of Price Administration, in its Washington office, was credited with having the most liberal hiring and promotion practices among the large agencies. The first administrator of the agency, Leon Henderson, began by using black workers only in traditional "Negro jobs," but he was open enough to let experience with those workers change his mind. In time, he even urged associates to "bring in some Negroes and give them a chance to show what they could do."[43]

A time soon came when many of the OPA offices had blacks working alongside whites in all levels of responsibility; some eventually became bosses of white secretaries. Even so, the OPA was not without its problems. Where whites were supervisors of all-black units, there were some tensions. Some white workers transferred when their units became predominately black.

The Commerce Department represented the other side of the issue, for it was a model of segregation and job insecurity for blacks. Of its 2,168 black employees in 1942, less than a quarter had permanent status. Commerce had black units, black sections, and black jobs. Blacks were virtually never in the business-related side of the department, except in clearly subordinate roles, but they were plentiful in the Census Bureau, where repetitive tasks—and segregation policies—were common. All of the known devices to keep blacks in their place were used at Commerce: quotas, restrictions on responsibilities, confinement to menial tasks, few promotions, supervisory roles only over other blacks, and segregated units.[44] The black jobs at the Census Bureau were, predictably, as sorters, cardpunch operators, and custodians. Equally predictable was the racial tension these arrangements generated.

The Justice Department, responsible for law enforcement throughout the land, did not manage much enforcement of antidiscrimination provisions in its own employment policies. In 1943, only 2 percent of Justice Department employees were black,[45] and these employees were required to eat in a carefully segregated cafeteria. Within the department, the FBI hired two blacks, one messenger who worked directly for Director J. Edgar Hoover, and one special agent.[46]

The State Department was very much a professional's organization, with little opportunity for advancement by others. Just before the war, the highest salaried black employee (excluding three black foreign service officers stationed overseas) was the secretary of state's chauffeur.[47] By 1944, State had acquired a few lower-level black clerical and administrative people, in part through pressure from the department's personnel office. The new positions actually represented promotions for black messengers with seniority in the department. Promotions of this sort were unusual enough that an FEPC investigation was launched and, as a result, additional promotions were made.[48]

When changes in the war theater required the State Department to have an authority on the political dynamics of African countries, their talent search turned up Dr. Ralph Bunche, a graduate of UCLA and Harvard who had pursued advanced studies in international affairs and specialized in colonization. At a time when the few blacks in policy-level positions tended to be race relations advisers, and against considerable hostility, Bunche succeeded in becoming an important figure in the development of State Department policy.[49] Despite high praise for his performance,[50] Bunche left the capital because of the segregated conditions there and his unwillingness to subject his family to its humiliating way of life.[51]

After the War

What little influence the first Fair Employment Practices Committee had under President Roosevelt disappeared when funding for its
operations was denied by Congress in 1946. After that, the plight of
black workers was occasionally taken up by individual federal officials or by officers of the United Public Workers of America (UPW),
a CIO labor union representing government employees.[52] Sometimes
through negotiations, other times by arguing and begging, they
helped black workers. In the Office of Price Administration (OPA),
a special unit was created to help displaced staff find jobs at the end
of the war. It was not easy. The administrator in charge of the unit
reported, "We have not found a single agency in which there has
been no evidence of racial discrimination in recruitment."[53] Employers felt free to use a host of rationales for not hiring or keeping black
employees, even in traditionally "Negro jobs."[54] Claiming everything, including the fear that hiring blacks would "start trouble,"
endanger "security," cause unhappiness to blacks who found themselves outnumbered, and be unacceptable to operating officials, some
administrators went so far as to admit that black people were only
hired during a time of war.[55]

Perhaps the classic case of agency discrimination occurred at the
end of the war, when the financial reporting division of one of the
war agencies was dissolved and the Federal Trade Commission was
ordered to absorb its 110 employees, among whom were 40 black
workers. Since the FTC had never hired blacks except as custodians,
their first act after hearing of the shift was to draw up a new organizational table, drastically cutting the financial reporting unit. With the
approval of the CSC and the Budget Bureau, all of the employees
chosen to fill the remaining vacancies were white. When the UPW
protested this decision, a new organization table was drawn up and
one black employee was retained. One month later, the FTC fired all
the personnel in the unit. Again the union appealed, and this time
32 employees, including 13 blacks with career status, were rehired.
This time the black accountants and financial analysts were all demoted to clerks and machine operators, and few were given any work
to do. Ultimately, they received low efficiency ratings, and when they
were fired, the CSC upheld the action.[56]

It is hard to know precisely what happened to the vast majority of black government employees in the period just after the war when white veterans began returning home in need of jobs. It is true that the government began to reduce the size of its wartime ranks, but it appears that black employment was not affected, at least not in numbers. The explanation lies in the jobs and working conditions of blacks. Returning white veterans were eager enough to come back home to the security of government employment, but not if it meant moving into all-black units in places like the Federal Works Administration. They were equally unlikely to apply at Freedman's Hospital or Howard University, both of which were largely run and staffed by blacks and experiencing an increase in employees of about one-third.[57] Those few blacks who held professional jobs in other parts of the government were far more likely to have their jobs threatened, but their numbers were too small to have much of a statistical impact on the totals. Blacks lost out in the kinds of jobs that reflected upward mobility during the war, but generally not in the numbers of custodians, maintenance people, or laborers.

In the aftermath of the war, some of the more blatant forms of discrimination crept back into practice, as they did when the FBI announced the need for 2,000 new clerical workers but made clear its refusal to hire any blacks,[58] and when five executive departments (Commerce, Treasury, Justice, State, and War), five independent agencies (the General Accounting Office, International Bank, Government Printing Office, Federal Security Agency, and Federal Works Agency) and the Bureau of the Budget posted their new vacancies for "white only" clerical workers.[59]

In 1947, the National Committee on Segregation in the Nation's Capital reported that discrimination remained as rampant as ever.[60] It showed that, all things being equal, black workers waited seven times as long as whites to be promoted, that they were systematically segregated in government agencies, and that they were still not permitted to supervise any but black workers. Agencies could easily slip back into old discriminatory patterns because, between 1946 and 1948, no federal body was charged with fair employment review.

Civil Service Reform and the McCarthy Years

President Truman finally acted in 1948, but only when there was the possibility of black civil disobedience in cities across the country, and the threat of black nonparticipation in the coming presidential election. When he did act, on July 26, 1948, Truman once again used the device of an Executive Order, 9980, to create a Fair Employment Board in the CSC, with fair employment officers for every department and independent agency.[61] Under the executive order, the CSC was charged with coordinating all the fair employment offices and with serving as the final review body for appeals from decisions made along the line.

Like its predecessors, this new review body had an organizational structure designed for failure, and no enforcement powers. The very personnel officers responsible for many of the discriminatory practices were to act as consultants when charges of discrimination were made.[62] Moreover, the CSC, in which the review board was lodged, had discriminatory staffing patterns: no black professionals, no black employees at all in three of its regions, and no black employee higher than a CAF–4 level clerk in the central office.[63] It was not a choice designed to inspire confidence in black workers that their rights would be protected. The absence of any black professionals within it to create internal pressure for reform was only one problem with the CSC in its new function. Its ability to influence equal employment opportunity throughout the government was hampered also because it had lower standing than the agencies it was meant to oversee.

Not all presidential orders were so little heeded as those affecting fair employment. At the same time that blacks' rights were frustrated by the lack of antidiscrimination enforcement, they were being very directly affected by the zealous (and often inappropriate) enforcement of another of Truman's executive orders which authorized a government-wide loyalty program. Black federal workers were fired for participating, after work, in NAACP-sponsored picketing of discriminating retail stores and on the strength of unproved allegations that they attended Communist-inspired meetings.[64] A black postal worker in Santa Monica who was also head of the local NAACP was fired from his job for organizing a drive, after hours, to increase black employment at a local department store.[65] His crime, and that of black postal and government employees in other states, was simply membership in the NAACP. These were the early cold-war years, and an atmosphere of prying and recrimination pervaded government. During the six-year life of the loyalty program (1947–1953), nearly 5 million federal employees were investigated by the FBI and the CSC.[66] In that atmosphere, fighting discrimination became nearly synonymous with disloyalty, and black employees everywhere became especially vulnerable—particularly since there was no need to prove the charges before firing a worker.[67] Time and time again, the NAACP was called on to defend black government workers accused of disloyalty after pressing for black rights.[68] By 1949, the situation had prompted the UPW to inform the president that, under the loyalty program, blacks were being fired at an alarming rate.[69] Truman had been known as a strong and personally committed supporter of equal rights, but, for blacks in government, the loyalty program undid much of the good will that his administration garnered elsewhere.

Setting the Federal House in Order

Dwight Eisenhower took office in 1952 with a definite set of ideas about the role of the federal government in racial matters. In general, he preferred to trust the intelligence and cooperation of people more than law, saying, "There are certain things that are not best handled by punitive or compulsory Federal law."[70] On that ground, he opposed a bill which would have prohibited discrimination in federal employment and private industry. Instead, promising to use all the power available to him to end segregation in Washington, D.C., in the armed forces,[71] and in the federal government, he wrote: "The very least the Executive could do would be to see first that the federal house itself was in order."[72]

Despite the fine words, Eisenhower did little or nothing to clean up the "federal house" during the first two years of his administration. When fair employment legislation to end discrimination in government service was being considered by the Senate, A. Philip Randolph testified:

> . . . the need for fair employment practice Federal legislation in the year 1954 is as imperative if not more so than on June 25, 1941 when . . . Roosevelt issued the first Executive Order on the subject of FEPC. . . . A Jim Crow "iron curtain" exists in the hiring practice of every Federal department, bureau, agency, board, or commission.[73]

A CIO indictment of government practices was just as strong. The union's newspaper said that job discrimination was still widely practiced and causing many blacks to lose their jobs.[74]

With the 1956 elections looming ahead, Eisenhower issued Executive Order 10590, establishing the President's Committee on Government Employment Policy (PCGEP) early in 1955.[75] Like other committees and commissions that had gone before, PCGEP was another moral persuader and presidential adviser, and like the others, it had no enforcement powers. The only difference from previous fair employment bodies was the appointment of the vice-president, Richard Nixon, to head the effort. Normally, this would imply strong White House support for fair employment but, in this instance, the signals were confused. While a congressman and senator, this vice-president had voted twice against an enforceable fair employment practices bill,[76] and had co-authored the minority report opposing the FEPC.[77]

During the course of the election year, the Republican National Committee issued statements that claimed credit for 316 black government appointees.[78] Their names and titles were circulated to the black media that year, and they reflected a wide range, all the way from a Supreme Court page (normally a high school student who carries messages) to chairman of the Federal Parole Board and a delegate to the United Nations. Of greatest credit to the Eisenhower administration were the appointments of Ernest Wilkins as the first black assistant secretary of labor, and Frederic Morrow as the first black presidential staff assistant.[79]

But that same year, when the federal government conducted a survey of salaried federal workers in five cities, including Washington, D.C., there were almost no black employees to be found in the higher-level positions of GS 12 through GS 15 (Table 4–4). The survey showed that it was not just higher-level jobs that were closed to blacks, but that the ranks of clerical workers remained all-white in many agencies. In Washington itself the Justice Department still had no black secretaries or accountants, the Civil Service Commission had no black stenographers, and the Labor Department had no black accountants or contract officers.[80] Yet these were the very agencies charged with fair employment enforcement responsibilities over private industry, as well as in state and federal government. They apparently had not been any more effective with other government agencies than with their own: 85 percent of the agencies in Washington still placed restrictions on hiring blacks, more than half of the agencies had yet to hire even black secretaries or stenographers, and one-fourth had no black typists.[81] In all five cities, black workers continued to be concentrated in the lower-level positions. But 1956 was a presidential election year, and while campaigning in Minnesota, the president managed to say that his administration had erased all vestiges of segregation and inequality of opportunity in all areas within the authority of the federal government.[82]

A follow-up study conducted four years later found that black employment had finally begun to improve in the middle levels of the government service. Blacks had moved from 7 percent of workers with jobs rated GS 5 through 8 in 1956, to 11 percent by 1960. That represented a significant improvement because it meant that blacks were no longer kept at the bottom of the ladder in the lowest-paid jobs in the government. Among jobs rated GS 9 through 11, the record was less impressive, but there too blacks had realized some improvements and had increased their numbers from 1 to 3 percent of all such workers. As before, almost no black employees were found in the higher-level jobs where policies are made and programmatic responsibilities are lodged (Table 4–4).

Near the end of Eisenhower's second term, 56 government agencies were asked to report their own progress on fair employment issues. When asked whether any units in their organizations were segregated on the basis of race, color, religion, or natural origin, 10 agencies declined to answer, and 3 reported that they still had some all-Negro units, but took the position that "this was not the result of deliberate intent."[83]

Despite this poor showing, administration officials were quick to take credit for the few bright spots in Eisenhower's civil rights record. They were careful to stress to black voters that the historic Supreme Court school desegregation decision was handed down during his administration and written by one of his appointees to the Court, Chief Justice Earl Warren.[84] And although little was done by Eisenhower to see that school desegregation was accomplished (that would have confronted his hands-off policy toward states' rights), he sent troops to Little Rock, Arkansas, to enforce a court order growing out of the desegregation decision.[85]

The 1961 Census

The first comprehensive federal employment census by race was taken in 1961. In that accounting, blacks were found to make up nearly one-fifth of all wage-board laborers and General Schedule employees at the lowest levels, GS 1 through 4. But blacks were only 1 percent of all workers in the higher, salaried jobs, those ranging from GS 12 through GS 18 at the very top (Table 4–5). Two agencies with large staffs of blacks in low-paying jobs, the Civil Service Commission and the Government Printing Office, had a particularly skewed staffing pattern. Despite a long history of having large proportions of black workers, they had no blacks to speak of in the upper-level positions by 1961 (Table 4–6).

When the middle and upper grades of the postal system were judged alongside the record of other parts of the government, opportunities for blacks proved to be much the same as everywhere else in 1961.[86] In one significant respect, the post office was still different: its jobs were located all around the country and, in many localities, provided some of the better-paying job opportunities open to blacks. A few years earlier, blacks were already a large proportion of the work force in the post offices of major cities like Chicago, Mobile, Los Angeles, and St. Louis.[87] Reports by FEPC's in states like Illinois and Minnesota,[88] and by *Ebony* magazine[89] after inquiring around the country, indicated that the postal system even had blacks in supervisory positions over white workers. And by 1961, 3 out of every 10 blacks employed by the federal government worked for the post office. (Table 4–7).

Outside Pressure

There is a sense in which government employees have never been as free as others to press for their rights and to make demands of their employers. All employees share the fear that any form of pressure may jeopardize a job or future promotions, but over the years, government workers have felt that sense of stricture even more keenly. In part, this stems from the language of the Hatch Act, which was long used (albeit inappropriately) to inhibit government employees from engaging in any activities that might be construed as "political."[90] And when black employees joined picket lines, civil rights organizations, or employee organizations working for fair employment, many of those activities were labeled "political." During the late forties and the fifties, when the loyalty program and McCarthyism held all of government in its grip, black government workers felt more than usually constrained to guard their words and actions. And, when some few blacks did win jobs in the middle ranks of the Civil Service, their own instincts and family interests operated to dampen their inclinations toward a more active role: government jobs were, after all, more secure than those usually available to black people.

But even government was not so removed from ordinary life that it could have been untouched by the civil rights protest that swept across the country in the early sixties. It made little difference that government workers themselves were not staging sit-ins in their agencies or outside the doors of personnel offices and agency officials. Government is after all presided over by men and women whose positions depend upon votes and public sentiment, and the presidents that held office at the height of the civil rights movement were very much attuned to political realities. After a March 1965 cabinet meeting spent discussing events in Selma, Alabama, the head of the CSC wrote to all department and administration heads, noting that the lack of black government employees in places like Alabama hampered "the effectiveness of the non-discrimination policy in Federal employment," and the president's "deep concern over these conditions."[91] As long as civil rights was an issue for the general public, it was an issue for government.

John Kennedy campaigned for the presidency with a deliberate focus on black votes. His speeches were filled with references to the need for equality and nondiscrimination in government, as part of his promise to get America moving again.[92] Black Americans were already on the move that year, staging sit-ins, wade-ins, pray-ins, picketlines, and demonstrations all across the South, and that fall they were moving into the voting booths of the urban North in unprecedented numbers to give Kennedy the margin that meant winning the election.[93] In return, Kennedy appointed blacks to positions in his administration: Robert Weaver became the first black to head a major agency, the Housing and Home Finance Agency (HHFA); Andrew Hatcher became the first black press secretary; and Carl Rowan was named first a deputy assistant secretary of state and later ambassador to Finland, the first time a black had been named U.S. ambassador to a white country. Clifton Wharton became ambassador to Norway, blacks began appearing as appointed members of the White House staff, and for the first time, a black was named to a regulatory board. There were enough senior-level staff from seventeen departments and agencies throughout the government to form an informal black subcabinet group.[94] They monitored internal hiring policies and the kinds of interpersonal problems that had rarely received attention in the past: the practices in cafeterias, lounges, and recreational activities.[95]

In March of 1961 Kennedy issued Executive Order 10925, establishing the newest version of a committee on equal employment opportunity and reaffirming the policies of previous executive orders forbidding discrimination in government. For the first time, the emphasis was shifted to affirmative action. This time the President's Committee on Equal Employment Opportunity (PCEEO) had built-in mechanisms for hearings, appeals procedures, review by independent authority, and the provision of counsel to employees who had grievances. In one significant respect, PCEEO was no different from all the committees that had come before: its enforcement provisions remained weak.[96] At least under PCEEO a census of federal employees was conducted each year to determine the effect of actual hiring and promotion policies with greater accuracy than had been possible before. The Federal Personnel Manual was revised to emphasize the importance of nondiscrimination in promotion, and equal employment activities finally became part of the normal review process for all federal agencies.[97]

By April of 1961 *Newsweek* magazine was extolling the Kennedy administration's "Search for Negro Talent: 'We Mean Business'."[98] *Newsweek* detailed the efforts in and out of government to overcome black skepticism and to find, recruit, and promote black talent willing to work in the government.[99] To Kennedy's credit, he was personally involved in the effort and attentive to detail, responding to complaints from private industry that some government regional offices were not behaving as industry was being expected to do, and personally ordering cabinet officers to ensure employment opportunity for minorities in their departments.[100]

But for all the activity and noble sentiments, the record of the Kennedy years is not much different from the early Eisenhower years: fine words but little actual change in black employment, which stayed at about 13 percent overall between 1961 and 1963, showed only the barest gains in middle-level government jobs, and none at all at the highest levels (Table 4–5). It may be, as the Leadership Conference On Civil Rights contended (and the record of the Eisenhower years seemed to show), that large, swift changes are not possible in an unresponsive bureaucracy.[101] The great improvements during the Johnson years may well have combined the legacy of the climate and machinery introduced in the Kennedy years with Johnson's continued commitment.

There was no mistaking Lyndon Johnson's commitment to civil rights. When he assumed office in 1963, President Johnson said:

No memorial or eulogy could more eloquently honor President Kennedy's memory than the earliest possible passage of the civil rights bill for which he fought so hard. We have talked long enough in this country about equal rights. We have talked 100 years or more. It is time now to write the next chapter—and to write it in the books of law.

I urge you . . . to enact a civil rights law so that we can move forward to eliminate from this nation every trace of discrimination and oppression that is based upon race or color. There can be no greater source of strength to this nation both at home and abroad.[102]

That same Civil Rights Act provided in the statute that, "it shall be the policy of the United States to insure equal employment opportunities for Federal employees without discrimination because of race, color, religion, sex or national origin."[103] Johnson's assault on inequality was grand in the way that much of what he did always seemed a little larger than life. His administration was responsible for the enactment of over one hundred laws, the majority of them dealing with social and domestic concerns of immediate importance to black Americans.[104] The "Great Society" programs stemming from the Economic Opportunity Act alone (Vista, Head Start, Job Corps, Neighborhood Youth Corps, Community Action, and more) were responsible for bringing some 15,000 new black workers into the federal government.[105]

Under Johnson the Equal Employment Opportunity programs were strengthened through Executive Order 11246 issued September 1965. Although the original Civil Rights Act of 1964 prescribed equal employment opportunity in the federal government, this policy was rescinded in 1966. The law gave no enforcement powers either to the CSC or any other government body.[106] Executive Order 11246 did, however, charge the CSC with the sole responsibility for enforcing nondiscrimination in the federal service.[107] With that, the CSC became responsible for training, upgrading, reviewing agencies, and establishing guidelines to govern the complaint process. But in two important respects even these changes included the same flaws already in the CSC civil rights process:[108] agencies were still to be allowed to investigate themselves, and systematic discrimination (rather than specific instances based on individual complaints) was still to be ignored.[109]

By setting up a President's Council on Equal Opportunity (PCEO), Johnson created the first umbrella organization for coordination of civil rights activities throughout the government.[110] The council's function was not so much to oversee equal employment opportunity in the government as to provide a means of ensuring coordination among the various federal agencies dealing with civil rights activities to make them more effective. For federal employment, the council provided a forum that proved important in two ways. First, it brought officials from over sixteen agencies together to discuss civil rights problems of mutual interest; second, the chairman of the Civil Service Commission was a member and so able to deal directly with high-ranking agency officials about civil rights problems in the agencies' field offices. The council was weakened by having, once again, inadequate staff and no enforcement authority.[111] But its potential as the first small superagency under a black administrator—Wiley Branton—and charged by the president with responsibility for discrimination problems wherever they might occur, was not lost on others. That power, and the threat it posed to others in the government, was thought to be the reason why the council was dismantled in 1965.[112] The immediate cause of the council's demise was the activist stance it chose to take whenever civil rights problems arose: it pressed for HEW to pursue desegregation of Chicago's schools,[113] and it tried to become involved in the racial strife in Selma, Alabama.[114] President Johnson may have been willing to twist arms in Congress to win passage of the Civil Rights Act, or to lean on his own cabinet officials to accomplish changes within the federal establishment, but even he was unwilling to confront directly the likes of Mayor Richard Daley in Chicago and Governor George Wallace of Alabama in their own political territory.[115] Ironically, the first time that the CSC was given administrative authority to set the rules and write the guidelines for EEO practices throughout the federal government, the new powers were included in the order abolishing the PCEO.[116]

The Johnson years were the first to witness the movement of blacks in significant numbers into the middle levels of the federal Civil Service, and in smaller numbers—but no less importantly—into the highest reaches of the government. By 1969, black workers held 13 percent of the positions rated GS 5 through 8, and 5 percent of those rated GS 9 through 11 (Table 4–5). Given the unusual stability of Civil Service jobs, there could be no turning back.

The impressive record of the Johnson years was no doubt a combination of many forces: Johnson's own personal commitment to civil rights, the pressure from the civil rights movement, the "multiplier" effect of bringing blacks into government in positions where they might influence who might be hired next, the gradual but inevitable result of having a civil service system that provides a mechanism for advancing the workers in it, and the impact of a developing system for handling complaints and exerting pressure. Perhaps as important as any other influence is the simple fact of attention. As the government agencies began to collect information on minority employees (and members of the press publicized it), as EEO officers became a presence in every agency (and those who hired or promoted knew their actions would be reviewed by someone), and as blacks themselves grew more confident that they had a right to bring in their recommended applicants just as white employees had been doing until then, things changed. No one piece of law or language could create such change the way a dozen or more forces impacting all at the same time in a variety of ways could do. The result was that black and white alike could believe Johnson, a southerner, when he said: "Their cause must be our cause too. Because it is not just Negroes, but really it is all of us, who must overcome the crippling legacy of bigotry and injustice. And we shall overcome."[117]

Turning Back

When Richard Nixon took office, there was some concern that his administration would mean a turning back from civil rights and fair employment in government. Civil rights leaders feared that Nixon "has consigned Negroes to a political doghouse whose roof leaks."[118] Presidential adviser Daniel P. Moynihan was learned to have counseled Nixon to give race problems a period of "benign neglect."[119] And, thirteen months into the administration, nine black representatives felt the need to meet with the president to learn his position on civil rights,[120] which they believed was influenced by his desire to build a new southern constituency based on old prejudices.[121]

Whether it was the "southern strategy" or the cumulation of a long list of small policy changes that seemed to be saying, "slow down," outspoken black officials and civil rights advocates did not stay long in the Nixon administration, and were difficult to recruit when posts became empty. In the first full year of office, Nixon either fired or asked for the resignations of the director of the Office for Civil Rights in HEW (to fill the job with someone less active), the chairman of the Equal Employment Opportunity Commission (EEOC) (just after he began a series of public hearings), a former director of CORE who had become an assistant secretary of HEW (and was dissatisfied with the pace of civil rights activities),[122] and other officials regarded as too vocal on civil rights matters.[123] The search for an acceptable black Republican to fill the vacant directorship of HEW's Office for Civil Rights lasted for the duration of the Nixon years.

Nonetheless, during these years, some of the same forces that operated to enhance the record of the Johnson years worked in the same way for the Nixon administration. Middle-level civil servants who had come into government under Kennedy and Johnson continued to move slowly upward. By 1975, 8 percent of the federal workers rated GS 9 through 11 and 4 percent of those over GS 11 were black (Table 4–5). Enforcement and monitoring procedures already in place kept a dimmed but steady spotlight on agencies' practices. When the pressure of civil rights complaints grew, Congress was persuaded to amend the Civil Rights Act to enable federal employees to pursue their discrimination claims in federal district courts.[124] Then black government workers had a powerful legal tool with which to press their rights. (The same amendment provided relief for the employees and punishment for the guilty officials.) And, whatever difficulty President Nixon may have had in finding acceptable appointees for agencies here at home, he appointed more blacks as chiefs of U.S. missions overseas than did any other president, although 10 out of 12 were appointed to black countries.[125]

In federal Civil Service terms, the Ford presidency was for the most part a continuation of patterns evident under President Nixon.

Changes over the Years

Over the years, three things stand out. First, by comparison with private industry, the fair employment record of the federal government looks fairly good (Table 4–8). The second is the extent to which even in recent years the federal Civil Service has resisted change, especially at higher levels (Table 4–5). And third is the striking way in which change, when it came, left things a good deal like the early years. Between 1938 and 1961, such gains as there were for blacks were chiefly in numbers (Table 4–9). Since 1961, blacks have moved slowly into middle- and higher-level Civil Service jobs; a few have moved into the "super grades"—the very top of the system in GS 16, 17, and 18 (Table 4–5).

For all the turmoil and pressure, the endless executive orders and presidential committees, the federal Civil Service has shifted remarkably little. The General Schedule (GS), the largest pay system, with 57 percent of all federal government employees in 1975 (Table 4–10), presents a checkered picture. In 1975 blacks occupied proportionally about the same position in the lowest grades that they had fourteen years before, but they held two-and-a-half times as many of the middle-level jobs as they did then. Blacks held only about 3 percent of the very top positions, the "super grades" (Table 4–5).

The postal service is the one place where a significant improvement occurred during those years. Blacks have come to occupy several times as large a proportion of the middle- and upper-level jobs as they did in 1961 (Table 4–5), and now hold some of the top positions in post offices across the country.[126]

But between 1961 and 1975, two of the federal pay systems have remained virtually unchanged. Blacks continue to be disproportionately found in the low-paying and least prestigious wage board jobs: although 11 percent of the total labor force, they continue to make up 20 percent of all federal wage board employees. And in the specialized pay systems that cover employers like the Foreign Service, the Atomic Energy Commission, and medical departments of the Veterans' Administration, the proportion of blacks was no greater in 1975 than it had been in 1961 (Table 4–7).

The most telling commentary of all is provided by grouping the agencies (and the positions) according to whether they are responsible for what are publicly identified as "black concerns." If equal employment and color-blind hiring and promotion policies had come to the federal government, then black employees should not only be found equally in the highest as well as the lowest positions, but equally in all of the agencies of government. There are, after all, black farmers and black coal miners, black housewives with consumer concerns, and black parents; there are black people who care about the quality of the air they breathe and the location of the lands set aside for recreation; black people have a stake in the policies arrived at by the Pentagon and the administration of our space exploration programs; black businesses and homeowners are as vitally affected by mortgage and financing policies as are their white counterparts; black families whose boy was lost or injured in Vietnam are every bit as much affected by our foreign policy as white people are. Yet the pattern of federal employment suggests something very different. It is almost as though poverty and unemployment, race relations and desegregation, were the only subjects about which black people ought to be concerned. Just as there were once "Negro jobs," and all black appointees found themselves assigned to "race relations," in 1975 an estimated one-third of all black supergrades in government filled equal-employment-opportunity-related positions.[127] Similarly, five agencies responsible for "black issues" (HEW, HUD, EEOC, the OEO, and the Department of Labor) accounted for only 20 percent of all black General Schedule federal employees in 1975, but for more than one-third of all black supergrades in that system, and for nearly as many of those in grades 12 through 15 (Table 4–11).

Most of the same agencies with discriminatory policies and poor hiring and promotion records in the forties still remained at the bottom of the fair employment list into the sixties and seventies: Justice, Interior, Agriculture, Defense. The Justice Department, with far-reaching influence on black lives and civil rights responsibilities, had fewer than 3 percent of its higher-level jobs filled by blacks (Table 4–6). As one coordinator of Government Employees United Against Racial Discrimination (GUARD) commented:

> . . . most blacks in the super-grades are not career government employees but Presidential appointees serving as equal employment officials, rather than in traditional policy-making posts. "It is misleading to count these people among the . . . supergrades."[128]

The grievance procedure is so tortuous that it is hard to see how conditions can improve without a drastic change in the rules and in basic civil rights commitment. Since the late sixties, black government employees, largely those in lower-level jobs, have been agitating for improvements in their various agencies' performance. GUARD was formed to take up the fight,[129] and angry black employees have been known to use every formal and informal complaint procedure available to them to press for their rights. But the complaint procedures on which black employees must rely are restricted in several important respects. The CSC has interpreted the EEOC guidelines to Title VII of the Civil Rights Act so that federal workers are not covered.[130] The burden of proof is put on the employee, who might have difficulty in gaining access to files or information necessary to prove a case.[131] Federal employees have only thirty days, one-sixth the time available to employees in private industry, to initiate a complaint.[132] If an employee should overcome all of these obstacles and lodge a formal complaint, the agency against which the complaint is filed becomes both defendant and judge.[133] Ultimately, there is little that will be done to discourage discriminatory practices even where they are proved (only one discriminating official has been dismissed in over a decade),[134] and little if any relief for "successful" employees. Civil rights lawyers contend that landmark cases which have been fought and won in the private sector could not have been won in the system set up for federal employees and, under most circumstances, would not even have been given a hearing on the merits.[135]

Despite that formidable obstacle course, in 1975 the CSC declared that one of the few effective tools in the fight against discrimination —the timetables and agency goals that were used since the late sixties —could no longer be employed.

With or without new legislation, the fate of black employees in the federal government will continue to depend in large measure, as it always has, on the depth of the chief executive's commitment to equal rights, and on the growing strength of black voters. Every president has the power to influence the civil rights climate in the country, in ways that touch the lives of virtually every worker. But that influence is largely indirect. The federal Civil Service is a different matter: the president is its boss and may both use its jobs to repay campaign assistance and make it accountable for its practices. Thus far, however, even those presidents who believe in equal rights and have large political debts to repay to black workers, have concentrated on making highly visible appointments of particularly gifted black men and women to top administration posts; none has yet made a campaign issue of the unreasonable preponderance of black men and women in the lowest-level government jobs, their opportunities for advancement, or the ability of the system to operate without discrimination. Numbers and visibility seem to be as far as most presidents have been willing to go. Without effective EEO machinery within the system, that is very likely where things will stay.

TABLE 4–1

The Federal Works Agency and the Government Printing Office Were Key Non-War Agency Employers of Blacks in 1944; These Manual Job Agencies Employed Many Blacks in Salaried Work

Percentage of Federal Workers Who Were Black,[a] by Agency and Pay Classification, 1944

Agency	Total	Salaried workers[b]		Craft, protective, custodial, clerical, mechanical
		Total	Professional[c]	
All agencies[d]	11	7[e]	1[e]	24
Federal Works Agency	42	41	[f]	56
Government Printing Office	31	17	[f][g]	60
Federal Security Agency	16	17	1	44
War[h]	13	6	1	17
Treasury	12	12	[f]	49
Civil Service Commission	11	11	1	74
TVA	11	6	[f]	25
Veterans Administration	10	10	1	12
Post Office	7	[i]	[i]	[i]
Commerce	6	7	1	48
Interior	3	3	[f]	7

[a] Negro only.
[b] Classified workers.
[c] In 1944 professional workers were 6 percent of total salaried employment.
[d] Does not include Justice, Labor, or Agriculture.
[e] Does not include Post Office, which had a different pay system.
[f] Less than 0.5 percent.
[g] Only two people—both white—held professional rank.
[h] Includes Navy Department.
[i] Not available.

Source: Derived from U.S. Committee on Fair Employment Practice, *The Wartime Employment of Negroes in the Federal Government,* 1945, Tables 1, 6, 8–10, pp. 28–9, 34, 36, 41, 43, 45.

TABLE 4–2

Most Black Federal Workers Were in War Agencies in 1944; Chiefly in Temporary Jobs

Percentage Distribution of Black[a] Federal Employees by Agency and Pay Classification, 1944

Agency	All workers	Salaried workers[b]		Hourly workers Craft, protective, custodial, clerical, mechanical
		Total	Professional[c]	
All agencies	100	100	100	100
Federal Works Agency	3	11	1	20
Government Printing Office	1	(d)	(d)	(d)
Federal Security Agency	2	6	11	8
War[e]	78	58	66	49
Treasury	4	14	(d)	16
Civil Service Commission	(d)	1	1	(d)
TVA	1	1	1	1
Veterans Administration	2	6	11	3
Commerce	1	2	7	2
Interior	(d)	1	2	1
Post Office	10	(f)	(f)	(f)

[a] Negro only.
[b] Classified workers.
[c] In 1944 professional workers were 6 percent of total salaried employment.
[d] Less than 0.5 percent.
[e] Includes Navy Department.
[f] Not available.

Source: Derived from U.S. Committee on Fair Employment Practice, *The Wartime Employment of Negroes in the Federal Government,* 1945, Tables 1, 8–10, pp. 28–9, 36, 41, 43, 45; 1940 Census of Population, *The Labor Force, Vol. 3, Pt. 1, U.S. Summary,* Table 76, pp. 188–9; 1950 Census of Population, *Characteristics of the Population, Vol. 2, Pt. 1, U.S. Summary,* Table 133, pp. 1–288–9; U.S. Bureau of the Census, *Historical Statistics of the United States, Colonial Times to 1957* (Washington, D.C.: Government Printing Office, 1960), Series Y 247, p. 710.

TABLE 4–3

Blacks in Federal Classified Positions in 1944 Were Half Maintenance Workers and Half Clerical and Subprofessional; White Workers Were 88 Percent Clerical or Higher

Salaried[a] Federal Workers by Occupation and Race, 1944

Occupation	Percentage distribution		Percent black[b] in each group
	Black[b]	White	
All occupations			
Number	81,816	1,094,515	[c]
Percent	100	100	7
Professional	1	6	1
Executive order[d]	1	4	1
Subprofessional	5	7	5
Clerical-administrative-fiscal (CAF)	43	71	4
Craft, protective, custodial	46	12	23
Clerical-mechanical[e]	4	[f]	61

[a] In 1944, during World War II, salaried (classified) workers were only half of all federal workers. The total in this table does not include such workers in the Post Office, Justice, Labor, and Agriculture Departments. The remainder were in the latter departments or were workers paid chiefly by the hour.

[b] Negro only.

[c] Not applicable.

[d] Employees not subject to competitive CSC requirements, hired at the discretion of agency head.

[e] Chiefly office machine operators and sorters.

[f] Less than 0.5 percent.

Source: Derived from U.S. Committee on Fair Employment Practice, *The Wartime Employment of Negroes in the Federal Government,* 1945, Tables 1, 6, 9, pp. 28, 34, 41, 45.

TABLE 4-4

Black Federal Workers in Five Major Cities Showed Almost No Gain in the Best Jobs, from 1956 to 1960

Percentage of Federal Workers Who Were Black[a] in Five Cities, by Grade, 1956 and 1960

City and grade	1956	1960
All five cities[b]		
Total[c]	4	6
GS 5-8	7	11
GS 9-11	1	3
GS 12-15	[d]	1
Washington, D.C.		
Total[c]	4	6
GS 5-8	8	13
GS 9-11	2	3
GS 12-15	[d]	1
Chicago		
Total[c]	4	8
GS 5-8	7	12
GS 9-11	1	6
GS 12-15	[d]	1
St. Louis		
Total[c]	2	4
GS 5-8	4	7
GS 9-11	1	3
GS 12-15	[d]	[d]
Los Angeles		
Total[c]	1	3
GS 5-8	2	5
GS 9-11	1	2
GS 12-15	[d]	[d]
Mobile		
Total[c]	[d]	1
GS 5-8	[d]	1
GS 9-11	0	[d]
GS 12-15	0	0

[a] Negro only.

[b] The five-cities sample for 1960 involved 6 percent of total federal employment and 4 percent of black federal employment. The number of agencies involved in 1956 and 1960 respectively were Washington, D.C., 53 and 53; Chicago, 24 and 27; St. Louis, 21 and 26; Los Angeles, 23 and 27; and Mobile, 16 and 15.

[c] GS 5-15.

[d] Less than 0.5 percent.

Source: Derived from U.S. President's Committee on Government Employment Policy. Unpublished data from its files available through the U.S. Department of Labor, Office of the Solicitor, Washington, D.C.

TABLE 4–5

Blacks Edged Up From 13 to 16 Percent of All Federal Workers in the Fourteen Years 1961–75; Largest Gains Were in Middle and Higher Postal Jobs and Lower GS Levels

Percentage of Federal Workers Who Were Black,[a] by Pay System and Grade, Selected Years, 1961–75

Pay system and grade	1961	1963	1969	1974	1975
All pay systems	13	13	15	16	16
General schedule	9	9	11	13	13
1–4	18	19	22	22	21
5–11	5	6	9	13	13
5–8	[b]	8	13	17	17
9–11	[b]	3	5	7	8
12–18	1	1	2	4	4
16–18	[b]	[b]	1	3	3
Wage system	19	19	20	21	20
Other pay systems	6	8	6	6	6
Postal Field Service (PFS)[c]	15	15	19	21	21
Low	16	17	21	22	22
Middle	6	7	12	23	23
Upper	[d]	1	4	9	10

[a] Negro only.
[b] Not available.
[c] Low is levels 1–5, except in 1961 and 1963, when it is levels 1–4. Middle is through level 11 in all years except 1974–75, when it is through level 12. Upper is all higher grades, 12 and over, in all but 1974–75, when it is 13 and over.
[d] Less than 0.5 percent.

Source: Derived from U.S. Civil Service Commission, "Minority Group Study, 1963," n.d., Table 1, n.p.; idem, "Study of Minority Group Employment in the Federal Government, 1963," n.d., Table 1, n.p. Unpublished surveys covering 1961–63 conducted by the commission at the request of the President's Committee on Equal Employment Opportunity: idem, *Minority Group Employment in the Federal Government, November 30, 1969* (Washington, D.C.: Government Printing Office, 1970), Table 1–1, p. 28; idem, *Minority Group Employment in the Federal Government, May 1974* (Washington, D.C.: Government Printing Office, 1976), Table 1–001, pp. 3–4; idem, "1975 Minority Group Study"; "All-Agency Summary, May 1975," n.d. (mimeographed); idem, "1975 Minority Group Study by Agency," n.d. (mimeographed).

TABLE 4-6

Blacks in 1975 Were 4 Percent or Less of All Salaried Federal Workers at GS 12 and Above in Several Old-Line Agencies with Important Missions, Including Especially the Department of Justice

Percentage of Federal Workers Who Were Black,[a] by Agency, for All Workers and Salaried Workers GS 12 and Over, 1961 and 1975

	1961		1975	
	All workers	Salaried only[b] GS 12	All workers	Salaried only[b] GS 12
Agency	Total	and over	Total	and over
All agencies	13	1	16	4
Government Printing Office	39	[c]	53	23
Labor	18	2	26	12
Housing and Urban Development[d]	10	2	23	11
Health, Education, and Welfare	18	1	24	10
State	9	1	15	9
Civil Service Commission	22	[c]	26	8
General Services Administration	36	[c]	36	7
Commerce	12	1	18	6
Veterans Administration	23	1	25	4
Treasury	12	[c]	15	4
Justice	3	[c]	12	3
Defense	11	1	12	3
Agriculture	5	[c]	7	2
Interior	4	[c]	5	1

[a] Negro only.

[b] Workers with classification of GS 12 and over were 15 percent of salaried employment in 1961 and 24 percent in 1975.

[c] Less than 0.5 percent.

[d] Housing and Home Finance Agency in 1961.

Source: U.S. Civil Service Commission, "Minority Group Study 1963," n.d., Tables 1–5, 7–12, 14, 15, 17–19, 21, n.p. Unpublished surveys covering 1961–63 conducted by the commission, made at the request of the President's Committee on Equal Employment Opportunity: idem, "1975 Minority Group Study: All Agency Summary," n.d. (mimeographed); idem, "1975 Minority Group Study by Agency," n.d. (mimeographed).

TABLE 4–7

Half of All Black Federal Workers Were Still in the Postal or Hourly Wage Pay Systems in 1975 (40 Percent of Whites); in the GS Group, the Percentage of Whites over GS 9 Was Several Times That of Blacks

Percentage Distribution of Federal Workers by Type of Pay System and by Race, 1961 and 1975

Pay system	1961		1975	
	Black[a]	White	Black[a]	White
All pay systems	100	100	100	100
Salaried[b]	32	48	45	59
GS 1–4	23	15	17	12
GS 5–11	9	25	25	31
GS 5–8	[c]	[c]	19	17
GS 9–11	[c]	[c]	6	14
GS 12–18	[d]	8	3	15
GS 12–13	[c]	[c]	3	11
GS 14–15	[c]	[c]	1	4
GS 16–18	[c]	[c]	[d]	[d]
Wage	38	24	25	18
Other pay systems[e]	1	2	1	2
Postal Service	29	25	30	22

[a] Negro only.
[b] General Schedule.
[c] Not available.
[d] Less than 0.5 percent.
[e] Includes employees not subject to competitive CSC requirements; hired at the discretion of agency head.

Source: Derived from U.S. Civil Service Commission, "Minority Group Study, 1963," n.d., Table 1, n.p.; idem, "All Agency Summary, May 1975," n.d. (mimeographed).

TABLE 4–8

Whether Black or White, Federal Workers Are Chiefly Clerks; Private Employees Are Mostly in Sales, Production, and Service, but the Federal Government Employs Black Professionals More Extensively than Private Industry

Percentage Distribution of Employees of the Federal Government and Private Industry, by Broad Occupation Group and by Race, 1970

Broad occupation group	Black[a] Federal	Private	White Federal	Private
All occupations	100	100	100	100
Professional and technical	11	4	23	11
Managers and administrators	3	2	10	8
Clerical	45	11	42	19
All other[b]	41	84	25	61

[a] Negro only.
[b] Includes sales, operatives, transport, laborers, and service workers.

Source: 1970 Census of Population, *Subject Reports, PC(2)–7D, Government Workers,* Table 2, pp. 7–12; idem, *Subject Reports, PC(2)–7A, Occupational Characteristics,* Tables 43, 44, pp. 693–714, 715–46.

TABLE 4–9

After Postwar Reductions, Black Federal Workers Increased 30 Percent to 390,000, and White Workers 20 Percent to 2 Million, in the Twenty-five Years from 1950 to 1975

Changes in Federal Employment by Race, Selected Years, 1938–75

Year	Total	Black[a]	Number (in thousands) White
1938	865	82	783
1944[b]	2,697	300	2,397
1950[c]	1,934	225	1,709
1961	2,197	283	1,915
1965	2,289	309	1,980
1970	2,572	391	2,180
1974	2,433	390	2,043
1975	2,438	387	2,051

[a] Negro only.

[b] Data for 1944 are based primarily on information from the U.S. Committee on Fair Employment Practice, *The Wartime Employment of Negroes in the Federal Government, 1945.* Data by race for the Departments of Agriculture and Labor could not be estimated with suitable reliability from this or other sources, and so have been excluded. These agencies employed 84,000 workers in 1944. Data for the Post Office were estimated by the authors, based on information from the 1940 and 1950 Censuses, and from the reference cited above. The Justice Department estimate is for 1943, also from the above reference, p. 7, notes.

[c] For 1950, data by race was available for wage-board employees only. An estimate for the total by race was derived by the authors, based on the ratio of known information on wage-board employees to total federal employment in 1961, using U.S. Civil Service Commission, *Employment in the Federal Government,* Agency Summary, Table 1. Wage-board employment in relation to the total has been stable over a long period.

Source: Derived from L. J. W. Hayes, *The Negro Government Worker* (Washington, D.C.: Graduate School, Howard University, 1941), p. 153; U.S. Bureau of the Census, *Historical Statistics of the United States, Colonial Times to 1957* (Washington, D.C.: Government Printing Office, 1960), Series Y–247, p. 710; U.S. Committee on Fair Employment Practice, *The Wartime Employment of Negroes in the Federal Government,* 1944, Tables 1, 2–A, pp. 28, 30; 1940 Census of Population, *Labor Force, Vol. 3, Pt. 1, U.S. Summary,* Table 76, pp. 188–9; 1950 Census of Population, *Characteristics of the Population, Vol. 2, Pt. 1, U.S. Summary,* Table 133, pp. 1–288–9; U.S. Civil Service Commission, "Minority Group Study 1963," n.d., Table 1, n.p. Unpublished surveys covering 1961–63 conducted by the commission at the request of the President's Committee on Equal Employment Opportunity; idem, "Study of Minority Group Employment, 1965," n.d., Table 1–1, p. 5 (mimeographed); idem, *Minority Group Employment in the Federal Government, November 30, 1970* (Washington, D.C.: Government Printing Office, n.d.), Table 1–1, p. 32; idem, *Minority Group Employment in the Federal Government, May 1974* (Washington, D.C.: Government Printing Office, 1976), Table 1–001, p. 3–4; idem, "1975 Minority Group Study: All Agency Summary," n.d. (mimeographed).

TABLE 4–10

Most Federal Workers Were in the Salaried GS Service by 1975. But Blacks Were Not: They Rose to 45 Percent GS, and Continued to Be About 30 Percent in the Postal Service

Percentage Distribution of Federal Workers by Pay System and Race, Selected Years, 1961–75

Year	All systems	Pay system			
		General Schedule	Postal	Wage	Other
		Total—all workers			
1961	100	46	26	26	2
1963	100	48	25	24	2
1965	100	49	26	23	3
1967	100	48	27	23	2
1969	100	50	27	21	2
1971	100	51	27	20	2
1973	100	53	26	19	2
1974	100	56	23	19	2
1975	100	57	23	19	1
		Black[a]			
1961	100	32	29	38	1
1963	100	34	30	35	1
1965	100	34	30	33	2
1967	100	34	34	31	1
1969	100	35	35	29	1
1971	100	38	34	27	1
1973	100	41	33	25	1
1974	100	44	30	25	1
1975	100	45	30	25	1
		White			
1961	100	48	25	24	2
1963	100	50	25	23	2
1965	100	51	25	21	3
1967	100	51	25	21	2
1969	100	52	25	20	2
1971	100	53	26	19	2
1973	100	55	25	18	2
1974	100	58	22	18	2
1975	100	59	21	18	2

[a] Negro only.

Source: Derived from U.S. Civil Service Commission, "Minority Group Study 1963," n.d., Table 1, n.p.; idem, "Study of Minority Group Employment in the Federal Government, 1963," n.d., Table 1, n.p. Unpublished surveys covering 1961–63 conducted by the commission at the request of the President's Committee on Equal Employment Opportunity; idem, "Study of Minority Group Employment in the Federal Government, 1965," n.d., Table 1–1, p. 5 (mimeo-

(Table 4–10, continued)

graphed); idem, *Study of Minority Group Employment in the Federal Government, November 30, 1969* (Washington, D.C.: Government Printing Office, 1970), Tables 2–1–2, pp. 184–5; idem, *Minority Group Employment in the Federal Government, May 31, 1971* (Washington, D.C.: Government Printing Office, 1972), Table 1–1, p. 15; idem, *Minority Group Employment in the Federal Government, May 1973* (Washington, D.C.: Government Printing Office, 1974), Table 1–001, pp. 4–5; idem, *Minority Group Employment in the Federal Government, May 1974* (Washington, D.C.: Government Printing Office, 1976), Table 1–001, pp. 3–4; idem, "1975 Minority Group Study: All Agency Summary," n.d. (mimeographed).

TABLE 4–11

Black Federal GS Workers in the Supergrades Are Concentrated in Just Five Agencies with Major Domestic Programs for the "Disadvantaged"

Percentage of Salaried Federal Workers[a] Who Were Black, by GS Grade, in All Agencies and in Agencies with Programs Directed at the "Disadvantaged," 1975

	Percent black[b]	
General Schedule (GS) grade	All agencies	Agencies with special programs[c]
All salaried workers	13	20
GS 1–4	21	19
12–18	4	31
12–15	4	31
16–18	3	36

[a] General schedule only.

[b] Negro only.

[c] Departments of Labor; Health, Education, and Welfare; Housing and Urban Development; the Office of Economic Opportunity; and the Equal Employment Opportunity Commission.

Source: Derived from U.S. Civil Service Commission, "1975 Minority Group Study: All Agency Summary," n.d. (mimeographed); idem, "1975 Minority Group Study by Agency," n.d. (mimeographed).

5

But Not Next Door

ONE OF THE CHANGES to come about with the end of World War II took place in the movies. Miraculously, it seemed, the patriotic women who a few years before donned overalls, kept the home fires burning for Jimmy Stewart, and took jobs in munitions factories, were transformed into full-skirted child brides whose only interest in life was a rose-covered cottage ringed by a picket fence. And, equally miraculously, they all seemed to get those rose-covered cottages—June Allyson, Doris Day, Dorothy Maguire—because the postwar housing boom was on, and loans from the Veterans Administration were helping to change America into a nation of homeowners. Millions of salespeople, clerks, and recent immigrants who never would have thought it possible found themselves with mortgages. It was the American Dream come true; we could not only mobilize for and win a war, but we could make homeowners out of ordinary workers when it ended.

But those miraculous transformations going on in white America's world were actually moving in the opposite direction for black Americans. With the end of the war, their boom seemed nearly over, and with vast numbers now crowded into urban ghettoes and housing opportunities of any kind severely limited, those rose-covered cottages remained more tantalizing but just as effectively out of reach as they had been before. In the long catalogue of victories in the field of civil rights, there is very little to be totted up in the column marked "housing."

Black Americans can now work at the same jobs, join the same unions, ride the same buses back and forth to work, eat at the same lunch counters, bowl in the same leagues, and see their children educated—some of the time—in the same schools, as whites. But still no black family has been permitted to move into the Chicago suburb of Cicero, and those black families that have breached the lily-white lines around the Ciceros across this nation must still expect to be shot at, firebombed, ridiculed, and harassed. White America still objects, after all these years, to having black people live next door.

One would like to think that the accommodation and egalitarian practices that we have worked out in other areas of life might be carried over here, that after fighting for the right to vote and work and go to school, there would not have to be yet another long fight for the right to buy a house or rent an apartment wherever one might choose. From the experience of black families, we know otherwise.

And yet, curiously, the surveys conducted over the years show white people to be increasingly tolerant on the matter of residential integration. In 1942, 6 in 10 of the whites polled answered "yes" when asked, "If a Negro, with just as much income and education as you have, moved into your block, would it make any difference to you?"[1] By 1965, only one-third were saying "yes," and by 1968, just one-fifth held out.[2]

But the polls themselves provide some clue as to why that is not the whole story, for at the same time that so few claimed it would "make any difference" to have black neighbors, only about one-third would say they favored residential desegregation.[3] That two-thirds of all Americans still could not bring themselves to be counted in favor of residential integration, in the same year that the most significant legislation on discrimination in housing was passed,[4] tells us a good deal. When the question was put even more explicitly in 1970, half the whites polled felt that "white people have a right to keep Negroes out of their neighborhoods if they want to and Negroes should respect that right."[5] Even so, that same year, only 21 percent of the whites agreed that they had the right to keep blacks out of their neighborhood when asked, "Which of these statements would you agree with: White people have a right to keep Negroes out of their neighborhoods if they want to, or Negroes have a right to live wherever they can afford to, just like anybody else?"[6] Somehow, the second question provoked a radically different response by linking the rights of blacks to the respondents' rights ("just like anybody else"). Because the results of public-opinion polls are difficult to interpret and there is wide variation between what people say and what they do about housing, the image of whites as ever more favorable to residential integration could be a mirage.

Housing and Prejudice

Housing has long been one of the areas of greatest white resistance to integration. Whites are most resistant to those forms of interracial contact that imply the greatest degree of social intimacy, and there is little doubt that white Americans find housing one of those intimate areas of life in which they fear contact with blacks. Perhaps this attitude is reinforced by the American image of romance between the boy and girl next door.[7] Whatever the reason, many whites who have black coworkers or even a black supervisor, ride the same buses as blacks, and sometimes even attend the same schools still feel threatened at the prospect of integrated housing. This aversion is expressed in both subtle and overt ways. Demonstrations where blacks march to dramatize the need for open housing continue to provoke violent white reactions. In July 1976, when about 100 black and white demonstrators marched for open housing in a Chicago neighborhood, a crowd of 1,000 angry whites lined the streets to jeer "go home, niggers" and to hurl rocks, bricks, and bottles.[8]

Because there are so few integrated neighborhoods, few Americans, black or white, have experienced interracial living, and white stereotypes about blacks remain intact.[9] Gordon Allport's classic study of the nature of prejudice in 1954 showed that white public-housing tenants who lived in integrated buildings were more likely to see blacks as being much the same as whites than were whites living in all-white projects.[10] In the seventies it was found that persons who had attended integrated schools when young were more likely to choose an integrated neighborhood to live in.[11]

The most effective way to alter the negative attitudes of whites toward integrated housing, as social psychologists note, is to have blacks and whites live successfully in such housing.[12] But this seems to be true only where the extremes of race sentiment (strong prejudice or race-mongering) do not exist. Gordon Allport concluded that four conditions are necessary if white resistance to integrated housing is to be eroded through interracial contact. Prejudice lessens when racial contacts are among groups (1) of approximately equal status, (2) seeking common goals, (3) actively depending on each other, and (4) in an interracial situation which is supported by positive social sanctions from authorities, law, custom, or peer group.[13] Each of these four points, Allport concluded, minimizes potential conflict by "making other things equal" aside from skin color. Equal status groups will have similar outlooks on common questions and will probably also have similar ways of communicating their concerns. Common goals furnish concrete points around which people can organize and work together. Working together will be more effective when mutual interdependence exists so that one group is not always on the giving or receiving end. Positive social sanctions provide support that whatever the group is doing or contemplating doing is "right."

Situations of relative racial harmony with these four criteria come readily to mind. Athletic teams are good examples. At the opposite pole, where none of the criteria holds, is the southern sharecropping system. White landowners and black sharecroppers were of radically different status, had conflicting goals, and depended on each other only at the extremes of status and authority and under social sanctions which reinforced prejudice even though the two groups lived in nearly constant contact.

At the heart of the problem remains the fact that these basic conditions cannot be found if whites assume that blacks are, by definition (because of their blackness), of unequal status and unsatisfactory neighbors.[14]

Segregation persists in housing also because housing is a very mixed bundle of situations and transactions and, as such, is uniquely unresponsive to protest. Mass protest works best when the issues are straightforward and the "bad guys" can be easily identified. The process of buying or renting a home has so many parts and so many possible villains along the way that they could hardly fit on a placard. How does one organize a picketline against all the banks, savings and loan associations, and private lending sources, plus all the realtors, brokers, rental agencies, listings offices, private agents, builders, zoning commissioners, housing authorities, and all those countless "others" who make up the housing process? Even if it were possible to get a pledge from all the bankers in an area, that would still leave holes in all the other parts of the process. Nor does the discrimination have to be overt to be effective. Realtors don't say that they won't handle rentals for black families; they just waste a black applicant's time going to obviously unsuitable apartments until it is the black applicant, not the white realtor, that chooses to do business elsewhere. Or, the management of an apartment complex insists that the unit is rented, or the bank says that the loan applicant's collateral isn't good enough, or . . . Proving discrimination in any of those instances, in ways that might sustain a protest movement, is no easy matter. Even if blame could be assigned and the culprit singled out, by the time a suit is carried through the courts or a complaint dealt with by the housing authorities, the apartment has been let or the house sold, and the complainant gets nothing but moral satisfaction for the time and effort involved, while the offending party gets no more than a little aggravation and perhaps an insignificant fine.

There is another element that makes housing unique, and that is the special vulnerability it imposes on those who try to cross the line. While there is no question of the bravery of those nine small black children in Little Rock over twenty years ago, of freedom riders on the buses traveling South, or of the hundreds of courageous voter registration workers, there is a terrible isolation that surrounds the lone black family in a hostile white neighborhood. There is no motel to retreat to or supportive black neighborhood to come home to; no one to cry out to when the shooting starts and the garbage is strewn all over the lawn. There is no defense against cars that speed up when your children cross streets on their way to school, no protection from the taunts. And so white prejudice against black neighbors is fed by the reluctance of black families to become those threatened and unwanted neighbors. When blacks were asked to name the conditions under which they most expected to receive a "hard time" in their daily encounters with whites, two-thirds of those interviewed cited housing—more than those expecting trouble when applying for a job or a bank loan; more than were concerned about enrolling a child in school.[15] And they were right. Even in 1975, newspapers across the country reported: the firebombing and vandalizing of a black Chicago college teacher's home;[16] crosses being burned on the lawns of black homes in white suburbs of Baltimore and New York;[17] rocks thrown through the windows of a black family in Cleveland Heights who were also victims of three separate arson attempts;[18] the burning of a vacant house in New Jersey when rumors spread that a black family had bought it;[19] the tale of two black families in Rockaway Beach, New York, whose duplex home was set afire nine times in a single year.[20] Sadly, the list could go on.

Fair Housing Legislation—a Latecomer

Fair housing legislation was the last of the federal civil rights political battles to be won, and the federal government took no active role towards fair housing until 1962. Lacking any success at the national level, black organizations used their local chapters to fight against local governmental bodies that tolerated or supported discrimination in housing. Typical of this was the March 1962 picketline thrown up around the New Haven, Connecticut, city hall by the local chapter of CORE. The issue was a fair housing ordinance before a board of aldermen who had already rejected one such resolution. Not daunted, the group expressed itself as being "committed to demonstrate until the ordinance is passed."[21] Similar protest was common elsewhere throughout the country that year, filling the columns of the *New York Times* and papers everywhere. By November, President Kennedy was willing to act, though with something less than vigor. He issued Executive Order 11063, prohibiting discrimination in new housing owned, operated, or subsidized by the federal government.[22] At best, the order was a symbolic gesture to put the administration "on record," for its exemptions covered 75 percent of new housing and 99 percent of the existing housing stock.[23] Enforcement was equally weak. By the following summer, it was clear that Kennedy's executive order had not been enough. Two hundred fifty members of a local CORE chapter joined a group called "Citizens United for Fair Housing" and jammed the galleries of the Rhode Island legislature to protest the failure of fair housing legislation that session. Despite their protest, the bill did not pass. In Columbus, Ohio, the same day, CORE members chained themselves to seats in the gallery of the Ohio legislature.[24] Strong local protest, in the face of a weak federal posture, began to be felt elsewhere that year. As CORE members continued to demonstrate at his Belair, Maryland, development, W. J. Levitt of the "Levittowns"— possibly the biggest home builder in the country—called on the president to widen his antidiscrimination order and to take steps to end discrimination. Only when all builders are forced to sell on a fair basis, he reasoned, would any of them be able to "afford" an end to discrimination.[25]

By 1964, the Civil Rights Act was passed after the most widespread mass protest movement experienced in this country, and in it was the first piece of national legal machinery for also dealing with fair housing. While still limited, it covered more federally assisted housing than had Kennedy's executive order.

Because of the 1964 act's inadequacies, a new wave of housing protest was mounted. This time, white reaction was often violent. In 1966, Dr. Martin Luther King led a series of open housing marches in all-white neighborhoods of Chicago to dramatize the barriers that kept blacks confined to the ghetto. Another highly publicized open housing demonstration in the Chicago area was a CORE march of 200 protesters into Cicero where, just as in 1951, they were attacked by a white mob.[26]

In the summer of 1967, national attention was again focused on the issue of open housing when a white Milwaukee priest, Father James Groppi, led the youngsters of the local NAACP Youth Council in a series of demonstrations to highlight the need for a local fair housing ordinance. On one occasion, the youthful marchers faced a mob of more than 1,000 whites who screamed obscenities and hurled bottles, stones, and chunks of concrete to register their opposition to open housing.[27]

Still, Congress failed, in both 1966 and 1967, to pass open housing legislation and following the ghetto rebellions of 1966 and 1967, the prospects for passage of legislation in 1968 were thought to be slight. But Dr. Martin Luther King's assassination that spring and the masterful legislative lobbying efforts of the NAACP combined to win passage of Title VIII (on housing) in the Civil Rights Act of 1968.

In his concern with the "perils of the situation"—the rioting that followed the assassination of Dr. King—President Johnson sought "something positive to carry to the people."[28] From this search, he later wrote in his memoirs:

> I decided that we should seize the opportunity and press for an open housing law. For two years we had struggled unsuccessfully for legislation to prohibit discrimination in the sale and rental of housing. We had lost our first battle in 1966. . . . We lost again in 1967. . . . In January 1968 observers overwhelmingly predicted a third defeat.[29]

But the angry rioting that came in response to Dr. King's assassination, and the sense of outrage on the part of many whites, created a national crisis that demanded action in much the same fashion that the 1965 voting rights demonstrations in Selma had provided the momentum necessary to pass the Voting Rights Act of 1965. When, one week after the assassination of Dr. King, Congress passed the Civil Rights Act of 1968,[30] the president wrote, "I thought to myself how different the mood of this day was from that just one week earlier."[31]

Still Not Next Door

Discrimination in housing is now officially illegal, yet, even by
conservative estimates, 81 percent of American households live in
segregated neighborhoods. Even that figure includes 10 percent of
households in neighborhoods that have almost no black households
among them, about half of which are in the North Central and
Western parts of the country.[32] It would be more realistic to regard
only 10 percent of all American neighborhoods as being integrated.
And, where large numbers of blacks are concentrated as a direct
result of racial discrimination, it is doubly apt to call such areas
segregated.

Even more telling is the degree to which racial concentration has
not changed since 1940. According to a widely accepted measure for
racial segregation in housing, the "index of dissimilarity,"[33] 109 of
the largest American cities were about as racially concentrated in
1970 as they were in 1940.[34] Only in 24 cities was there any evidence
of a meaningful decline in concentration and, aside from New York
City, these cities represent relatively few blacks.[35] The level of concentration in these 109 cities is very high. In 1940, 93 of the cities
scored over 80—meaning that 80 percent of the households of either
race in those cities would have had to move in order to achieve
complete integration. In 1970, 67 had scores over 80. (Zero would
have represented perfect integration.) This seeming decline is a technical artifact; none of it may have really happened. Since these are
central cities in which the black population has been expanding
rapidly, the ghettoes would be expanding also. When ghettoes expand, their borders become longer and create more transitional
blocks and neighborhoods. Thus, the black population could be no
less segregated, but expansion of the ghetto leads to a seeming decline
in racial segregation in the areas undergoing racial change. Ghettoi-
zation is actually taking place within cities.[36]

For 1960–70, the years of active protest and open housing legislation, we have an even better set of estimates because they cover 136
Standard Metropolitan Statistical Areas (SMSA's), which include
suburban areas as well as the cities. These 136 SMSA's account for
over half the population in 1970, and almost 85 percent of those
living in SMSA's.[37] And again, the degree of racial concentration is
constant and high: 75 on the index of dissimilarity both years.[38]

Although only for one decade, this presents a more accurate picture because an SMSA is more representative of the housing market than is just the central city.

It may be tempting to argue that race alone (the basis for the index of dissimilarity) is only one of the ways to characterize a neighborhood. Blacks and whites may differ in other respects, such as income or education, that might influence where they will choose to live. But that is too simplistic an explanation for nationwide patterns of separation. In a study of residential integration, Hermalin and Farley have shown that, given black family incomes and suburban housing prices, more than three times the number of blacks would have lived in the suburbs as actually did, if income were the issue.[39] Consequently, only a small amount of the underrepresentation of blacks in the suburbs could be explained by income alone. These results and other evidence led the authors to conclude:

> . . . economic criteria account for little of the observed concentration of blacks in central cities and their relative absence from the suburbs.
> . . . We believe then that the current level of residential segregation must be attributed largely to action and attitudes, past and present, which have restricted the entry of blacks into predominately white neighborhoods.[40]

Forces That Keep Black and White Apart

The dramatic split between nearly all-white suburbs and increasingly black central cities did not just happen. This movement has been promoted by public policies, including Federal Housing Administration (FHA) approval of loans to restricted subdivisions, local restrictive zoning laws, and the efforts of the private real estate industry to avoid racial integration. Many of these policies have been reformed or modified since the 1960s, but their nearly unrestricted operation for the first twenty years after World War II has left a gulf that would take many years to close even if all the discrimination still existing were to end at once.

Although economic differences do not account for racial concentration, some believe that blacks prefer to "live with their own kind," treating concentration as a matter of free choice. One way to test whether separation is voluntary is to ask people about their preferences. A 1963 opinion study showed that almost two-thirds of the blacks surveyed preferred an integrated neighborhood, and by 1969, three-fourths expressed this preference.[41] Over the same period, the percentage preferring an all-black neighborhood declined slightly from 20 to 16 percent. The rest had no opinion.[42] Another test, using the statistical technique called multiple regression analysis, found that preferences could account for little of the racial separation in the San Francisco Bay Area in 1965.[43] If the self-segregation thesis were true, blacks would have to be willing to pay a very high price for it. The quality of the central-city ghetto environment is continuously described as inferior to that outside the ghetto, while the taxes, especially the property taxes, are generally higher.[44] It is absurd to assume a preference for such conditions by black Americans, any more than by white Americans. All in all, the economic disadvantages of staying in the ghetto are large, and there is no evidence that more than a small minority of blacks would voluntarily pay them.

Segregated housing patterns are no accident. Residential separation rests on a system of formal rules (though no longer worded in racial terms—the words are illegal) and informal but carefully adhered-to practices which no amount of legislation has been able yet to penetrate. The fact that no significant antidiscrimination legislation could be won in housing until 1968, and that no national administration has been willing to confront the open housing issue directly, demonstrates that there has been little progress. More important, it gives powerful evidence of just how close to the surface racial prejudice remains.

One of the most widespread grounds for white resistance to black homeowners rests on the myth that, as blacks buy homes in the neighborhood, property values will fall. That fear has never been supported by the facts.[45] If anything, the opposite is more likely to occur because black housing opportunities are limited; these more limited opportunities cause prospective black home buyers to pay higher prices than whites for the same homes. The result is that prices in the neighborhood rise. That happens whenever white realtors engage in "blockbusting" to drive white families out and artificially raise housing prices. (See pages 176–7.) Despite the overwhelming weight of the actual record, the myth continues to be widely believed. When people choose to deny simple facts, the emotional need to do so must be great. And the most obvious need in this case is a thinly veiled rationale for prejudice.

Black Americans in need of housing continually see the segregated system at work, including the practices and processes that maintain it. From the first visit to a realtor, up through the various institutional levels locally, and even shaping the many layers of governmental policy which underwrite so much of the housing financially, separation is virtually ensured. The result, with few exceptions, is a two-tiered housing market: one for black families and another for white, and a housing stock that differs with the race of its occupants, black and white.

How Black and White Lived—1940–74

Even the most casual observer knows that the general prosperity since 1940 has improved housing conditions greatly for all Americans. In 1940, one-third of white and nearly three-quarters of black households were without running water, flush toilet, bathtub, or shower, or lacked some combination of these. By 1974, these serious deficiencies had been nearly eliminated for whites, and reduced to 10 percent for blacks. The improvements have been substantial (Figure 5–1). This thirty-four-year span also saw a significant reduction in overcrowding for owners and renters of both races. Nonetheless, by 1974 about 13 percent of all black households still lived in overcrowded housing units.

While these physical improvements were being made, prosperity created progressively more homeowners who were assisted by the greatly liberalized mortgage terms initiated by the government in the thirties. More than just the realization of a goal, the movement toward increasing homeownership is important for the financial security of families, because building equity in a home is the single most important form of savings for middle- and working-class families.[46] Although the trend has been generally upward for both blacks and whites, the substantial gap between the races in 1940 was about the same decades later, in 1974.

These general trends appear to be contradictory because they show great improvement as well as a continuing gap in the quality of housing occupied by blacks and whites. They do not reveal discrimination in any direct way, since the differences in ownership or overcrowding could be caused by the generally lower incomes of black households. After all, white median household income in 1974 was $11,604, while the black median was $7,180.[47]

FIGURE 5–1

All American Housing Improved Dramatically 1940–74, but A Sizable Black-White Gap Remained in Key Conditions

Selected Housing Characteristics by Race, 1940 and 1974

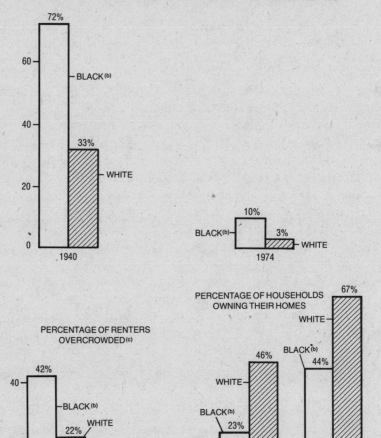

(a) No running water, flush toilet, or bathtub or shower.
(b) Negro only.
(c) More than 1.00 person per room.

Source: Derived from 1940 Census of Housing, *General Characteristics, Vol. 2, Pt. 1, U.S. Summary,* Tables 1, 10, 66, pp. 7, 38; U.S. Bureau of the Census, *Annual Housing Survey: 1974 United States and Regions, Pt. A, General Housing Characteristics, Advance Report,* Series H–150–74A (Advance) (Washington, D.C.: Government Printing Office, 1976), Tables A–1, A–3, pp. 1, 2, 13, 14.

What Black and White Housing Dollars Buy

The usual approach to quantifying what the housing dollar buys is to use statistical methods showing the price that blacks and whites pay for comparable housing. Although many studies have been done on this question, and the results are by no means unanimous, the most sophisticated and persuasive ones show a range of "discrimination markup" for blacks, from not less than 3 percent to as much as 20 percent, depending on the city and on whether blacks are renters or buyers.[48]

Another way to compare what black and white housing dollars buy is to look directly at the amenities and disamenities present in white and black homes. The issue is whether black and white householders paying the same rent or owning homes of equal value get comparable conditions for their money. This avoids focusing the issue of "housing dollars" on the rents paid, or on the value of owner-occupied homes, and instead looks at what people get for their money. The "disamenities" are conditions as basic as having to live with shared or no bathrooms, too little space, no central heating, or rents that absorb more than 35 percent of a household's income. Amenities are judged in part by the same measures, that is, no overcrowding or shared baths, and the presence of central heating, and also by whether a unit has air conditioning or two or more baths. Investigation into this question reveals that, in both 1960 and 1970, black owners and renters of units comparable to those of whites found that their housing dollars bought consistently less in amenities and that they endured more disamenities (Table 5–1). For instance, they were less likely, for the same owner or renter dollar, to have air conditioning or two or more baths. By contrast, their housing dollars bought more crowding, more units with a shared or no bath, and more often no central heat. In addition, blacks more often had to pay an excessive amount of the family income for rent (if they were tenants).

What this exercise so graphically demonstrates is that blacks simply get less for their housing dollars. The facts are absolutely consistent. The black housing dollar never buys the same good, or absence of bad, features as the white housing dollar in a single case for any amenity or disamenity, for either rented or owned housing, in either year. Discrimination is the only plausible explanation for why the same housing expenditures lead to such consistently unequal results. In housing as in so many other areas, prosperity and economic change improve conditions generally, but they do not eliminate the black-white gap.

Yet ultimately, it is not going without air conditioning that causes black people to feel so angry over housing. The physical differences —bathrooms, air conditioning, central heating, space—are real enough, but they are far from the heart of the matter. For housing is also a matter of neighborhoods and communities, and the degree to which public authorities act responsibly toward those who live there. The housing issues that leave black people particularly frustrated are both more elementary and less measurable, and they reach beyond the number of rooms and type of heating system.

At some level, the issue is services: garbage collection, police protection, schools, street repair, lighting maintenance, and efficient water mains and sewer systems. What is involved is the politics that leave black tenants at the mercy of uncaring absentee landlords, in city blocks riddled with abandoned apartments that become the haven of junkies and vandals. The issue is unenforced city building codes and recalcitrant housing departments; it is neighborhoods so poorly patrolled that children must be locked inside their apartments as soon as school is out; it is a matter of multistory structures in which the heat doesn't work for months at a time, the water supply is unreliable, and garbage is routinely left to pile up outside; it is something as callous as untended sewer lines that spawn a meningitis epidemic serious enough to send fifty people to the hospital.[49]

Black people in search of housing continue to be without the power to control discrimination in private transactions and so to be at the mercy of a system largely in private hands. At every step of the process, from the simplest encounters between individuals and local brokers to the most sophisticated workings of the federal financial regulatory machinery, the deck is stacked against the black client. At each level, it takes a different form, although since 1968 every level theoretically operates under antidiscrimination law. But the effect is the same whether the methods used are subtle or obvious.

The Gatekeepers
The Real Estate Agent

The first step in the process is the private real estate agent. Agents and the organizations representing them have been adamant in enforcing residential segregation in the past, and there is little evidence to suggest that that has changed. At times, their determination has had a "Keystone Kop" quality, as the files of the Leadership Council for Metropolitan Open Communities reveal. In one case the white investigators going to the rental or real estate office against which a complaint of discrimination had been leveled, reported:

> . . . each time the [real estate] agent spotted the complainant approaching the rental office, she would lock all of the doors and close shop for the day. On one occasion, the complainant spotted her locking the front door, and raced around to the rear to slip in the back door. He arrived just in time to hear the door slam and a lock click. The investigator suggested that the complainant approach the office door five minutes after the investigator entered the building. While the investigator discussed available apartments, the defendant spotted the complainant approaching the building. With a rush, she charged past the investigator, kicking his ankles and stepping on his feet in her successful attempt to lock the doors, front and back. Suit was filed on the basis of that unusual office procedure.[50]

However comical such behavior may seem, the results are no laughing matter for black people in need of housing. Real estate agents have perpetuated segregation, not just in their individual actions, but through their trade association, the National Association of Realtors (NAR, which was the National Association of Real Estate Boards until 1974). The NAR is a powerful influence on brokers' behavior and standards throughout the country. NAR agents handle most real estate sales. Its code of ethics is the broker's standard for business behavior. The association has influenced the adoption of real estate law in many states and carries on an active education program within the profession and in real estate courses offered by most college departments of business administration.[51]

The NAR openly supported racial—and, for that matter, class, religious, and other ethnic—discrimination until 1948. In 1924, it adopted Article 34 of its Code of Ethics, which stated:

> A Realtor should never be instrumental in introducing into a neighborhood a character of property or occupancy, members of any race or nationality, or any individuals whose presence will clearly be detrimental to property values in that neighborhood.[52]

The primary tool enforcing this standard was the racially restrictive covenant, until it was invalidated by the Supreme Court in 1948. This restriction prohibited an owner from selling or renting to blacks and was effective in enforcing residential segregation.[53]

The battle against the restrictive covenant was the single most important legal battle between 1917—when racial zoning was outlawed—and 1968, when all racial discrimination in housing was forbidden. The effectiveness of these covenants lay in their enforceability in courts of law. Blacks who took possession of property governed by covenants were subject to suits to divest them of title.[54] A typical agreement used for many years and initially drawn up in 1935 reads:

> We, the undersigned . . . do hereby agree that the following restriction be imposed on our property above described to remain in force until January 1st, 1960, to run with the land, and to be binding on our heirs, executors and assigns:
>
> This property shall not be used or occupied by any person or persons except those of the Caucasian race.
>
> It is further agreed that this restriction shall not be effective unless at least eighty percent of the property fronting on both sides of the street in the block where the above property is located is subject to this or a similar restriction.[55]

The NAACP developed a national strategy to attack the covenant in 1945. The strategy used paralleled the procedure adopted in preparing for the historic 1954 ruling on school segregation. Experts on housing and the impact of segregated housing on the life chances of blacks were consulted and asked to develop supporting materials. Civil rights supporters were encouraged to submit *amici curiae* briefs, and scholars were encouraged to write about the issue of restrictive covenants to educate the general public.[56] The attorneys prepared themselves by conducting "dry runs" of their arguments before faculty and students of the Howard University Law School. A 1955 *Life* magazine article described this process:

> These are arduous, all-day rehearsals at the law school, where Marshall (NAACP chief legal counsel) and his assistants try their arguments on a simulated Supreme Court made up of professors. Nine of them sit at a long table, and each one tries to act as much as possible like a specific Supreme Court justice, sticking the lawyers with tough questions that might crop up in the court itself. Law students form the audience and are encouraged to ask rough questions too.[57]

On May 3, 1948, the Supreme Court ruled in the cases known as *Shelley v. Kraemer* that racially restrictive covenants were unenforceable in a court of law and could not be used to exclude blacks from occupying property sold to them. This decision was elaborated and expanded on when the court ruled in 1953 that whites could not be sued for selling to blacks property governed by the restrictive clause.[58] Awarding damages, said the court at that time, would amount to indirect court enforcement of the restrictive agreement.[59]

With the effectiveness of racial covenants officially removed from the arsenal of weapons used to maintain residential segregation, whites did not hesitate to rely on other formal and even extralegal practices such as ostensibly nonracial covenants which relied on a variety of class-related restrictions. Such covenants were actively initiated by local neighborhood associations and real estate developers.[60] Three days after the Supreme Court decision, the *Chicago Tribune* aptly noted:

> Nothing in the decision prevents neighbors from agreeing on maintaining standards of occupancy, such as limiting the number of persons per room or requiring proper care of the premises.
>
> Such agreements are enforceable in the courts. They can preserve the neighborhood values perhaps more effectively than restrictive covenants have succeeded in doing.[61]

Realtors in particular assumed a new and increased importance in the day-to-day maintenance of residential segregation. Within a month of the 1948 Supreme Court decision, real estate agents were actively assuming the increased responsibility thrust upon them. Thus, in St. Louis, where one of the restrictive covenant cases had originated, a realtor soon informed an interested Virginian:

> The method now being employed here in St. Louis . . . is to have the Real Estate Exchange zone the city and forbid any member of the exchange under pain of expulsion to sell property in the white zone to a Negro. If the real estate men refused to participate in the sale, the breaches will at least be minimized to those who deal with each other directly or through a . . . non-member of the exchange who could be easily identified and boycotted more or less by all the people to whom the knowledge comes.[62]

And, just as black doctors and lawyers were barred from medical and legal professional associations, black realtors were excluded from membership in the real estate associations.

In 1950, the NAR got around to revising Article 34 to read:

> A Realtor should not be instrumental in introducing into a neighborhood a character of property or use which will clearly be detrimental to property values in that neighborhood.[63]

While this action removed explicit reference to race, there is evidence that the change was only formal.[64] Local real estate boards were confused by the change, and some of them expressed surprise that realtors could no longer be disciplined for selling a home to a black family in a white area.[65] More important, the association newspaper noted that, despite the change, there was no general change among real estate agents in the policy of racial exclusion,[66] and the NAR actively opposed the passage of fair housing laws in many states and localities where they were proposed. The California state branch of the NAR, for example, waged an active campaign against California's fair housing law in 1964. The California group hinted that fair housing had something to do with communism and distorted the law's meaning to imply that homeowner rights would be grossly abridged. Typical of their campaign rhetoric was the following:

> Proponents of housing legislation to force regulation of the rights of owners point to other states that already have such law as the Rumford Act. They claim these laws have worked. They are saying, in effect: "Other states have taken away freedoms from their people and the people have not rebelled, so we have the right to take them from the people of California."[67]

The 1948–68 period was basically like pre-1948. The only differences were minor changes in formal written policies in response to *Shelley v. Kraemer,* and adjustments to the changing etiquette in real estate dealings which moved away from open acts of bigotry.

The passage in 1968 of the landmark civil rights in housing bill and, within weeks, the Supreme Court decision in *Jones v. Mayer Co.* combined to make the most important advances in open housing law in U.S. history. Yet the NAR did not adopt a pro–fair housing position until 1972, and it is still not clear to what degree this position is being translated into action by brokers around the country. Some limited studies in California[68] and Massachusetts[69] show little change. A more comprehensive study in the New York Metropolitan area, by the National Committee Against Discrimination in Housing, exposed some of the many ways used to discriminate that do not involve a direct refusal to sell. Misrepresenting the price or availability of houses, saying the customer does not qualify financially, delaying the submission of an offer until a white buyer can be found, saying a house is not available for inspection, and breaking appointments to show houses are only some of the devices used by the determined realtor. There are many other ways the knowledgeable agent can influence the result. A broker can simply fail to encourage the prospective purchaser by not "selling" the house as he would to a white buyer, by not pursuing financing strongly, by not alerting the black client when a house comes on the market, or by interpreting the buyer's needs so strictly as to be able to say, "Sorry, I don't have anything for you."[70]

This kind of behavior can make it almost impossible for black families to buy the house of their choice, since the nature of the real estate agent's function makes these subtle acts effective. All that an agent has to do is provide either less information than usual or misinformation, and the transaction process is likely to be aborted. The real estate industry is competitive, and brokers are in a constant struggle for both listings and buyers. Brokers who feel that the white community (the largest group of potential customers) is prejudiced discriminate to avoid any loss of business that they think might come from selling to blacks. They are sensitive to professional pressure from other brokers, and particularly from lenders who reject black applicants for financing and might make it more difficult for even the broker's white customers to get loans.[71] Actions like these seriously affect the nondiscriminatory broker's livelihood and the degree to which the customers can rely on a broker for housing leads.

Given the pressures within the industry that support discrimination, outside enforcement of antidiscrimination laws becomes imperative. The causation is circular. Pressure at any one point could influence the entire process in the move toward open housing. As fewer brokers discriminated, their colleagues would find it harder to practice discrimination; as fewer brokers discriminated, lending institutions inclined to indulge in discriminatory practices would be put at a competitive disadvantage vis-à-vis nondiscriminatory lenders.

Financial Institutions

For prospective buyers, financial institutions become the next barrier to overcome, and it is not one to be taken lightly. Blacks have always found it difficult to obtain home loans. Before the Civil Rights Act of 1968, financial institutions could openly discriminate in granting mortgages. Blacks living in San Francisco in the 1940s found themselves in a typical but inescapable double bind: lenders refused them loans in white areas, and would not lend in black areas.[72] In the

1950s, the U.S. Commission on Civil Rights found that it was often nearly impossible for a black family to get a mortgage to buy a house in the white neighborhoods of Cleveland, Columbus, Dayton, Detroit, and Los Angeles.[73] Almost no part of the country was immune. Institutional financing has been so difficult to get that, in the past, blacks in many cities were forced to accept "land contracts," an arrangement in which the seller holds the deed to the property until the last payment has been made. To make matters worse, land contracts typically carried higher interest rates and shorter terms than did conventional mortgages,[74] making monthly payments higher than they would have been with a conventional mortgage.

Even with the 1968 act outlawing discrimination in financing, many practices still exist that continue to place black home buyers at a disadvantage. Brokers can also be critical in obtaining mortgages, screening applicants before actual application is made, and working closely with one or more financial institutions to secure loans for their clients. If brokers do not look kindly on black home buyers, or feel that "their" lenders do not, this prejudice combines with the conservatism typical of such institutions and acts to screen out a disproportionate number of minority borrowers.[75] This informal type of discrimination is hard to prove —a matter of "opinion" about such nebulous criteria as "suitability" or the "appropriateness" of neighborhoods. Another important point in the home-buying process when discrimination can take place occurs during the interview with the loan officer of a financial institution, who has wide latitude to encourage or discourage formal application for a loan. The loan officer is in much the same position as the broker, since personal prejudice and ideas of what is "appropriate" for black home buyers can easily result in diminished opportunities to obtain financing.[76]

The real starting point of the process for most white applicants is the formal loan application. This is the point at which questions of creditworthiness, ability to pay, property value, and regularity of income should be the only determinants of whether a loan will be granted. Even so, some of these "objective" criteria can be applied inconsistently, and with prejudice. For example, family incomes may come from more than one source and when, as is common, the secondary source, usually the wife's income, is not fully counted, the loan may be denied. Although less a difference between the races today, working wives traditionally were more common in black families, and such theoretically "objective criteria" had very practical discriminatory effects. Many financial institutions are also known to automatically disqualify an applicant with a poor credit report without looking into the circumstances surrounding the evaluation. This can be especially damaging to black applicants because credit bureaus have often made discriminatory judgments on the basis of race.[77]

Mortgage discrimination is shown by objective evaluations of institutional behavior. Special studies of member institutions by the responsible federal financial regulatory agencies[78] were conducted to gauge the extent of discrimination in eighteen SMSA's[79] from June through November 1974.[80] Even though the studies are not uniform in statistical consistency, they show a clear pattern of discrimination against all but white applicants.[81] A substantially higher percentage of black applicants for mortgage loans were rejected than were white applicants with the same financial characteristics. Another study by the comptroller of the currency—which permits comparisons by income class, years in the same job, and size of the loan rejected—reflects this sharp difference; equally matched blacks were rejected at rates almost invariably much higher than their white counterparts (Table 5–2).

These results are particularly sound because both denials of written applications and preliminary oral reports were recorded.[82] The actual degree to which brokers informally screen blacks more than whites in advance could not be recorded, and so, if anything, the total amount of discrimination in the financing process may be understated.

Red-lining

All of these policies on the part of brokers and lenders are typified by the practice known as "red-lining," or drawing a line (presumably in red) around areas of the city where financial institutions will not make real estate loans. Red-lining is nothing more than the logical extension of mortgage discrimination. Less arbitrary but no less discriminatory practices have similar effects: charging higher interest rates, refusing long-term loans, and requiring higher down payments relative to property value for black applicants. If it is riskier to lend in certain areas, less favorable terms in those areas are economically justified. However, if one of the criteria used to determine risk is the borrower's race or the racial makeup of the neighborhood, then the lending practice is illegal.

Red-lining is not new, but its existence is now more widely known and understood; its prevalence has been documented and mortgage lenders are now required by law to disclose their loans by geographic area.[83] Most studies of the practice have been local.[84] A congressional investigation of the practice showed:

In Milwaukee: 63 percent of loan requests made in a racially changing area were rejected;[85]

In Chicago: 15 communities in metropolitan Chicago lodged red-lining complaints with the Governor's Commission on Mortgage Practices;[86]

In the Bronx, New York: A significant minority presence in neighborhoods was shown to have a direct negative bearing on lending policies;[87]

In Philadelphia: Of two areas which were nearly identical in all respects save racial composition, only the black area was experiencing difficulty in securing conventional mortgages;[88]

In Baltimore: Red-lining was shown to exist and to be particularly severe in black neighborhoods;[89]

In Los Angeles: Whole areas of the city were red-lined, including the entire central city and East Los Angeles;[90]

In Washington, D.C.: Although 70 percent of the city's population is black, city savings and loan institutions gave 88 percent of their loans outside the District of Columbia, and only 4 percent in areas of the District which were majority black;[91]

In Indianapolis: A community group documented the pattern of applicants for loans turned down because of the area in which the property was located;[92]

In Oakland, California: A community group found that East Oakland was red-lined by California's largest savings and loan institutions, all of which had offices in that part of the city;[93]

In Cincinnati: Local institutions were found to be investing very little in black or transitional areas.[94]

This is only a small sample of the mass of evidence establishing the seriousness of discrimination in home financing. In the face of it, the accuracy of denials by mortgage lenders can only be assessed definitively when state and federal regulatory bodies take it upon themselves to enforce the law, review compliance, and publish their findings.

Red-lining is serious not only because it is discriminatory. It is a direct cause of neighborhood decay. It does not stop real estate transactions in a neighborhood, but it causes black neighborhoods to depend on the least reliable and most exploitive methods of financing. This leads to a process of neighborhood decline with some or all of the following stages:

STAGE 1: Financial health. Conventional mortgage and home repair loans are readily available.

STAGE 2: Savings institutions begin to perceive greater risk. They tighten loan criteria and impose stricter terms, making loans more difficult to get and harder to carry. Property assessments begin to decline, reinforcing the perception of risk.

STAGE 3: Conventional loans become unavailable. The only financing granted is now through an individual or government insured, primarily the FHA.

STAGE 4: All institutional financing is curtailed. Foreclosures rise, abandonment takes place, and absentee landlords and speculators take over the market.

STAGE 5: The area may be declared for urban renewal and completely demolished, rebuilt in several years as a high-rise-townhouse area for affluent residents—the former residents having been crowded into another red-lined area.

Red-lining, then, is a complex process, with many actors—banks, savings and loan associations, mortgage bankers, speculators, federal housing authorities, and still others.

Three studies—in Philadelphia, Cincinnati, and Chicago—have tried to answer how much of red-lining occurs for economic or racial reasons by taking two or more neighborhoods, very similar in all socioeconomic dimensions except their racial makeup, and comparing their residential finance patterns. In Philadelphia, a stable white area and an area that went from 18 to 46 percent black between 1960 and 1970 were chosen. In that case, the proportion of conventional loans stayed constant—about three-quarters—in the white neighborhood, while the proportion of conventional loans made in the changing area dropped from three-quarters to one-third between 1962 and 1972.[95] Three socially similar Chicago neighborhoods, two in the process of racial change and one remaining nearly all white, were examined. In this case, the white neighborhood also did not change significantly in financing patterns. In the two changing neighborhoods, conventional loans fell from 90 percent in 1964 to 15 percent in 1970.[96] As nonconventional financing took over these neighborhoods, the foreclosure rate also rose sharply, from almost zero in the early 1960s to over five times the conventional foreclosure rate in the early 1970s.[97]

The Cincinnati experience was similar. In the white neighborhood, the flow of local conventional financing continued, while in the changing and majority black areas, local conventional monies declined substantially.[98] As the authors of the Cincinnati study noted, "the racial composition of the neighborhoods has been the determining factor in whether Cincinnati lending institutions invested monies in the three sample communities at all."[99] And the Philadelphia study concluded, in a similar vein:

> One thing does seem more clear than ever in all this, and that is there is simply no validity to the oft-heard claim that race does not have any bearing on disinvestment patterns of institutional lenders.[100]

Yet, despite such evidence, bankers have been reluctant to admit that red-lining exists and, especially, that it is widespread. In recent congressional hearings, Grover J. Hansen, a director of the National Savings and Loan League and president of the First Federal Savings and Loan Association of Chicago, insisted:

> Red-lining—which we take to mean the arbitrary withholding of funds from an area simply because of its geographic location—has not been proved to be a common or ordinary practice. In Chicago and Milwaukee, which are centers of antired-lining efforts, not one single case has been substantiated by competent public authority. All there has been is assertion of red-lining, and we should be reminded that assertion, no matter how often repeated, is not proof.[101]

In a more specific case, William A. Beasman, Jr., president of the Savings Bank of Baltimore and chairman of the Committee on Mortgage Investments of the National Association of Mutual Savings Banks, asserted:

> . . . contrary to statistics or studies that I have heard, in my own particular experience in the city of Baltimore I know of no instance where a loan has been turned down because it happened to be in the center of the city of Baltimore in a decaying neighborhood.[102]

Beasman's statement was made *after* publication of a study by the Baltimore city government that showed red-lining by conventional lenders to be a serious problem in that city.[103]

All of the evidence points to a close relationship between race and red-lining. Where blacks are present or soon will be, red-lining is very likely to occur. Although both economics and race are involved, race has been shown to be by far the more important.

The history of the National Urban League—which has lodged

stubborn protest over discrimination in housing—sums up the difficulties that the housing arena posed:

> A tougher area of activity could not have been chosen, for it was in
> the private market that there was least leverage and most latitude for
> every kind of prejudice, ignorance and manipulation to be exercised
> by financing institutions, real estate operators, dealers, sellers, build-
> ers and unions.[104]

Suburban Zoning and Black Residents

Black people in search of housing also find their choices circum-
scribed by the actions of local governmental bodies. The main policy
instrument of localities is zoning power, which prescribes land use
in designated areas in order to separate incompatible land usage.
Zoning is what keeps slaughterhouses out of residential neighborhoods, but it can easily be applied to have other, discriminatory
effects. When zoning limitation operates to eliminate whole categories of housing, it is called "exclusionary zoning." The phrase is apt:
usually apartments, mobile homes, or even single-family homes on
lots of less than a given size are covered, and the people who would
live in such housing are effectively excluded.

When it is widespread, exclusionary zoning can be a controlling
factor in housing patterns, as it is in the New York area, where 99
percent of the undeveloped residentially zoned land is reserved for
single-family houses. Across the river, in Newark's suburbs, the same
proportions prevail.[105] Where apartments are allowed, they are
confined largely to low-density, one-bedroom, spacious units; even
mobile homes are subject to floor-area[106] and lot-size minimums.
Probably the most widely known exclusionary zoning device is large-
lot zoning. Suburban lot sizes are commonly limited by ordinance to
at least one acre and sometimes to as many as four. In Connecticut,
more than 70 percent of residentially zoned land carries a one-acre
minimum lot size.[107] Large-lot zoning increases the price of housing,
limits the supply of land for apartments and other kinds of more
dense settlement, and results in areas devoted almost exclusively to
high-cost, single-family, and luxury multiple-family housing which
only the affluent can afford.

Local officials defend these practices with the rationale that low-
or moderate-cost housing imposes a disproportionate burden on public service expenditures compared with the tax revenue it generates

(the opposite is said to be true of expensive single-family homes). Thus, exclusionary policy is really a matter of "fiscal zoning," which only permits uses that bring in more taxes than they cost in services. At least one study has attempted to test this notion, and finds that the results suggest

> such controls are not typically imposed for fiscal reasons, i.e., to increase the taxable value of real property in the jurisdiction and to exclude low income residents who would heavily burden the jurisdiction's public services.[108]

Since it is no longer legal to identify races that a community might wish to exclude, zoning laws are the next best thing. They keep out a whole class of people, like the poor who cannot afford private homes on big lots, among whom minority groups are disproportionately represented. Some communities defend large-lot zoning on aesthetic grounds; others give environmental reasons, arguing for the need to preserve natural habitats and reduce the load on sewer and water systems, recreational facilities, and streets. They argue in terms of maintaining property values, keeping up public school quality, or preserving the "character of the community." The intention of keeping "undesirable elements" out of a community is not stated. While we do not know in any detail the relative extent of race and class discrimination involved, investigations into the subject usually assign racial discrimination a prominent role.[109]

Litigation under the civil rights laws has found racial motives to be more prominent when the poor or working-class people who would be excluded by local policies are also expected to be black. But to be successfully appealed zoning decisions must involve specific actions by local officials which can be proved to have violated the civil rights of blacks (or other minorities). One important and relatively early case is *Dailey v. City of Lawton, Oklahoma.* It concerned the proposed rezoning of a white neighborhood to permit construction of a subsidized housing project. The land was zoned for single-family dwellings, but was surrounded by land zoned for apartments. The town denied the request for rezoning and the developer sued, contending that the town had acted from racial motivations. The developer won.[110]

Broadly exclusionary provisions like large-lot zoning have been challenged successfully in state courts, particularly in New Jersey and Pennsylvania. But in this and other successful cases against zoning ordinances the evidence must be very strong, and the racially discriminatory conditions must be blatant indeed. Few ordinances have been invalidated as racially discriminatory, in part because such intentions are virtually impossible to prove in a legal sense, and in part because other influences—fiscal, environmental, class—may be considered to dominate the legislators' motives. While in a general sense suburbs have been closed to blacks, different suburbs exclude to different degrees, and even vary their policies at different points of development. A suburb may include a large stock of relatively low-cost housing that was built before a more exclusionary period.

Exclusionary zoning has the effect of raising housing prices. To the degree that blacks have lower incomes, they are more affected by such policies, but again it is important to underline that economic differences between the races explain only a very small part of observed racial segregation. And if the different incomes of blacks and whites do not explain racial segregation, then exclusionary zoning alone cannot be responsible for the lower rate of black suburbanization. One thing is known with some certainty: black suburbanization has been minimal in comparison with the rush to the suburbs that has taken place among whites in recent years.

In the period 1965–70, nearly 4 million white households, representing nearly 10 percent of all white households in SMSA's, moved from the central cities and nonmetropolitan areas to the suburbs.[111] In absolute numbers, they "outsuburbanized" black households 23 to 1. Even when their greater numbers are taken into account, they were still three times more likely than blacks to move to suburbia. During that period of mass suburbanization, the number of black families moving to the suburbs was only about 160,000—something less than a flood.[112] While it is not possible to quantify the movement from central city to suburb for the years before 1965 as precisely as for the later period, we have some facts about it.

In 1950, blacks occupied 4.6 percent of the housing units outside of central cities but still within SMSA's. By 1970, that figure had actually dropped to 4.2 percent, despite the growing prosperity and generally rising incomes of black families; for white families, that period of prosperity meant a move out of the crowded cities and into nicer homes with good schools and municipal services. The number of white-owned and rented suburban dwelling units between 1950 and 1970 increased by almost 12 million, or 120 percent. By 1970, only 45 percent of all the white households in the country remained in central cities, while the proportion of black households in the city actually rose. Blacks as well as whites were moving off the farms in unprecedented numbers during those years, but without open sub-urbs—where most of the new housing was being built—blacks had little choice but to go to the cities.

The black households living in the suburbs actually are composed of two quite different groups. The "old-timers" didn't move to the suburbs; the suburbs moved to them. These are the people who were residents of all-black towns or, more often, of black enclaves that were really rural settlements perched on the edges of major cities. As the suburbs grew in the post–World War II period, these enclaves were surrounded by all-white, mostly affluent subdivisions. Some black enclaves were obliterated by urban renewal or highway con-struction.[113] But others survived, becoming the "poor sections" that remain on the fringes of so many urban centers.[114]

Black newcomers to suburbia are an entirely different matter. Their median income in 1969 was nearly $9,000, not so very different from the $11,700 median income of white homeowners then living in suburbia.[115] (On the basis of income alone, it is estimated that three times the number of blacks as could have lived in the suburbs actu-ally did.)[116] And, if the findings of one unpublished study are any indication, they are largely two-parent families in which the wife is working and the family income is solidly middle-class. That study examined a very special group, black veterans who had qualified for Veterans Administration mortgage guarantees to purchase homes in the suburbs around Washington, D.C. Even there, where the pres-sure to obey civil rights laws is greater than in many other locations, and where there is a long history of a black middle class, occupancy proved to be a good deal less than "open." Black homeowners with dependable (often government) jobs and government-backed financ-ing, tended overwhelmingly to go to areas in which black families already lived.[117] The new black suburbanites had the incomes, the financing, the stability, the right characteristics—including service to their country—but they did not have equal access.

Housing Policy and Segregation

Over the years, whether a black family could get a loan or find an apartment to move into may, however, have been determined in Washington, far from the local zoning board or realtors' association. Four areas of federal policy are particularly important: the mortgage programs of the Federal Housing Administration (FHA); direct subsidy programs, like public housing; the financial benefits made available through the tax system; and fair housing activities (the formulation and enforcement of civil rights laws, as they apply to housing).

The first of these areas of federal policy, the FHA mortgage program, has touched the lives of more American families than any other federal housing program. Between 1934 and 1973, FHA insured mortgages on 13.4 million homes, and insured 30.9 million property improvement loans.[118] The FHA insures the mortgage loans made by private lenders through a variety of programs, but the largest is a basic insurance program authorized by Section 203 of the National Housing Act of 1934. Since its inception in 1934, the FHA has clearly led the way toward making mortgage terms for home-buyers more liberal. In the 1920s, mortgages granted by savings and loan associations required a 40 percent down payment and ran only for an average of eleven years.[119] On those terms, a $10,000 loan at 9 percent interest would have required monthly payments of nearly $120 at a time when such sums were beyond most families. In 1976, that same mortgage under FHA rules would require much less down, extend over thirty years, and involve monthly payments of only $80. Lower down payments and easier terms with FHA financing made homeownership possible for young and working-class families, and stimulated high rates of homeownership in the United States (Table 5–3).[120] From 1940 to 1974, homeownership went from 44 percent of all households to 65 percent, a minor revolution made possible largely by easy mortgage terms begun under FHA.[121] Best of all, it cost the government nothing[122] and did much to improve housing conditions, but only for white households. The program overlooked or specifically denied benefits to qualified black purchasers.

From its beginnings until 1948, FHA policy was unabashedly segregationist. The official FHA *Underwriting Manual* stated that "the presence of incompatible racial elements results in a lowering of the rating, often to the point of rejection (of insurance applications)."[123] Another part of the *Manual* cautioned appraisers to be sure that properties were protected from "adverse influence," including "lower class occupancy and inharmonious racial groups."[124] Until it was declared legally unenforceable by the Supreme Court in 1948, the *Manual* contained a model restrictive covenant, which it promoted.[125] In 1948, Assistant FHA Commissioner W. J. Lockwood could boast that "FHA has never insured a housing project of mixed occupancy."[126]

Although the FHA revised its *Manual* when the Supreme Court acted, actual working policy changed at a slower rate, and open occupancy was not supported by the FHA until 1954.[127] In 1959, the U.S. Commission on Civil Rights estimated that less than 2 percent of new housing built since 1945 with FHA insurance was available to minorities.[128]

Policies that reinforced residential segregation prevailed well into the 1960s. A 1968 survey showed that only 3 percent of subdivision housing had gone to black families between 1962—the date of the first executive order on equal opportunity in housing—and 1968.[128] FHA had insured a substantial part of subdivision housing, and during much of the time, it officially continued the practice of redlining (until 1966).[129]

When not actively promoting discrimination, the FHA has been passive. The U.S. Commission on Civil Rights, which studied the FHA's administration of the program to subsidize purchases of homes by low- and moderate-income families (Section 235 of the Housing Act), noted in 1971:

> Officially, FHA officials have taken little note of racial residential patterns under the 235 program, but, unofficially, many FHA staff members have expressed awareness of the segregated and unequal 235 buying pattern. No local FHA insuring office, however, has been willing to undertake affirmative action to prevent such a pattern from occurring in the absence of specific directives from Washington. No such directives have been forthcoming. FHA staff members in Washington also have been aware of the discriminatory 235 buyer patterns but have allowed them to continue without instituting corrective or preventive measures.[130]

The Subsidized Programs

A casual observer of the American housing scene is easily confused about subsidized housing programs because of the odd name-and-number designations of the many programs and because publicly assisted housing is commonly associated with big projects in ghetto areas of large cities where only poor people live. There are, in fact, two main kinds of publicly assisted housing. The earliest program is commonly called "public housing"; it is built and operated by local public housing authorities, and the rents are subsidized by the federal government. Other publicly assisted housing is privately built with a variety of subsidies, including low-interest rates or tax exemptions.

Publicly assisted housing as a whole has served mostly white and lower-middle-income or near-poor families. Only a small part of all such housing is in so-called public housing, which truly serves poor families, half of whom are black. Contrary to popular impressions, public housing is scattered in small apartment projects or single-family dwellings. The public housing program was established in 1937. Since then, activity has always been low relative to total construction, and the somewhat more than 1.3 million public housing units existing in 1974 made up only 2 percent of the nation's housing supply.[131] After forty years, there is still less than 1 public housing unit for every 10 households with incomes under $4,000 per year.[132]

About half of all units are located in the North, one-third in the South, and the remainder in the West.[133] But, public opinion aside, most public housing is not in large cities. As many units are in small towns as are in large cities, and the remainder are split about evenly between moderate- and middle-sized cities (Figure 5–2).[134] High-rise public housing is rare except in the large cities, especially since the Housing and Urban Development Act of 1968, in which the construction of high-rise public-housing elevator buildings for family occupancy was forbidden.[135]

There has always been a strong black presence in the projects. In 1952, blacks made up 38 percent of the tenants; by 1961, 46 percent; and in 1973, 47 percent.[136] Both white and black tenants were very poor (Table 5–4). The income of black families was higher than white-family income, but among blacks the income per household member was lower, since the average black family in public housing was nearly twice as large as the average publicly housed white family. Relative to the rest of the population, public housing tenants were poorer in the 1970s than they were in 1952. In 1952, the median income of all families was 80 percent above that of public housing families, but in 1970, the median family income had risen to 340 percent above median public housing income.[137] A partial explanation may be that in 1952, 71 percent of public housing tenants were able to get all their income from working, but by 1974, only 27 percent could.[138]

The principal differences between black and white public housing tenants stem from differences in their ages. White tenants are usually elderly; black tenants are not (half the white families received Social Security either with or without other benefits, compared to only 13 percent of blacks). Therefore, black tenant families are twice as likely as white families to contain workers (42 percent versus 22 percent) and children.[139] At the same time, nearly twice as many blacks receive assistance (chiefly welfare), sometimes supplemented by other benefits. But whatever the differences, both black and white public housing tenants are at the bottom of America's economic heap.

Public housing rents are subsidized so that tenants will not have to pay more than 25 percent of their incomes for rent.

Outside the public housing program, another rent subsidy program is authorized under Section 236 of the National Housing Act of 1934. These rent subsidies[140] are intended for moderate-income, not poor, families. At the start of 1975, nearly 400,000 units were either occupied or being built under the 236 program.[141]

Tenants subsidized under Section 236 differ markedly from those in public housing (Table 5–5). Median incomes are about twice as high; tenants are much younger, especially the whites; families are smaller; about half have both husband and wife present; and a smaller proportion receive any kind of public assistance.

The popular impression of public housing tends to be unrelievedly bad: a depressing picture of marauding gangs, prostitutes, and dope peddlers plying their trades in gloomy halls and rooms with cracked windows and peeling paint. Whatever occasional truth there may be to that picture, a 1973 Harris Survey discovered that the residents find public housing an improvement over earlier housing and, usually, good places to live. There is usually a long waiting list for public housing accommodations, and the vacancy rate is very low: nationwide, it was less than 3 percent in 1974.[142] The quality of the units is much better than the tenants would have been able to afford in the private market. Public housing tenants in a sample of seven major cities were found to have housing substantially better than they would have had in the absence of the program.[143] When they cite their chief complaints, the subjects are very ordinary: poor maintenance, noisy neighbors and children. Crime, violence, and social disorganization are not among the three main problems of public housing tenants; even stealing and break-ins were mentioned by only a small proportion (2 to 8 percent). Another study shows that although black residents were generally less positive about living in a public housing project than were white residents, blacks living outside the project areas expressed more concern about their neighborhoods than their counterparts in the projects.[144] For many people, a project is a decent home.

FIGURE 5–2

Less than One-Third of All Public Housing Units Are in Large Cities

Distribution of Public Housing Units by Size of Locality, 1970

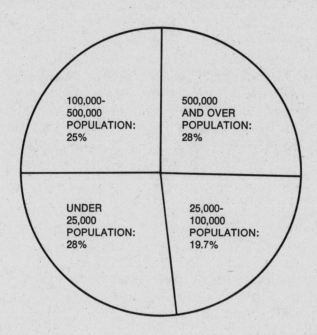

100,000-
500,000
POPULATION:
25%

500,000
AND OVER
POPULATION:
28%

UNDER
25,000
POPULATION:
28%

25,000-
100,000
POPULATION:
19.7%

Source: U.S. Department of Housing and Urban Development, *1970 HUD Statistical
Yearbook,* (Washington, D.C.: Government Printing Office, 197?). Data from
Journal of Housing 30 (April 1973): 183.

Subsidies and Segregation

The problems of integration confronting both administrators and tenants of subsidized housing projects are, to some degree, un-resolvable. Site selection outside the ghetto is fraught with con-troversy, and the use of controls of some kind to ensure a ra-cially integrated community is no easier. To overcome such obstacles, the commitment to integration must be truly overriding on the part of housing professionals, local political leadership, and at least a substantial part of the citizenry. Rarely is such an overriding commitment present.

Attitudes toward integration among public housing officials have varied. The federal Public Housing Administration made real efforts at integration, even in the earliest years of public housing:

> Wherever it could, PHA [the federal Public Housing Administration] went beyond the policies of insuring racial equity to promoting inte-gration. By 1960 it was able to report that thirty-two states operated their public housing projects on an open-occupancy basis.[145]

"Wherever it could" did not include the South, where the majority of poor blacks lived. In order to preserve the program, southern votes were needed in the House of Representatives, and so segregation in all projects was total in that region.[146] At the local level, public housing authorities have a varied history. Some have been openly discriminatory, while others have worked hard for integration.

A key to integration in public housing is site selection. While the placement of public housing units in non-ghetto areas does not guar-antee integrated projects, placing a project in the ghetto leads to exclusive minority occupancy, a point which has not been lost on local authorities. In Chicago, where the city council had effective veto power over site selection by the housing authority, members of the council from white areas would only approve sites in ghetto areas because the waiting list for units was composed mainly of blacks.[147] During the 1950s, 31,000 public housing units were built in these areas.[148] These practices and the use of quotas continued in the 1960s, in order to keep black tenants out of public housing located in white areas.[149]

Although such measures were patently illegal after passage of the Civil Rights Act of 1964, HUD did not force the Chicago authority to stop its practices. Even after the authority was found guilty of racial discrimination in 1969 and refused to abide by a court order, HUD still did nothing.[150]

In Cleveland, a newly elected city government revoked the building permits for low-income housing in white areas of the city in 1971, and had to be sued in order to get the permits reinstated.[151] In New York City during 1971 and 1972, a furor was caused by the decision to place three 24-story towers (842 units) of public housing in the predominantly white Forest Hills section of Queens.[152] The ultimate compromise struck is instructive. The buildings were to be reduced to 12 stories each, for a total of 430 units in all. Forty percent of the units were reserved for elderly households, and the entire complex was to be turned into a cooperative. Finally, all residents were to come from the immediately surrounding neighborhoods, making the tenant population about 70 percent white.[153] Even though the original design had the support of the mayor, the City Housing Authority, and the Board of Estimate, community opposition changed the project's size, nature, and projected racial character.

In many large cities, the waiting lists for public housing are composed largely of blacks, so a "first come, first served" policy leads to a nearly all-black enclave in a white area. This is integration in only the most limited sense of the word. To avoid this result, a "benign housing quota" has been suggested to ensure stable integrated projects. Under this idea, a certain proportion of units in the project would be allocated to each ethnic group and the "first come, first served" principle would apply only within the number of units reserved for each group. New York City instituted this policy on the Lower East Side of Manhattan in the early 1970s in order to keep a complex of new low- and middle-income housing from becoming segregated.[154] The City Housing Authority was then sued by a group of black and Puerto Rican tenants who felt that minority households that had been displaced by the construction should have had priority. The court found for the authority and stated:

> . . . the Authority may limit the number of apartments to be made available to persons of white or non-white races, including minority groups, where it can show that such action is essential to promote a racially balanced community and to avoid concentrated racial pockets that will result in a segregated community.[155]

While a benign quota might indeed guarantee a stable integrated community, it is open to serious criticism on other grounds. Blacks are discriminated against much more in housing than are whites, and there is a chronic shortage of low-cost housing in most cities. These two facts make it much harder for a black family excluded under however "benignly" intended a quota to find alternative decent housing than for a comparable white family.

A much newer program which had much better chances of avoiding racial discrimination is the homeownership plan enacted as Section 235 of the Housing Act. Section 235 is by far the largest, although not the first, direct homeownership subsidy of the federal government. The program aids moderate-income buyers (median income of participants was $6,500 up to 1973)[156] and was assisting about 400,000 households in 1974.[157] Blacks make up 22 percent of the participants; whites, 66 percent; and other groups, 13 percent.[158]

The Section 235 family is not poor, is of moderate size (4.2 persons, on average), and is young (average age in 1973 was thirty-one), so that it would presumably "blend in" with most community concepts of what a new homeowner should be.[159] The subsidies can be for either new or existing housing, giving the participant a potentially wide choice of house type and location. And the program can operate in any community. It was essentially an arrangement between the federal government, the mortgagee, and the mortgager, with no local veto over the housing units beyond what existed over single-family units in general under zoning and similar powers.[160]

Despite these positive features, including sizable participation of blacks in the program, the U.S. Commission on Civil Rights showed in 1971 that purchases under the program followed the general lines of segregation already present in the cities they studied. The commission pointed out that all actors in the Section 235 drama—the broker, the mortgage lender, the FHA—share responsibility for the segregated pattern of purchases.

As the commission noted:

> FHA staff, although frequently aware of the racial residential patterns developing as a result of the 235 program, disclaimed responsibility for them. No FHA office visited by Commission staff had taken any affirmative action to assure that the 235 program was opening up new housing opportunities for minority families. . . .
>
> Most FHA insuring office personnel interviewed by Commission staff expressed surprise that anyone should be interested in documenting the segregated buying patterns of minority and white 235 buyers. To them, this segregated pattern was both obvious and inevitable.[161]

FHA developed no meaningful counseling for prospective buyers. Clients were simply referred to a broker, who, in turn, had little interest in promoting integration and used techniques such as biased advertising and steering clients to "their own" areas to maintain segregation.

At the time of a sale, mortgage lenders took no action to discourage racial concentration.[162] As the commission summed up:

> FHA's past reputation has been that of an anti-poor, anti-inner-city, antiminority agency. One year before the 235 program was established FHA officials had been severely criticized by the National Commission on Urban Problems for the Agency's operation of a low-income housing program [rent supplements]. Nonetheless, when the Section 235 low-income homeownership program was enacted, FHA took no special steps to insure its successful operation. The 235 program, like all FHA programs, has been largely entrusted to the private housing and home finance industry. When complaints have been received regarding the location and quality of Section 235 houses, local FHA officials have justified inaction on grounds that such factors were not their responsibility. The only direct contact FHA had with FHA buyers, including Section 235 buyers, has been through an understaffed counseling service which has referred the buyers back to the real estate industry.[163]

Considering the lack of governmental interest and the history of private agents, brokers, and bankers, the segregation of Section 235 buyers is hardly surprising.

Beneficiaries of Housing Subsidies and the Tax System

The federal government operates two housing subsidy systems. The one limited almost entirely to the poor and near-poor is among the most controversial of government program areas. The other subsidizes people roughly according to their income—the richer you are, the more you get. This program is four times as large and arouses practically no comment at all outside of academic circles. Public housing is the largest of the direct-subsidy housing programs for the poor and, in 1972, it cost $1.3 billion.[164] Only $800 million more went into the other direct subsidy program for lower-income households. Together, then, the federal government spent about $2.1 billion on low- and moderate-income housing subsidies in 1972.

The other, far larger, housing subsidy program cost $9.6 billion in 1972, and is limited to people who are not poor. These subsidies operate through the tax system by permitting homeowners to pay lower taxes. They are "tax subsidies." To a homeowner, paying $10 less in taxes is the same as receiving a $10 check from the government —in both cases, the homeowner has $10 more to spend. In the same way, $10 not collected in taxes leaves the government with $10 less to spend. The net result to the Treasury is the same, whether the transaction is a check or a tax deduction. The most familiar preferential taxes are the income tax deductions for mortgage interest and property taxes paid. One deduction which is not as well known, but which amounts to more than the first two put together, is nontaxation of the imputed net rent on owner-occupied dwellings. If a homeowner is thought of as a landlord who is also the tenant, the concept of imputed net rent is easy to understand. If another tenant were living in the house and paying rent, the landlord would subtract the expenses of keeping the house—such as taxes, insurance, mortgage payments, depreciation, and repairs. If these costs were less than the amount of rent collected, which is usually the case, the landlord would have to pay taxes on these profits. If the homeowner lives in the house, the same costs and income can be assumed, but there is no tax liability since the net rent—"imputed" because no money changes hands—is not taxed in the case of the owner-occupant.[165] In 1966, property tax and mortgage interest deductions cost the U.S. Treasury $2.9 billion in uncollected taxes, and nontaxation of imputed net rent cost $4.0 billion.[166]

These homeowner tax subsidies are, like other tax deductions (such as losses from fire and theft, medical payments over 3 percent of income, and all others) more valuable as a person's income rises. For example, if a family's taxable income were $5,000, an additional $100 in homeowner deductions would save $19 in taxes; if taxable income were $50,000, the savings would be $50.[167]

The amount of homeowner preferences at different levels of income in 1972 shows how valuable they are (Table 5–6). They are essentially worthless to the poor, while the wealthy receive hundreds or thousands of dollars per family in tax subsidies. Therefore, they encourage homeownership to a greater degree among those with higher incomes. Their relationship to the problems of race is twofold. First, to the extent that blacks are excluded from good owner-occupied housing, they are not able to take advantage of homeowner preferences in the tax law. Second, discrimination in other spheres has meant lower incomes for blacks. Since homeowner subsidies vary directly with income, blacks benefit less than proportionately from the tax system in this respect.

Subsidies outside the tax system, on the other hand, are largest at the lower end of the income scale, and become insignificant to families making more than $10,000 per year (Table 5–7). Combining this information on all types of housing subsidies with data on race, housing tenure, and income provides estimates of both kinds of housing subsidies that blacks and whites in the various income classes receive (Table 5–8).

Blacks get quite a bit more in direct subsidy per household at lower incomes, but considerably less at higher income levels, because subsidies at higher incomes consist entirely of homeowner tax subsidies. Blacks have considerably lower rates of homeownership at all income levels, and this lower rate is especially significant at higher incomes where the tax subsidies are largest.

There is a relationship between where black people live and the subsidies they receive. That is, blacks live more than proportionately in those areas which have a large amount of directly subsidized housing. These areas are HUD regions IV and VI, which take in the states of the old Confederacy, minus Virginia and plus Oklahoma and New Mexico. In addition, each of the different programs produces a southern orientation.[168] Thus a larger share of subsidized units in the South leads to greater black subsidies overall, since a bit more than one-half of all blacks live in the South and black incomes are lower there than in any other part of the country.

The higher rate of direct subsidization for low-income blacks stems also in part from their lower rate of homeownership. The great majority of subsidized homes are rental units, and blacks are disproportionately renters.[169] Thus, other things being equal, blacks would receive direct nontax subsidies more often. Also, while they get higher housing subsidies per household, their higher subsidy average is the result almost entirely of their being half the tenants in public housing. Black representation in other direct-subsidy programs is about proportionate to their presence in the various income classes.

While public housing and other housing that receives direct subsidies are an important help for those who need them, it would be far better to be among those who do not need them—those who can benefit from high tax preferences in home ownership—and who can select freely the neighborhoods and homes where they would like to live.

Effectiveness of Fair Housing Laws

Given the history of both the private and the public housing sectors, it is not surprising that fair housing activities had to be included in HUD's general equal opportunity effort.

That role was strengthened by Title VIII of the 1968 Civil Rights Act, which charges HUD with enforcing prohibitions against racial discrimination in the sale, rental, advertising, or financing of housing, or in brokerage services. But, like so much civil rights legislation, it conveys no direct powers of enforcement. HUD can only conciliate or persuade builders, brokers, agents, officers of financial institutions, and others to stop the discriminatory practices.[170] It cannot issue cease-and-desist orders or institute litigation. When conciliation doesn't work, HUD can refer a case to the Department of Justice, which then decides whether to press it.

HUD is also charged with enforcing Title VI of the 1964 Civil Rights Act and Executive Order 11063. Both of these prohibit discrimination in federally assisted housing, although they differ in their various provisions. HUD has the same weak enforcement powers under Title VI, but it can withhold or withdraw funds from those who violate the provisions.[171] This power is hardly ever used, however. No agency or authority has ever been "debarred" (lost funds from an ongoing program), and only one agency, the Capital Region Planning Agency of Hartford, Connecticut, has ever been "decertified" (made ineligible for future funds).[172]

The U.S. Commission on Civil Rights points out that reliance on complaints, the only basis for HUD action, is inferior to conducting area-wide compliance reviews since complaints are spotty and may not include the worst cases of discrimination. The complaint process is also inefficient because of the inordinate amount of time necessary to pursue each case. During the first 9 months of fiscal year 1973, HUD received 2,053 Title VIII complaints, and took an average of 5.5 months to process each one.[173] From July 1972 to March 1973, the department also received 232 Title VI complaints and, at the end of that period, had a 9-month backlog.[174]

Great power to act against racial discrimination in housing lies potentially with the federal financial regulatory agencies: the Federal Reserve System (FED), the Federal Home Loan Bank Board

(FHLBB), the Comptroller of the Currency (COC), and the Federal Deposit Insurance Corporation (FDIC). Title VIII of the 1968 Civil Rights Act requires these agencies to promote equal housing practices in the financial institutions under their jurisdiction.[175]

The great majority of banks and savings and loans are examined by one or more of these agencies which review their financial condition and business practices. There are about 3,600 examiners involved, in contrast to the 427 equal opportunity staff at HUD, 4 at VA, and 20 Department of Justice lawyers responsible for Title VIII. Significant equal housing opportunity would result if this already existing, comprehensive regulatory program were used actively for enforcement, but it has not been.[176]

These four agencies did virtually nothing to ensure nondiscrimination in lending before passage of the 1968 Civil Rights Act.[177] Even afterward, action was taken only reluctantly, prodded by lawsuits and administrative petitions filed by outside organizations. At best, each of these agencies has assumed a small part of the job: only the FHLBB had adopted general nondiscrimination regulations by 1972, and then it instituted a regular compliance reporting system. Only FED and FHLBB started civil rights training programs, and only the FDIC held hearings on the subject. The only action taken by all four agencies as of June 1973 was to require all institutions to advertise affirmatively and to have an equal opportunity poster in their lobbies.[178]

In the spring of 1976, hearings were held by the Senate Committee on Banking, Housing, and Urban Affairs, on the agencies' fair housing efforts. Despite the passage of eight years, numerous meetings, petitions and lawsuits, and formal requests to the agencies by HUD and the Justice Department,

> The Committee finds the record in fair lending enforcement of the three commercial bank regulatory agencies to be lacking and believes it could be greatly improved by the agencies working in cooperation with one another to assure a consistent approach to combating discrimination.[179]

Specifically, the committee found that no agency had set up the record-keeping system needed to expose possible cases of discrimination; that none of them had ever formally found that even one of their regulatees had discriminated; that no agency had ever required adoption of an affirmative-action plan or referred a case to the Justice Department for investigation; that there was no cooperation between the agencies and HUD or Justice; and finally, that all but the FHLBB considered equal opportunity in lending "to be an extremely low supervisory priority."[180]

In theory all racial discrimination in housing has been illegal since 1968. But, because the enforcement machinery is weak and the possible avenues of redress so unsatisfactory, open housing remains little more than theory, eight years later. Litigation is costly, time-consuming, and unlikely to result in any satisfaction because the fines levied against discriminatory builders or sellers have been minimal. The administrative machinery is cumbersome and slow.[181] Even when discrimination has been proven, HUD's only power is "conciliation." Because HUD cannot hold contested property vacant while discrimination charges are being considered, the winners in discrimination proceedings cannot even expect to get the housing denied them in the first place.[182] It is a no-win situation:

> In spite of the obvious drawbacks to seeking judicial redress, private litigation appears preferable to administrative remedies for obtaining the complainant's primary goals, housing and compensation. However, private civil litigation seems particularly ill-suited to achieve the other goals, because of high court costs, the complexity of litigating a successful suit, and the uncertainty of an award of attorney fees.[183]

Blockbusting

"Blockbusting" offers a case in point. The practice can take a number of forms, but it is usually caused by white real estate agents who solicit sales on a door-to-door basis by telling white homeowners that they are about to be inundated by blacks, that their property will lose value, that crime will rise, and that the quality of education in the school system will soon be poor.[184] The blockbuster then offers a quick cash deal for the property, buys it, and soon after sells it to a black family at a much higher price. Sometimes the blockbuster only handles the sale, without buying the property, making his profit on commissions generated by the rapid turnover.

Both races are victimized by the blockbuster. Whites receive too little for their property, and blacks are forced to pay an exorbitant price for it. The social goals of racial harmony and equal justice are dealt a heavy blow.

Administrative and judicial processes are open to the victims of blockbusting, but here, too, HUD can only conciliate disputes. Since the blockbuster is consciously out to make a profit at the expense of the victims, and since HUD cannot assess any penalties, conciliation is almost certain to fail. If conciliation is tried and fails, the next avenue of redress is suing.[185] Victims who decide to go to court are faced with the high costs and delays of protracted litigation. Attorney's fees are likely to be substantial, and award of fees is unlikely.[186] The most serious problem is compensation. When suit is brought to *prevent* blockbusting, no punitive or other damages will be awarded, since no losses have occurred.[187] When suit is brought after the fact, punitive damages are limited to $1,000, an amount that a blockbuster would likely view more as overhead than as a deterrent.[188] Both types of suit, even if brought together, are unlikely either to deter the blockbuster or to compensate the victim. An injunction would immediately halt a blockbuster and prevent any further damage. However, the plaintiff would have to oversee compliance with the injunction, and few plaintiffs have the resources and time necessary to monitor a realtor's activities.

The problem is not words; the language of the antiblockbusting law is clear and forthright. Under it, it is unlawful,

> "For profit, to induce or attempt to induce any person to sell or rent any dwelling by representations regarding the entry or prospective entry into the neighborhood of a person or persons of a particular race, color, religion, or national origin." The forbidden representations do not have to be false to be actionable, nor do they have to be limited to direct references to Negroes. Indirect references to a "changing neighborhood," to undesirables, and to fear of a rising crime rate have also been found to violate the Act.[189]

The difficulty arises because the same law that forbids the action leaves the aggrieved without effective remedy. In housing, as in any part of life where prejudice exists, words are simply not enough.

No Choice

The sobering facts are that residential integration in this country is insignificant and there has been little change over thirty-five years. Most frustrating of all are the institutional and social mechanisms in place, which are often maintained by the very government agencies charged with ending discrimination. Together, all agents in the process have made housing almost impervious to the forces promoting desegregation in other spheres of our national life. Inequities in the housing of black and white Americans prove indisputably that we live in a deliberately segregated society based on race.

The moral of the housing story is that for black families there has been no choice. At every step of the way, their choice is made for them. The federal government has contributed programs and policies that have at times actively promoted separation and at other times avoided taking action to prevent it. The real estate industry and mortgage financiers have made large contributions to our dual housing system, promoting separation actively in the past and doing little to change old patterns in the present. Lending discrimination, redlining, and blockbusting have been particularly effective tools at their command. Local governments have used their zoning and taxing powers to act indirectly, slowing the desegregation of the largely white suburbs. Black families that do move into white neighborhoods often find themselves victims of mobs and threats, and local police often fail to protect them. The exclusion of black families from many places, even though their income and education are comparable to those of whites, leaves little doubt that separation is not an artifact of income or education differences. Finally, it can be no accident that the housing dollars of black people consistently buy less in convenience and in an escape from poor conditions than the same dollars in the hands of white citizens like them. Blacks cannot choose where to live, in what conditions, at what price, in what safety.

TABLE 5–1

Blacks Are More Likely to Have Poor Housing Conditions and Are Less Likely to Have Superior Facilities in Housing of the Same Rent or Value

Percentage of Owners and Renters Having Selected Housing Amenities and Disamenities, by Tenure and Race, Standardized by Rent and Value of Owner-Occupied Home[a]

Amenities or disamenities		Percent owners		Percent renters	
		Black[b]	White	Black[b]	White
Amenities					
Air conditioning	1960	6	10	3	8
	1970	27	36	13	28
2 or more complete baths	1960	(c)	(c)	(c)	(c)
	1970	10	22	2	3
Disamenities					
Shared or no bath	1960	31	16	41	24
	1970	14	7	16	11
More than 1.01 persons per room	1960	20	10	31	14
	1970	16	8	21	9
No central heat	1960	(c)	(c)	(c)	(c)
	1970	39	30	39	30
35 percent or more of household income goes for rent	1960	(c)	(c)	28	18
	1970	(c)	(c)	29	23

(a) Rent and home value standardized to the population of blacks. This means that the white rates for particular rent/value groups have been applied to a population distribution exactly like the black population of the same year. The result is that the differences in the table are not caused by differences in the distribution of rents or values of the black and white housing units. The fact that blacks pay less rent and live in homes of lower value is *not* responsible for these differences.

(b) Negro and other nonwhite races in 1960; Negro only in 1970.

(c) Data not available or not applicable.

Sources: Derived from the 1960 Census of Housing, *Metropolitan Housing, Vol. 2, Pt. 1, United States and Divisions,* Tables A1–2, 11–2, pp. 1–3–4, 1–12–3; 1970 Census of Housing, *Metropolitan Housing Characteristics, HC(2)–1, United States and Regions,* Tables A1–2, 11–2, pp. 1–3–4, 1–12–3; idem, *Subject Reports, HC(7)–4, Structural Characteristics of the Housing Inventory,* Tables A–9, 24, pp. 19, 56.

TABLE 5–2

Blacks Are Denied Mortgage Loans Much More Often than Whites, Even When Income, Stability of Employment, and Loan Amount Are Similar

Percentage of Loan Applications Denied in Six SMSA's, by Income Class, Years at Present Occupation, and Amount of Loan Requested, and by Race, June–November 1974

Characteristic	Black[a]	White
All borrowers	25	15
Gross annual income		
Less than $5,000	40	34
$5,000–9,999	33	22
10,000–14,999	27	16
15,000–24,999	21	14
25,000 and over	23	12
Years at present occupation		
Less than 1 year	31	17
1 year	23	15
2 years	24	15
3–5 years	26	14
Over 5 years	23	14
Amount of loan requested		
Less than $5,000	26	11
$5,001–$15,000	34	17
15,001–25,000	23	15
25,001–45,000	22	14
45,001–60,000	15	17
Over $60,000	35	19
Number of cases	320	1,693

[a] Negro and other nonwhite races.

Source: Derived from U.S. Comptroller of the Currency–Administrator of National Banks, *Fair Housing Lending Practices Pilot Project, 1975,* Tables 1, 2, and 6.

TABLE 5–3

Homeownership Is More Common in the United States than in Other Highly Industrialized Nations

Percentage of Homeownership in the United States Compared with Industrialized Western Nations

Country and year	Percent
United States (1970)	63
Austria (1971)	41
Belgium (1970)	56
France (1968)	43
Germany (1968)	34
Sweden (1970)	35
Switzerland (1970)	28
United Kingdom (1971)	50

Sources: United Nations, Department of Economic and Social Affairs, Statistical Office, *United Nations Statistical Yearbook, 1973* (New York: United Nations, 1974), Table 198, pp. 740–8; 1970 Census of Housing, *Metropolitan Housing Characteristics, HC(2)–1, United States and Regions,* Table A–3, p. 5.

TABLE 5–4

Black Public Housing Tenants Differ Markedly from White: Blacks Are Working Younger Families with Children and Many Receive Public Assistance, Whites Are Elderly and Receive Social Security

Characteristics of Public Housing Tenants Re-examined for Continued Occupancy, October 1973–October 1974

Characteristic	Black	White
Family income		
Percent less than $5,000	71	82
Median income	$3,400	$2,800
Approximate income available per person	919	1,333
Age of family head		
Median age	41	67
Percent older than 62	16	56
Mean number of minors per family	2.3	.8
Mean number of persons per family	3.7	2.1
Receiving assistance[a] and benefits[b] (percent)[c]		
None	32	17
Assistance with or without benefits	49	28
OASDI[d] with or without benefits or assistance	16	52
Number of cases	266,131	224,245

[a] Assistance = funds given on the basis of need by organizations, some private, primarily public.

[b] Benefits = nonsalary funds not given on the basis of need by government agencies —unemployment insurance benefits, for example.

[c] Does not add up to 100 because a small miscellaneous category is omitted.

[d] OASDI = Old Age, Survivors, Disability Insurance, commonly known as Social Security.

Source: Derived from U.S. Department of Housing and Urban Development, *1974 HUD Statistical Yearbook* (Washington, D.C.: Government Printing Office, 1976), Tables 63, 65, 69, pp. 70, 72, 74.

TABLE 5–5

Black and White Tenant Families Are Similar in Moderate-Income
Subsidized Housing; Exceptions Are that Whites Tend to Be Older, to Be
Receiving Social Security, and to Have Fewer Children at Home

Characteristics of Low- and Moderate-Income Families Certified for Occupancy in Subsidized Rental Housing[a], October 1973–October 1974

Characteristics	Black	White
Family income		
Percent with less than $5,000	31	40
Median income	$5,900	$5,500
Approximate income available per person	2,034	2,200
Age of family head		
Median age	27	29
Percent older than 62	5	21
Mean number of minors per family	1.5	1.0
Mean number of persons per family	2.9	2.5
Receiving assistance[b] and benefits[c] (percent)[d]		
None	47	44
Assistance with or without benefits	45	35
OASDI[e] with or without benefits or assistance	5	17

[a] Under Section 236.
[b] Assistance = funds given on the basis of need by organizations, some private, primarily public.
[c] Benefits = nonsalary funds not given on the basis of need by government agencies.
[d] Does not add up to 100 because a small miscellaneous category is omitted.
[e] OASDI = Old Age, Survivors, Disability Insurance, commonly known as Social Security.

Source: Derived from U.S. Department of Housing and Urban Development, *1974 HUD Statistical Yearbook* (Washington, D.C.: Government Printing Office, 1976), Tables 71, 73, 77, pp. 75, 77, 79.

TABLE 5-6

The Higher the Income, the Larger the Homeowner Tax Benefits per Household, Up to $2,347 for the Richest Group in 1972

Homeowners' Tax Preferences,[a] Total and per Household, by Income Class, 1972

Income class	Number of households (in thousands)	Tax preferences Total (in millions)	Per household (in dollars)
Total	68,251	$9,641	$141
Less than $3,000	9,350	4	less than $1
$3,000– 4,999	7,644	41	5
5,000– 9,999	18,155	625	34
10,000–14,999	15,698	1,588	101
15,000–24,999	13,172	3,630	276
25,000–49,999	3,754	2,631	701
50,000 and more	478	1,122	2,347

[a] Preferences are limited to those stemming from provisions in the federal income tax. Many states and localities have parallel provisions in their tax laws. Because the subject here is federal housing subsidies, these are not counted. Inclusion of state and local preferences would tend to widen the gaps exposed by this analysis.

Source: Derived from Joseph Pechman and Benjamin A. Okner, *Individual Income Tax Erosion by Income Class*, Reprint No. 230 (Washington, D.C.: Brookings Institution, 1972), p. 34; CPR, Series P-60, No. 89, *Household Money Income in 1972 and Selected Social and Economic Characteristics of Households*, Table 3, p. 20; 1970 Census of Housing, *Metropolitan Housing Characteristics, HC(2)-1, U.S. and Regions*, Table A-3, p. 1-5.

TABLE 5–7

Direct Housing Subsidies Excluding Tax Benefits Go Only to Low- and Moderate-Income Families; Lowest-Income Households Get the Highest Direct Housing Subsidies, but the Subsidies Averaged Less than $100 per Household in 1972

Federal[a] Direct Housing Subsidies—Seven Programs[b]—by Income Class, 1972

Income class	Direct subsidies Total[c] (in millions)	Per household (in dollars)
Total	$1,836	$27
Less than $3,000	810	87
$3,000– 4,999	583	76
5,000– 9,999	438	24
10,000–14,999	5	less
15,000–24,999	less	than
25,000–49,999	than	$1
50,000 and over	$1 million	

[a] Localities contribute indirectly to public housing by collecting less in payments in lieu of taxes than would have been paid on private projects. This amount is $374 million and is not included here since the subject is federal subsidies (*Housing in the Seventies,* pp. 4–87).

[b] Programs covered are: Section 235, Lower Income Homeownership Program (National Housing Act of 1934 as amended), Section 236, Rental and Cooperative Housing Assistance (National Housing Act of 1934 as amended), Veterans Loan Guarantee Program (38 U.S.C. sec. 1810 (1970)), FHA Mortgage Insurance (Sec. 203, National Housing Act of 1934 as amended), Rent Supplement Program (Sec. 101, Housing and Urban Development Act of 1965), Sec. 221(d)(3), Below Market Interest Rate Loans (National Housing Act of 1934 as amended), Sec. 502, Low and Moderate Income Housing for Rural Areas (Housing Act of 1949 as amended).

[c] Total direct subsidies are adjusted to take account of significant costs in the public housing program which push total costs above market value. Subsidy recipients get no benefits from these expenditures since they would be able to rent comparable housing if they received the total subsidy in cash minus costs. The costs are $9.5 million in management costs over and above what costs would be in the private sector and $28.5 million due to housing production inefficiency (*Housing in the Seventies,* pp. 4–87). Inefficiencies in the various other programs are small—less than 2 percent of the total subsidies—and therefore were not incorporated in this analysis.

Sources: Derived from U.S. Department of Housing and Urban Development, *Housing in the Seventies* (Washington, D.C.: Government Printing Office, 1973), pp. 4–47, 4–59, 4–90–1; Henry J. Aaron, *Shelter and Subsidies: Who Benefits from Federal Housing Policies?* (Washington, D.C.: Brookings Institution, 1972), p. 162.

TABLE 5–8

*Total White Housing Subsidies Were Ten Times the Black in 1972
(Including Tax Benefits Plus Housing Programs); Blacks Received More
per Household than Whites at Incomes Below $15,000, but Much Less at
Higher Incomes*

All Housing Subsidies and Subsidies per Household, by Income Class and Race, 1972

Income class	Black[a]	White
	Total housing subsidies (in millions)	
All households	$1,181	$10,385
Less than $3,000	394	419
$3,000– 4,999	282	315
5,000– 9,999	242	935
10,000–14,999	72	1,524
15,000–24,999	127	3,503
25,000–49,999	45	2,586
50,000 and over	19	1,103
	Housing subsidies per household (in dollars)	
All households	$ 173	$ 171
Less than $3,000	223	56
$3,000– 4,999	238	49
5,000– 9,999	119	59
10,000–14,999	69	106
15,000–24,999	190	285
25,000–49,999	441	711
50,000 and over	1,357	2,601

[a] Negro only.

Source: Derived from Joseph Pechman and Benjamin A. Okner, *Individual Income
Tax Erosion by Income Class,* Reprint No. 230 (Washington, D.C.: Brookings
Institution, 1972), p. 34; CPR, Series P–60, No. 89, *Household Money Income
in 1972 and Selected Social and Economic Characteristics of Households,* Table
3, p. 20; 1970 Census of Housing, *Metropolitan Housing Characteristics,
HC(2)–1, U.S. and Regions,* Table A–3, p. 1–5; U.S. Department of Housing
and Urban Development, *Housing in the Seventies* (Washington, D.C.: Government Printing Office, 1973), pp. 4–47, 4–90–1, 4–101; Henry J. Aaron,
Shelter and Subsidies: Who Benefits from Federal Housing Policies? (Washington, D.C.: Brookings Institution, 1972), p. 162.

6

Second-Class Medicine

When at birth the black child's chances, by virtue of . . . skin color alone, for a long and comfortable life are statistically different from the white child's, then racism is causing [the] problems.[1]

IN THE 1940s, in the nation's capital, a black woman in labor on the sidewalk outside a white hospital was refused admission[2]; nearby, the publicly supported Gallinger Hospital (now D.C. General) had a patient-load that was 70 percent black but permitted no black medical students from Howard University to get clinical training there.[3]

In the 1950s, a public health nurse working in Chicago wrote of a black infant whose hand was chewed by rats during the night. Wakened by the baby's cries, his mother found two rats on top of him and his hand "a bleeding mass of mangled flesh." She gathered up her other children to rush the baby to Cook County Hospital for emergency care, more than an hour's ride and an expensive taxi fare away, because no other emergency room in South Side Chicago hospitals would treat black patients.[4]

Until 1963, the fathers of black infants born in the St. Dominic-Jackson Memorial Hospital in Jackson, Mississippi, could not see their babies until they left the hospital. Most black patients were in the "colored wards" on the first floor, but the newborn nursery happened to be located among the "white wards" on the second, and black fathers were not welcome there. In 1963, the rule was changed to permit black fathers to visit their infants in the nursery—but only once.[5]

In the 1970s, civil rights investigations revealed that black patients

187

across the South were still being admitted to doctors' offices through separate doors[6] and assigned to separate wings and rooms of hospitals.[7] The attitude behind such practices was much in evidence in 1976, when a white doctor tore newly sewn stiches out of a black youth's arm after he learned that the boy had $5 less than the $25 fee. An all-white jury later awarded the boy just the $20 it had cost to have the stitches replaced by another doctor.[8]

Whatever else these vignettes may suggest, they only hint at the cost black people have paid in pain and suffering, in humiliation and foreshortened lives. "Of all forms of inequality," Martin Luther King has said, "injustice in health is the most shocking and most inhuman."[9]

The story of black people in the American health care system has two parts: one of them concerns black people who are sick and in need of the care the system can provide, while the second is largely an employment issue, because it deals with how black people have had to struggle to win jobs and professional status in that system. Both issues are double-edged: real progress has been made as discrimination has been reduced, though real disparities remain, stemming in large part from continuing discriminatory practices. Black Americans are still less well than white Americans, but they are demonstrably healthier than their parents and grandparents, chiefly because more medical care and a higher standard of living have become available to them. Discrimination still imposes limitations, but their access to doctors, clinics, and hospitals, to lab tests, x-rays, and medicines, have improved. Full equality is still elusive, but black people now have better nutrition, housing, and jobs, plus the incomes and insurance plans that go along with them. Taken together, all of these elements show up in the gradually improving profile of black people's health.

It is a somewhat different matter for black people seeking to make a career in medicine. Their struggle has been like the struggle of every other group of blacks attempting to gain entry to an occupation or profession which was previously closed, is well-organized, and is resistant to change. It has been uphill all the way. Black people wishing to work in health care have had to fight to win places in the schools and training programs, for the right to train in the hospitals, to be accepted among their professional peers, and for the right of black patients to the same quality of care given by white health professionals to white patients.

The link between black health status and more equal opportunity for black professionals is not clear. The improvements in black health status have not come about because there are more black doctors now than there were thirty years ago. For many individual patients that would be true, but it could not explain the steady trend toward improved black health status, particularly in the face of the small number of black professionals and their scarcity in much of the country even now. But the hospital is an important link between the two. At the same time that black doctors were winning the right to admit patients and practice medicine in white hospitals, black people were gaining access to a kind and level of care they had not had before. And that circumstance must be credited with some of the improvements that show up in many of the indices of good health.

Black Health Status

Discriminatory treatment in the American health care system is reflected in almost every set of health care indices. By virtually every measure, black Americans were and are less well than white Americans. While the degree of difference between the health status of black and white has grown smaller with time, it is more remarkable that it remains so significant. Well into the seventies, life expectancy for the average young black American was still a full six years shorter than for whites, giving blacks the expectation of fewer years in the seventh decade than whites had twenty years before (Table 6–1). Black people do not only die younger, they live lives that are less healthy: they have more days of disability, of illness, and of work loss (Table 6–2); greater unmet dental needs (Table 6–3); almost twice as much likelihood of being in poor or only fair health (Table 6–3). "Day after day," reports the director of the Howard University Hospital, "I see evidence that the medical problems of blacks are more acute, more complicated and more neglected than those of other Americans."[10] Despite their greater need for care, at every age black Americans are less likely to get it.

Even before birth, blacks are less likely to get the health care that they need. When the National Academy of Sciences (NAS) conducted a special study of prenatal care in New York City in 1968, it found that only 5 percent of the black women in a sample of 140,000 received adequate medical care, although 43 percent of the white women did (Table 6–4).[11] Black women were more likely to get poor care, even though their pregnancies more often involved medical risk. And poor care meant more low-birthweight babies and higher death rates[12] (Table 6–5).

Our national statistics have been making the same point for many years. The infant death rate, long regarded as one index of "the effectiveness of prevailing medical care" as well as "an indirect measure of the adequacy of prenatal care programs,"[13] has been one-and-a-half to almost two times as high for black infants as for whites since 1940[14] (Table 6–6). For much of this time, black women had little access to medical care of any kind. Over half of all black births in the forties took place outside of a hospital, without a doctor present (Table 6–7). An associate chief of the Children's Bureau estimated that, in 1941, 90 percent of Negro births in the rural South were attended by untrained midwives with "primitive methods,"[15] a tragedy compounded by the insensitivity of some of those in charge. One white health professional expressed the callous view that the problem was not the lack of care, but

> Negroes who are generally satisfied with health conditions as they find them and often look with placid resignation upon the loss of a mother in childbearing or the death of her baby shortly after birth.[16]

Low birthweight is linked to poor care, and shows up in the infant mortality rates—which are highest for lightweight babies.[17] (About 60 percent of infant deaths occur in low-birthweight infants.[18]) In 1974, for example, more than twice as many black babies as white were born to mothers who had little or no prenatal care, and more than twice as many black babies as white were born low in birthweight,[19] suggesting that, even into the seventies, black mothers were still getting less adequate prenatal care. When black mothers have gotten good care, black infant death rates have fallen.[20]

Well into the century, just having a baby was dangerous for mothers as well as babies because so many women died from fevers and infections contracted during childbirth. Since the adoption of antiseptic techniques and of in-hospital and professionally assisted deliveries, the deaths from childbirth have become increasingly rare[21] (Table 6–8). With proper care, maternal mortality is almost entirely avoidable today, so it is significant that when the rates for black mothers are compared with those for white mothers, they reveal a persistent variance. Over these thirty-five years, two-and-a-half to four times as many black as white mothers have died from causes associated with childbirth.[22]

Whether a baby survives the first month of life is very much a matter of the mother's health and the adequacy of her medical care.[23] The babies that survive the first month but die before the end of the first year tend to be victims of conditions that are caused by environmental factors, but for which medical science has answers: parasitic and infectious diseases, flus, pneumonia, congested lungs, intestinal disorders.[24] The children who continue to die from these causes are often from poor families for whom adequate health care cannot be assumed. Since 1940, the deaths of black children during these early eleven months have consistently been two to three times what they have been for white children.[25]

What is true for the beginning of life is true for black people of every age: black Americans are less well and get less care. As children, blacks are more often found without the basic vaccinations that reflect the most rudimentary level of care (Table 6–3). As adults, they show up in the statistics with dramatically higher death rates for conditions which are now, and for the most part have long been, susceptible to proper medical management. In the hands of good health professionals, with medication and medical supervision, Americans need not be dying of diabetes or tuberculosis today, nor should they have to fear death from flu or pneumonia (unless the underlying cause is something else). Just as with maternal mortality, medical science has brought the absolute number of victims from such conditions down substantially. But today just as surely as thirty-five years ago, significant differences of two to four times remain between black and white victims of all of them (Table 6–9).

Some conditions have a higher incidence among blacks than among whites; with those conditions, a higher death rate might be expected. What does occur are death rates far in excess of their incidence. Hypertension, for example, is diagnosed two-thirds more often in blacks than in whites, yet deaths due to hypertension— which can be controlled—are recorded seven-and-a-half times more often in blacks than in whites (Table 6–10). It would seem that treatment is more available to white victims of hypertension than to black victims. It may be a matter of not having early treatment, and, when help is sought, a more seriously advanced and more disabling case. Reported chronic diseases show less incidence among blacks, but more likelihood of disability for those who have the illness. The explanation lies in the better medical care and socioeconomic level of white people, which results in more frequent and more accurate diagnosis and reporting of chronic conditions.[26] The reverse of that is also true: black people get less frequent medical attention, which results in fewer diagnosed chronic conditions and less treatment, leading eventually to more disability and limited activity among blacks and the greater likelihood[27] of not being able to go about their daily activities as usual—at work or at home. Blacks are only slightly more likely to have diagnosed heart conditions, but are one-and-a-half times more likely to die of heart disease; they are 75 percent more likely to be diagnosed as having diabetes, but three times more likely to die of it (Table 6–10). All of these conditions—hypertension, diabetes, heart conditions—require careful monitoring and proper treatment, without which the patients die.[28] And it is inescapable that, in disproportionate numbers, blacks with these conditions die.

The difference between average incomes of blacks and whites is frequently offered to explain the differences in their health status. It is true that poor people of whatever race are more likely to be in poor health than are those who can afford and who get better medical care. But, whenever health-status information is collected by income group, the anomaly remains that blacks still tend to be less well than whites.[29]

Not only are black people apparently less likely to get the care that might prevent death; in the last year of life, blacks are less likely to have hospital care and, if hospitalized, are likely to have such care for shorter periods of time than white people. If all those who die are in some sense in comparable health in their last year of life, then equally sick black people have not been getting equal care (Table 6–11).

Getting Care from Hospitals

It is never pleasant to be sick, and always a little frightening to be hospitalized. But hospitals are the foundation of any modern medical system, and for the seriously ill they are critical. A private physician working out of an office, however elaborately equipped, can only do so much. Sophisticated equipment, major surgery, continuously monitored in-patient care, special diets, or batteries of tests are all beyond the capabilities of the doctor's office when patients need them. On the physician's part, there is the need to talk with colleagues, to take advantage of new techniques, and to remain current with new procedures.

For black people, being sick and frightened has only been part of the problem. Until well into the sixties, many hospitals and doctors refused to treat black patients altogether, or they maintained separate rooms and facilities for blacks and whites. Hospitals that accepted black patients routinely refused to allow them to be treated by their own black doctors.[30] (Hospital privileges were given only to physicians who were members of local medical societies, and in some places they refused to admit black physicians until the sixties.) This situation, and its logical outcome, was reported on in 1940 in the only all-black unit of the Virginia Statewide Writers' Project, organized under the Works Project Administration:

> Although Negro patients are admitted to separate wards in most hospitals, Negro doctors are uniformly excluded, even when their own patients are admitted. The St. Phillip Hospital of the Medical College of Virginia, with more than two hundred beds for Negro patients, has Negro nurses but no Negro interns or staff members. . . . Denied the privilege of attending their own patients, Negro physicians in the larger cities have united to establish hospitals of their own, staffed by Negroes (Richmond, Roanoke, Norfolk, and Newport News).[31]

For as long as and wherever black doctors were excluded from white hospitals being seriously ill was a special problem for black people.

The details differed from place to place. Some hospitals maintained clearly segregated facilities and others denied admission to black patients, or designated some wards or beds as "colored beds"; in still other places, the racial separation was informal but no less effective. In 1946, the U.S. Public Health Service estimated that only approximately 15,000 out of a total of 1,500,000 hospital beds in the country were available to black patients.[32]

By the early 1940s, 110 black-owned and -operated hospitals, primarily in urban areas, had been established to meet black needs.[33] Where there were no black hospitals and severely limited access to white hospitals, black physicians' offices were commonly equipped to operate as small clinics.[34] There, black physicians could perform many of the procedures that white patients might routinely get at a hospital, private laboratory, or public clinic.[35]

Many of the black hospitals had fewer than 100 beds, and all of them together provided fewer than 10,000 beds.[36] Seventy percent of those hospitals were privately owned, and only 22 of the 110 were fully approved hospitals (5 were provisionally approved). Just 13 of the hospitals were approved for training interns, and about 20 for training nurses. The situation was worse in some areas than in others. By 1950 the black residents of four still-segregated southern states

(Georgia, Mississippi, North Carolina, and Virginia) were nearly half the population, but had access to fewer than one-third of the available hospital beds.[37]

Probably the most common experience for black patients was to be in segregated wards, rooms, or floors within hospitals.[38] The physicians treating them were almost always white,[39] and many did not even think that black patients were entitled to be treated alongside whites. A survey of nearly 6,000 southern white physicians in 1953 revealed that only 17 percent of them supported the notion of admitting black patients to hospitals on a nonsegregated basis; nearly two-thirds favored admission to the same hospitals, but on a segregated basis; and 11 percent still wanted separate hospitals.[40] Their Hippocratic oath was not color-blind.

Black patients needing treatment would be admitted to "colored beds" until those were filled. Additional patients would be turned away or crowded into hospital corridors no matter how much space there was in the "white" wards.[41] For those who were hospitalized in the forties:

> The basement "colored ward" is notorious. Here no attempt at an acceptable hospital set-up is made. Negro patients are admitted for what attention the white physicians will give them, often with a single untrained attendant as the nursing staff.[42]

In urban areas, black people could usually get care only at clinics. In Chicago, for example, all hospitals except Cook County General Hospital either segregated their black patients or refused them admission entirely.[43] Cook County took black patients, but in the early forties it was only able to handle about one-half of those in need of hospital accommodations.[44] Obviously, a hospital system that refused black patients, or accepted only a limited number, left a serious gap in health care.

In time, large municipal hospitals came under black control. The process in these instances reflected what was happening to the residential character of the cities. As neighborhoods changed and became increasingly black, the hospitals in their midst—which had been built to serve white patients, white physicians, and a white community—found themselves surrounded by an increasingly black community. One choice for such hospitals was to remain in the same location, but to serve the new clientele. The other, more common choice would be for the hospital's board of directors to vote a fund drive to support the building of a new hospital in a "better" location. But the old hospitals represented a dilemma: it seemed wrong and

wasteful to think of abandoning or razing a hospital. The solution
was to turn the hospital over to the black community. That solved
many problems at once: the board would not have continued responsibility for a piece of real estate that it no longer wanted; the black
community would seem to be getting something better than they
presently had; there would be a feeling of having done something
good for these poor, black people; public support would be virtually
assured; and any subsequent deterioration in the old hospital plant
or any lack of an adequate financial base could be blamed, not on the
whites who had abandoned it, but on the inability of blacks to run
a major institution competently.[45] The process was most perceptively
described by an early president of the National Medical Association,
Montague Cobb. "All over the country," Cobb wrote in 1947,[46] "the
secondhand hospital stands as a symbol of what the system means."
He likened the transfer of old hospitals in changing neighborhoods
to the mental process that goes on when a man gives away an old
suit that he can no longer use. The giver very quickly becomes
convinced of the generosity of the deed and the expectation that the
beneficiary would have to be a fool to be ungrateful for the gift. "I'll
just tell him [Sam] frankly that his needs have been recognized and
received a great deal of thought for a long time. In his economic
position, he will understand that he can't have everything at once
and something as good as this is ten times better than nothing."
According to Cobb, these are the kinds of rationalizations that accompany the transfer of many "secondhand products of modern
American culture to Negro hands as the brown population increases
in an urban community."[47] Not only do the vacating whites have to
sell their homes, they also have institutions, schools, churches, and
hospitals to dispose of.

Sydenham Hospital in New York began as an overwhelmingly
white but mixed hospital that became black, first in patients and later
in staff, as Harlem expanded.[48] Carver Memorial in Tennessee was
originally a private hospital for white patients; as a black hospital,
it became the first place in Chattanooga where a black doctor could
treat private patients.[49] Union Memorial Hospital in Baltimore was
white until the neighborhood changed and Union left for newer
buildings—what remained became the black Provident Hospital.[50]
Wheatley-Provident Hospital in Kansas City was a Catholic school
that was abandoned when the neighborhood changed.[51] With minor
variations, the basic pattern was repeated in major cities everywhere.[52]

For the black community, the choice posed by the secondhand hospitals, or any other all-black hospital, was not an easy one. Those who supported expanding the black hospitals did so out of fear that they would never have access to the white hospitals, and this way, at least they might have something—a facility over which they could exert some control. From the beginning, many opposed establishing all-black hospitals—whether new or second-hand—on the grounds that it was better to have no care than to accept a segregated system. They were convinced that facilities for black patients served by black doctors would always be severely limited and would also reduce the pressure needed to as-sure access to all available medical resources.[53]

Without ready access to doctors (and hospitalization insurance also), the medical care of black people could only have been made worse by the steady movement of white-controlled hospitals out of the central cities. As neighborhoods became predominantly black, some hospitals did not revert to black control but were simply shut down, leaving large areas with little or nothing in the way of medical facilities. In the fifties, while black Chicagoans were increasing sub-stantially as a proportion of the city's population, Chicago Memorial Hospital, Mercy Hospital, and St. Luke's all left Chicago's black South Side for whiter, more suburban locations. That left over 1,000 fewer hospital beds to serve an area where an estimated half-million southern blacks had settled since World War II.[54] By the late sixties, only 13 physicians remained to serve the 63,000 black residents of the East Garfield Park area of Chicago. Nearby, in the Kenwood-Oakland area, 45,500 black people had only 5 physicians to meet their needs by 1968. According to one estimate, there were more physicians in one suburban medical building than in the whole west-side ghetto, which housed 300,000 blacks.[55] Into the sixties, Cook County General still remained the major source of care for black Chicago families, a kind of mammoth family doctor, simply because clinics and doctors' offices were so scarce. In a single typical day, Cook County General's admitting examining room dealt with 1,200 patients.[56]

The magnitude and seriousness of the exodus of white-controlled hospitals from black neighborhoods did not become widely known until the ghetto uprisings of the 1960s forced attention on the prob-lem. When the Los Angeles area called Watts exploded, studies discovered what community people had known all along—there were no hospitals in Watts.

In 1965, the Watts-Willowbrook area—large sections of which were 90 percent black—contained about 380,000 people.[57] For this large, predominantly poor, badly housed, sicker-than-average population, there were few doctors and no hospital. Six small (18 to 67 beds) proprietary hospitals and several small nursing homes were located on the periphery of the area, but the only comprehensive facility was Los Angeles County General Hospital, a two-hour bus or $10 taxi ride away. Three public health district centers and two subcenters were in the local area, but they offered only preventive care.[58] The McCone Commission, set up in the aftermath of the violence in Watts, specifically recommended "a new and comprehensively equipped hospital" for the area.[59] By 1967, the University of Southern California Medical School, using OEO money, had opened the Watts-Willowbrook multipurpose Neighborhood Health Center to serve the area with its first primary and comprehensive care medical facility, and a larger hospital facility was being planned.[60] Black protest rather than health planning had been necessary to force a solution. Watts was not unique. The hospitals that may be open to Negroes, Whitney Young wrote in 1964,

> are generally unattractive if not repellent, and the ailing Negro avoids them if he is able. Usually he has no choice. Anxiety-ridden as to his chance of finding decent hospital facilities and apprehensive of the quality of care he will receive if and when admitted, is it any wonder that the Negro in ill health holds out against hospitalization until the last possible moment?[61]

Federal Support for Segregated Hospitals

In 1941, Congress considered a Wagner-George Health Bill that proposed spending $10 million over six years for hospital construction, primarily in underserved rural areas, to be administered without racial discrimination.[62] It did not pass. After the war, it had become apparent that the demands of a wartime economy had exacerbated an already serious hospital situation by limiting badly needed hospital construction to veterans' facilities. The serious postwar shortage of hospital beds was especially acute in small towns and rural areas.

The landmark Hill-Burton Hospital Survey and Construction Act of 1946[63] was an attempt to encourage all states to survey the facilities available, to assess their hospital needs in the coming years, and to draw up coordinated plans that would equitably distribute hospital beds in a statewide system. In that way, normally underserved areas would be taken into account. In addition, the legislation provided terms on which federal funds would become available to pay one-third of the cost of new construction or of the renovation and expansion of existing facilities.

When the act was taken up by Congress, a clause was inserted which specified that no federal funds could be used for facilities that discriminated "on account of race, creed or color." But the principal sponsor of the bill was Senator Lister Hill of Alabama. A prohibition against the use of any funds for facilities discriminating on the basis of race would have disqualified all the hospital facilities in his home state of Alabama. As the price for his continued support and championship of the legislation, he added an exception to the nondiscrimination clause. It provided that localities where separate health facilities were planned for separate population groups might be eligible for funds if the facilities and services were of like quality for each group. With the passage of Hill-Burton, Congress had written the "separate but equal" philosophy into the law affecting hospitals.

Under the law, hospitals exclusively for one race or the other were designated "discriminatory," but were not disallowed; seventy single-race hospitals were built with Hill-Burton funds in the first seventeen years of the program.[64] All other facilities were classified as "nondiscriminatory," but under the law as interpreted by the general counsel of HEW, such facilities were permitted to deny admission on the basis of race to sections of a facility not constructed with federal funds (important where the money was used to build additions to segregated facilities). They could separate patients within a facility, deny staff privileges to professionally qualified people, and deny training opportunities to residents and interns, on account of race.[65] Discriminatory policies with respect to staff were permitted under that part of the law which specified that the federal government would have no control over the hiring policies of the hospitals built with federal aid. That Hill-Burton would be underwriting hospital segregation was conceded in 1949 by the federal security administrator, who said that

> 214 [hospitals] are being built to serve both races and four are to be exclusively for Negroes. It is true that the 214 hospitals will be operated on a policy of segregation. . . . Under the present law the Federal Government cannot interfere.[66]

Because it was such an important source of funding for hospital construction and improvement, the Hill-Burton legislation had a profound effect on maintaining segregation in the medical care system. Its financing requirements, as well as its policies, contributed to segregated care in white-controlled hospitals. Applicants for Hill-Burton funds had to put up two-thirds of hospital construction costs.[67] Few black communities or doctors could afford the matching requirement.

It was not until the *Simkins v. Moses Cone*[68] decision was handed down in 1963 that the "separate but equal" doctrine was found unconstitutional in the field of health. By March of 1964, HEW had revised its regulations to provide that:

1. Patients must be admitted and have access to all of a hospital's facilities and not just the parts built with Hill-Burton funds;

2. Patients could no longer be segregated within the facilities;

3. Qualified professionals were to be admitted as staff and with hospital privileges without respect to race, color, or creed;

4. Projects under way or in planning were required to give assurance of nondiscrimination in order to remain eligible for federal funds.

Of 835 "nondiscriminatory" facilities being built or already receiving federal funds, 700 agreed to give the necessary assurances.[69]

The change in Hill-Burton was soon dwarfed in importance by the impact of three pieces of legislation passed in less than a year: the Civil Rights Act of 1964, and the Medicare and Medicaid programs enacted as Titles XVIII and XIX of the Social Security Act in 1965. Between them, they provided the carrot and the stick. The Civil Rights Act stipulated that federal funds could not be used to discriminate. The Medicare and Medicaid programs held out the promise of virtually unlimited federal reimbursement to medical personnel and facilities for services provided to participants in either of those programs. But Medicare and Medicaid funds could not, in theory, be used to reimburse services given by hospitals or doctors that continued to segregate their waiting rooms or in any way give discriminatory care. To ensure that the civil rights requirements were obeyed, 500 HEW staff were employed to review the policies of some 9,000 hospitals,[70] and more than 3,000 actually changed discriminatory practices in order to comply with the Civil Rights Act and qualify for federal reimbursement.[71]

HEW's civil rights compliance efforts focused largely on the institutional side of health care, the hospitals and nursing homes, rather than on what happened to black patients in individual doctors' offices. Another important aspect of discrimination was ignored altogether in formal guidelines—the location of hospitals. When federal dollars are used to relocate hospitals from the inner city with its predominantly black population to distant suburbs with their predominantly white populations, for patients the effect is the same as it was in the days when black people had no hospitals to which they could turn.[72] Negotiation alone, without the force of sanctions and unsupported by official policy, is a weak reed on which to lean, and has been used with mixed results. Hospital relocations were prevented in Connecticut.[73] But, when a 120-bed hospital adjacent to a black community in Alexandria, Virginia, was closed and moved to expanded facilities several miles away in a mostly white community, HEW did not even know about the move[74] (presumably in official terms only; Alexandria is a Washington, D.C., suburb that houses many HEW officials). HEW's Chicago regional office, which is responsible for health compliance in five states,[75] identified twenty intended relocations which would make hospitals less accessible to minority communities, though as late as 1974 there was no indication that HEW had any effective plan for acting on the problem.[76]

The Medicare law itself provides a way around compliance for those hospitals that wish to avoid it, because hospitals will be reimbursed for treating patients who come as emergencies, even though the hospital is not otherwise in compliance. What constitutes an emergency admission is apparently subject to regional variation. In 1968 there were 466 facilities in the South designated as "emergency hospitals." Most of them failed to comply with the civil rights guidelines.[77] These emergency hospitals of the South accounted for 17 percent of all hospitals and 26 percent of all hospital beds,[78] as well as over 85 percent of all claims for emergency payments made to noncomplying hospitals in the late sixties.[79] Some care may be better than none, but a hospital that uses public money and refuses to comply with the Civil Rights Act cannot be a very pleasant place for black patients.

When Money Is Not Enough

How black people are treated by the health care system is not just a function of their being poor. Even in recent years, when public and private insurance plans are more available, two to three times as many black as white people get their medical care through hospital emergency rooms or clinics (Table 6–12). In the forties and fifties, black people who could afford to pay for their hospital care sometimes found themselves in the most awkward position of all: no private hospital would take them and they were too "rich" to qualify for free clinic care. In the forties, Atlanta was such a place. Indigent patients there could get good care at Grady Memorial Hospital, but Grady and all other hospitals were closed to black patients who could afford to pay. The choice was either to pretend poverty and suffer the indignities that went with being a charity patient, or to leave the city in order to enter a black hospital somewhere else. The practice had a debilitating effect on patient and doctor alike. Black physicians lost their only paying customers to another doctor's care whenever something serious arose, and black patients lost the consolation of familiar surroundings, doctors, and friends just when they most needed that kind of support.[80] A special addition, completed in 1952, had to be built so that Grady would have a place for nonpoor black patients.[81]

In the mid-1950s, blacks with union or job-related hospitalization plans presented an awkward problem for the exclusionary hospitals in Chicago, and the hospitals developed an elaborate system for dealing with it. One device was to limit the admission of black patients to those who could pay for private rooms, because it was known that the Blue Cross Plan only reimbursed for semiprivate accommodations. Or, member hospitals might admit the black patients and then immediately transfer them to Cook County General, so that Blue Cross could reimburse the member hospital, which in turn would have to pay Cook County for the care that was actually received. A more direct route to hospital care for those who could pay, and who were therefore not really eligible for care in a charity hospital like Cook County General, was to have middle-class black patients admitted as emergencies, even when they were not.[82] Thus, even in that northern urban center, middle-income black families with hospital insurance coverage were forced to accept charity care —and had to pay for it—crowding the facility and preventing all from getting as good care as was available. In 1955, blacks constituted the vast majority of paying patients at Cook County General.[83]

Health insurance, so important to increasing numbers of Americans, remained beyond the reach of black Americans for much longer than for others. In the mid-sixties, when private insurance had already become fairly common, far more white married couples had hospital insurance to help defray the cost of having a baby (Table 6–13). With today's rapidly rising medical care costs, insurance coverage may well make the difference between getting care or not, and at what stage that care is obtained. Yet as late as 1974, only about three-fifths of black Americans (compared with four-fifths of whites) had hospital and surgical insurance to protect them against at least the economic side of poor health (Table 6–14). It may well be that the only sense in which blacks and whites have reached medical parity is that, white or black, the higher the income, the larger the amount spent on medical care (Table 6–15).

For black people who are old or poor, the enactment of the Medicare and Medicaid programs in 1965[84] has had an important impact on their ability to get care. The two programs operate differently. In Medicare there was a conscious decision to reimburse patients for their medical expenses rather than to pay the physicians directly. The political basis for this decision stemmed from the claims of organized medicine that a direct financial relationship with the federal government would open the door to government control of medical practice. Their concern might seem more genuine if it were not that, at the same time that the Congress enacted Medicare, it also enacted Medicaid, a program to pick up the cost of providing medical care to poor people directly. In Medicaid, the patients were not to be reimbursed; instead, the government would indeed have a direct payment relationship with the physicians, hospitals, and nursing homes participating in the program. The medical community accepted the government tie when the alternative was to trust poor people.

In theory, there should be no difference between the benefits available to black and white participants in Medicare and Medicaid. The law makes no distinctions. Medicare is available to all Social Security beneficiaries who have reached the age of sixty-five,[85] simply by enrolling. The program has two parts. "Part A" entitles the enrollee to hospitalization insurance at no additional cost to all those who sign up. It pays a large portion of hospital costs.[86] Ninety-seven percent of the white population over sixty-five, and 91 percent of the black, were signed up for "Part A" within two years of its enactment (Table 6–16). "Part B" extends insurance coverage to medical-care costs,[87] but involves a monthly charge (about $6.70 in 1974).[88] (People who are not otherwise eligible for Social Security can buy into both parts.[89]) For whites, participation in medical and hospital insurance is about the same, over 95 percent, but only 86 percent of elderly blacks were covered under medical insurance in 1973 (Table 6–16).

Although the differences in coverage are not great for "Part A," they occur largely because blacks are less likely to have been in occupations covered by Social Security and are therefore less likely to be eligible to enroll. "Part B" differences are further explained by the black elderly being disproportionately of low income, so that even the seemingly modest monthly payment required to participate seems too great a burden when they are well.

Blacks' disadvantage in the system does not end with lower rates of enrollment; as a group, blacks get lower benefits as well (Table 6–16). Under medical insurance (Part B) blacks who seek medical help get less than 80 percent of white dollar benefits. But fewer blacks than whites seek medical help under Medicare. Why blacks use Medicare less is not entirely clear. It may be a matter of provider status—hospitals and doctors must be willing to comply with the Civil Rights Act in order to be reimbursed for services under Medicare. Or it may be a matter once again of cost. This coupled with the lower enrollment of blacks in Medicare means that for every person sixty-five and over in 1969, blacks were receiving dollar benefits less than 75 percent as high as whites under hospital insurance, and less than 60 percent as high as whites under medical insurance.

Medicare does not pick up all of the costs for those who participate. Under Part A, the patient is responsible for the first part of medical bills run up each year (in 1974, this "deductible" was $84),[90] and patients must also share in the costs if they are hospitalized for a long period of time. In 1972, Medicare only paid about three-fourths of the cost of hospitalization for its beneficiaries.[91] One-fourth of a $2,000 hospital bill, $500, is a great deal of money for someone who is old and not well-off.

Under Part B, Medicare pays only 80 percent of charges that it considers reasonable, beginning after the patient has paid initial costs.[92] If a doctor actually charges more than what Medicare accepts as reasonable, the patient is responsible for paying the deductible, the 20 percent not covered by Medicare, and the doctor's additional charges. For elderly people beset by ailments that are troublesome over many months, the costs associated with Medicare can quickly mount up, and could discourage them from seeking care. Medicare does not meet any of the costs of many services important to the elderly, including routine foot care and examinations for hearing aids.[93]

Lower Medicare (and Medicaid) benefits for blacks may also be tied to the kinds of services available to blacks. The highest costs in medical care reimbursement programs are from institutional settings, hospitals and nursing homes, and blacks are less likely than whites to receive care in the most expensive of these—the long-term nursing homes.[94] Since they are more likely to receive the less expensive services, their per person cost to the program will average less.

Medicare has contributed substantially to the health care of all of the elderly, for the most part without removing disparity between black and white (Table 6–17).

Medicaid is a program usually quite separate from Medicare. The two overlap at times when the benefits from Medicare are exhausted for those who are both elderly and poor. In general, Medicaid is the federal program that pays the cost of medical care provided to welfare recipients and, in half the states, to people who have incomes slightly above the welfare limit (a group referred to as the medically needy).[95] Here, too, the dollar benefits going to blacks are lower.[96] Blacks of all ages, in all parts of the country, cost the Medicaid program less than whites do, and the largest gap between the two is found among the elderly, and recipients living in the South. It is not that the doctors are paid different fees for people of different colors but rather that, under Medicaid as under Medicare, many fewer blacks get the more expensive services provided in nursing homes, hospitals, and intermediate care facilities. State after state has indicated in reports and other documents, as the National Urban League found in 1965, that

> because there is literally no other place for them to go, chronically ill
> Negroes have been condemned to live out their lives in custodial care
> mental hospitals![97]

Because welfare varies from place to place (and Medicaid is closely linked to welfare), Medicaid has widely varying coverage and benefits from state to state, and sometimes within states as well. Many of the poor are not covered at all: they do not fall into the welfare categories, or are living in states which limit welfare and Medicaid to people with incomes well below the poverty line. For those poor who can use Medicaid, not all states reimburse for the same services. In all states, a mother can expect Medicaid to pay the doctor for diagnosing her child's strep throat, but in 4, not for the medication that is prescribed to cure it; all states will pay for a patient in a private doctor's office, but 13 will not pay for the same service in a clinic;

10 states refuse to pay for poor people who get their care from hospital emergency services.[98] Only 18 states have opted to cover Medicaid costs for all the needy children in families with incomes lower than their welfare limit.[99] Over 20 states refuse to pay for the prenatal care of a woman who is pregnant for the first time.[100]

For those black people who now seek and get care from hospitals or doctors, when they would not have before, Medicaid and Medicare have made an important change that shows up in the diminishing differences between black and white using the medical care system. Those who are still priced out of the system, discriminated against, or excluded from the Medicaid categories despite their poverty show up in the differences that remain between black and white, rich and poor. For those who are left out, the old fears of meeting medical expenses still loom large and must be added to the indignities that go along with being a black patient in a largely white and insensitive medical world.

Black patients may have less difficulty finding doctors and hospitals that will treat them, but finding a white doctor who gives care only grudgingly, and with prejudice, creates another set of problems. The power wielded by white physicians over black patients is not only used to heal. In Aiken, South Carolina, in 1973 only one of the county's obstetricians would accept Medicaid patients.[101] It was his stated policy to deliver a third or later baby for a Medicaid patient only if she agreed to sterilization. A poor black woman in labor, or having a troubled pregnancy, is in a weak position to argue ethics with the only white doctor in the county who might help her. One patient was told by the physician that he would refuse to attend her or her infant, would have her barred from the hospital, and would see to it that she lost her entitlement to welfare. Feeling herself without alternatives, she reluctantly agreed. Another patient refused to be sterilized after giving birth to her baby and was sent out of the hospital without any postnatal care. When these two women brought suit against the doctor, he was only made to pay $5 in damages.[102] In the course of congressional hearings on Aiken's doctors, one woman asked:

> Now, how can he set himself up as a god to do this type of thing. I thought his job was to bring life into the world and keep us here a bit longer. . . .[103]

There have been instances in which black patients proved useful to the system. In the sixties, when black mothers in a North Carolina county were found to have fewer than the recommended number of child care visits for their children, it was learned that they had little choice. The university-related services on which they relied reduced or suspended services while the medical students were on vacation or taking examinations. In such circumstances, the patients would seem to be serving the needs of the medical students rather than the other way around.[104] And in 1938, when the U.S. Public Health Service wished to make a long-term observation of untreated syphilis, six hundred black men (who were not told the nature of the study or its possible consequences for them) were chosen as the research subjects. The study only ended in 1973—long after a cure for syphilis was known—and as a result of public protest.[105]

Black people are certainly not the only people to be practiced on by medical students or used in medical experimentation without their full knowledge and informed consent, but they are more likely to be poor, and it has been estimated that "possibly 80 percent of all human experimentation which has occurred in this country involved the poor."[106]

It is not difficult to understand why some black people go without care. Black patients are not likely to seek out doctors who only see black patients on Tuesdays,[107] or who, as late as the mid-seventies, expect black patients to remain fully clothed during physical examinations.[108] Black people have all heard the stories about black accident victims being taken to distant hospitals while the white victims of the same accidents get help immediately from "white" hospitals nearby.[109] The only doctor available to the black people of one area was described in the following terms:

> I heard that he done killed two or three girls up that way. Women with babies. He done said many times he don't want to look up any nigger. He would rather look up a dog than a colored person. When he first come up here he was good, but now he done got rich and he don't want to wait on colored people.[110]

Whatever the situation, however short-term the anxiety, humiliation, or pain, the outcome is the same: second-class care, and worse.

Blacks in Medicine
Training Black Doctors

At least part of the problem faced by black patients stems from the ways in which blacks have been excluded from the medical professions and the medical care system. It is perhaps ironic that the nature and extent of segregation in health care is most easily documented in the training and education opportunities open to black students wishing to become doctors. If white physicians were reluctant to treat black patients, and that were the only issue, then they should have welcomed black men and women into the professional ranks who might relieve them of that burden. Instead, the medical profession was staunchly resistant to black medical professionals.

Because so few black physicians were being trained, the black physician/population ratio has been about 27 per 100,000 since 1940. For whites, that ratio was five times higher in the forties, and almost six times higher by 1970 (Table 6–18). In a world without discrimination, physician/population ratios would be meaningless by race. Black men and women would have equal opportunity to join the profession of their choosing. But, in a world in which white doctors choose whether or not to treat black patients, or treat them only with reluctance, the number of black doctors is of paramount importance to black people. In the 1940s, the two principal medical schools training black doctors were Howard University in Washington, D.C., and Meharry Medical College in Tennessee. The other seventy-odd medical schools in the country admitted only a few black students or none at all.[111] Harvard University regularly took one or two—but never more than three—black medical students, among them people like the brilliant surgeon and developer of Aureomycin, Louis T. Wright.[112]

The changing pattern of legal segregation, token integration, and then partial integration is reflected in the statistics of white medical school policies and actions on the admission of black medical students. In the late 1940s, 26 of 76 medical schools in the United States openly stated that they did not admit black students. The remaining 50 theoretically were open to black medical students but, in practice, only 27 had ever enrolled a black student (Table 6–19). Gradually, more white medical schools admitted black students. By 1961, 55 of the 83 medical schools in the country had admitted at least one black student.

Admitting a token black student in a given year is different from a sustained policy to admit a considerable number of black medical students every year. And by 1971, only 13 of 101 predominantly white medical schools admitted twenty or more black medical students for training (Table 6–19). Proportionally, black students were still just 3 percent of all medical students around that time (Table 6–20).

Over the years, the South, the region with the largest black population, has been most resistant to training black physicians. In 1948,
the region contained 26 medical schools, in addition to Howard and
Meharry—yet none of the 26, even when tax-supported, admitted
any black students.[113]

Rather than train black medical professionals themselves, the
eleven southern states worked out an arrangement by which they
would pay the tuition of black students from their areas who were
accepted by Meharry. Meharry, hard-pressed for a sound financial
base, and committed to educating black physicians who might return
to serve black southerners, accepted the money and the educational
burden it represented.[114] That decision incurred the wrath of those
who felt that such a posture reduced the pressures on those same
southern states to open the doors of their tax-supported institutions
to black as well as white residents. By 1948, the *Gaines* and *Sipuel*
decisions had been handed down, stating clearly the opinion of the
Supreme Court that the states had a responsibility to provide professional education for their black students desiring it.[115] In that context, the decision of Meharry to accept the money and unwanted
students of the southern states was viewed by some as a cruel sell-
out.[116]

The idea that the agreement with Meharry gave southern states a
way to avoid training black doctors was unequivocally rejected by
the courts. A test case in Maryland established that interstate agree-
ments on education did not eliminate the obligation of states to
provide professional training to all their citizens in schools within
their own borders.[117] Getting southern schools to admit black students was another matter.

By 1956, Meharry had come to reserve 75 percent of the places
in each freshman class for southerners. Nearly twenty years later,
Meharry was still responsible for training 40 percent of all the black
medical students being trained in the nineteen medical schools of
these nine southern states.

As predominantly white schools in the North, West, and finally
the South admitted more black medical students, the proportion of
black medical students attending schools other than Howard and
Meharry gradually rose. In 1938–39, there were 350 black medical
students. All but 45 attended Howard or Meharry. By 1969–70, only
about half of the 1,042 black medical students attended Howard and
Meharry; the rest went elsewhere.[118]

Even more closed to blacks than the medical schools in the 1940s were opportunities for training beyond medical school—internships, residencies, and specialization. In 1947, 18 hospitals accepted black interns; 14 accepted black residents.[119] Opportunities had been so few that there were only 87 living, board-certified black specialists in the United States.[120] While the ordinary practitioner does not need to be board-certified, medical school faculty members must be if the school is to be accredited.[121]

Through continual effort, advanced training opportunities slowly opened up to black medical students. By 1952, 46 hospitals were willing to take black interns.[122] By 1963, the number had grown to 82.[123] In 1973, 303 of the country's 1,681 hospitals had either black interns or residents.[124]

Although greater numbers of medical schools and hospitals were willing to train black medical students and black interns, blacks remained a constant 2 to 3 percent (Table 6–20) between 1940 and 1970, since total medical school enrollment was growing at the same pace as black student enrollment (Table 6–20). In the first half of the seventies, the number of black students enrolled tripled, making them 6 percent of all medical students. More open entry has given black young people one of the opportunities they have long sought.

Doctors were not the only black medical personnel in short supply. The details vary, but the end result of a system of exclusion and discrimination has been much the same with pharmacy and dentistry (Table 6–18).

Nursing

Initial exclusion in nursing was somewhat less than with physicians, and greater progress has been made. But even so, opportunities for student nurses have been severely limited. In 1941, 29 accredited schools accepted black nurses for training, and another 11 accredited white schools accepted a few black women each year.[125] The St. Phillips School attached to the Virginia College of Medicine trained black women from states that would pay their tuition and a small stipend. It was an arrangement much like the one worked out by the southern states for training black medical students at Meharry.[126] By 1948, about 275 of the 1,200 schools of nursing admitted black students.[127]

The American Nursing Association voted to admit black nurses in 1946, and agreed to take black nurses into the national organization from those states where they were barred from local chapters.[128] By 1950, only six state nurses' associations still excluded black nurses, and the National Association of Colored Graduate Nurses voted to disband its 11,000-member organization.[130]

Opportunities for black student nurses have improved, so that by 1970 black nurses were 8 percent of all nurses, though the nurse-to-population ratio for blacks is still much lower than for whites (Table 6–18).

The Professional Societies

The exclusion of blacks, begun in medical schools, was followed through in the segregationist policies of the medical profession. In the 1940s, one black member was elected to the policymaking body of the American Medical Association—Dr. Peter Marshall Murray of Harlem Hospital,[131] and the medical societies of St. Louis, Baltimore, and Florida voted to accept black physicians as members.[132] But many local chapters of the American Medical Association continued to discriminate against blacks. In the 1950s, the AMA recommended to its member chapters that they review their policies of discriminating on the basis of race, but took no strong action to impel a review.[133] It was not until 1968 that the AMA voted sanctions against chapters that would not admit blacks and other minority groups.[134] Medical societies were important because hospital segregation often was the result of

> the private action of doctors, hospital boards, and medical societies. It reflects the arrangement which links the right to practice in a hospital to membership in the local medical society.[135]

Hospital staff privileges, including the right to admit and treat patients, to make rounds, and to acquire specialty training, were confined to members in good standing of the local affiliate of the American Medical Association. Those medical societies could practice strict policies of discrimination: no black physicians could be admitted as members. The medical societies were private organizations, often social or educational in purpose, and not subject to regulation, state law, or—even when it might have become appropriate—any form of federal law or public policy. But the direct effect of such "social practices" was that black physicians could not admit black patients to white hospitals, and those patients either had to go elsewhere, if they could, or be admitted under the care of white physicians.[136]

The director of the largest publicly supported hospital in New Orleans defended its policy of refusing appointments to black doctors because they were excluded from the medical society by saying, "We are a state agency and must conform to state rules, regardless of what the Federal Government says."[137]

In the early 1960s, in thirteen southern and border states, approximately 817 black doctors still could not get hospital privileges, largely because they were still denied admission to local medical societies. In those thirteen states, medical society membership was open to black doctors only in Nashville, Tennessee; a few counties of North Carolina; Jefferson County in Texas; Fulton County in Alabama; Dade County in Florida; and Baltimore, Maryland.[138]

Being formally barred from the AMA also meant that black physicians were often informally barred from all of those positions, honorary and remunerative, which were controlled by the local professional society. It was common in Connecticut, for example, for the AMA to approve appointments to positions open under the federally supported maternal and child health programs, including that of state commissioner of health.[139] In the sixties, when the oil refineries of Baton Rouge, Louisiana, instituted health plans for all of their workers, black doctors found themselves worse off than before. Louisiana still refused to admit any black doctors into its local medical societies, and so black doctors were automatically excluded from the new medical insurance plan by virtue of not being accredited.[140] And when, in the 1950s, southern medical societies began offering to open up the "scientific" part of their medical society meetings to black doctors—provided the black doctors left when the social part of the meeting began—they could not understand why the black doctors refused their terms.[141] Treatment like that was one reason a young board-certified pediatrician who had grown up in New Orleans and had come home in the fifties to practice felt that he had to leave. He said, in part:

I had spent . . . over twenty years preparing myself to be a qualified pediatrician, and I returned to New Orleans with high hopes. Approximately 95 percent of Negro infants born in New Orleans are delivered at Charity Hospital, a tax-supported institution. Yet no Negro physician had been admitted through its doors, much less on its staff.

[The Department Chairman] working on my behalf... met opposition on every front. [The] final request, that I be permitted to make ward rounds—in the Negro wards *only*—and stand quietly at the foot of the bed and listen to the discussions, was also flatly refused.

... there were few medical meetings, few discussions, few forums in the city that a Negro physician might attend. ...

And so I left.[142]

Fighting Back

Something in the deeply personal and profoundly vulnerable nature of illness may explain why black people have not been more vocal in protesting the kind of medical care they've received. No patient, black or white, feels inclined to protest discourtesy on the part of doctors holding the power of life and death; few patients of any color, however angry or aggrieved, feel competent to challenge the professional care meted out by the practitioners of the medical arts. It is not surprising, then, that the kind of protest that is recorded with respect to health involved the professionals more than the patients.

Black protest in the medical arena goes back to the earliest attempts to win black membership in the AMA in the 1800s, and to the formation at the end of the nineteenth century of the National Medical Association (NMA) as a forum for black medical interests.[143]

By the 1940s the concerns of the black medical community still revolved around admission to national professional associations like the AMA,[144] but they also embraced the war-related issues that affected so many blacks in those days. For medical professionals, the question was not so much the right to wartime jobs as it was acceptance as medical professionals in the various branches of the still-segregated armed forces.[145] A committee was formed early in the war to speed acceptance of black medical personnel, but it was not until 1943 that the armed forces agreed to take five hundred black doctors. The response from the black community was immediate and, by war's end, 16 percent of all the black doctors in the country were serving in the armed forces.[146]

On the home front, the issues were still the interrelated ones of membership in medical societies and admission to hospital staffs. As early as 1940, there was a successful protest lodged in Knoxville, Tennessee, to win hospital privileges for black doctors in a general hospital that had been built with funds from both blacks and whites.[147] Elsewhere, individual doctors and local chapters of the NMA everywhere petitioned local medical societies for membership and pressed the national AMA to change their bylaws, giving each local society control over membership policies.[148] But the national AMA was not yet ready to yield, and local medical societies opened their doors only when black physicians joined forces with local chapters of the NAACP, the Urban League, and perhaps an interracial committee, as they did in Kentucky in 1948.[149]

The NMA and NAACP formed a useful alliance in those years. Together, they opposed the plan agreed to by the southern governors in 1948, which provided for training and tuition payments in other states for black medical and nursing students unable to get medical training in their own, still-segregated school systems.[150] Their representatives in Washington also began to lobby for other health-related legislation affecting blacks.[151]

Beginning in 1950, the *Journal of the National Medical Association* (JNMA) formally took up the civil rights fight in a regular feature called "Integration Battlefront," which kept members informed of developments in health.[152] That same year, when national health insurance was being debated by the Congress, the AMA expected the NMA to join them in opposing the bill, and nearly succeeded in winning their support—until the JNMA reminded black doctors everywhere, "you'll get a pat on the back from the AMA, and a kick in the pants from the NAACP and 11 million blacks."[153]

Their stand on health insurance, as well as growing pressure around the states, caused the AMA to take more notice of their black counterparts, and although they were not yet prepared to take a strong stand, in 1950 the AMA did pass a resolution urging local societies to review their restrictive membership policies. This was hardly a total victory in the eyes of the NMA. The NMA physicians may always have chosen tactics befitting the image of professionals, but the pressure they exerted for equal rights in health grew steadily.

In 1956, the NMA and the NAACP joined together with the Urban League to form "Imhotep" to specifically address the problems of hospital discrimination. Imhotep was an Egyptian physician who lived in 3000 B.C. and whose name means "He who cometh in peace"; the organization Imhotep hoped to use peaceful means to

end the effects of discrimination on the black community, medical
and lay. From the first, the organization extended invitations to the
AMA, the American Hospital Association, and other major health
organizations to attend the conferences which were to be held annually in Washington, D.C. Although the invitations were renewed
each year, none of the white organizations sent representatives to
Imhotep.[154]

The sixties brought a new mood of militancy that swept over
everyone fighting for civil rights, including the usually more staid
medical community, and black medical professionals stepped up
the amount and urgency of their protest. In 1960, the first and
most significant case to come before the courts in the health area
was filed in a North Carolina district court by George Simkins and
other doctors and dentists who, like him, had been denied staff
privileges in hospitals receiving federal support under the Hill-Burton Hospital Survey and Construction Act.[155] The following year,
black physicians in Chicago filed suit to win hospital staff privileges
as well as the right of black patients to treatment.[156] The Imhotep
conference of 1961 urged the creation of local Imhotep committees
across the country to press for an end to hospital discrimination,[157]
and eight Atlanta physicians became the first medical professionals
to be arrested for participation in a demonstration "stand-in"—this
one staged to protest their exclusion from eating facilities at a medical conference.[158] Within two years, still other legal approaches
were being pursued: in Atlanta, the NAACP and black doctors
sued to win admission to the local medical society and staff privileges at Grady Hospital;[159] in Chicago and in Greensboro, North
Carolina, physicians brought lawsuits challenging discrimination
against patients and doctors in Hill-Burton facilities;[160] and in the
Congress, amendments were offered for the first time, though un-
successfully, to forbid discrimination under Hill-Burton.[161] CORE
protested in Alabama against the use of federal money for a new
hospital with separate entrances and rooms and blatant segregation
policies.[162] As one newspaper of the health care industry, *Medical
Tribune,* commented:

> The drive for integration in medicine . . . promises to become even
> stronger in coming months, what with the increased militancy of the
> National Medical Association, the probability of more public demon-
> strations and direct action by the Medical Committee for Civil Rights,
> and increased pressure from civil rights groups. . . .[163]

At the seventh annual meeting of Imhotep, to which other groups still failed to send their representatives, Chairman Montague Cobb reflected the increasingly militant mood of black health professionals everywhere:

> Their representatives are not here. For seven long years we have come in peace. For seven years we have invited them to sit down with us and solve the problem. . . . By their refusal to confer they force action by crisis. And now events have passed beyond them. The initiative offered is no longer theirs to accept.[164]

Black leaders of the profession were the first to acknowledge that there had been real progress, but they were equally quick to emphasize their long patience. Within a few weeks, black doctors had mounted picketlines around the Atlantic City headquarters of the AMA convention. Wearing three-piece suits and professional demeanors, they carried their picket signs first at the AMA convention, and then at the AMA's offices in Chicago. The picketlines helped to focus public attention on the incongruity of a profession pledged to help relieve the suffering of all humanity, but applying that commitment only to some. Joining in the picketlines were white members of the organizing group, the newly formed Medical Committee for Civil Rights, and the picketlines made their point. In less than a month, the AMA and the NMA were holding meetings and had established a working committee with three representatives each. Nevertheless, the national organization still would not impose a policy of nondiscrimination on its local affiliates. For that and other reasons, formation of the joint committee left many black doctors skeptical or openly critical. They would not be pacified by anything less than a commitment by the AMA's policymakers to work for full integration wherever racial segregation and discrimination in medicine and medical services remained.[165] The march of events had moved black doctors beyond polite exchanges.

New events and new issues had demanded their attention in the mid-sixties. When Martin Luther King led a march from Selma to Montgomery, Alabama, in 1965, the Alabama chapter of the NMA saw to it that medical care was available to participants along the way. Nearly one hundred black physicians and nurses gave their time and skills to support the march, and mobile vans and ambulances were donated by black groups across the state.[166] A year later, the

NMA members of Mississippi stepped in with their medical support of the march begun by James Meredith in Mississippi.[167] Before long, a retiring president of the NMA could refer to "our traditional role of protesting and fighting every form of discrimination against physicians and their patients."[168] For black doctors, protest had become a tool of the profession.

Health protest constantly took new forms. In the Los Angeles (Watts) riots of 1965, a lack of health facilities was one of the issues, and the Watts-Willowbrook multipurpose health center was one of the results.[169] Black medical students put pressure on the NMA to be more aggressive on matters like medical school admission, hospital staff privileges, and federal aid for black students.[170] Through the years, lone black students had braved the isolation and hostility of being the only black medical student, or one of only two or three, in all-white institutions. Theirs was a hard and lonely effort for many years. But in the sixties, when their numbers had grown, black medical students organized and began to exert group pressure. In Philadelphia in 1968, black medical students formed a Committee for Black Admissions to win more places in the area's six medical schools.[171] Taking a cue from the students, in 1970 the NMA taxed each of its members $100 to help aid recruiting efforts and later set up a program for legal action against medical schools that remained closed.[172]

At the AMA's convention in 1969, black doctors, nurses, and students staged a takeover of the podium. At issue were the conservative leadership of the AMA and the exclusionary policies which had contributed to the shortage of health personnel.[173] Their protest broke down barriers of long standing. By the next convention, students were given full membership, and by 1971, a resolution finally was passed by the House of Delegates agreeing to suspend any state or local society that refused membership to black physicians because of race.[174]

Protest of the traditional variety continued into the seventies, as when blacks organized against the inadequate care and lack of opportunity for black staff at the Hall-Mercer mental health center of Pennsylvania Hospital,[175] and a black community group in Chicago formed to monitor its neighborhood hospital and change its discriminatory practices.[176] But an important new effort emerged in the seventies when blacks in science and public policy positions made a public, national issue of sickle cell anemia. That disease affects 1 black birth in 500, but had received little attention from the white medical and scientific community. Sickle cell anemia occurs twenty times as frequently in blacks as PKU (phenylketonuria, an inherited metabolic disease) occurs in whites.[177] Testing is mandatory in all infants for PKU, yet it required a major effort to win enactment of the National Sickle Cell Anemia Control Act in 1972. Protest had found its way from the medical societies to the medical laboratories.

Over the years, the issues have remained essentially the same: the exclusion of black professionals, the lack of quality health care for black patients, official inattention to the medical problems faced by black people. If history is any measure, as long as the issues remain, so will the protest.

Civil Rights Enforcement

Until the mid-sixties, black people had to make their fight for a nondiscriminatory health system virtually alone. Court decisions were not enough by themselves to effect a major change, and the hospitals and professional health associations made little effort to improve the system without prodding. But when the Civil Rights Act and the Medicare and Medicaid programs became law, there was a strong, though temporary, federal commitment to civil rights enforcement in health.

Since the sixties, there has been a tendency to assume that somehow the job of eliminating bias from our institutions is taken care of because there are laws that prohibit discrimination. Health, however, provides a good example of how critical enforcement efforts can be, for when they were strong and actively pursued, changes were indeed being made; when enforcement was relaxed, further change was forestalled and some parts of the system reverted to their former ways.

HEW's initial attempts to win compliance from hospitals across the country have been described as "a model of affirmative action." Within months 8,000 facilities were reviewed, 2,500 by on-site inspection.[178] That flurry of activity lasted less than three years. By 1968, civil rights advocates had reason to be concerned that the desegregation effort in HEW was already on the decline.[179] During that entire year, only 60 hospitals in seven southern states were visited for on-site reviews.[180] By the mid-seventies, enforcement staff for the entire United States had been reduced to fewer than 70 people with responsibility for health and social services combined. As staff was being reduced, so was the business of enforcement: guidelines to about 250 state agencies were not promulgated; guidelines for hospitals and nursing homes under Medicare were incomplete; some Medicaid providers were ignored altogether. Although the law required that minorities be included among the various programs' advisers, no instructions were issued on the subject, and hospitals, doctors, and other participants in federal programs were never required to determine that their services were equitably distributed to minority people.[181] Hospitals cleared for participation in Medicare did not even have to file the forms showing the extent of their compliance until the summer of 1969.[182]

Without adequate staff and commitment, the civil rights enforcement effort in health has plainly suffered. When reviews were conducted, they missed blatant discrimination, such as segregated facilities,[183] or they permitted discriminatory agencies to continue to receive federal money.[184] When problems were documented in Louisiana, Michigan, Indiana and elsewhere, no enforcement action was taken. Although hospitals are required to give assurance that they are open to people of all races, they were put under no obligation to monitor the referral patterns of the doctors on their staffs. These patterns take the form of legalized discrimination as to who is being treated.[185] More important, by 1969 no action had ever been taken against a facility for failing to grant staff privileges to minority physicians.[186]

Overall, what began as an exemplary effort has become progressively weaker and weaker. By the seventies, HEW's role was small. Fiscal year 1973 saw only 1 percent of medical facilities getting federal funds subject to an on-site review, a figure hardly designed to strike fear in the hearts of others not yet in compliance. Where noncompliance was known, the necessary remedial steps never followed: in Louisiana, Florida, and Michigan, defiance of the law went unpunished.[187] In 1975, the department tried to eliminate handling individual complaints, even though the Civil Rights Commission concluded that

> complaint handling appears to be the principal compliance tool with which HEW has produced any positive results in the area of health and social services.[188]

Fortunately, the outcry by civil rights groups and their supporters squelched the department's proposal.[189]

For most practical purposes, civil rights compliance in health had ground to a halt by the mid-seventies. The Civil Rights Commission noted:

> Despite the large number of unresolved Title VI problems in HEW health and social service programs, HEW has not referred any instances of discrimination prohibited by Title VI to the Department of Justice for action. As of January 1975, there were no outstanding orders terminating HEW assistance to recipients of health or social service programs and administrative proceedings for fund termination have been initiated against only five recipients who were formally considered to be in noncompliance.[190]

We are left with a system that is like a net with as many holes as it has string. While the health needs of many black people manage to be caught in the net and are dealt with (improving health measures reflect that), urgent needs still fall through the holes. Black people remain more sick, more likely to be left untreated, more disabled, more likely to lack institutional care when they need it, more likely to die young.

As the comptroller general of the United States found when he reviewed the situation in 1972:

> ... this country has essentially a dual health care system for minorities and nonminorities. . . . minority group patients often received their health care from public hospitals . . . were sometimes unaware that their Medicare or Medicaid coverage entitled them to use private hospitals; and . . . many hospitals and nursing homes were treating patients of only one race. . . .[191]

TABLE 6-1

Blacks Live Shorter Lives than Whites—at Least Five Years Shorter on the Average, and the Difference Has Not Changed Much Since 1960

Life Expectancy at Birth and at Age 20, by Race, 1940–73

Year and age	Black[a]	White	Years whites live longer than blacks
At birth—1940	53	64	11
1950	61	69	8
1960	64	71	7
1970	65	72	7
1973	66	72	6
At age 20—1940	[b]	50	[b]
1950	45	52	7
1960	48	53	5
1970	48	54	6
1973	49	54	5

[a] Negro and other nonwhite races.
[b] Not available.

Source: Derived from NCHS, *Vital Statistics Rates in the United States, 1940–1960* (Washington, D.C.: Government Printing Office, 1968), Tables 50–1, pp. 308–9; NCHS, *Vital Statistics of the United States, 1970, Vol. 2, Mortality, Pt. A* (Washington, D.C.: Government Printing Office, 1974), Table 5–3, pp. 5–7; NCHS, *Vital Statistics of the United States, 1971, Vol. 2, Mortality, Pt. A* (Washington, D.C.: Government Printing Office, 1975), Table 5–3, pp. 5–7; unpublished data from National Center for Health Statistics.

TABLE 6-2

Blacks Are Laid Up by Illness More Days than Whites

Restricted Activity, Bed Disability, and Work Loss Days from Illness, by Race, 1973

Disability days and activity loss	Black[a]	White	Days blacks are ill longer than whites
Restricted activity days All ages[b]	19	15	4
Bed disability days All ages[b]	8	6	2
Work days lost (among employed) 17 years old and over	8	5	3

[a] Negro and other nonwhite races.

(Table 6–2, continued)

(b) Age standardized to the 1973 population for Negroes and other nonwhite races. This means that the rates for whites for particular age groups have been applied to a population exactly like the black population. The result is that the differences seen in the table are caused by something other than the difference in the age structures of the black and white populations.

Source: Derived from CPR, Series P–25, No. 614, *Estimates of the Population of the United States by Age, Sex and Race: 1970 to 1975,* Table 3, pp. 25–7; NCHS, *Health, United States, 1975,* 1976 Tables CD.I. 35, CD. II. 30, CD. III. 28–9, CD. IV. 6, pp. 253, 403, 491, 493, 561.

TABLE 6–3

Blacks Feel Less Well and Are More in Need of Care than Whites

Percentage of Persons with Selected Health Conditions, by Race, Selected Years, 1960–74

Health indicators	Black[a]	White
Severely disabled[b] (1972)	11	7
Personal health assessment[c] (1973)[d]		
Excellent	37	53
Good	44	37
Fair	14	8
Poor	4	2
Dental needs		
Adults need care soon (1960–62)	62	38
Teeth decayed, age 12–17[e] (1966–70)	3.2	1.5
Youth immunized (1974)		
Polio vaccine (under age 20)[d]	54	69
Rubella vaccine (under age 12)[d]	58	63

(a) Negro and other nonwhite races.
(b) Persons unable to work at all or only intermittently.
(c) Based on questionnaire of the National Health Interview Survey.
(d) Age standardized to the population for Negroes and other nonwhite races for the year to which the data relate. This means that the rates for whites for particular age groups have been applied to a population exactly like the black population. The result is that the differences seen in the table are caused by something other than the difference in the age structures of the black and white populations.
(e) Average number of decayed teeth per person.

Source: Derived from NCHS, *Health, United States, 1975,* 1976, Tables CD. II. 17, CD. III. 1, CD. III. 2, CD. IV. 1, pp. 377, 437, 439, 551; CPR, Series P–25, No. 614, *Estimates of the Population of the United States by Age, Sex and Race, 1970 to 1975,* Table 2, pp. 18–19; NCHS, *Need for Dental Care Among Adults, United States, 1960–62,* Vital and Health Statistics, Series 11, No. 36, Table 2, p. 12.

TABLE 6–4

In New York City—Abounding in Obstetricians and Gynecologists—Most Black Mothers Did Not Receive Adequate Health Care in 1968

Percentage Distribution of Mothers by Quality of Health Care and by Race, New York City, 1968

Quality of care[a]	Black[b]	White[b]
All mothers	100	100
Adequate	5	43
Intermediate	49	41
Inadequate	46	16

[a] Quality-of-care categories are based on the time of first prenatal visit, on the number of prenatal visits, and on the hospital service, whether ward or private.

[b] Native-born black and native-born white.

Source: Derived from National Academy of Sciences, Institute of Medicine, Panel on Health Services Research, *Infant Death: An Analysis by Maternal Risk and Health Care* (Washington, D.C.: National Academy of Sciences, 1973), Table 1–1, p. 22.

TABLE 6–5

Black Infants Were About Twice as Likely as White Infants to Die or Weigh Too Little (in New York City in 1968). Adequate Care of the Mother Helps, but Does Not Close the Gap

Infant Mortality Rate and Percentage of Low-Birthweight Babies, by Adequacy of Mother's Health Care and by Race, New York City, 1968

Infant viability and quality of mother's care[a]	Black[b]	White[b]	Ratio: black to white
Infant mortality rate			
All mothers	35.7	15.2	2.4
Adequate	21.0	12.6	1.7
Intermediate	25.4	13.7	1.9
Inadequate	48.1	25.8	1.9
Percent of low-birthweight babies			
All mothers	16	8	2.0
Adequate	11	7	1.6
Intermediate	13	8	1.6
Inadequate	19	12	1.6

(Table 6–5, continued)

[a] Quality-of-care categories are based on the time of first prenatal visit, on the number of prenatal visits, and on the hospital service, whether ward or private.

[b] Native-born black and native-born white.

Source: Derived from National Academy of Sciences, Institute of Medicine, Panel on Health Services Research, *Infant Death: An Analysis by Maternal Risk and Health Care* (Washington, D.C.: National Academy of Sciences, 1973), Tables 1–1, 1–8, pp. 22, 38.

TABLE 6–6

Black Infants Remain, Since 1940, Almost Twice as Likely to Die as White Infants Even Though Mortality Rates Have Dropped Sharply—by Two-Thirds—for Both

Infant Mortality Rates[a] by Race, Decennial Years 1940–70, and 1974

Year	Black[b]	White	Ratio:[c] black to white
1940	74	43	1.7
1950	45	27	1.7
1960	43	23	1.9
1970	31	18	1.7
1974	25	15	1.7

[a] Deaths per 1,000 live births of infants under 1 year old.

[b] Negro and other nonwhite races.

[c] Rates were rounded to the nearest whole number for easy reading, but ratios are based on data correct to the nearest tenth.

Source: Derived from NCHS, *Vital Statistics Rates in the United States, 1940–1960* (Washington, D.C.: Government Printing Office, 1968), Table 38, p. 206; NCHS, *Vital Statistics of the United States, 1971, Vol. 2, Mortality, Pt. A* (Washington, D.C.: Government Printing Office, 1975), Table 2–1, p. 2–3; unpublished data from the National Center for Health Statistics.

TABLE 6–7

Half the Black Babies but Few White Ones Had No Doctor to Deliver Them in 1940; by the Seventies a Doctor Delivered Almost All Babies

Percentage of Live Births Without a Physician Present, by Race, Selected Years, 1940–71

Year	Black[a]	White
1940	49	4
1945	38	2
1950	28	1
1955	17	1
1960[b]	12	1
1965[b]	8	1
1971[b]	2	[c]

[a] Negro and other nonwhite races.
[b] Based on 50 percent sample of births.
[c] Less than 0.5 percent.

Source: Derived from NCHS, *Vital Statistics of the United States, Vol. 1, Natality* (Washington, D.C.: Government Printing Office, 1975), Table 1–35, p. 1–35.

TABLE 6–8

Black Mothers Are Over Three Times as Likely to Die in Childbirth as White Mothers, at Least Since 1950; but the Danger Has Fallen to Low Levels in Both Groups

Maternal Mortality Rates[a] [c] by Race, Decennial Years 1940–70, and 1974

Year	Black[b]	White	Ratio:[c] black to white
1940	774	320	2.4
1950	222	61	3.6
1960	98	26	3.8
1970	56	14	4.0
1974	35	10	3.5

[a] Maternal deaths per 100,000 live births.

[b] Negro and other nonwhite races.

[c] Rates were rounded to the nearest whole number for easy reading, but ratios are based on data correct to the nearest tenth.

Source: Derived from NCHS, *Vital Statistics Rates in the United States 1940–1960* (Washington, D.C.: Government Printing Office, 1968), Table 45, pp. 296–7; NCHS, *Vital Statistics of the United States, 1971, Vol. 2, Mortality, Pt. A* (Washington, D.C.: Government Printing Office, 1975), Table 1–16, p. 1–72; unpublished data from the National Center for Health Statistics.

TABLE 6-9

*Death from Chronic Illness and Flus Has Dropped Markedly Since 1940,
but the Black Rate Far Exceeded the White Even in 1974*

**Death Rates from Several Major Diseases, by Race, for 35–44-Year-Olds, 1940
and 1974**

Disease and year		Death rates[a] Black[b]	White	Ratio:[a] black to white
Diabetes	1940	16	6	2.9
	1974	11	3	3.1
Flu and	1940	92	21	4.3
pneumonia	1974	17	4	4.0
Hypertension	1950[c]	19	2	7.8
	1974	5	[d]	11.8
Tuberculosis	1940	174	46	3.8
	1974	5	[d]	12.3

[a] Rates are per 100,000 population. They were rounded to the nearest whole number
for easy reading, but ratios are based on data correct to the nearest tenth.

[b] Negro and other nonwhite races.

[c] Data for 1940 were not available.

[d] Less than 0.5.

Source: Derived from NCHS, *Vital Statistics in the United States, 1940–1960* (Wash-
ington, D.C.: Government Printing Office, 1968), Tables 63, 69, pp. 378, 542,
778–85; U.S. Bureau of the Census, *Vital Statistics of the United States, 1940,
Pt. 1, Natality and Mortality Data for the United States Tabulated by Place of
Occurrence with Supplemental Tables for Hawaii, Puerto Rico and the Virgin
Islands* (Washington, D.C.: Government Printing Office, 1943), Table 11, pp.
210–11; "Advance Report, Final Mortality Statistics, 1974" *Monthly Vital
Statistics Report* 24 (3 February 1976), Table 8, pp. 16–7; unpublished data
from the National Center for Health Statistics.

TABLE 6–10

Blacks in Middle Age Are More Likely than Whites to Have Treatable
Chronic Diseases, and Much More Likely to Die of Them

Incidence of Illness and Death from Diabetes, Heart Disease, and Hypertension
in 45–64-Year-Olds, 1972

Disease	Illness			Death		
	Rates[a]		Ratio: black to white	Rates[a]		Ratio: black to white
	Black[b]	White		Black[b]	White	
Diabetes[c]	70	40	1.8	54	18	3.0
Heart disease	92	88	1.1	561	395	1.4
Hypertension	197	119	1.7	15	2	7.5

[a] Rates per 1,000 population. They were rounded to the nearest whole number for easy reading, but ratios are based on data correct to the nearest tenth.
[b] Negro and other nonwhite races.
[c] Data are for 1973.

Source: Derived from NCHS, *Prevalence of Chronic Circulation Conditions, United States, 1972,* Vital and Health Statistics, Series 10, No. 94, 1974, Tables 1, 8, pp. 20, 27; NCHS, *Health, United States, 1975,* 1976, Tables CD II. 27, CD III. 23, CD III. 26, CD IV. 4, pp. 397, 481, 487, 557; NCHS, *Vital Statistics of the United States, 1972, Vol. 2, Mortality, Pt. A* (Washington, D.C.: Government Printing Office, 1976), Tables 1–8, 1–26, pp. 1–14–7, 1–216–21; NCHS, *Vital Statistics of the United States, 1973, Vol. 2, Mortality, Pt. B* (Washington, D.C.: Government Printing Office, 1975), Table 7–5, pp. 7–154–5; unpublished data from National Center for Health Statistics; CPR, Series P–25, No. 614, *Estimates of the Population of the United States by Age, Sex and Race, 1970 to 1975,* Table 2, pp. 19–20.

TABLE 6–11

*Blacks Have Tended to Receive Less Hospital Care than Whites During
the Year Before Their Death*

**Extent of Hospital Care During Last Year Before Death, by Race,
1961 and 1965**

Extent of hospital care and year	Black[a]	White
Percent hospitalized		
1961	64	73
1965	66	74
Hospital days, per hospitalized person		
1961	45	65
1965	55	84

[a] Negro and other nonwhite races.

Source: Derived from NCHS, *Expenses for Hospital and Institutional Care During the
Last Year of Life for Adults Who Died in 1964 or 1965, United States,* Vital
and Health Statistics, Series 22, No. 11, 1971, Tables 2, 12, pp. 23, 35; NCHS,
Hospitalization in the Last Year of Life, United States, 1961, Vital and Health
Statistics, Series 22, No. 2, 1966, Tables 7, 12, pp. 20, 28.

TABLE 6–12

*Black Patients Are Much More Likely than White Patients to Get Their
Medical Attention in a Hospital Clinic or Emergency Room*

**Percentage of All Doctor Visits in Hospital Clinic or Emergency Room, by
Race, Selected Years, 1963–73**

Year	Black[a]	White	Ratio: black to white
1963–64	32	10	3.2
1966–67	26	8	3.3
1969	23	9	2.6
1973	23	9	2.6

[a] Negro and other nonwhite races.

Source: Derived from NCHS, *Physician Visits by Place of Visit and Type of Service,
United States, July 1963–June 1964,* Vital and Health Statistics, Series 10, No.
18, 1965, Table 12, p. 24; NCHS, *Volume of Physician Visits, United States,
June 1966–June 1967,* Vital and Health Statistics, Series 10, No. 49, 1968,
Table 15, p. 30; NCHS, *Age Patterns in Medical Care, Illness, and Disability,
United States, 1968–1969,* Vital and Health Statistics, Series 10, No. 70, 1972,
Table 11, p. 32; NCHS, *Health, United States, 1975,* 1976, Table CD. I. 52,
p. 293.

TABLE 6–13

Mothers of Black Infants Were Less Likely to Have Insurance for Maternity Care than Others at Almost Every Income Level in the Mid-Sixties; Most Black and White Mothers Had Insurance at Incomes Above the Average

Percentage of Mothers Without Insurance for Maternity Care, by Family Income and Race of Infant, 1964–66

Family income[a]	Black[b]	White
All mothers	62	37
Less than $1,000	88	81
$ 1,000–2,999	75	76
3,000–4,999	59	55
5,000–6,999	33	26
7,000–9,999	30	17
10,000 or more	35	18

[a] Median income in 1965 was $6,957.
[b] Negro and other nonwhite races.

Source: Derived from NCHS, *Health Insurance Coverage for Maternity Care: Legitimate Live Births, United States, 1964–1966,* Vital and Health Statistics, Series 22, No. 12, 1971, Table 1, p. 19.

TABLE 6–14

Hospital and Surgical Insurance Remains Much Less Prevalent Among Blacks than Whites, and Coverage Rose Only Moderately in a Decade

Percentage of Persons Under 65 Covered by Hospital and Surgical Insurance, by Race, 1962–63, 1968, and 1974

Type of insurance and year	Black[a]	White	Difference
Hospital insurance			
1962–63[b]	55	76	21
1968	56	81	25
1974	58	81	23
Surgical insurance			
1962–63[b]	48	71	23
1968	54	80	26
1974	56	79	23

[a] Negro and other nonwhite races.
[b] For families and persons of all ages.

Source: Derived from NCHS, *Family Hospital and Surgical Insurance Coverage, United States, July 1962–June 1963,* Vital and Health Statistics, Series 10, No. 42, 1967, Table 7, pp. 28–9; NCHS, *Hospital and Surgical Insurance Coverage, United States, 1968,* Vital Statistics and Health, Series 10, No. 66, 1972, Table 2, p. 17; "Hospital and Surgical Coverage Among Persons Under 65 Years of Age in the United States, 1974," *Monthly Vital Statistics Report* 25 (19 May 1976), Table 3, p. 4.

TABLE 6–15

Health Expenses Rise with Income and Are About the Same, Black or White, at Comparable Incomes[a]

Health Expenses per Person, by Family Income and Race, 1970

Family income	Black[b]	White
Total	$143	$189
Under $5,000[a]	97	154
$5,000–9,999	165	170
10,000 and over	219	222

[a] The disparity in expenditures of incomes below $5,000 in 1970 reflects the larger proportion of whites than blacks close to the upper limit of the income interval.
[b] Negro and other nonwhite races.

Source: Derived from NCHS, *Personal Out of Pocket Health Expenses, United States, 1970,* Vital and Health Statistics, Series 10, No. 91, 1974, Table F, p. 7.

TABLE 6–16

Blacks Are Less Likely to Be Covered by Medical than Hospital Insurance Under Medicare, and Are Less Likely to Be Served than Whites; Once Served, Dollars Reimbursed Are Equal for Hospital Care but Less for Medical Care

Percentage Covered and Served by Medicare and Dollars Reimbursed, by Race, 1967, 1969, and 1973

Item	Black[a]	White
Percent of 65+ persons enrolled		
Hospital insurance—Part A		
1967	91	98
1969	91	98
1973	91	97
Medical insurance—Part B		
1967	77	92
1969	83	95
1973	86	96
Percent of 65+ persons using, 1969		
Hospital insurance	15	21
Medical insurance	23	42
Dollars reimbursed, 1969		
Hospital insurance		
Per person served	$1,019	$1,019
Per person enrolled	170	216
Per person 65+	159	214
Medical insurance		
Per person served	$ 182	$ 211
Per person enrolled	62	91
Per person 65+	52	87

[a] Negro and other nonwhite races.

Source: Derived from U.S., Social Security Administration, Office of Research and Statistics, *Medicare: Health Insurance for the Aged, 1967, Sec. 2, Persons Enrolled in the Health Insurance Program* (Washington, D.C.: Government Printing Office, 1972), Table 2.1, pp. 2–2, 2–11; idem, *Medicare: Health Insurance for the Aged, 1969, Sec. 2, Persons Enrolled in the Health Insurance Program* (Washington, D.C.: Government Printing Office, 1972), Table 2.1, pp. 2–2, 2–10; idem, *Medicare: Health Insurance for the Aged and Disabled, 1973, Sec. 2, Persons Enrolled in the Health Insurance Program* (Washington, D.C.: Government Printing Office, 1975), Table 2.2, pp. 2–4, 2–13; CPR, Series P–25, No. 519, *Estimates of the Population of the United States by Age, Sex and Race, April 1, 1960–July 1, 1973,* Table 30, p. 2; CPR, Series P–25, No. 614, *Estimates of the Population of the United States by Age, Sex and Race,* Table 2, p. 19; U.S. Social Security Administration, Office of Research and Statistics, *Medicare: Health Insurance for the Aged, 1969, Sec. 1, Summary Utilization and Reimbursement by Person* (Washington, D.C.: Government Printing Office, 1975), Table 1.12–3, pp. 1–21–1.

TABLE 6–17

Hospitalization Rates Have Risen Markedly Among the Elderly Since the 1960s—Doctors' Visits Less So; a Quarter of Black and White Elderly Had Not Seen a Doctor in 1972–73

Persons 65 Years Old and Over Who Were Hospitalized and Percentage with No Physician Visits, Selected Years, 1963–73

Item and year	Black[a]	White	Ratio: black to white
Hospitalized (persons per 1,000 population)			
1965–66	79	134	.59
1968	126	158	.80
1972	136	170	.80
	Black[a]	White	Difference
No physician visits in past year			
1963–64	36	31	5
1969	33	28	5
1973	25	23	2

[a] Negro and other nonwhite races.

Source: Derived from NCHS, *Persons Hospitalized by Number of Hospital Episodes and Days in a Year, United States, July 1965–June 1966,* Vital and Health Statistics, Series 10, No. 50, 1969, Table D, p. 9; NCHS, *Persons Hospitalized by Number of Hospital Episodes and Days in a Year, United States, 1968,* Vital and Health Statistics, Series 10, No. 64, 1971, Table B, p. 5; American Public Health Association, *Minority Health Chart Book,* prepared for its 102nd Annual Meeting, New Orleans, October 1974, and published by the U.S. Public Health Service, p. 67; NCHS, *Physician Visits: Intervals of Visits and Children's Routine Checkup, United States, July 1963–June 1964,* Vital and Health Statistics, Series 10, No. 19, 1965, Table 14, p. 29; NCHS, *Age Patterns in Medical Care, Illness and Disability, United States, 1968–1969,* Vital and Health Statistics, Series 10, No. 70, 1972, Table 15, p. 36; NCHS, *Health, United States, 1975,* Table CD. IV–8, p. 565.

TABLE 6–18

*Blacks Rose in Relative Numbers Only in the Lower-Paid Health
Professions in the Thirty Years 1940–70*

**Proportion of Black and White Medical Personnel, by Profession,
1940 and 1970**

Profession and year	Black[a] as percent of total	Medical personnel (per 100,000 population)	
		Black[a]	White
Physicians			
1940	2	27	136
1970	2	27	152
Dentists			
1940	2	11	57
1970	2	9	49
Nurses			
1940	2	53	294
1970	8	276	425
Pharmacists			
1940	1	6	63
1970	2	11	59
Technicians— medical and dental			
1950[b]	3	17	54
1970	9	107	130

[a] Negro only.
[b] Data for 1940 were not available.

Source: Derived from 1940 Census of Population, *The Labor Force, Vol. 3, Pt. 1, U.S. Summary,* Table 62, p. 90; idem, *Characteristics of the Population, Vol. 2, Pt. 1, U.S. Summary and Alabama,* Table 4, p. 19; 1950 Census of Population, *Characteristics of the Population, Vol. 2, Pt. 1, U.S. Summary,* Table 128, pp. 1–276, 1–278; idem, *Characteristics of the Population, Vol. 2, Pt. 1, U.S. Summary,* Table 35, pp. 1–87; 1970 Census of Population, *Characteristics of the Population, Vol. 1, Pt. 1, Sec. 2, U.S. Summary,* Table 223, p. 1–739; idem, *Subject Reports, PC (2)–1B, Negro Population,* Table 1, p. 1.

TABLE 6–19

Almost All Chiefly White Medical Schools Have Moved from Outright Refusal to Admit Blacks to Enrolling Some—Not Many—in a Generation

Integration Policy of Predominantly White Medical Schools, 1948 and 1971 School Years

Integration policy about black[a] enrollment	1947–48	1970–71
All schools	76	103
Schools saying:		
Blacks refused	26	0
Blacks admitted	50	103
Blacks enrolled	27	91
Over 20 blacks being trained	0	13

[a] Negro only.

Source: Derived from Montague Cobb, *Progress and Portents for the Negro in Medicine* (New York: National Association for the Advancement of Colored People, 1948), p. 33; Association of American Medical Colleges, *Minority Student Opportunities in United States Medical Schools, 1971–72* (Washington, D.C.: Association of American Medical Colleges, 1971).

TABLE 6–20

It Took Almost Four Decades for Black Medical Students to Increase from 2 to 6 Percent of the Total; Most of the Increase Came After 1970

Number and Percentage of Blacks in Total Enrollment in Medical Schools, Selected School Years, 1939–76

Year	Total	Number Black[a]	Percent Black[a]
1938–39	21,302	350	2
1948–49	23,670	612	3
1955–56	28,639	761	3
1969–70	37,756	1,042	3
1975–76	55,818	3,456	6

[a] Negro only.

Source: Derived from James L. Curtis, *Blacks, Medical School and Society* (Ann Arbor: University of Michigan Press, 1971), Table 3, p. 34; T. L. Gordon and W. F. Dube, "Medical Student Enrollment, 1971–72 Through 1975–76 (Datagram)," *Journal of Medical Education* 51 (1976): 146.

7
Making Do

I got plenty o' nothin'
And nothin's plenty for me.
Got no car
Got no mule
Got no misery.
(From *Porgy and Bess* by George Gershwin)

THOUGH WHITE AMERICANS eagerly accepted the picture of Porgy in Gershwin's 1935 opera, black Americans weren't content with plenty of nothing. Along with other Americans they wanted a steady job, decent wages, and some security.

The Income-Security System

In that desire they recognized a central fact of economic life: the most important source of income, past or present, for the great majority of Americans is wages and salaries. Economic security can be loosely described as a system that includes all the many ways that people have of acquiring income. Some are so informal as scarcely to be identified as belonging to a system (like mowing lawns or baby-sitting), but others are carefully planned and administered by vast public and private bureaucracies established for that purpose. Three forms of income maintenance tie future incomes to past and present salaries—Social Security, private pensions, and unemployment insurance. Together with wages these four sources of income represent nearly all the money middle-income people are likely to have. For all of the very rich, and some of the very poor, "the system" includes two additional elements: wealth and welfare.

The institutionalized income security programs are virtually all products of the thirties, when the Depression jolted America into the

236

realization that devastating economic conditions could occur even here. The basic concern of those years was to provide a framework in which most people could be protected against precipitous drops in income, whether from unemployment, retirement, disability, or death of a breadwinner. Reflected in large measure in the Social Security Act of 1935, the development of that system brought about a remarkable change in the lives of ordinary Americans. But it took time.

In 1940, the average worker had to assume that old age would mean work as usual, except probably for fewer hours and at lower pay. Old age meant the fear of being alone and without resources, the fear of having no way to buy medicine or even food, the danger of having no way to hold on to a home or the accumulated possessions of a lifetime, the indignity of having to be a burden on a struggling son or daughter. That is perhaps the biggest difference between 1940 and the present. Social Security benefits are still low, but they have bought us some relief from the terrible fear of being old and destitute.

For black Americans that security has come more slowly and less consistently, just because they held jobs that were not covered by the system until later, and because they worked for wages that yielded lower benefits in the end. But for black as well as white there is now some measure of income security. The same things might be said for most of the component parts of the system: workmen's compensation, unemployment insurance, disability insurance, survivors' insurance, and the minimum wage.[1] All of them are tied either to previous work experience and wages or to the industries or firms covered. As time has passed, each has contributed to a growing sense of security against the anxiety that an accident or a layoff might mean automatic poverty or a job that paid virtually nothing. Veterans' benefits added yet another layer of security for those who had served in the armed forces.

Over the years each of these programs has developed along similar lines. Typically, they started out covering less than half of the labor force, and then broadened to include nearly all workers. Since blacks were disproportionately in employment that was not covered by the laws originally, they were less likely to be eligible for benefits than whites; and because the same industries that had no coverage tended to pay lower wages, coverage yielded small payments when it did come. Today the differences between black and white are closing slowly.

By 1966 this system of economic security had had nearly thirty years to mature. Many of the hopes of its designers for a comprehensive system were being borne out. Social Security retirement benefits had become almost universally available, even though it was not easy to live on those benefits alone. Survivors' and disability benefits—added to the program in 1939 and 1954 respectively[2]—had also grown, and by then were part of the "securities" in the portfolio of every American. And as they grew, their counterparts in the welfare system—the Old Age Assistance program and the welfare program for those who were both poor and disabled—carried less of the burden for poverty from those causes. Soon those whose disabilities were related to work, and virtually all the elderly, found themselves covered by Social Security disability and retirement benefits. One welfare program that did not decline was the one providing aid for children in families too poor to care for them.[3] By 1966 Aid to Families with Dependent Children (AFDC) had become the bane of virtually every taxpayer and politician in the country as well as the exasperation of every social policy designer. AFDC not only showed no signs of withering away, even with the economy growing and low unemployment, it grew faster during the sixties than it had at any time in the past.

These public income support mechanisms reached out to large numbers of those who remained poor even with benefits, as well as to many who would have been poor without them. In 1966, nearly 29 million Americans were found in families with incomes below the officially defined poverty line, and by 1974, 24 million still had incomes so low as to be counted poor. Falling into this category were about a third of all black Americans, including 40 percent of all black individuals living alone and half of the families in which a black woman was the breadwinner.[4]

When HEW looked at its programs in 1965, they saw that many of the poor were not being helped by them. A large proportion of those living below the poverty line—80 percent—received no public assistance. One-third of that 80 percent were thought to be eligible by the strict welfare standards of the day, yet had not received financial aid.[5] The gaps in coverage between blacks and whites were significant. Virtually every public income support device—including Social Security, unemployment insurance, veterans' benefits, as well as public assistance—was reaching a larger proportion of poor whites than poor blacks. Or, the benefits brought more whites who were poor out of poverty or reduced the extent of their poverty more (Table 7–1). Even where blacks seem to have been the more frequent beneficiaries, as in the unemployment insurance program, the payments that went to whites filled more of their income needs and were more likely to lift them out of poverty.[6] The system was working relatively well and as expected for whites; it worked less well for blacks. And because they were less well served by the more acceptable major security programs (the automatic kind that require no means test), blacks had more need of the less acceptable, more demeaning, more grudgingly bestowed part of the system—welfare. Excluded longer from other forms of support, or given lower benefits when covered, blacks were forced into a greater dependence on welfare, and then roundly condemned for that dependence. Even the fact that the welfare system was only half as likely to lift blacks out of poverty as whites did not free blacks from the charge of being freeloaders on the public coffers.

The income security system was developed to serve most ordinary Americans by ultimately covering all current and past workers. Although the very rich and very poor might participate, it was expected to give economic security primarily to that three-fourths of the population in the middle-income category. And, as judged by the most commonly used measure, median income,[7] the black middle-income group is poorer by nearly $6,000 ($14,268 versus $8,779 in 1975) than the white (Table 7–2).

White family income has always been substantially higher than black, though the amount of white advantage has varied somewhat over the years[8] (Table 7–2). In 1947 blacks had slightly more than half of white median income. This grew to 57 percent during the Korean War, but slipped back quickly after the war. Black median family income hovered around 52 to 53 percent of whites' until well into the prosperous sixties, when it peaked at 62 percent of whites'; by 1973 it had fallen back to 58 percent, and again rose to 62 percent in 1975.

What causes the gap in median incomes is a somewhat different matter from what causes changes in the gap from year to year. Discrimination that takes the form of denying jobs to blacks because of their race has a direct and obvious effect on incomes. But that kind of discrimination is not the only cause. Some causes of the income gap have only a very tenuous or no direct relation to racial discrimination—basic features like the age structure of the population or region of residence. Other forces involve discrimination but affect income only indirectly. The role of discrimination in something like health status provides a good example. Blacks may have lower incomes in part because they are more often ill or disabled, but illness or disability itself may be the result of blacks' having been confined by discrimination to more dangerous or debilitating jobs. Or, wages that are set lower because of discrimination may have left blacks with less access to medical care, and poorer health—and, once again, lower incomes. It matters little whether the discrimination is direct or indirect if the result is lower incomes.

Working people with incomes in the middle range (from $7,000 to $25,000 in 1969) derive almost all (about 75 percent) of their incomes from labor.[9] That is true for both black and white. Even people who are retired may be said to be living on earned incomes, because their pensions and Social Security benefits are wage-related and based on past labor income. It is only in the economic lives of the richest and the poorest that wages and salaries account for less. The incomes of the poor draw heavily on a combination of Social Security and other government sources; and much of the income of the rich comes from profits, rents, and the returns from property ownership (Table 7–3). Because blacks are more dependent on wage and salary income, as a group they are more exposed to economic risk than whites. Layoffs, short hours, illnesses, and generally bad economic times hit blacks harder than whites, whose incomes are more often from several sources.

Not only do blacks rely more heavily on labor income, they must put forth considerably more effort to achieve the same income as whites. That means that, typically, more black family members than white must work just to reach the same level of family income (Table 7–4).

All of the differences—greater dependence on wages, greater vulnerability to economic conditions, the need for more wage earners—are part of what translates into lower family incomes. Each year the Bureau of Labor Statistics publishes family budgets at three levels of living, an "intermediate" and two that represent standards somewhat higher and lower. In 1974 the intermediate budget for an urban family of four was set at $14,333 while the lower budget was set at $9,198.[10] That year the median income of white families was not quite $1,000 lower than the *intermediate* budget level, while black median family incomes were $1,200 less than the *lower* budget level. Black incomes permit families a life-style substantially below what the BLS and most Americans would regard as a moderate standard of living. In practical terms, that means that most black families are likely to have 25 to 40 percent less to spend on such basic budget items as food, rent, and clothing than white families with nothing more luxurious than an "intermediate" style of life.

Social Security and Unemployment Insurance

The principal income security program for workers and their dependents is Social Security (Old Age, Survivors, and Disability Insurance—OASDI). Among social welfare programs, Social Security is the most objective and the least arbitrary, cumbersome, or demeaning. It is also the largest, and has had a greater impact on preventing and alleviating poverty than any other income maintenance program.

Social Security was established in 1935 as a means of insuring against the largest unavoidable causes of reduced income—old age and retirement. Workers and their employers pay equal amounts into the Social Security fund, regardless of whether the workers are janitors or professionals. Workers receive these social insurance benefits on retirement as a matter of right without regard to how rich or poor they may be. Rockefellers who have worked in covered employment are just as entitled to receive Social Security benefits at age sixty-five as their family chauffeurs.

The right to OASDI benefits is conditioned only on previous participation in the system. Everyone participates by paying into the fund for a given period of time, and benefits are set with some relationship to earnings. What workers earn determines how much they get. Because Social Security depends in the first place on earnings (and on whether the industry or establishment was always covered under the system), it indirectly perpetuates the wage discrimination operating in the labor market.[11]

Social Security began making payments in 1940, but only to workers sixty-five years old or over who had worked in covered establishments of a certain size, and in commerce or industry for a year and a half.[12] Many blacks got jobs in covered industries during World War II, but then quickly lost them and so lost much of these gains after 1945.[13] A major liberalization of the act came in 1950, when workers with six quarters (one-and-a-half years) of covered employment became fully insured, although at very low benefits. Thus,

700,000 elderly people were made eligible for benefits. The 1950 amendments covered workers in many additional industries: regularly employed farm and domestic workers, self-employed persons not in agriculture, federal employees not under the civil service retirement system, people employed by U.S. firms outside the continental United States, and state and local government workers at the option of their employers.[14] Just after the 1950 amendments applications from blacks, particularly from black women, rose dramatically. The *Social Security Bulletin* for November 1951 noted:

> The extension of coverage to domestic employment under the 1950 amendments resulted in an unprecedented rise in the number of accounts established for Negroes, particularly for Negro women. During January–March 1951, 240,000 account numbers were issued to Negroes; for the corresponding quarters of the years 1947–1950, the average was 58,000. Negroes represented 18 percent of all applicants, a percentage that was larger than for any other quarter on record.[15]

But these new eligibles had earned low wages, had correspondingly low wage credits in the fund, and so received low benefits. Their benefits averaged $25.37 per month, while those eligible under the earlier rules averaged $49.02, or almost twice as much.[16]

The black elderly have always been more likely to continue working well into old age simply because they were always less likely to have income from wealth to fall back on, or from pension plans and other retirement arrangements. Yet despite their traditionally higher labor-force participation, the proportion of elderly blacks receiving OASDI benefits has always been substantially lower than the proportion of whites. During the fifties this disparity increased as more of the population reaching retirement age were entitled to Social Security based on earnings from before 1950 when most blacks were still not found in covered employment. But then it narrowed appreciably when the effect of coverage extensions, particularly the 1950 expansion, began to be felt and caused the number of black recipients to rise sharply. The difference between the two groups had still not disappeared by 1975, when 95 percent of elderly whites and 87 percent of elderly blacks were drawing benefits from what most Americans had come to regard as a universal retirement insurance system (Table 7–5).

For those on the receiving end the most important thing about Social Security is the size of the retirement check. Because OASDI is the only source of income for many elderly people (68 percent of the black elderly and 35 percent of the white in 1967), it plays a critical role in their economic lives.[17] The size of these benefits is related to race in two ways. Because blacks tend to have lower wages during their working lives, the retirement benefits they receive tend to be lower than the benefits received by whites. But another feature of the system compensates for the relatively poor position of black workers. Benefits are set relatively higher for those who earned less during their working lives; thus, their so-called replacement ratio (the benefits replacing a proportion of previous income) is high. Though blacks suffer relatively less of a drop in their lower incomes than others, the "compensation" is as much a reflection on their poor wages during their working years as it is on the equity of the Social Security system, which takes relatively more from their salaries than from the salaries of others. The "better deal" that lower-income workers could be said to get out of Social Security is one "deal" that many blacks would gladly trade for better wages during a lifetime of work. The dollars they receive are barely enough to buy groceries and pay the rent; landlords are not interested in "replacement ratios."

Even though the benefits low-income retirees receive may be relatively generous in actuarial terms, they turn out to be so low that too often they leave beneficiaries below the official poverty line (Table 7–6). Retired black workers, who generally had lower earnings, would be concentrated in the lower reaches of the benefit distribution. Considering the benefits and poverty thresholds in Table 7–6, many workers and families who were middle-income during their working years must be in poverty or close to it in their old age.

The relationship of black benefit levels to white has been rather stable over the years, usually fluctuating between 70 and 80 percent of white (Table 7–7). In that, as in so many ways, Social Security reflects our discriminatory society, even though the discrepancies are gradually diminishing, in OASDI as in other aspects, between the lives of black and white workers.

The other income security mechanism available to Americans who lose their jobs is unemployment insurance (UI). Established by the Social Security Act of 1935, the states set up programs financed by a payroll tax on employers.[18] UI was seen both as a mechanism for maintaining an individual worker's purchasing power, and as a countercyclical force that would automatically pump buying power into the national economy during recessions. It began by paying a relatively high proportion of average wages. In 1938, benefits equaled 43 percent of the average weekly wage, at that time a princely $10.94 per week.[19] In the 1940s, benefits rose slower than wages, and by 1951 they were only 32 percent of average weekly earnings. Since then, benefits have been between 32 and 36 percent of average weekly wages, and in 1974 averaged $64.25 per week.[20]

State administration has meant that many provisions, especially benefit levels, vary considerably. In 1975, maximum benefits ranged from $60 per week in Mississippi to $127 per week in the District of Columbia.[21] Across the country, until the prolonged recession of the mid-seventies, benefits were usually available for 26 weeks; in 1976, Congress temporarily extended that right to an additional 39 weeks.

In theory the UI program means that workers will not be plunged into poverty if their jobs disappear. While they look for work, UI is expected to keep food on the family table and creditors from the family door. But the practice has left some holes in the theory. The most serious gap was created when Congress chose only to cover the workers in certain industries, leaving more than one-half (53 percent in 1938) of the civilian labor force without UI protection when the program began in the thirties. Even in the mid-seventies, some 20 percent of all workers were still not covered by the protections that the UI program had to offer.[22] For blacks those omissions in coverage have had serious implications. Particularly in the early years of the program when discrimination kept blacks out of the very industries in which UI was available, the lack of UI coverage left blacks much more vulnerable when unemployment hit. At least until 1960 there was always a sizable difference in the degree to which black and white knew the protections of UI, and in 1970 there was still an estimated gap of 7 percentage points between the two (Table 7–8).

Even though industry coverage has now become almost universal, nevertheless, startling as it may seem, most of the unemployed at any one time do not receive UI benefits. Workers are not eligible for benefits unless their circumstances meet more than the single criterion of being unemployed from a job they held in covered employment. In addition, they must not have left their jobs voluntarily without good cause, must have been working and their employers paying into the system for a statutory minimum number of months, must have been earning above a state-determined minimum, must not have been discharged for job-related misconduct, and must not have exhausted their period of benefits. New entrants into the labor force cannot collect UI; to collect, a worker must have had a job in covered employment for a period of time first.

The largest proportions of unemployed actually collected benefits in the periods immediately following both World War II and the Korean War, because in both instances former service personnel were covered by special, temporary programs.[23] In the years since 1954, only rarely have more than half the unemployed received unemployment insurance benefits (Table 7–9).

An even lower proportion of black than white unemployed have collected UI benefits. While blacks made up between 18 and 21 percent of the unemployed between 1969 and 1975, only 13 to 15 percent of UI benefit recipients were black.[24] What causes this gap? Again, some of it can be accounted for by fewer black than white workers being covered by the system. A small amount may be due to blacks being unemployed longer and so exhausting their benefits, and to a somewhat larger proportion of blacks newly entering the labor force. Slightly more whites leave their jobs voluntarily, so voluntary quitting cannot cause the difference.

These results parallel those of the larger OASDI system. There is no reason to believe that outright racial discrimination is taking place in unemployment insurance offices. However, all the discriminatory mechanisms in the job market which hurt blacks when it comes to retirement benefits also cause them to get less out of the UI system than whites.

Private Pensions

Despite its advantages, the Social Security system does not provide benefits high enough to support retired workers and their families at an adequate enough level, and so increasing numbers of workers have turned to private pension plans. Between 1945 and 1972, the number of workers covered by private pension plans had grown from a little less than 5 million to more than 23 million.[25] But despite high hopes, the growing assortment of private pension offerings has not made a significant difference in the economic lives of more than a few of the elderly. And for many of the same reasons that Social Security proves less than adequate for the black elderly, so do the private pension plans.

Perhaps the most important difference between Social Security and private pensions is eligibility. Any worker with one-and-a-half years of experience in covered employment is entitled to some Social

Security benefits, but many workers in jobs covered by private pensions will never get any benefits at all. The explanation lies in what is called "vested" rights to a pension. Once a worker has a vested right, he cannot lose his pension benefits even if he retires early or is let go. Social Security is a fully vested retirement program.[26] Once a worker has qualified for benefits, they cannot be withheld even if the worker changes jobs or stops working altogether. Before the pension reforms enacted by Congress in 1974, and made effective January 1, 1976, many private plans did not provide for vesting on any terms, or provided for vesting only after long years of work. One-third of whites and only one-fourth of blacks who were in jobs covered by private pensions were in vested systems in 1972.[27] In 1971, a Senate Labor Subcommittee investigation into private pension plans revealed that out of 87 plans covering 3.1 million workers, 51 plans required eleven or more years of employment for vesting.[28] Because white workers, particularly white men, tend to have longer job tenure than blacks, they can more often rely on future benefits from their contributions to a pension plan, though the proportion who benefits is not very large in either case. In the 51 plans investigated in 1971, 70 percent of all participants over the twenty-year period covered in the study had forfeited their benefits by leaving or being let go, and 23 percent of this group had already had five or more years of work under the plan.[29] If the results were not so tragic, certain restrictive vesting requirements would simply be ludicrous:

> Mr. X began employment for a Midwest meat-packing company in 1927, at one of the employer's two plants in the same city. During World War II, he was sent to work in the other plant in the city because of the need to fulfill government contracts. He remained there until 1965 when the plant closed. The employers would not permit him to transfer back to the former plant as a regular employee, but only as a casual and intermittent laborer at the former plant. When the plant was closed, Mr. X was paid a total of $231.55 for his accrued pension benefits, despite 38 years of continuous employment with the same employer. Since he was reemployed in his old plant as a casual laborer, he was not eligible for any pension benefits after 1965. In 1970, he was dismissed because he was overage at 65. He did not receive any pension benefits. In sum, this employee was dismissed at age 66 after 43 years of continuous employment with the same employer and with no benefits to him except $231.55 paid to him in 1965. Had he been permitted to carry his pension benefits and credits from both plants with the same employer, which were located a few streets apart, Mr. X would have been eligible for a pension.[30]

Largely because the requirements for vesting are so stringent, few of the elderly receive private pension benefits. Only 6 percent of the black elderly (singles or married couples) and 12 percent of the white received anything from private pensions in 1968,[31] and they did not get very much. The year before, median benefits from private plans yielded $900.[32] Only 7 percent of the elderly recipients drew $3,000 or more as the result of the long years it had taken to be vested.[33] Much as they do under Social Security, blacks, who usually earn less, also fare less well under the private plans. A sample of new retirees in 1969–70 showed that blacks with private pensions got only about 60 percent of what white pension beneficiaries received.[34]

Private pensions are still far less common than Social Security coverage (only about half of full-time white workers were covered by private plans in 1972, and just two-fifths of blacks),[35] and the differences that exist between black and white under the private plans are largely accounted for by their differing occupations. Black workers are disproportionally found in the labor and service occupations, which have low levels of coverage, and whites continue to be found more often in the professions, in which coverage is high.[36]

The operation of private pension plans is still another illustration of how racial discrimination can hurt blacks at many points along the way, even when the institution responsible in the end does not actively discriminate. What shows up for the black at the point of retirement as a lower rate of coverage or a smaller check began many years before with lower-level jobs, lower earnings, and the "last in, first out" syndrome. In the end, blacks forfeit private pension rights more often than whites, and even when collecting, draw benefits that are lower.

Taxes

Nothing is more certain, the saying goes, than death and taxes. Taxes fall on black and white alike, making no distinctions at the gas pump or the drugstore counter; assessing equally all who choose to buy what society regards as luxuries; making demands without distinction on those who operate a car; adding to the cost of telephone service and utilities no matter what the color of the users; and taxing nearly everyone's income. It is certainly true, as the poor understand instinctively and so well, that the rich often manage to avoid a fair share of their income taxes, but the white poor are just as shabbily treated in that way as the black. The important distinction occurs because blacks as a group have lower incomes, and taxes bear more heavily on lower-income people; that means that blacks carry a disproportionate share of our national tax burden.

Among our more popular national myths is the notion that ours is a progressive tax system, taking more from those who have more and requiring less from those who have little. As income rises, the percentage of income paid back in taxes is supposed to rise. A proportional tax system in which everyone pays the same percentage of income in taxes sounds "equal" but works out unfairly. Taking $1,200 from the income of a worker who is struggling to raise a family on $6,000 a year seems plainly harsher than taking $12,000 from the banker living comfortably on $60,000, even though the proportion of tax would be the same.

Yet the realities of the American tax system are such that when federal, state, and local taxes are all combined, the system turns out to be not progressive but proportional (actually taking the same percentage of income) for 90 percent of the American people. Under a variety of reasonable assumptions about who actually pays the corporate, personal, property, and Social Security payroll taxes, the record shows that nearly all American households lose the same proportion, about 19 to 25 percent, of their incomes to taxes. Only those with the very lowest and highest incomes carry a tax burden higher than twenty-five percent.[37]

The proportional system is unjust to low- and middle-income people because, in gross terms, to raise a certain amount of total national revenue, a proportional system takes more from them and less from the well-off than a progressive system will. As a nation we shift more of the tax burden onto those citizens who are least able to bear it. And blacks, who are rarely rich and disproportionately poor, fall more often into this group. Once again a neutral system proves not so neutral in its effects.

Black middle-income families are at a greater disadvantage than the simple dollar gap between them and middle-income white families suggests. The three largest income maintenance programs that primarily serve such families—Social Security, private pensions, unemployment insurance—and the tax system contribute to a thoroughgoing economic inequality. Middle-income blacks live much closer to poverty than middle-income whites and have less security to fall back on during old age or unemployment. Furthermore, because of their income position, they pay an unfair share of taxes.

Wealth, Power, and Race

Rich, wealthy, well-to-do, moneyed, affluent, loaded, in the chips: we all know it when we see it, but it isn't just money. Most people would agree that there is more to being wealthy than having a steady income. Being wealthy means, besides that income, owning real estate, stocks, bonds, securities, and flourishing enterprises, and having social and political power or having access to it. For most black people, discussion about wealth is largely academic, because they have little beyond income from earnings. But even if "rich" is defined narrowly in terms of income alone, it helps at least to give a sense of scale.

In 1971, Bostonians considered a family rich if they had an income (excluding other assets) of about $26,000 or more that year.[38] Nationally in that year, the lowest income a white family could have and still qualify as one of the top 5 percent of all white families in the country was $25,890. The Bostonians were more accurate than they could have known: those they called "rich" proved to be the 5 percent of American families taking in the most money annually.

Blacks who were rich in money terms alone were not as well-off as the whites since the ratio of black to white incomes in that lucky 5 percent had stayed below 70 percent until 1956, and by the mid-seventies had only reached 76 percent (Table 7–10). Family income grew for both groups in the years between 1947 and 1975, but blacks as a group were making far less than whites through all of that time. In fact, while the ratio of black to white incomes among the richest earners has improved a little, the actual dollar gap, in both current and real dollars, has widened.

If rich blacks appear to be doing better relative to rich whites than other black families to comparable whites (for whom, as shown above in Table 7–2, the black to white ratio was not even 2 to 3 in 1975), appearances are once again deceiving—a matter of how statistics are kept. The top 5 percent of the families for whom data are available by race[39] include, disproportionally, nonwhite people who are not black but are Chinese and Japanese. In both 1959 and 1969 nonwhite, nonblack families were only 6 to 10 percent of all nonwhites, across all income categories, but made up about one-third of families with more than $15,000 per year.[40]

Looked at objectively, the uppermost 5 percent of blacks are not so much rich as they are middle-income. The wealthiest black families generally have low incomes by any standard for defining "rich": about $20,000 to $22,000 per year in the early seventies, a period when such incomes were not considered "rich" by most Americans. The black rich differed greatly from their white counterparts in the source of their money as much as just in the number of dollars: more of the black income was from labor rather than wealth (Table 7–3). Since part of what it means to be "wealthy" involves having income from business and property rather than income from a job, blacks at the upper end of their income range do not qualify in this important respect. For it is not the size of yearly money income that makes the wealthy so secure, but the amount of wealth they hold and the power that yields. Wealth offers the most economic security, and it is the kind that is least available to blacks.

Over the years even though income has been rising, the concentration of great wealth in a few hands has scarcely changed at all. By the seventies, just as was true in the fifties, the richest one-half of 1 percent of the population (about 1 million people in 1969) has held about 20 percent of the nation's personal wealth. This extremely powerful, exceptionally wealthy elite owns well over two-fifths of all corporate stock, one-third of all bonds, nearly all of the trusts, and a substantial amount of other income-producing assets.[41]

The status of black wealth appears in sharp contrast. In 1967, when blacks' median income was 62 percent of whites', their famiily accumulation of wealth was only 19 percent that of white families.[42] Thus the average white family had wealth (that is, a backlog of assets) worth $20,153, whereas the average black family had only $3,779.[43]

Even this description overstates the position of black families. The wealth that blacks hold tends to be found in consumer assets such as homes and cars to a greater degree than is true of whites. Wealth is generally thought of as equity in business, stocks, bonds, and real estate—all of which are continually producing more wealth or income—rather than a home and the usual accumulations of everyday consumers. Technically the latter are wealth too, but they do not produce cash income and are not readily turned into cash when emergencies arise. Yet these kinds of wealth are nearly two-thirds of average black wealth holdings, compared with only one-third of whites'. Twice as much of the wealth in the hands of whites tends to be income-producing, the kind that produces more wealth in turn (Table 7–11).

These differences are evident even in a predominantly black city like Washington, D.C., where blacks have long owned businesses and have been middle-class for generations. In 1967, the average wealth holdings of whites in Washington was almost six times that of blacks.[44] Washington blacks held 82 percent of their net worth in real estate, mostly in their homes; white Washingtonians held only 18 percent of their wealth that way. On the other side, the white wealthy had 35 percent of their holdings in stocks and bonds, while blacks had only 5 percent of their wealth invested in this way.[45] Even in Washington, white wealth was both larger and more lucratively invested than was black wealth.

Another way of measuring family wealth is to compare the incomes derived from it. Very few families of either race can claim a substantial amount of such "property" income.[46] Only about 10 percent of black families and upwards of 20 percent of white families had property income of $1,000 or more in 1969 and 1974. Even among the few blacks who have so small a share of it, the maldistribution of property income is substantial. Less than 15 percent of black families (and about half of white families) had any property income at all (Table 7–12). And of those who have it, the blacks' average is only about one-third of whites'. This almost complete lack of representation among the propertied is especially important because such families are certainly the richest, the most economically secure, the best able to support worthy causes while amassing still more wealth and passing the accumulated riches on to their heirs.[47] Because of the nature and limitations of black wealth holdings, black families had only about an estimated 1 percent of total U.S. property income in 1974, assuming that black and white holdings of a similar nature realized the same returns. In 1967, black families' share of holdings of stocks, cash in banks, government bonds, and equity in real estate other than homes was estimated about the same: 1 percent.[48] The number of very wealthy families is small in both groups, but it is striking that virtually no blacks enjoy the most exclusive, and most secure economic status.

The fact that some few white families have big houses and yachts and Maseratis, or that they get their incomes from clipping coupons rather than holding down jobs, might invite the envy of poorer whites and blacks alike, but by itself it would not necessarily be significant. But wealth is far more important than just the dollars it represents, because wealth is synonymous with power.

Wealth conveys many privileges. The power of wealth has meant light sentences for white-collar criminals who steal millions, while petty thieves spend years in jail. And the political corruption known as Watergate was almost exclusively the result of the interplay of power and wealth. Ambassadorships were sold to the highest of the campaign bidders: Luxembourg went to Mrs. Ruth Farkas for $300,-000; Denmark went to Fred J. Russell for $50,000; and J. Fife Symington contributed $100,000 for a post that was never conferred.[49]

It is one of the ironies of Watergate that the villains of the piece were white. That must have been heartening to black Americans. But if there were no black criminals among the politician/participants, or among the many wealthy who made secret and illegal campaign contributions in the hope of future favors, the reason may have been as much that blacks had neither the money, nor the access to the White House in the terms that might have won them shame as well as power.

Not all of the power of wealth is wielded in the rarefied air of presidential politics and diplomatic postings. Wealth also means influence over legislators on matters of personal interest to the wealthy. Wealthy individuals and corporations have contributed countless special provisions to the tax code. Buried in the small print of voluminous tax proposals are the special provisions passed on behalf of the very wealthy.

> The estate of Charles E. Merrill, of Merrill Lynch fame, is the beneficiary of another anonymous provision of the tax code—to wit, Section 512(b) (13). At his death on October 6, 1956, Mr. Merrill willed an interest in his firm to a charitable trust. Under the generally applicable law, the trust's share of the firm's income would be taxable. But, thanks to Section 512(b) (13), the general rule does not apply in the case of a partnership interest willed by "an individual who died afer August 16, 1954 and before January 1, 1957."[50]

And when Mary Hill Swope died in 1955, her will was found to have been drawn in such a way as to make her estate liable for $4 million in taxes, probably through oversights of her attorneys; therefore:

> At the behest of a bipartisan pair of New York Congressmen—Democrat Eugene Keogh of Brooklyn and Republican Daniel Reed of Sheridan—Congress reopened the past and expunged the consequences of unprescient decisions. The measure Messrs. Keogh and Reed shepherded through made, of course, no mention of Mr. and Mrs. Swope or the perfectly understandable human frailties the meas-

ure sought to remedy. Instead, it bestowed a special power on husbands (and wives) who are over eighty at the time of the spouse's death (Mr. Swope was one month short of eighty-three when his wife died). If such a surviving spouse (no one younger than eighty may qualify), within a year of his wife's death, exercises the power under her will to transmit her property to charity, the law will treat this as if she had decided to do this herself. Thus, the charitable gifts may be subtracted from her taxable estate and not subjected to tax.[51]

Since wealth confers power, it is just one more dimension of the relative powerlessness of black people that they have so little of it.

Poverty

Blacks, who are underrepresented among the very rich, are overrepresented among the very poor. In 1959 well over half of all black people living in America were poor. In 1974, nearly 3 in 10 black Americans, but only 1 in 10 white, were counted as poor (Table 7–13). For people who were elderly or very young, or were in families with a woman breadwinner, the likelihood of poverty among blacks was double and triple what it was for whites. As America approached its Bicentennial, 4 of every 10 black children were being raised in poverty.

Poor Americans are at any one time in one of two groups, and sometimes in both. The first are people who can and do work, but who are poor because their wages are low, or because their wages were so low in the past that Social Security entitlements are not enough to raise them out of poverty; this group also includes the long-term unemployed, and those whose unemployment has outlasted unemployment insurance benefits. The second group are those who temporarily or permanently cannot work, and who are "lucky" to be on public support that is not related to work, usually welfare. The two groups are not static, as people cross frequently between them, moving over the line that separates the near-poor from those who are officially poor. Black Americans are found disproportionately in both groups.

Even the stringent federal criteria for designating poverty are able to catch a large proportion of blacks each year. In fact, the proportion of blacks among the poor has stayed about the same since 1959 (Table 7–14). In 1975 an income of less than $5,500 put a family of four into the count of the poor.[52] Because these poverty levels constitute an "absolute standard" (referring to constant dollars adjusted for inflation), as society becomes better off the number of poor will automatically fall. If incomes do not improve or the economy stagnates, the number of people counted as poor either remains the same, or, if unemployment rises, will possibly rise as well. From 1959 to 1969 real median income rose substantially and the number of the officially poor also declined substantially. Comparing 1970 and 1975, the real income of people did not change significantly, and the number of poor stayed about the same, increasing and decreasing along with the business cycle (Table 7–14).[54]

The effects of prolonged high rates of unemployment (from the late sixties to the middle seventies) have been devastating to poor blacks, for whom wages and salaries are the most important forms of income. The number of blacks counted as poor has risen since 1969, and blacks were the same percentage of the poor in 1975 as in 1969. White America may think it has been doing much for blacks who are poor, but there is little evidence that this is so.

Welfare

One of the economic aids available to some of the poor is the now much maligned program known as welfare. It was not always so. When the largest of the federal welfare programs[55]—Aid to Families with Dependent Children (AFDC)—began in 1935 (as Aid to Dependent Children, or ADC),[56] its passage was viewed as a victory because it provided some measure of economic security for otherwise helpless children. Originally just for poor children (mothers and other family members were not included in the grants until 1950), the program was enacted as just one part of the historic Social Security Act, which embodied a national commitment to the relief of suffering from economic want.

Making public welfare available to needy children seemed a good and reasonable thing. That was easier in the early years because originally the program was relatively small (only 351,000 families nationwide in 1940[57]), and its little, fatherless beneficiaries seemed especially worthy of public sympathy. Like other parts of the welfare system, the AFDC program was expected to diminish in size and cost as other parts of the Social Security system reached maturity; as more and more workers' families became eligible for survivors' benefits, fewer and fewer children would need welfare because of the death of a parent. In 1942, "death was the most important single factor in the dependency of families aided,"[58] and such families could be expected to be covered in subsequent years by the "Survivors' Insurance" provisions of the same Social Security Act that included welfare. Although in recent times public pressure has been bent on reducing welfare costs and efforts, initially almost the opposite was true. In 1942, the Federal Bureau of Public Assistance chided the states for not making greater use of the AFDC program for "moral attitudes" that made it difficult for the children of unmarried mothers to get aid, or for defining "incapacity" in ways that might deprive needy children of aid when they needed it most.[59] The federal administrators of the program in the early years saw AFDC as something of social importance, and their jobs as including the promotion and expansion of an obviously needed service.

The official view of welfare had changed dramatically by the 1960s. Officials and the public with them had come to regard it as a program for the "undeserving." Clearly welfare had not "withered away" as other parts of the system had expanded, so the poor on welfare were numerous and became uncomfortably noticeable.

Children whose parents died were increasingly covered by survivors' insurance; that meant not fewer children on welfare but only a different sort of dependent child needing welfare: the children of parents who had never married, or who were alive but absent from the home. Such children and their mothers found the public far less sympathetic to their plight than it had been to orphans and widows thirty years before. And when, in addition, the public thought AFDC benefits were going largely to black families, whose numbers on welfare appeared to them to be increasing daily, a host of prejudices combined in vociferous opposition to the program. It mattered little that only about a third of poor black families were getting any welfare aid at the height of the sixties' "welfare crisis," or that those who did usually got too little to escape from poverty (Table 7–1). The public perception has been that idle black welfare recipients lived on Easy Street, despite the fact that in the only terms that count—money—welfare took only a little over 10 percent of the black households it helped out of poverty, but two times as many of the whites.

Although there were always black welfare recipients, until the seventies blacks were more likely to get lower benefits.[60] And there have always been other anomalies in the system: fewer black men approved for welfare on the basis of incapacity despite demonstrably higher rates of disability[61]; fewer black children approved for benefits despite their being in needy families of the same or larger size.[62]

Three early policy decisions determined whether black families would fare the same as whites on welfare. The first came when

Under pressure from Southern congressmen, any wording that might have been interpreted as constraining the states from racial discrimination in welfare was deleted from the Social Security Act of 1935.[63]

The second critical choice was made when the Congress rejected language that would have required all states to make payments assuring a minimal "level of health and decency."[64] And the third involved the decisions to permit states and even localities to design and administer their own welfare programs in return for sharing in their costs.[65]

The combined effect of those three policy choices was virtually to ensure that racial discrimination would exist in the system and be sanctioned. And, since the legislative history showed that the notion of curtailing racial discrimination had been considered and rejected, that was tantamount to bestowing a blessing on discriminatory practices. If, in addition, racial discrimination was to be sanctioned in a system that left states free to pay as little or as much as they chose, and even different amounts to different groups among those they might find eligible, then differentials were being invited. One version of the congressional debate on that issue reported that equality in welfare payments was most opposed by southern congressmen who feared northern standards of relief would disrupt the wage scale for black and white tenant farmer families.[66]

When the states were left free to determine need and to decide who might be eligible, free from any federal standards or active supervision, to hire and supervise personnel, and to monitor program administration, they were in effect being given federally collected tax dollars from the pockets of white and black taxpayers to discriminate as much as they always had. Since the states were further permitted to turn actual administration of the programs over to local administrative units (usually in return for a local contribution to the cost of the program), the possibility that local prejudices might become a matter of official practice was guaranteed.

Perhaps equally important, particularly for blacks, welfare was not set up to respond to needs, especially those caused by rising unemployment. There have always been many more poor than welfare recipients, and welfare programs have been remarkably impervi-

ous to unemployment hikes and declines, and to periods of social
dislocation that might have signaled a need for expanded welfare[67]
(Figure 7–1). The availability of welfare for poor black people particularly has been a function, not of need, but of the state of the
economy, political forces, and the ability of blacks to press for their
rights.

From the first there were obvious differences in the treatment of
poor blacks living in states with official policies of segregation. In
1940, seven of the southern states with large black populations had
black welfare populations that were proportionally much smaller.[68]
In Georgia, where 38 percent of the children were black, only 12
percent of the children on welfare were black.[69] One southern welfare
supervisor was quite candid about the reasons more poor black
families were not accepted:

> The number of Negro cases is few due to the unanimous feeling on
> the part of the staff and board that there are more work opportunities
> for Negro women and to their intense desire not to interfere with local
> labor conditions. The attitude that "they have always gotten along,"
> and that "all they'll do is have more children" is definite. . . . There
> is hesitancy on the part of lay boards to advance too rapidly over the
> thinking of their own communities, which see no reason why the
> employable Negro mother should not continue her usually sketchy
> seasonal labor or indefinite domestic service rather than receive a
> public assistance grant.[70]

When the Bureau of Public Assistance (a predecessor of the
agency now responsible for welfare in HEW) conducted its first
major survey of the AFDC program in 1942, it was concerned to find
that the degree to which black children were helped varied widely.
Black and white families already on welfare tended to be treated
differently in the sixteen states studied. Even when the families were
equally large and poor, fewer black than white children in those
families would actually receive aid. Among the sixteen states, Illinois
was an exception at the top of the scale; there, black children were
ten times more likely to get aid though they made up only 5 percent
of the population under eighteen. By contrast, the dramatically
poorer but segregationist state of North Carolina had a child population that was 30 percent black, yet black children were far less likely
to be aided than white.[71]

Systematic federal records have never been kept that would show
how many people apply for welfare, by race, and of that number how

FIGURE 7–1

The Unemployment Rate Does Not Affect the Welfare Rolls

Unemployment and AFDC Rates, 1950–75

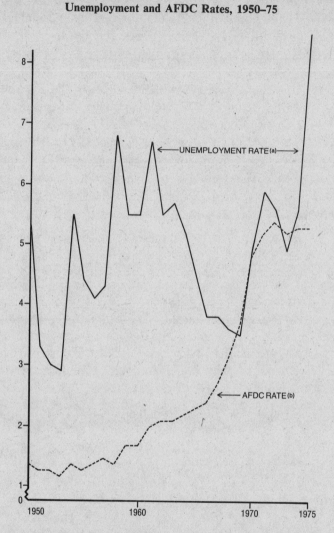

(a)Unemployed as a percentage of the civilian labor force.
(b) AFDC recipients as a percentage of the civilian population.

Source: Unemployment derived from U.S. President, *Economic Report of the Presi-dent, 1976* (Washington, D.C.: Government Printing Office, 1976), Table B–24, p. 199.

AFDC derived from *Social Security Bulletin,* "Annual Statistical Supple-ment, 1973," Table 142, p. 157; Idem., 39 (April 1976), Table M–31, p. 55; U.S. Bureau of the Census, *Statistical Abstract of the U.S., 1974* (Washington, D.C.: Government Printing Office, 1974), Table 2, p. 5; CPR, *Estimates of the Population of the United States to January 1, 1976,* n.p.

many of each race are accepted. But black families and needy individuals were bound to be affected by the generally uncontrolled situation surrounding the application process. The first special report of the Bureau of Public Assistance in 1940 noted:

> An unknown number of families in financial need . . . have requested such assistance, but have been turned away because agencies either through legislation or rule and regulation interpret the Federal act less broadly than the act permits. Agencies often refer to this group of families as the "obviously ineligible," and little if any record is kept of their inquiries.[72]

The record of the states had been uneven enough, and poor enough in some places—particularly the deep South—that in 1947 the Bureau of Public Assistance began to exert pressure to reduce the discriminatory effect of state practices. As a start, formal application procedures were required of all the states to reduce the arbitrary nature of the application and denial process that had been noted.[73]

By 1948 the boom years of the war were over and such economic gains as had been made by black families were fast disappearing. Since the 1942 bureau report, only 9,000 families had been added to the public assistance rolls nationally, and wide state variations remained. For example, fewer than 2 in 100 black children received aid in Georgia and Mississippi, but more than 10 in 100 in Florida, Illinois, New York, and Pennsylvania.[74] When the bureau reported on the same states as six years earlier, it found "an increase in nonwhite recipients was the most conspicuous change occurring."[75] Six states, five of them in the South, now had welfare rolls that were half or more black.[76]

The needs of black welfare recipients in the still segregated South were met largely by white social workers, working under white administrators, in buildings that had separate waiting rooms or rooms with clear indications as to where white and black recipients should sit.[77]

Nor did discrimination end at the Mason-Dixon Line. In December of 1948 the Chicago Relief Administration reported that it was

> carrying about 2,000 Negro families on relief budgets, despite the fact that there was a person in each family for whom work opportunities were being sought and could not be found on account of discriminatory hiring policies in the Chicago labor market.[78]

Discrimination took many forms. Although the number of black recipients was still small throughout the forties, their growing number prompted some states to institute policies ostensibly applicable to everyone, but in practice applying almost exclusively to black families. One such policy held that aid could be given only if the children were living in a "suitable home." Gunnar Myrdal had noted such policies with concern:

> Such regulations . . . may easily lend themselves to rather arbitrary interpretations whereby, in particular, many Negro families can be cut off from any chance of receiving this kind of assistance. According to popular belief in the South, few Negro low-income families have homes which could be called "suitable" for any purpose. . . . And since often practically all Negroes are believed to be "immoral" almost any discrimination against Negroes can be motivated on such grounds.[79]

Some years later, a close look at the AFDC program revealed a distinct pattern of exclusion of the children of black unwed mothers, and in particular found that, "where the suitable home philosophy prevailed, their exclusion was endemic."[80]

In the same way, states with rules denying aid to mothers when "suitable work" was available applied the rule with less than an even hand. In 1952, Georgia began a policy of denying assistance to mothers of children over three years of age when "suitable work" was available, no matter if the wages were lower than what welfare would provide.[81] County welfare boards were directed to deny all applications and close all existing cases during periods when hands were needed in the fields to pick cotton.[82] Decades later, the same practice was routinely applied to food-commodity applicants across the South during the picking or chopping seasons.[83]

Over the course of the fifties, the general attitude toward welfare became openly punitive and antagonistic, although in actual numbers the program only grew by 150,000 families.[84] The proportion of blacks in the program grew slowly, but in what struck some as alarming spurts: from 36 percent of families in 1953 to 43 percent in 1961.[85] Black recipients still accounted for less than half of those in the program, but they were much more visible. While over half of white welfare families were still scattered in small towns and outside of metropolitan areas, two-thirds of black welfare families were living in the central cities of the metropolitan areas.[86] Thus there were growing, visible concentrations of people who were black, poor, and living in the cities, and whose needs might more readily be ignored if it were not for the dependence of some of them on public assistance. In a country where separate schools, hospitals, and neighborhoods were still the rule, black welfare recipients aroused more hostility than sympathy.

Between the end of World War II and the sixties, the country experienced profound social changes that were reflected by the incumbents of the White House. Truman's strong activist commitment to civil rights was replaced by Eisenhower's eagerness to protect states' rights, just as the forceful protest of the war years gave way to the status-quo politics and anticommunist demagoguery of the cold-war era. In such a climate, those who sought to help the poor, were critical of American society, or protested its practices were suspiciously regarded as the tools of communism.

Antiwelfare feeling ran high. When federal officials ruled that "suitable home" policies were inappropriate, variants of them appeared in the guise of policies denying aid to any mother presumed to have a "man in the house" who might be a "substitute parent" capable of contributing to her children's support. During the fifties white welfare officials felt little compunction to prove the case they were making against black families (whether under "suitable home" or "substitute parent" policies), or to prove that AFDC funds were being misused. Public pressure to keep welfare costs down justified these policies in the eyes of public officials. The fact that there was little pressure to be equally zealous in protecting the rights of the poor, and particularly of poor black mothers and children, gave welfare officials little cause to champion the rights of their clients. As the *Arkansas Gazette* noted, "Nobody, of course, wants to be put in the light of defending both bastardy and Negroes in the same breath.[87] So children lost their welfare entitlement because a man's truck happened to be parked outside the apartment building in which they lived ("evidence" of a substitute father who might contribute to their support), and recipients might be subjected to midnight raids (in search of more "evidence" of substitute fathers), arbitrary terminations of assistance, and a host of large and small indignities.[88]

Everything the country imagined about welfare was heightened by the sheer numerical increases of the sixties. In a few years' time the size and cost of the program had changed dramatically. In the first half of the 1960s the AFDC program expanded by 1.3 million persons, and in the second half by another 5.3 million—more than three times the number added to the welfare rolls in the twenty years between 1940 and 1960 (Table 7–15). By the end of the sixties the black families made up 47 percent of welfare families, only 5 percent more than a decade before.[89] But with almost 75 percent living in large cities,[90] as their numbers grew, so did their visibility (Table 7–16).

That sudden increase in the welfare rolls was the product of a unique combination of forces. The same burgeoning economy that opened up jobs for many also put more tax revenues in the public coffers that might be used for new social initiatives and expanded social welfare efforts. They were actually used for that purpose in part because welfare came to be recognized as a civil rights issue, and the forces of black protest were directed toward its improvement. That there was any response to those pressures was due to the disposition of the White House as well as the Congress. Both Kennedy and Johnson had reason to believe that black votes had been critical to their election, and both were personally persuaded of the basic legitimacy of the civil rights struggle. When all forces came together—civil rights, welfare rights, effective political pressure, a healthy economy, and political leadership willing to respond— changes in how the welfare programs were run became virtually inevitable.

Civil rights and welfare rights moved hand in hand, and in their wake the welfare population grew. Borrowing leadership and tactics from the civil rights movement, welfare rights advocates and recipients themselves began to take action against discriminatory welfare policies.

A new activist welfare posture among blacks began to take form in the autumn of 1959 when the National Urban League announced a "new militancy" and translated this into action on behalf of the discontinued welfare recipients of Louisiana.[91] Almost as soon as 29,000 predominantly black AFDC recipients were struck from the rolls in 1960, the National Urban League went into action.[92] Protesting and applying pressure everywhere they could, NUL members went to the state legislature, the governor, and eventually to Washington. The struggle lasted nearly a year, but the program was restored, the statute cutting the mothers and children off was repealed, and a new federal policy was announced forbidding applications of the "suitable home" policy.[93]

The interests of the poor and blacks were most explicitly combined when a former associate director of CORE, George Wiley, formed the Poverty Rights Action Center (PRAC) in 1966 to meld civil rights and poverty activities in a common cause. Within a year,

PRAC had become the National Welfare Rights Organization (NWRO), representing welfare clients and their advocates in twenty-four cities in eleven states.[94] By mid–1969 NWRO was serving approximately 100,000 welfare recipients nationwide, but concentrated in nine major industrial states.[95] The NWRO testified before Congress, demonstrated, and protested on its own. Working together with legal services lawyers and community action agencies, it won both dollar increases in benefits and court decisions affirming and protecting the rights of welfare recipients. Most important, it created a new climate of public recognition that even welfare recipients are citizens with rights under law, and that was no small accomplishment.

Some part of the welfare expansion of the sixties was the result of legislative changes. Without always realizing the effect of their actions, Congress liberalized the welfare laws in ways that worked to increase the welfare rolls. A 1967 amendment to the Social Security Act[96] was intended to encourage welfare mothers to work by permitting them to keep some of what they earned (rather than have welfare benefits offset dollar for dollar by earnings, as before); the effect was to expand welfare by keeping welfare mothers on the rolls even after they found some work. In a similar fashion, an amendment passed in the same year required states to make their payment standards reflect increases in the cost of living, which had the effect of making more families eligible for welfare.[97] More obvious in its implications was the 1961 amendment[98] permitting states (under stringent conditions) to make payments to families with an involuntarily unemployed father still in the home.

These amendments added to civil rights and welfare rights pressures, and the existence of an emerging cadre of poverty lawyers,[99] produced an atmosphere in which once again there was pressure to expand welfare, and welfare administrators approved an increasing number of eligible applicants for welfare. Even with all that, many of the needy poor still did not get any aid from the welfare system.

The struggles of this period had another measurable effect; they seem to have removed discrimination from the area in which it counts the most: how much money a family on welfare gets. By 1973 the only consistent nationwide figures showed that families of the same size and living in the same state received about the same size welfare grant irrespective of whether they were black or white (Table 7–17). In that year the average grant was $54 per person per month.[100] Black recipients appeared to have come a long way from the days when fewer of their children were approved for welfare, and those who were approved got less.

Other evidence indicates that discrimination continues in the welfare system. Since 1948 states with a large proportion of blacks on their AFDC rolls have consistently paid lower benefits than states with few blacks drawing AFDC benefits, even when the differing wealth of the states is taken into account. Benefits continue to be set by state legislatures, and as a rule that has meant that the more blacks on the rolls, the lower the benefits (Table 7–18). Thus, black and white recipients within the same state seem to receive the same average benefits, but states pay lower benefits when they have large numbers of black recipients.

In addition, figures are kept only on what recipients receive, not on what they need. The black poor may have greater needs than the white; if that is true, equal benefits may actually be discriminatory. By ignoring the "need" part of the question, the statistics give only a partial answer; although it would seem that black and white recipients in the same state are treated alike, it is not really possible to know. There have certainly been many individual cases of discrimination within states documented, and these support the idea that prejudice exists. A U.S. district court decision in 1975, for instance, dealt specifically with the issue of whether AFDC rates were set lower in Alabama because most of the recipients were black. The three-judge panel learned that over the years, state officials and legislators had been aware of the racial composition of the various welfare programs and had taken that into account in setting benefit levels. As AFDC became increasingly black and Old Age Assistance (OA) remained predominantly white, grants to Old Age Assistance beneficiaries grew so much faster that the grant to a single individual on OA was higher than the grant to an entire family on AFDC.[101] Ruben King, the official in charge of both programs between 1963 and 1974, testified that the legislators were critical of AFDC because it was predominantly black.[102] The court concluded: "The message is plain . . . AFDC benefits had to be smaller because AFDC was considered to be a program for Negroes."[103]

A 1969 study of the AFDC program in Virginia found that policies differed substantially from one county to the next depending on whether the population (and welfare clientele) was predominantly white or black. AFDC benefits were significantly lower and equally needy children were less likely to be approved for benefits in counties with mostly black recipients.[104] Among twenty-one equally poor rural counties, 1,500 more children, most of them black, would have been aided by AFDC if the rates applying in the white counties had applied throughout the state. Moreover, Virginia authorities knew about these discriminatory variations and accepted them.[105]

The South was not the only part of the country to be guilty of discrimination. The U.S. Civil Rights Commission went to Cleveland and found that black welfare recipients there usually received less cash, food stamps, and medical benefits than whites in the same size families.[106]

In the days when segregation was officially sanctioned, different and discriminatory treatment of black recipients dominated day-to-day practices and were characteristic of the programs. Official segregation has disappeared but many of the practices from those days persisted well into the sixties: black welfare recipients were not addressed as Mr. or Mrs. or Miss; their rights to hearings were ignored; "suitable jobs" for black women still included chopping cotton at $3 per day[107], or domestic work for less; white staff continued to determine black needs in segregated offices, and routinely used discriminatory hearings and complex eligibility criteria to deny black applicants assistance.[108]

One observer of the system in the South noted in 1971:

> When civil rights activism disturbed the calm of Southern rural life, the welfare system was available for, and easily adapted to, discouraging "troublemakers." County officials systematically suspended (food) commodity distributions and warned that benefits would be restored only when local blacks surrendered their "uppity" ideas about changing the local balance of power . . . the discretionary power of county welfare boards continues to keep many a would-be activist from political involvement, and to put off indefinitely the time when hundreds of thousands of black Southerners can begin to exercise their rights without fear of reprisal.[109]

By the end of the sixties many poor women and children were still in need of help and not yet getting it, but times had changed once again. A new and more conservative president and Congress reflected a political climate in which the federal government would not press for the rights of blacks. With an end to the economic growth of the sixties, and the dissipation of the civil rights and welfare rights causes as mass protest movements, much of the impetus for a more equitable and better welfare system for needy families disappeared.

In the seventies the most striking feature of AFDC—almost constant and usually dramatic increases—is gone; instead program growth has decelerated (Table 7–15). The proportion of recipients who are black continues to change little from year to year.[110] For blacks who need help, some of the changes of the seventies are particularly serious ones. Procedural safeguards that had been so painstakingly won a short decade before were whittled away by administrative rulings in the seventies, while public support even for the concept of welfare rights virtually disappeared. Antipoverty lawyers working with public financial support found their activities curtailed by a Congress and administration that found every victory adding to program costs,[111] and many among them, lacking continued support, turned to new fields. Without protection for their rights, without procedural safeguards, without the possibility of capable legal defense, welfare recipients find their grants arbitrarily cut or denied. Perhaps the greatest irony of the early seventies is that it should continue to seem a victory to win for black people the least dignified, least reliable, least respected means of income support this country has to offer.

Welfare is, after all, a residual program. Not in the way imagined forty years ago, when the expansion of social insurance was expected to cause welfare programs to wither away until only a few in need remained, but in a larger sense. Those early reformers also assumed that government would never again permit the widespread unemployment that had prompted the reform measures in the first place. And indeed, if everyone who needed and wanted to work could, and could earn above-poverty wages, then our work-oriented insurance programs would cover many more people and the welfare program would operate as it was intended, picking up the support and service needs of only that small group of poor who are unavoidably without attachment to the work force.

An Inadequate Offering

Instead, welfare has been left to deal with problems created by inadequate jobs and wages policies, and persistent discrimination in the workplace. In that sense welfare is a residual program, helping those whom the economic system has left behind, and for whom the more socially accepted forms of aid are not available or do not even provide poverty-level subsistence. They are the old who have worked in low-wage, unstable jobs, the children of women for whom there are no jobs at wages that would support a family and no means to care for children during a work day, and they are people for whom there is only part-time work or seasonal jobs, or work at less than a living wage. Blacks are found disproportionately in all of these categories. For them, welfare is still the only and inadequate offering of our income security system.

TABLE 7-1

Poor Black Households Benefit Less than Poor White Households from the Federal Government's Social Insurance Programs

Poor Households Receiving Public Insurance and Effect on Reducing Poverty, by Program and Race, 1966

Program and race[a]		Of those receiving benefits	
	Percent receiving benefits	Percent of poverty gap[b] filled	Percent of households brought out of poverty
All programs			
Black	66	59	25
White	79	79	55
OASDI			
Black	32	60	22
White	60	85	48
Unemployment insurance			
Black	4	33	22
White	3	41	31
Workmens' compensation			
Black	2	47	33
White	2	47	37
Veterans' compensation			
Black	1	58	35
White	2	73	67
Veterans' pension			
Black	6	56	40
White	8	69	55
Public assistance			
Black	36	51	12
White	21	62	23

[a] Negro and other nonwhite races.
[b] Gap between income before and after the benefit payments.

Source: Derived from Irene Lurie, "The Distribution of Transfer Payments Among Households" in *Technical Studies of the U.S. President's Commission on Income Maintenance Programs* (Washington, D.C.: Government Printing Office, 1970), pp. 153, 156–7.

TABLE 7–2

Blacks Still Average Less than Two-Thirds Whites' Family Income; the Ratio Has Fluctuated Within a Narrow Range Since 1947—from 51 to 62 Percent

Median Family Income by Race, and Black-White Income Gap in Current and Constant 1947 Dollars, 1947–75

Year	Black[a] median family income	White median family income	Ratio: black to white	Income gap (white minus black)	Income gap in constant dollars (1947 = 100)
1947	$1,614	$ 3,157	.51	$1,543	$1,543
1948	1,768	3,310	.53	1,542	1,428
1949	1,650	3,232	.51	1,582	1,479
1950	1,869	3,445	.54	1,576	1,459
1951	2,032	3,859	.53	1,827	1,575
1952	2,338	4,114	.57	1,776	1,492
1953	2,466	4,398	.56	1,932	1,610
1954	2,416	4,338	.56	1,922	1,602
1955	2,544	4,613	.55	2,069	1,724
1956	2,632	5,002	.53	2,370	1,943
1957	2,763	5,168	.53	2,405	1,909
1958	2,715	5,300	.51	2,585	2,004
1959	2,915	5,643	.52	2,728	2,098
1960	3,230	5,835	.55	2,605	1,959
1961	3,191	5,981	.53	2,790	2,082
1962	3,328	6,237	.53	2,909	2,155
1963	3,465	6,548	.53	3,083	2,250
1964	3,838	6,858	.56	3,020	2,173
1965	3,993	7,251	.55	3,258	2,311
1966	4,691	7,825	.60	3,134	2,161
1967	5,094	8,234	.62	3,140	2,107
1968	5,360	8,937	.60	3,577	2,293
1969	5,999	9,794	.61	3,727	2,273
1970	6,088	10,236	.61	3,948	2,269
1971	6,440	10,672	.60	4,232	2,338
1972	6,864	11,549	.59	4,685	2,505
1973	7,269	12,595	.58	5,326	2,676
1974	8,006	13,408	.60	5,402	2,444
1975	8,779	14,268	.62	5,489	2,287

[a] Negro and other nonwhite races for years 1947–67. Negro only 1968–75.

Source: Derived from CPR, Series P–60, No. 101, *Money Income in 1974 of Families and Persons in the United States,* Tables 10, 16, pp. 19, 27; CPR, Series P–60, No. 103, *Money Income and Poverty Status of Families and Persons in the United States, 1975 and 1974 Revision (Advance Report),* Table 1, p. 10.

TABLE 7-3

Blacks Are More Dependent on Earnings from Work than Whites at All Levels of Income

Percentage of Total Family Income from Wages and Salaries, by Race, 1959 and 1969

Income	Black[a]	White
1959		
Less than $2,000	39	14
$2,000–$4,999	79	58
5,000– 6,999	87	78
7,000– 9,999	86	81
10,000–14,999	81	71
$15,000 and over	57	42
1969[b]		
Less than $4,000	56	41
$4,000– 6,999	84	70
7,000– 9,999	92	85
10,000–14,999	93	88
15,000–24,999	92	85
$25,000 and over	75	62

[a] 1959 figures are for Negro and other nonwhite races.
[b] 1969 income distribution is roughly equivalent to that for 1959, adjusted for price change since 1957.

Source: Derived from 1960 Census of Population, *Subject Reports, PC(2)–4C, Sources and Structure of Family Income,* Table 7, pp. 122–3; 1970 Census of Population, *Subject Reports, PC(2)–8A, Sources and Structure of Family Income,* Tables 5 and 7, pp. 169–80, 315–17.

TABLE 7–4

It Takes More Black than White Earners in a Family to Make the Same Family Income

Ratio of Average Number of Black to White Earners per Family, by Income Class, 1960 and 1970

Income class	(white = 1.00)	
	1960[a]	1970[a]
Less than $3,000	1.41	1.24
$3,000– 6,999	1.19	1.22
7,000– 9,999 ·	1.25	1.47
10,000–14,999	1.26	1.22
15,000–24,999	1.40	1.24
25,000 and over	1.40	1.45

[a] Black in 1960 is for Negro and other nonwhite races; in 1970, for Negro only.

Source: Derived from 1960 Census of Population, *Characteristics of the Population, Vol. 1, Pt. 1, U.S. Summary,* Table 227, pp. 1–605–6; 1970 Census of Population, *Characteristics of the Population, Vol. 1, Pt. 1, Sec. 2, U.S. Summary,* Table 252, pp. 1–923–6.

TABLE 7–5

A Smaller Proportion of Black than White Aged Receive Social Security Benefits, but the Gap Has Been Closing, Especially Since 1960

Percentage of Aged Receiving OASDI, by Race, Selected Years, 1945–75

Year	Black[a]	White	Gap—white minus black
1945	4	8	4
1950	13	21	8
1955	30	45	15
1960	49	67	18
1975	87	95	8

[a] Negro and other nonwhite races.

Source: Mollie Orshansky, "The Aged Negro and His Income" in *Social Security Bulletin* (February 1964): 9. Our special thanks to Ms. Orshansky, who provided us with an unpublished set of figures for 1975.

TABLE 7–6

At Least Half of All Social Security Recipients Do Not Get Benefits Above the Poverty Line

Distribution of Retired Social Security Beneficiaries, by Average Monthly Benefits, Compared with Poverty Level, 1974

Monthly benefit amount	Percent receiving monthly benefit[a]
All beneficiaries	100
Beneficiaries receiving less than $120	20
$120–159.90	17
$160–199.90	16
$200–239.90	21
$240 or more	26
Average benefit	$188.50
Poverty threshold for	
Elderly couple	$249
Elderly single person	$199

[a] Retired workers and dependent spouse and children.

Source: Derived from USDHEW, Social Security Administration, *Social Security Bulletin, Annual Statistical Supplement, 1974,* Table 78, p. 114; U.S. Bureau of the Census, *Characteristics of the Population Below the Poverty Level, 1974,* P–60, No. 102, January 1976, Table A2, p. 145.

TABLE 7–7

*Average Social Security Benefits Are Lower Among Blacks than Whites,
and the Gap in 1973 Was Almost as Large as in 1950*

**Average Monthly Benefits of Retired Workers by Race, Selected Years,
1950–73**

Year	Black[a]	White	Ratio: black to white
1950	$35.76	$47.95	.75
1955	50.46	68.59	.74
1960	57.13	81.11	.70
1965	64.55	93.66	.69
1970	90.52	113.64	.80
1973	129.23	161.53	.80

[a] Negro and other nonwhite races in 1950–65; Negro only in 1970–73.

Source: Derived from *Social Security Bulletin* 14 (September 1951), Table 22, p. 33;
idem, "Annual Statistical Supplement, 1955," Table 33, pp. 24–8; idem, "Annual Statistical Supplement, 1960," Tables 50, 51, pp. 37–46; idem, "Annual
Statistical Supplement, 1965," Tables 64, 67, pp. 56–66, 69; idem, "Annual
Statistical Supplement 1970," Tables 67, 68, pp. 73–85; idem, "Annual Statistical Supplement, 1973," Tables 66, 69, pp. 88–98, 102.

TABLE 7–8

*Unemployment Insurance Has Always Covered Proportionately Fewer
Blacks than White Workers, but the Gap Has Been Closing*

**Estimated[a] Percentage of Workers Covered by Unemployment Insurance,
by Race, Decennial Years 1940–70**

Year	Black[b]	White
1940	33	56
1950	47	60
1960	54	69
1970	67	74

[a] Coverage estimated by assuming each group was covered in proportion to the
percentage of workers covered in each industry and the employment of each race
in each industry.
[b] Negro and other nonwhite races.

Source: Derived from BLS, *Employment and Wages of Workers Covered by State
Unemployment Insurance Laws and Unemployment Compensation for Federal
Employees by State and Industry,* Table 2, pp. 5–7; 4th Quarter and 1960
Average, Tables 2, 4, pp. 10, 12–19; 4th Quarter 1970 and Annual Summary,
Tables 4A–4D, pp. 19–28.

TABLE 7–9

Seldom Do as Many as Half the Unemployed Receive Unemployment Insurance Benefits

Percentage of Unemployed Workers Receiving Unemployment Insurance Benefits, Selected Years, 1939–74

Year	Percent receiving benefits
1939	11
1942	25
1945	69
1948	64
1951	49
1954	58
1957	55
1960	54
1963	48
1966	39
1969	42
1972	46
1973	42
1974	48

Source: Derived from BLS, *Employment and Wages of Workers Covered by State Unemployment Insurance Laws and Unemployment Compensation for Federal Employees by State and Industry,* 4th Quarter 1973, Table A1, p. 3; 4th Quarter 1974, Table A1, p. 3.

TABLE 7–10

The Difference in Income Between the Richest 5 Percent of Black and White Families Is Large and Persistent

Difference in Black and White Income of the Richest 5 Percent of Families, Selected Years, 1947–75[a]

Year	Black[b]	White	Ratio: black to white	Income gap —white minus black (current $)	Income gap (constant $) (1947 = 100)
1947	$ 5,398	$ 8,383	.64	$2,985	$2,985
1950	5,200	8,877	.59	3,677	3,405
1953	7,117	10,495	.68	3,378	2,815
1956	7,340	11,874	.62	4,534	3,716
1959	8,722	13,050	.67	4,328	3,329
1962	10,000	15,159	.66	5,159	3,821
1965	11,800	17,067	.69	5,267	3,735
1968	15,800	21,000	.75	5,200	3,333
1969	17,238	23,298	.74	6,060	3,695
1970	18,521	24,941	.74	6,420	3,690
1971	19,411	25,890	.75	6,479	3,580
1972	20,400	28,500	.72	8,100	4,332
1973	23,000	30,645	.75	7,645	3,842
1974	24,500	32,966	.74	8,466	3,831
1975	26,600	35,000	.76	8,400	3,500

[a] Using the lower limit of the top 5 percent of families. These income data are in current dollars, thus providing realistic figures. If adjusted for price increases since 1947, 1975 family income limits of the upper 5 percent of blacks would be $11,083; for whites, $14,583.

[b] Negro and other nonwhite races.

Source: Derived from CPR, Series P–60, No. 101, *Money Income in 1974 of Families and Persons in the United States,* Tables 10, 22, pp. 19, 37; CPR, Series P–60, No. 103, *Money Income and Poverty Status of Families and Persons in the United States, 1975 and 1974 Revisions (Advance Report),* Table 5, p. 17.

TABLE 7–11

White Wealth Is Much More Often in Income-Producing Assets than Is Black Wealth

Percentage Distribution of Family Net Wealth,[a] by Type of Wealth and by Race, 1967

Type of wealth	Percent of total holdings	
	Black	White
Total assets	100	100
Financial assets[b]	10	30
Other assets[c]	26	33
Equity in homes and autos	64	37

[a] Net wealth unencumbered by debt.
[b] Value of stocks, government bonds, and cash in banks.
[c] Equity in other real estate, farms, and businesses.

Source: Derived from Henry S. Terrell, "Wealth Accumulation of Black and White Families: The Empirical Evidence," *Journal of Finance* 26 (May 1971): 367.

TABLE 7–12

Few Black Families Get Large Incomes from Property

Distribution of Property Income[a] of Families by Race, 1969 and 1974

Amount of property income	1969		1974	
	Black	White	Black	White
Total[b]	100.0	100.0	100.0	100.0
Loss, to $999	90.5	78.9	88.6	75.2
$1,000 – 4,999	9.3	17.7	10.4	19.9
$5,000 –24,999	0.3	3.8	0.8	4.5
$25,000–49,999	[c]	0.2	[c]	0.3
$50,000 and over	[c]	0.1	[c]	0.1
Mean property income	$339	$990	$417	$1,194
Families with property income	571,000	20,589,000	167,000	26,089,000
Percent of all families with income	12	45	14	53

[a] Property income is the total of dividends, interest, net rental income, income from estates or trusts, and net royalties.

[b] Entries may not add up to 100 because of rounding.

[c] Less than .05 percent.

Source: Derived from CPR, Series P–60, No. 75, *Income in 1969 of Families and Persons in the United States,* Table 38, pp. 80–2; CPR Series P–60, No. 101, *Money Income in 1974 of Families and Persons in the United States,* Table 50, pp. 97–9.

TABLE 7-13

Poverty Hits Blacks Much More Often than Whites in All Types of
Families and Among Different Age Groups

Incidence of Poverty—Percentage of Persons Who Are Poor—by Family Type
and Age Group and by Race, 1959, 1969, and 1974

Group	1959 Black[a]	1959 White	1969 Black	1969 White	1974 Black	1974 White
All persons	56	18	32	10	31	9
In families						
Man at head	51	15	21	6	17	6
Woman at head	76	40	58	29	55	28
Unrelated individuals	57	44	47	32	41	23
Persons over 65 years old	(b)	(b)	(b)	(b)	36	14
Related children[c]	67	21	40	10	41	11

(a) Negro and other nonwhite races.

(b) Data not available.

(c) Related children are all children in a family who are related to the family head by blood, marriage, or adoption.

Source: Derived from CPR, Series P-60, No. 102, *Characteristics of the Population Below the Poverty Level, 1974*, Table 1, pp. 14–15.

TABLE 7–14

*The Trend Toward Reduction in Poverty Has Been Stalled or Reversed
for Both Blacks and Whites During Most of the Seventies*

**Number of Persons in Poverty by Race, and Percentage of Poor Persons Who
Are Black, 1959 and 1966–75**

Year	Total	Black[a]	Percent black
	(in thousands)		
1959	39,490	11,006	28
1966	28,510	8,867	31
1967	27,769	8,486	31
1968	25,389	7,616	30
1969	24,147	7,095	29
1970	25,420	7,548	30
1971	25,559	7,396	29
1972	24,460	7,710	32
1973	22,973	7,388	32
1974	23,370	7,182	31
1975	25,877	7,545	29

[a] Negro and other nonwhite races in 1959; Negro only 1966–75.

Source: Derived from CPR, Series P–60, No. 102, *Characteristics of the Population
Below the Poverty Level, 1974,* Table 1, p. 13; CPR, Series P–60, No. 103,
*Money Income and Poverty Status of Families and Persons in the United States,
1975 and 1974 Revisions (Advance Report),* Table B, p. 3.

TABLE 7–15

Welfare Growth Was Slow in the Forties and Fifties, Fast in the Sixties, and Has Slowed Again During the Seventies

Number of AFDC Recipients and Their Percentage of the Civilian Population, Selected Years, 1940–75

Year	Total (in thousands)	Percent of civilian population
1940	1,222	1
1945	943	1
1950	2,233	2
1955	2,192	1
1960	3,073	2
1965	4,396	2
1970	9,659	5
1975[a]	11,112	5

[a] Average through November.

Source: Derived from *Social Security Bulletin*, "Annual Statistical Supplement, 1973," Table 142, p. 157; idem, 39 (January 1976), Table M–31, p. 70; CPR, Series P–25, No. 621, *Estimates of the Population of the United States to January 1, 1976,* n.p.

TABLE 7–16

Black Welfare Families Are Increasingly Concentrated in Large Cities,
Whereas Most White Families on Welfare Are Dispersed Among Smaller
Places

Percentage of AFDC Families, by Location and Race, Selected Years, 1953–73

Year	All places	Metropolitan Total	Large cities[a]	Nonmetropolitan
			Black[b]	
1953	100	64	56	37
1956	100	65	58	36
1961	100	75	66	25
1967[c]	100	80	70	20
1971[c]	100	81	71	18
1973[c]	100	84	73	16
			White	
1953	100	38	25	62
1956	100	40	28	60
1961	100	48	29	53
1967[c]	100	65	42	34
1971[c]	100	71	44	30
1973[c]	100	73	43	26

[a] Cities of 50,000 or more in years before 1961 and the central cities of SMSA's in 1961 and later.
[b] Negro and other nonwhite races in 1953; Negro only in all other years.
[c] Excludes families living out of state where assistance is given.

Source: Derived from U.S. Bureau of Public Assistance, *Characteristics of Families Receiving Aid to Dependent Children, November 1953,* Table 2, 3, pp. 13–14; idem, *Characteristics of Families Receiving Aid to Dependent Children in Early 1956,* n.d., Tables 2, 3, n.p.; U.S. Welfare Administration, Bureau of Family Services, *Study of Recipients of Aid to Families with Dependent Children, November–December 1961: National Cross-Tabulations, 1965,* Table 32, n.p.; unpublished data from the 1967 AFDC study of the National Center for Social Statistics; U.S. National Center for Social Statistics, *Findings of 1971 AFDC Study, Pt. 3, National Cross-Tabulations, 1973,* Table 65, n.p.; unpublished data from 1973 AFDC study of the National Center for Social Statistics.

TABLE 7-17

*There Was Little Variation in the Welfare Benefits Received by Blacks
and Whites Within Individual States in 1973*

**Thirty-one States: Number of These States Reporting Benefit Amounts by
Race, by Black to White Mean AFDC Benefits, and by Number of Persons in
the Assistance Groupings,[a] 1973**

Ratio of black to white AFDC benefits	Size of assistance groups in 31 reporting states				
	All size assistance groups	2 persons	3 persons	4 persons	5 persons or over
All reporting states[b]	31	31	31	31	31
Between .90 and 1.10[c]	29	28	28	30	29
Less than .90	2	1	3	1	2
More than 1.10	0	2	0	0	0

[a] Having one adult plus a dependent child or children and no other income.

[b] Covers 31 states: Alabama, Arizona, Arkansas, California, Colorado, Florida, Georgia,
Illinois, Indiana, Iowa, Kansas, Kentucky, Louisiana, Maryland, Michigan, Minnesota,
Mississippi, Missouri, Nebraska, New Jersey, New York, North Carolina, Ohio, Oklahoma, Pennsylvania, Rhode Island, Tennessee, Texas, Virginia, West Virginia, Wisconsin.

[c] This is virtual parity.

Source: Derived from analysis of unpublished data from the 1973 AFDC study provided
by the National Center for Social Statistics.

TABLE 7–18

States with a High Proportion of Blacks on Welfare Rolls Usually Pay Less Benefits than States with Mostly White Recipients

Percentage Distribution of States by Low and High State Contribution to AFDC Benefits and by Low and High Percentage of Blacks on AFDC Rolls, 1948, 1961, and 1973

Monthly AFDC benefit levels[a] per recipient	Percent of AFDC families black	
	Low[b]	High[b]
1948 All states	100	100
Low-paying[c]	33	67
High-paying[c]	67	33
1961 All states	100	100
Low-paying[c]	30	75
High-paying[c]	70	25
1973 All states	100	100
Low-paying[c]	32	60
High-paying[c]	68	40

[a] Benefits include only those actually supplied by each state. Federal funds are not included. Benefits were adjusted by an index of state per capita income (U.S. = 100) to reflect the resources of each state available for AFDC payments.

[b] 1948: low = 0–16 percent, high = 17–83 percent; 1961: low = 0–36 percent, high = 37–93 percent; 1973: low = 0–34 percent, high = 35–98 percent.

[c] 1948: low = $3–9, high = $10–20; 1961: low = $3–10, high = $11–27; 1973: low = $3–19, high = $20–43.

Source: Derived from U.S. Federal Security Agency, *Annual Report 1948* (Washington, D.C.: Government Printing Office, 1949), Table 7, p. 251; U.S. Bureau of Public Assistance, *Source of Funds Expended for Public Assistance Payments, Calendar Year Ended December 31, 1948,* 1949, Table 4, n.p.; U.S. Bureau of the Census, *Summary of State Government Finances in 1948,* G–SF48–No. 1, 1949, Table 2, p. 6; Robert B. Bretzfelder, Q. Francis Dallavale, and David A. Herschberg, "Personal Income, 1968 and Disposable Income, 1929–68 by States and Regions," *Survey of Current Business* 49 (April 1969), Table 5, p. 26; Frances Piven and Richard A. Cloward, *Regulating the Poor: The Function of Public Welfare* (New York: Pantheon Books, 1971), Source Table 4, n.p.; U.S. Department of Health, Education, and Welfare, *1961 Annual Report* (Washington, D.C.: Government Printing Office, 1962), Table 7, pp. 122–3; U.S. Social Security Administration, Bureau of Family Services, *Source of Funds Expended for Public Assistance Payments, Calendar Year Ended December 31, 1961,* 1962, Table 7, n.p.; U.S. Bureau of the Census, *Governmental Finances in 1961,* G–GF61–No. 2, 1962, Table 14, pp. 28–30; Bretzfelder, Dallavale, Hirschberg, *Personal Income,* Table 5, p. 27; Piven and Cloward, *Regulating,* Source Table 4, n.p.; U.S. National Center for Social Statistics, *Public Assistance Statistics,* June 1973, Table 7, n.p.; U.S. Social and Rehabilitation Service, Office of Financial Management, *Fiscal Year 1973: State Expenditures for Public Assistance Programs Approved Under Titles I, IV–A, X, XIV and XIX of the Social Security Act,* n.d., p. 17; U.S. Bureau of the Census, *Governmental Finances in 1973–74,* GF 74–No. 5 (Washington, D.C.: Government Printing Office, 1975), Table 17, pp. 31–3; "State and Regional Personal Income, 1958–1973," *Survey of Current Business* 54 (August 1974, Pt. 1), Table 1, p. 32; U.S. National Center for Social Statistics, *Findings of the 1973 AFDC Study: Pt. 1, Demographic and Program Characteristics,* NCSS Report AFDC–1 (73), 1974, Table 7, n.p.

Epilogue

"What is Past is Prologue." So it says, inscribed in granite on the National Archives on Constitution Avenue in our nation's capital. Those five words from Shakespeare also tell in shorthand how change takes place and the way black Americans have progressed since 1940. Past history, all of it, favorable and unfavorable, has created the stage for new beginnings. Whatever has promoted equality between black and white Americans requires strong support to preserve those gains in the present, and to improve a future that will not wait. Whatever has retarded or impeded progress remains a heavy weight containing the seeds of retrogression. These lessons from the past are clearly delineated in every area essential to life itself —getting and keeping a job and some economic security, having the home of one's choice, and staying well.

The sweeping gains in American levels of living since 1940 have improved the condition of black and white alike. White Americans have made as much or more progress than any others and, under these circumstances have become increasingly more tolerant. At each stage they have become less patient with the signs of racism of earlier periods. Laws now prohibit all of the most blatant forms of discrimination. What is considered correct or proper in everyday, face-to-face relations has also changed, bringing a general climate of congeniality in the workplace and in other formal and informal meetings. But while the etiquette by which we live, especially that supported by law, gives black Americans greater access to a better life than ever before, it is too often forced. It successfully masks stereotypical ways of thinking, and the bureaucratic manipulations that sustain them. These have persisted and come through clearly in the many ingenious ways we circumvent civil rights laws intended

284

to ensure basic human rights, which are themselves renegotiated over and over again, reminders that the right to vote or defend one's rights in court might still be denied.

Many would solve the problems of continuing discrimination and lawlessness by improving enforcement of the civil rights laws we have. Of course enforcement should be infinitely more stringent. But the very inadequacies of the enforcement provisions to begin with, and the need for them at all, speak volumes about the resistance of white Americans to accepting black Americans as equals.

It is important now, when we regard ourselves as a civilized and mature people, that we acknowledge not just how much has been achieved in civil rights, not just how much is yet to be accomplished, but how fragile is the result.

We are an aggressive and competitive people. When the economy is working so that nobody loses on the way up, black Americans achieve enough to maintain and even reduce a little the relative distance between them and white Americans. But depending too much on the economy to reduce the disparity between the races leaves black Americans vulnerable to the kind of progress that quickly vanishes in hard times. Besides, the economic system has built-in limits that tie later comfort to early and continuous high earnings which are not yet commonly the lot of black American workers. When competition for basic needs becomes keen in a stagnant or receding economy, and when at the same time, the push for equality comes closer to home, the film of civility disintegrates. Such times are perilous; newly learned manners give way; retrogression sets in, sometimes egged on by an indifferent or opportunistically neglectful government.

The cutting edge of black Americans' progress, therefore, has been protest. Our findings are unequivocal that vigilant, aggressive protest is necessary at all times—good or bad—to maintain gains, to prevent losses, and to make progress. The gains by black Americans since 1940 have been truly theirs, with relatively few outside champions who have spent a lifetime in their struggle. If "the Lord helps those who help themselves," black Americans would long since have achieved equality with white Americans. Intense effort has been an integral part of their lives. That even so persistent and creative an effort has not yet achieved its goal is testimony to the power and influence of the white majority. This is not just because of their wealth, or because of the ordinary restrictions societies impose on minorities; it is also because black and white Americans still live out their lives in separate social worlds. That separateness is no accident; it is managed, contrived, and not yet resisted actively by either group. Residential segregation is only the physical manifestation of the way American society as a whole is organized. This way of living leads to separate communications networks that operate continuously to the advantage of the majority in maintaining their better-than-equal life chances. The majority controls public and private institutions and the management that opens doors. This adds heavily to the odds when the prevailing sentiment is that white is better, regardless of any other criterion.

The separate social worlds of black and white Americans is only one manifestation of how racism has become institutionalized in America. We have seen how blacks are denied employment regardless of merit; denied housing regardless of credit worthiness; and receive less from income security systems regardless of characteristics similar to white fellow citizens. Institutionalized racism, that which is built into organizations' ways of proceeding, eases the burden of personal guilt, and so is readily perpetuated.

Our predominantly white institutions—public and private—and the individuals in them do not take it on themselves to remove barriers or to act forcefully on behalf of black Americans without pressure being brought to bear. The managing white world continues to be ingenious in finding ways to resist change even under the restraints of law. Only persistent protest, using equally ingenious ways of carrying on the struggle has been an equally powerful way of meeting and overcoming that resistance.

It is our hope that white Americans will join black Americans in increasing numbers in the struggle for a more equal society. Such humanism would be a natural outgrowth of this nation's long concern with social equity. Ultimately total national commitment to these values, together with continued pressure, will break through what until now have been apparently unbreachable walls.

*Bibliographical Note**

The research for this book was based on upwards of 1,500 references, too many to cite individually in a publication designed to reach a large audience with limited budgets. The references range in character all the way from thirty-five-year-old and current newspaper or journal articles to previously unexamined materials in the National Archives, and in the archives of various federal executive departments, using the authority of the Freedom of Information Act. Most of the references are old and new books, articles from professional journals over a wide span of years, and articles from the popular and scholarly black press. Unpublished statistics were analyzed from many sources, but especially from parts of what is the present Department of Health, Education, and Welfare, the Civil Service Commission, the Bureau of the Census, and the Department of Labor.

We refer those interested in assembling a working bibliography to the notes for each chapter. These notes contain many of the more important works, old and new.

*Footnote conventions:
CPR: Current Population Reports
BLS: Bureau of Labor Statistics
NCHS: U.S. National Center for Health Statistics

Notes

Chapter 1: Making a Difference

1. Walter White, *A Man Called White* (1948; reprint ed., New York: Arno Press and The New York Times, 1969), pp. 325–8.
2. This chapter only highlights facts such as these, which are developed in detail in later chapters. For this reason precise references come later.
3. Hortense Powdermaker, *After Freedom: A Cultural Study in the Deep South* (New York: Viking Press, 1939), pp. 93–4, 117–8.
4. Gunnar Myrdal, *An American Dilemma: The Negro Problem and Modern Democracy,* 20th ann. ed. (New York: Harper and Row, Publishers, 1962), pp. 485, 947–8.
5. Langston Hughes, *Fight for Freedom: The Story of the NAACP* (New York: W. W. Norton and Co., 1962), p. 94.
6. U.S. Congress, Full Employment Act of 1945, S.380, 79th Cong., 1st sess., 1945.
7. Ibid., Sec. 2.
8. 15 U.S.C. Sec. 1021 *et seq.* (1970).
9. 15 U.S.C. Sec. 1021 (1970).
10. U.S. Congress, Joint Economic Committee, *Economic Policy and Inflation in the United States: A Survey of Developments from the Enactment of the Employment Act of 1946 through 1974,* by Edward Knight, Studies in Price Stability and Economic Growth, No. 2 (Washington, D.C.: Government Printing Office, 1975), p. 83.
11. Ibid., pp. 23–9.
12. This theory was developed by A. W. Phillips using 1862–1957 data for the United Kingdom. The relationship was between wages and unemployment and not prices and unemployment, was for Britain not the United States, and covered a period during which drastic changes in the economic structure had taken place. See A. W. Phillips, "The Relation Between Unemployment and the Rate of the Change of Money Wage Rates in the United Kingdom, 1862–1957," *Economica* 25 (November 1958): 283–99.
13. Robert Lekachman, *Economists at Bay: Why the Experts Will Never Solve Your Problems* (New York: McGraw-Hill Book Co., 1976), pp. 44–53. Bradley R. Schiller writes: "The goal most often deemed in direct competition with full employment is that of price stability. It is widely believed that we cannot have both price stability and full employment at the same time, thereby implying that the pursuit of one objective necessarily means abandonment of the other." In *The Economics*

of Poverty and Discrimination (Englewood Cliffs, N.J.: Prentice-Hall, 1973), p. 47.

14. Many modern economists favor the latter approach, including, for example, Robert Lekachman, *Economists at Bay;* Lloyd G. Reynolds, *Economics: A General Introduction,* 4th ed. (Homewood, Ill.: Richard D. Irwin, 1973); Bradley R. Schiller, *The Economics of Poverty and Discrimination.*

15. U.S. President, *Economic Report of the President, 1974* (Washington, D.C.: Government Printing Office, 1974), pp. 58–9.

16. "The President's News Conference of June 25, 1975," *Weekly Compilation of Presidential Documents* 11 (30 June 1975):677.

17. The states were California, Colorado, Connecticut, Illinois, Indiana, Iowa, Kansas, Massachusetts, Michigan, Minnesota, Nebraska, New Jersey, New York, Ohio, Pennsylvania, Rhode Island, Washington, and Wisconsin.

18. Richard Bardolph, ed., *The Civil Rights Record: Black Americans and the Law, 1849–1970* (New York: Thomas Y. Crowell Co., 1970), pp. 257, 260.

19. President of the Brotherhood of Sleeping Car Porters, the first black trade union group in organized labor.

20. Herbert Garfinkel, *When Negroes March: The March on Washington Movement in the Organizational Politics for FEPC* (Glencoe, Ill.: Free Press, 1959), and Louis C. Kesselman, *The Social Politics of FEPC: A Study in Reform Movements* (Chapel Hill: University of North Carolina Press, 1948), discuss in detail the wartime movement by blacks for jobs and the particular role of A. Philip Randolph.

21. Walter White quoted in Garfinkel, *Negroes March,* p. 39.

22. White, *A Man,* pp. 191–2.

23. U.S. President, "Reaffirming Policy of Full Participation in the Defense Program by All Persons, Regardless of Race, Creed, Color or National Origin and Directing Certain Action in Furtherance of Said Policy," Executive Order 8802, 25 June 1941, *3 Code of Federal Regulations, 1938–43 Compilation* (Washington, D.C.: Government Printing Office, 1968), p. 957.

24. Garfinkel, *Negroes March;* Kesselman, *Social Politics.*

25. Malcolm Ross, *All Manner of Men* (New York: Reynal and Hitchcock, 1948), p. 24.

26. Kesselman, *Social Politics,* p. 23n.

27. Philip S. Foner, *Organized Labor and the Black Worker, 1916–1973* (New York: Praeger Publishers, 1973), p. 265.

28. Kesselman, *Social Politics.*

29. Ross, *All Manner,* describes a large variety of complaints.

30. John Hope Franklin, *From Slavery to Freedom,* 4th ed. (New York: Alfred A. Knopf, 1974), pp. 363–4.

31. 321 U.S. 649 (1944); ibid., p. 364.

32. Thomas R. Brooks, *Walls Come Tumbling Down: A History of the Civil Rights Movement 1940–1970* (Englewood Cliffs, N.J.: Prentice-Hall, 1974), p. 54.

33. Ibid., p. 122.

34. Henry Lee Moon, *Balance of Power: The Negro Vote* (Garden City, N.Y.: Doubleday and Co., 1948), pp. 31–2; White, *A Man,* pp. 187–9.

35. Kirk H. Porter and Donald B. Johnson, *National Party Platforms, 1840–1968* (Urbana: University of Illinois Press, 1970), pp. 404, 412.

36. William C. Berman, *Politics of Civil Rights in the Truman Administration* (Columbus: Ohio State University Press, 1970), pp. 97–9.

37. U.S. President, "Establishing the President's Committee on Equality of Treatment and Opportunity in the Armed Services," Executive Order 9981, 26 July 1948, *3 Code of Federal Regulations, 1943–1948 Compilation* (Washington, D.C.: Government Printing Office, 1957), p. 722.

38. Berman, *Politics,* pp. 73–7.

39. Ibid., pp. 79–135.

40. 347 U.S. 483 (1954).

41. Jack Greenberg, *Race Relations and the Law* (New York: Columbia University Press, 1959); William Hastie, "Toward an Equalitarian Legal Order" in *Blacks and the Law: Annals of the American Academy of Political and Social Science,* Vol. 407, ed. by Jack Greenberg (Philadelphia: American Academy of Political and Social Science, 1975), pp. 18–31; Langston Hughes, *Fight For Freedom: The Story of the NAACP* (New York, W. W. Norton and Co., 1962); and Randall W. Bland, *Private Pressure on Public Law: The Legal Career of Justice Thurgood Marshall* (Port Washington, N.Y.: Kennekat Press, 1973), pp. 38–40, discuss the long-term strategy of the NAACP leading up to the Brown decision.

42. *Missouri ex rel. Gaines v. Canada* 305 U.S. 337 (1938); *Sipuel v. University of Oklahoma* 332 U.S. 631 (1948); *Fisher v. Hurst* 333 U.S. 147 (1948); *Sweatt v. Painter* 339 U.S. 629 (1950); *McLaurin v. Oklahoma State Regents* 339 U.S. 637 (1950); *Gray v. University of Tennessee* 342 U.S. 517 (1952). See Jack Greenberg, *Race Relations and the Law.*

43. Hastie, "Toward an Equalitarian"; Greenberg, *Race Relations.*

44. *Brown v. Topeka* was not one case but five. The cases were *Brown v. Board of Education of Topeka* 98 F. Supp. 797 (D., Kan. 1951); *Briggs v. Elliot* 103 F. Supp. 920 (E.D.S.C. 1952) from South Carolina; *Davis v. County School Board of Prince Edward County* 103 F. Supp. 337 (E.D.Va. 1952), Virginia; *Gebhart v. Belton* 33 Del. Ch. 144, 91 A. 2nd 137 (1952) from Delaware; and *Bolling v. Sharpe* 347 U.S. 397 (1954) from the District of Columbia. The *Bolling v. Sharpe* case from D.C. was ruled upon, in the same day as the others, but in a separate decision because of the peculiar federal status of the District of Columbia. See Greenberg, *Race Relations.*

45. Robert H. Brisbane, *The Black Vanguard: Origins of the Negro Social Revolution, 1900–1960* (Valley Forge, Pa.: Judson Press, 1969), p. 237.

46. Martin Luther King, Jr., *Stride Toward Freedom: The Montgomery Story* (New York: Harper and Bros., 1958). See especially Chaps. 3–9.

47. Brooks, *Walls,* pp. 84–5.

48. Ibid., pp. 78–81.

49. Greenberg, *Race Relations,* p. 193.

50. Brooks, *Walls,* p. 85.

51. August Meier, "Civil Rights Strategies for Negro Employment," in *Employment, Race and Poverty,* ed. by Arthur M. Ross and Herbert Hill

(New York: Harcourt, Brace and World, Harbinger Book, 1967), pp. 185–90; Foner, *Organized Labor,* pp. 293–331.

52. Walter White quoted in Brooks, *Walls,* p. 87.

53. Porter and Johnson, *Party Platforms,* p. 487.

54. Ibid., p. 504.

55. Ibid., pp. 541–2, 554.

56. James L. Sundquist, *Politics and Policy: The Eisenhower, Kennedy and Johnson Years* (Washington, D.C.: Brookings Institution, 1968), pp. 222–38.

57. Martin Arnold, "There Is No Rest for Roy Wilkins," *New York Times Magazine,* 28 September 1969, p. 41.

58. Theodore H. White, *The Making of the President, 1960* (New York: Atheneum Publishers, 1961), p. 323.

59. Chuck Stone, *Black Political Power in America* (Indianapolis: Bobbs-Merrill Co., 1968), p. 53.

60. Howard Zinn, *SNCC: The New Abolitionist* (Boston: Beacon Press, 1964); Pat Watters and Reese Cleghorn, *Climbing Jacob's Ladder: The Arrival of Negroes in Southern Politics* (New York: Harcourt, Brace and World, 1967); August Meier and Elliott Rudwick, *CORE: A Study in the Civil Rights Movement, 1940–1968* (New York: Oxford University Press, 1973); James Forman, *Making of Black Revolutionaries* (New York: Macmillan Co., 1972).

61. Howard Zinn, *Postwar America 1945–1971* (Indianapolis: Bobbs-Merrill Co., 1973), p. 207.

62. One authority writes: "The television networks made an incalcuable contribution to public enlightenment on the racial issue simply by supplying extensive spot news coverage of racial strife. The spectacle of . . . an enraged Lester Maddox driving young theological students from the Pickwick Restaurant with ax handles, could hardly fail to bring in converts to the cause. Television also devoted a great deal of prime time to documentaries . . . (like the 1963 March on Washington . . .) concerning the Negro's plight and the crusade to resolve it." He goes on to write about reaction to the "Battle of Oxford" when the University of Mississippi was compelled to register James Meredith under the eyes of the attorney general and federal troops; the shooting of Medgar Evers and the release of his accused murderer; the bombing of the homes of Negro civil rights workers; the 1963 murder, by bombing, of four Negro children in a Birmingham Sunday school; the use of clubs, tear gas, dogs, and high-powered hoses on demonstrators in Birmingham by the police commissioner, Eugene "Bull" Connor; brutish treatment of marchers, freedom riders, and voter-registration volunteers; and the murder of three young civil rights workers. Bardolph, ed., *Civil Rights Record,* pp. 330, 405.

63. Benjamin Muse, *The American Negro Revolution: From Nonviolence to Black Power, 1963–1967* (Bloomington: Indiana University Press, 1968), p. 67.

64. Rudwick and Meier, *CORE;* Muse, *Negro Revolution.*

65. U.S. National Advisory Commission on Civil Disorders, *Report* (Washington, D.C: U.S Government Printing Office, 1968); California,

Governor's Commission on the Los Angeles Riots, *Violence in the City—An End or a Beginning*, 1965; "Urban Problems and Civil Disorder," *Congressional Quarterly Weekly Report*, 8 September 1967, pp. 1707–67.

66. August Meier and Elliott Rudwick, *From Plantation to Ghetto*, new ed. (New York: Hill and Wang, 1970), pp. 271–98; Brisbane, *Black Activism*; Joseph S. Himes, *Racial Conflict in American Society* (Columbus, Ohio: Charles E. Merrill Publishing Co., 1973), pp. 77–96; Forman, *Making*.

67. Himes, *Race Conflict*, p. 94.

68. Bardolph, ed. *Civil Rights Record.*, pp. 311–15.

69. These were not always or necessarily entire segments of a curriculum, but emphasis within curricula on the history and contributions of black Americans, that had previously been omitted and ignored. They correspond to the drive for "women's studies" today. Brooks, *Walls*; Robert H. Brisbane, *Black Activism: Racial Revolution in the United States, 1954–1970* (Valley Forge, Pa.: Judson Press, 1974); Armstead L. Robinson, Craig C. Foster, and Donald H. Ogilvie, *Black Studies in the University: A Symposium* (New Haven: Yale University Press, 1969).

70. Stokely Carmichael and Charles V. Hamilton, *Black Power: The Politics of Liberation in America* (New York: Random House, Vintage Books, 1967), p. 47.

71. *Washington Post*, 30 December 1975, 6 January 1976; U.S. Congress, Senate Select Committee to Study Governmental Activities with Respect to Intelligence Activities, *Final Report Book B: Supplementary Detailed Staff Reports on Intelligence Activities and Rights of Americans* (Washington, D.C.: Government Printing Office, 1976), pp. 11–270; U.S. Commission on CIA Activities Within the United States, *Report to the President* (Washington, D.C.: Government Printing Office, 1975).

72. Bayard Rustin, "From Protest to Politics: The Future of the Civil Rights Movement," *Commentary* 39 (February 1965): 29.

73. Maynard Jackson quoted in Edward Brooks, "Black Business, Problems and Prospects," *Black Scholar* 6 (April 1975): 2.

74. *Washington Post*, 25 July 1976, p. H3.

75. *New York Times*, 1 June 1976.

76. *New York Times*, 1 June 1976; Joint Center for Political Studies, *National Roster of Black Elected Officials, Vol. 5* (Washington, D.C.: Joint Center for Political Studies, 1975).

77. *New York Times*, 1 June 1976.

78. CPR, Series P–23, No. 54, *The Social and Economics Status of the Black Population in the United States, 1974*, Table 95, p. 146.

79. Alex Poinsett, "Why Blacks Don't Vote," *Ebony* 31 (March 1976):38; 42 U.S.C. sec. 1973 *et seq.* (1975 supp.).

80. Milton D. Morris, *The Politics of Black America* (New York: Harper and Row, Publishers, 1975), p. 169.

81. Ibid., pp. 172, 174–5.

82. Congressional Quarterly Service, *Revolution in Civil Rights* 4th ed. (Washington, D.C.: Congressional Quarterly Service, 1968), pp. 32–52.

83. Morris, *Black America*, p. 172.

84. U.S. Congress, Senate, *Nomination of Ellsworth, Greener, Perry and Reed,* Hearings held 16 December 1975, 94th Cong., 1st sess., 1975, pp. 3–5.

85. Frederick Douglass quoted in Lerone Bennett, *Before the Mayflower: A History of the Negro in America 1619–1964,* rev. ed. (Baltimore: Penguin Books, Pelican Book, 1966), p. 274.

Chapter 2: Unequal Employment Opportunity

1. Richard M. Nixon, "Address to the Nation on Labor Day, September 6, 1971," in the *Public Papers of the President Richard M. Nixon, Containing the Public Messages, Speeches and Statements, January 1 to December 31, 1971* (Washington, D.C.: Government Printing Office, 1972), p. 935.

2. Work created under special programs, such as the Works Progress Administration (WPA) and the Civilian Conservation Corps (CCC).

3. Estimated from 1940 Census of Population, *The Labor Force, Vol. 3, Pt. 1, U.S. Summary,* Table 4, p. 18.

4. Walter White, *A Man Called White* (1948; reprint ed., New York: Arno Press and The New York Times, 1969), pp. 191–3.

5. Jessie P. Gazman, *Negro Year Book: A Review of Events Affecting Negro Life 1941–1946* (Tuskegee, Ala.: Department of Records and Research, Tuskegee Institute, 1947), pp. 141, 144; Richard H. Jefferson, "Negro Employment in St. Louis War Production," in *The Black Urban Condition,* ed. by Hollis R. Lynch (New York: Thomas Y. Crowell Co., 1973), pp. 324–5; Robert C. Weaver, *Negro Labor: A National Problem* (New York: Harcourt, Brace and Co., 1946), pp. 20–3; U.S. Committee on Fair Employment Practice, *Final Report,* cited in Louis C. Kesselman, *The Social Politics of FEPC: A Study in Reform Pressure* (Chapel Hill: University of North Carolina Press, 1948), p. 18. This practice of segregated employment offices in the USES continued until the 1960s. See U.S. Commission on Civil Rights, *Jobs and Civil Rights: The Role of the Federal Government in Promoting Equal Opportunity in Employment and Training,* by Richard Nathan (Washington, D.C.: Government Printing Office, 1969), p. 159.

6. Gunnar Myrdal, *An American Dilemma: The Negro Problem and Modern Democracy,* 20th ann. ed. (New York: Harper and Row, Publishers, 1962), pp. 388–96; Donald Dewey, "Negro Employment in Southern Industry," *Journal of Political Economy* 60 (August 1952): 282–5; Herbert R. Northrup and Richard L. Rowan, "Concluding Analysis," in *Negro Employment in Southern Industry: A Study of Racial Policies in Five Industries,* by Herbert L. Northrup and Richard L. Rowan (Philadelphia: Industrial Research Unit, Wharton School of Finance and Commerce, University of Pennsylvania, 1970), p. 14; Herman J. Bloch, "The Employment Status of the New York Negro, 1920–1964," *Interracial Review* 37 (December 1964): 229–38; National Committee on Segregation in the Nation's Capital, *Segregation in Washington* (Chicago: National Committee on Segregation in the Nation's Capital, 1948), p. 55; Jefferson, "Negro Employment," p. 324.

7. Bloch, "Employment Status," p. 231.

8. " 'N' for Negro," *Crisis* 48 (November 1941): 355.

9. George M. Johnson, "The Segregation of War Workers Because of Race, Creed, Color or National Origin." From his files, which are part of the U.S. Committee on Fair Employment Practice's records in the National Archives, Washington, D.C.

10. Nine major occupational groups are given a numerical value by multiplying the percentage of workers in each occupational group in each race by an index representing the earnings value for the occupational group, using median 1969 earnings. (See Table 2–4 for median 1969 earnings.)

11. The authors are indebted to Gary S. Becker for this method. (See Gary S. Becker, *Economics of Discrimination* 2nd ed. [Chicago: University of Chicago Press, 1971], pp. 135–52.) Changes from Becker's original work include using nine occupational groups instead of three (skilled, semiskilled, and unskilled), including all workers—women as well as men and farm as well as nonfarm workers.

The authors agree with Becker that a fixed earnings weight (1969 earnings) helps to reveal year-to-year differences more than variable earnings would—as suggested by Elton Rayack. (See Elton Rayack, "Discrimination and the Occupational Progress of Negroes," *Review of Economics and Statistics* 43 [May 1961]: 209–14.) However, we applied 1949 earnings in one set of data to assess the difference in the decennial years 1950–70 and studied results for decennial years 1940–70 when farm workers were excluded. (Table 2–5). The argument in this study is supported by each of these techniques. The authors concluded that, to understand the dynamics of race in the ever-changing labor force in this century, all workers should be included. Also applying the earnings weight as one point in time does not obscure changes in occupational structure and status, since relative position in the occupational hierarchy remains fixed over very long periods. (See Peter M. Blau and Otis D. Duncan, *The American Occupational Structure* [New York: John Wiley and Sons, 1967], pp. 120–1.)

12. The statistical analysis on which these industry data are based reflects a set of comprehensive indicators of attainment within industry to juxtapose against the same kind of indicators for occupational position, discussed earlier in the text. In this case, however, the data are not a summary for the nation, but are for each of the four main census regions—Northeast, North Central, West, and South. For industry as for occupation, the proportion of workers within each of seventeen industry groups (for each race and region) was weighted (multiplied) by an index of the comparative importance of the industry group. That index is based on the average annual 1969 full-time earnings in each industry group.

13. Ray Marshall, "Summary, Conclusions and Recommendation" in *Negro Employment in the South,* Report prepared for U.S. Manpower Administration (Austin: Center for the Study of Human Resources, University of Texas, 1973), p. 1.

14. Ibid., pp. 44–5.

15. Sar Levitan, William B. Johnson, and Robert Taggart, *Still a Dream: The Changing Status of Blacks Since 1960* (Cambridge: Harvard University Press, 1975), pp. 310–3.

16. In 1948, 1954, 1958, 1961, 1971, and 1975. The most severe were in 1954, 1958, and 1975.

17. BLS, *Handbook of Labor Statistics 1975, Reference Edition,* Bulletin 1865 (Washington, D.C.: Government Printing Office, 1975), Table 158, p. 389; unpublished data from BLS.

18. See, for instance, M. W. Reder, "Wage Structure and Structural Unemployment," *Review of Economic Studies* 31 (October 1964): 309–22; Robert M. Solow, "Technology and Unemployment," *Public Interest,* Fall 1965, pp. 17–26; Harold Wool, *The Labor Supply for Lower Level Occupations* (Washington, D.C.: National Planning Association, 1973), pp. 34–5.

19. See Chapter 3 for an expansion of this point.

20. Carol S. Greenwald, "The Changing Composition of the Unemployed," *New England Economic Review,* July–August 1971, pp. 2–10; Robert E. Hall, "Why Is the Unemployment Rate So High at Full Employment?" *Brookings Papers on Economic Activity,* No. 3, 1970, pp. 369–402; Irwin L. Kellner, "Counting the Employed, Not the Unemployed," *New York Times,* 26 October 1975, Sec. 3, p. 12. U.S. President, *Economic Report of the President, 1975* (Washington, D.C.: Government Printing Office, 1975), pp. 102–16.

21. U.S. President, *Economic Report, 1975,* p. 111.

22. Ann R. Miller, "The Black Migrant—Changing Origins, Changing Characteristics," paper presented at W. E. B. Dubois Conference on the American Black, Atlanta University, Atlanta, Georgia, October 1974, App. Table 1, p. 1.

23. Karl E. Taeuber and Alma F. Taeuber, "The Black Population in the United States," in *The Black American Reference Book,* ed. by Mabel M. Smythe (Englewood Cliffs, N.J.: Prentice-Hall, 1976), p. 171.

24. Miller, "The Black Migrant," App. Table 1, p. 1.

25. Ibid., p. 4.

26. 1940 Census of Population, *Labor Force, Vol. 3, Pt. 1, U.S. Summary,* Table 77, pp. 190–3; 1950 Census of Population, *Characteristics of the Population, Vol. 2, Pt. 1, U.S. Summary,* Table 161, pp. 1–407–12; 1960 Census of Population, *Characteristics of the Population, Vol. 1, Pt. 1, U.S. Summary,* Table 260, pp. 1–728–9; 1970 Census of Population, *Characteristics of the Population, Vol. 1, Pt. 1, Sec. 2, U.S. Summary,* Table 299, pp. 1–1376–81.

27. Calvin L. Beale, "The Black American in Agriculture," in *The Black American Reference Book,* ed. by Mabel M. Smythe (Englewood Cliffs, N. J.: Prentice-Hall, 1976), p. 287; 1959 Census of Agriculture, *General Report, Vol. 2, Chap. 10, Color, Race, and Tenure of Farm Operators,* Tables 5, 7, pp. 1032, 1034; 1969 Census of Agriculture, *General Report, Vol. 2, Chap. 3, Farm Management and Farm Operators,* Table 35, p. 98.

28. BLS, *Handbook,* Table 107, pp. 264–5.

29. Beale, "Black Americans," p. 291.

30. Lester M. Salamon, *Black Owned Land: Profile of a Disappearing*

Equity Base: State Level Analysis, Report of the U.S. Office of Minority Business Enterprise (Durham, N.C.: Institute of Policy, Science, and Public Affairs, Duke University, 1974), Table 5, p. 11.

Blacks were much more likely to have lost their land than were whites. Many were cheated by white entrepreneurs who took advantage of title disputes arising from absence of formal wills. Others were enticed by unscrupulous land profiteers as the value of farm land close to developing urban centers soared in many places. Ibid., p. iii; Black Economic Research Center, *Only Six Million Acres: The Decline of Black Owned Land in the Rural South* (New York: Black Economic Research Center, 1973), pp. F1–3, G3–10; Michael J. Piore, "Negro Workers in the Mississippi Delta: Problems of Displacement and Adjustment," in *Perspectives on Poverty and Income Distribution,* ed. by James G. Scoville (Lexington, Mass.: D. C. Heath and Co., 1971), pp. 151–7.

31. Homer G. Hawkins, "Trends in Black Migration from 1863 to 1960," *Phylon* 34 (Summer 1973): 150; Miller, "The Black Migrants," pp. 6–9; Taeuber and Taeuber, "Black Population," p. 181.

32. Miller, "Black Migrants," p. 25; Gene B. Petersen, Laure M. Sharp, and Thomas F. Drury, *Southern Newcomers to Cleveland: Work and Social Adjustments of Recently Arrived Residents of Low-Income Neighborhoods,* Report prepared for U.S. Manpower Administration (Washington, D.C.: Bureau of Social Science Research, 1975), especially pp. 373–83, is another recent study with similar findings.

33. James L. Sundquist, *Politics and Policy: The Eisenhower, Kennedy, and Johnson Years* (Washington, D.C.: Brookings Institution, 1968), pp. 85–110.

34. U.S. Bureau of the Census, *Historical Statistics of the United States, Colonial Times to 1957* (Washington, D.C.: Government Printing Office, 1961), Series D8, H201, 204, pp. 70, 200.

35. Myrdal, *American Dilemma,* pp. 360–1, 1282–3.

36. Alden F. Briscoe, *The WPA: What Is to Be Learned,* Issues Paper No. 2 (Washington, D.C.: Center for Governmental Studies, 1971), p. 19.

37. Herbert Hill, "Employment, Manpower Training and the Black Worker," *Journal of Negro Education* 39 (Summer 1969): 205.

38. Bernard E. Anderson and Charles R. Perry, presenting a prepared statement in *Employment Problems of Women Minorities and Youths,* Hearings held by the U.S. Congress Joint Economic Committee, Subcommittee on Economic Growth on July 7–8, 1975, 94th Cong., 1st sess., 1975, pp. 21–35, especially pp. 22–5 and pp. 31–5.

39. Eli Ginzberg, *The Manpower Connection: Education and Work* (Cambridge: Harvard University Press, 1975), p. 173.

40. Garth L. Mangum and John Walsh, *A Decade of Manpower Development and Training,* quoted in ibid., p. 175.

41. Ewan Clague and Leo Kramer, *Manpower Policies and Programs: A Review, 1935–75* (Kalamazoo, Mich.: W. E. Upjohn Institute for Employment Research, 1976), p. 65.

42. Ibid., p. 43. The authors summarize one of the major conclusions of

the study by E. Wright Bakke, *The Mission of Manpower Policy* (Kalamazoo, Mich.: W. E. Upjohn Institute for Employment Research, 1969).

43. Ginzberg, *Manpower,* p. 175.

44. BLS, *Handbook,* Table 57, pp. 142–4, is the basis for the estimate.

45. An educational position index was constructed to compare with the occupational position index (described on pages 35 and 294, note 10). Instead of the median years of schooling attained, the usual measure, it takes into account the rising importance, or the added weight of each attainment level. For schooling, the importance, or a weight, was assigned to each class or group of years of school attained: 0–4 years (.86); 5–8 (1.24); 9–11 (1.61); 12 (1.82); 13–15 (2.03); 16 and over (2.24). For comparative purposes the numerical range of the weights for schooling groups from none to 16+ is the same as for the nine occupation groups in the occupational index. That range was used, first to get a weight for a single year of schooling, as follows. The range for occupation groups of 1.68 (from .56 to 2.24) was divided by 16—the total years of school, excluding the open end above 16, which includes relatively few persons. The result—.105—is the weight for a single school year. Zero school years begins at .56—the bottom of the occupational weight range. Weights were derived for the middle year of each schooling level of group of years. For 0 to 4 years of school, for instance, the weight came out this way—2.5 (middle of 0–5) $\times$ .105 (weight for one year) + .56 (the weight for zero years) = .86.

The percentage distribution of persons at each schooling level multiplied by the appropriate weight, totaled, for each race separately, gives the index of educational position in each of the years shown. The ratio of the results —black to white—gives the relative educational position in each year. This ratio is comparable to the occupational position index. They appear together in Table 2–12.

46. Based on calculation of relative educational and occupational indices for the twenty-five- to thirty-four-year-old group of black and white persons in the labor force using the same techniques as for the labor force as a whole. See notes 11 and 45 for the method. Data were derived from unpublished data from the BLS. See also Becker, *Discrimination,* pp, 112–4.

47. Guichard Parris and Lester Brooks, *Blacks in the City: A History of the National Urban League* (Boston: Little, Brown and Co., 1971), p. 333.

48. National Urban League, *Annual Report* (New York: National Urban League, n.d.). See the 1969–74 reports particularly.

49. Parris and Brooks, *Blacks,* pp. 331–36.

50. August Meier, "Civil Rights Strategies for Negro Employment," in *Employment, Race, and Poverty,* ed. by A. M. Ross and Herbert Hill (New York: Harcourt, Brace, and World, Harbinger Books, 1967), pp. 186–8.

51. National Association for the Advancement of Colored People, *Annual Report* (New York: n.d.). (Hereafter cited as *NAACP Report.*) See the reports from 1945 to 1975.

52. Herbert Garfinkel, *When Negroes March: The March on Washington Movement in the Organizational Politics for FEPC* (Glencoe, Ill.: Free Press,

1959), pp. 161, 192; U.S. President, "Regulations Governing Fair Employment Practices Within the Federal Establishment," Executive Order 9980,
26 July 1948, *3 Code of Federal Regulations: 1943–1948 Compilation*
(Washington, D.C.: Government Printing Office, 1957), pp. 720–1.

53. Garfinkel, *When Negroes March,* p. 162.

54. Ibid., p. 163.

55. U.S. President, "Authorizing the Department of Defense and The
Department of Commerce To Exercise The Functions and Powers Set
Forth in Title II of the First War Powers Act, 1941 as Amended by the Act
of January 12, 1951 and Prescribing Regulations for The Exercise of Such
Functions and Powers," Executive Order 10210, 2 February, 1951, *3 Code
of Federal Regulations: 1949–1953 Compilation* (Washington, D.C.: Government Printing Office, 1958), pp. 390–2; ibid., p. 176.

56. U.S. President, "Improving The Means for Obtaining Compliance
with the Nondiscrimination Provisions of Federal Contracts," Executive
Order 10308, 3 December 1951, *3 Code of Federal Regulations: 1949–1953
Compilation* (Washington, D.C.: Government Printing Office, 1958), pp.
837–8.

57. U.S. President, "Establishing the Government Contract Committee,"
Executive Order 10479, 13 August 1953, *3 Code of Federal Regulations:
1949–1953 Compilation* (Washington, D.C.: Government Printing Office,
1950), pp. 961–2; U.S. President, "Establishing the President's Committee
on Equal Employment Opportunity," Executive Order 10925, 6 March
1961, *3 Code of Federal Regulation: 1959–1963 Compilation* (Washington,
D.C.: Government Printing Office, 1964), pp. 448–54.

58. U.S. Commission on Civil Rights, *The Federal Civil Rights Enforcement Effort–1974: Vol. 5: To Eliminate Employment Discrimination,* 1975,
p. 510.

59. Ibid., pp. 532–3.

60. *NAACP Report,* 1966, pp. 55–60.

61. 401 U.S. 424 (1971).

62. 446 F.2d 652 (C.A.2, 1971); Herbert Hill, "Black Labor, the NLRB,
and the Developing Law of Equal Employment Opportunity," *Labor Law
Journal* 26 (April 1975): 217.

63. *Stamp et al. v. Detroit Edison,* 365 F. Supp. 87 (D.C. Mich., 1973);
Hill, "Black Labor," pp. 214–6.

64. August Meier and Elliott Rudwick, *CORE: A Study in the Civil
Rights Movement, 1942–1968* (New York: Oxford University Press, 1973),
pp. 236–7.

65. Ibid. describes the range of job-related protest activities of this period.

66. *NAACP Report,* 1964, pp. 56–7.

67. Meier, *"Rights Strategies,"* pp. 196–201.

68. "Ham and Eggs on Earth: Opportunities Industrialization Centers
See Profit Motive As Key to Helping the Poor," *Manpower* 3 (June 1971):
3.

69. *NAACP Report,* 1965, p. 46.

70. *NAACP Report,* 1966, p. 54; *NAACP Report,* 1970, pp. 85–6.

71. Philip S. Foner, *Organized Labor and the Black Worker, 1619–1973*
(New York: Praeger Publishers, 1974), pp. 334, 345–6.

72. Ibid., pp. 295, 300–10.

73. Ibid., pp. 300–1.

74. Hill, "Black Labor," pp. 212–13.

75. Foner, *Organized Labor,* pp. 397–424.

76. CPR, Series P–23, No. 46, *The Social and Economic Status of the Black Population in the United States, 1972,* Table 42, p. 54.

77. Hill, "Black Labor," p. 214.

Chapter 3: Learning Without Earning

1. Just before World War II the USES was in the Social Security Board; it was under the War Manpower Commission during wartime, and moved to the Labor Department in 1945, where it has remained.

2. E. Lanham, *Job Evaluation* (New York: McGraw-Hill Book Co., 1955), pp. 6–12, contains a history of this technique and its uses.

3. U.S. Employment Service, *Job Analysis in the United States Employment Service, 1935–1972,* 1973, pp. 2–5.

4. BLS, *Occupational Outlook Handbook, 1976–77 ed.,* is the latest of this series.

5. Table 3–2 compares schooling requirements of occupations and the educational levels of workers for fifty jobs common to the major occupation groups, from 1950 to 1970. The comparison is in terms of mental requirements for the job (years of schooling) and the median years of schooling of the labor force, using information about worker traits required for the former from the U.S. Employment Service (USES) and census data for the latter.

The translation of mental traits required for jobs into years of schooling appears in a range, and is according to the recommendations of the USES in its 1971 publication, *Relating General Educational Development to Career Planning,* pp. 5–17. Median years of schooling means that half the experienced civilian labor force for whom each occupation was reported in the applicable census was below the figure shown, and half was over. Analysis of the census education data shows substantial concentration around the median for the occupations shown.

6. BLS, *Occupational Outlook Handbook, 1975–76 ed.,* Bulletin 1875 (Washington, D.C.: Government Printing Office, 1976).

7. Harry J. Gilman, "Economic Discrimination and Unemployment," *American Economic Review* 55 (December 1965): 1077–96; James Gwartney, "Discrimination and Income Differentials," *American Economic Review* 60 (June 1970): 396–408; William M. Landes, "The Economics of Fair Employment Laws," *Journal of Political Economy* 76 (July–August 1968): 507–52; Leonard Weiss and Jeffery G. Williamson, "Black Education, Earnings and Interregional Migration: Some New Evidence," *American Economic Review* 62 (June 1972): 372–83, are representative of the articles with this point of view.

8. This is not to say, however, that individuals and American society in

general deny the value of what high schools teach for citizenship and enjoyable living.

9. Dixie Sommers, "Occupational Rankings for Men and Women by Earnings," in *Monthly Labor Review Reader* by the BLS (Washington, D.C.: Government Printing Office, 1975); pp. 327–44; 1970 Census of Population, *Characteristics of the Population, Vol. 1, Pt. 1. Sec. 2, U.S. Summary,* Tables 227–8, pp. 766–77; Peter M. Blau and Otis Dudley Duncan, *The American Occupational Structure* (New York: John Wiley and Sons, 1967), pp. 122–3.

10. BLS, *Occupational Outlook Handbook, 1948–49 ed.,* Bulletin 940 (Washington, D.C.: Government Printing Office, 1948), p. 167; BLS, *Occupational Outlook Handbook, 1957–58 ed.,* Bulletin 1215 (Washington, D.C.: Government Printing Office, 1957), pp. 224–5; BLS, *Occupational Outlook Handbook, 1961–62 ed.,* Bulletin 1300 (Washington, D.C.: Government Printing Office, 1961), pp. 336–7; BLS, *Occupational Outlook Handbook, 1968–69 ed.,* Bulletin 1550 (Washington, D.C.: Government Printing Office, 1968), p. 316; BLS, *Occupational Outlook Handbook, 1974–75 ed.,* Bulletin 1785 (Washington, D.C.: Government Printing Office, 1974), p. 25

11. U.S. National Commission of Technology, Automation, and Economic Progress, *The Employment Impact of Technological Change, Appendix, Vol. 2* (Washington, D.C.: Government Printing Office, 1966). See especially James E. Bright, "The Relationship of Increasing Automation and Skill Requirement," pp. II–207–21 and Morris A. Horowitz and Irwin L. Hernstadt, "Changes in the Skill Requirements of Occupations in Selected Industries," pp. II–227–87.

12. Lewis Corey, *The Crisis of the Middle Class* (New York: Covici Friede, 1935), p. 250.

13. Gloria P. Greene, "Employment Data for Detailed Occupations, 1975," *Employment and Earnings* 22 (January 1976): 11.

14. Whitney M. Young, *To Be Equal* (New York: McGraw-Hill Book Co., 1964), pp. 54–5; Mahlon T. Puryear, "Technology and the Negro," in *Negroes and Jobs,* ed. by Louis A. Ferman, Joyce L. Kornbluh, and J. A. Miller (Ann Arbor: University of Michigan Press, 1968), pp. 203–4; A. Philip Randolph, "Foreword," in *Negroes and Jobs,* p. v.; Vivian W. Henderson, "The Economic Imbalance: An Inquiry into the Economic Status of Negroes in the United States, 1935–1960, with Implications for Negro Education," *Journal of Negro Education* 38 (Winter 1961): 13–16.

15. Benjamin Muse, *The American Negro Revolution: From Nonviolence to Black Power* (Bloomington: Indiana University Press, 1968), p. 64.

16. Arthur Goldberg, "Editorial," *NEA Journal* 50 (April 1961): 9.

17. Arthur Goldberg, transcript of interview for the Westinghouse Broadcasting Company radio program, *Washington Viewpoint,* for 5 September 1961, p. 12.

18. D. J. Giese, "I Was a High School Dropout," *Reader's Digest* 79 (December 1961): 203–7.

19. "School Dropouts Called Great American Tragedy of Our Times," *Science Digest* 52 (July 1962): 32.

20. "The Tragedy of Dropouts," *Ebony* 16 (September 1961): 48; "The Dropout Campaign," *School Life* 46 (October 1963): 2–3.

21. "The Tragedy," p. 48.

22. Ibid.

23. Jacob Schiffman, "Employment of High School Graduates and Dropouts in 1962," *Monthly Labor Review* 86 (July 1963): 772–9; Vera C. Perrella and Elizabeth Waldman, "Out-of-School Youth—Two Years Later," *Monthly Labor Review* 89 (August 1966): 860–6; and Elizabeth Waldman, "Employment of High School Graduates and Dropouts in 1966," *Monthly Labor Review* 90 (July 1967): 15–21, are representative of the type of articles available in the *Monthly Labor Review.*

24. BLS, *Handbook of Labor Statistics 1975—Reference Edition* (Washington, D.C.: Government Printing Office, 1975); U.S. President, *Manpower Report of the President, 1976* (Washington, D.C.: Government Printing Office, 1976), are the latest editions of annual series which contain data that reflect this dichotomy.

25. U.S. Manpower Administration, *Credentials and Common Sense: Jobs for People Without Diplomas,* by Rose Wiener, Manpower Report No. 13, 1968, p. 2.

26. U.S. Office of Management and Budget, Statistical Policy and Management Information Systems Division, *Occupations of the Labor Force According to the Dictionary of Occupational Titles,* by Ann R. Miller, Statistical Evaluation Report No. 9, 1971, p. 3.

27. U.S. Department of Health, Education, and Welfare, Special Task Force, *Work in America* (Cambridge: MIT Press, 1973); James O'Toole, "The Reserve Army of the Unemployed," *Change* 7 (May–June 1975): 26; Richard Freeman and J. Herbert Holloman, "The Declining Value of College Going," *Change* 7 (September 1975): 24; Martin Trow, "Reflections on the Relations Between the Occupational Structure and Higher Education," in *An International Perspective: Higher Education: Crises and Support* by The International Council for Educational Development, 1974, pp. 35–42; Harold Wool, "The Labor Supply for Lower Level Occupations" (Washington, D.C.: National Planning Association, 1973).

28. Wool, "The Labor Supply," p. 100.

29. White House Conference on Youth, 1971, Recommendations and Report; Gene I. Maeroff, "New Look at the 'Quitting Age'," *New York Times,* 18 January 1976, Sec. E4, p. 18; David A. Wise, "Academic Achievement and Job Performance," *American Economic Review* 65 (June 1975): 350–66.

30. Ivar Berg, *Education and Jobs: The Great Training Robbery* (New York: Published for the Center for Urban Education by Praeger Publishers, 1970), pp. 105–20; U.S. Manpower Administration, *Credentials.*

31. John C. Flanagan et al., *Project Talent: Five Years After High School* (Pittsburgh: American Institute for Research and University of Pittsburgh, 1971); Janet Coombs and William W. Cooley, "Dropouts: In High School and After School," *American Education Research Journal* 5 (May 1968): 343–63; Jerald G. Bachman, *Youth in Transition: Dropping Out—Problem* *or Symptom, Vol. 2* (Ann Arbor: Institute for Social Research, University of Michigan, 1971).

32. Maeroff, "New Look"; W. Willard Wirtz, *The Boundless Resource* (Washington, D.C.: New Republic Press, 1975); National Commission on Reform of Secondary Education, *The Reform of Secondary Education: A Report to the Public and the Educational Profession* (New York: McGraw-Hill Book Co., 1973), pp. 127–8.

33. CPR, Series P–20, No. 295, *Educational Attainment in the United States: March 1975,* Table 1, pp. 9–16.

34. According to the educational index discussed in Chapter 2, page 00, the index for twenty-five-to-thirty-four-year-old white youth went from 1.63 (on a base of 1.00) in 1940 to 1.91 in 1975; the index for black youth went from the relatively low level of 1.25 in 1940 to 1.84, which was 96 percent of the index for white youth in 1975.

35. Gunnar Myrdal, *An American Dilemma: The Negro Problem and Modern Democracy,* 20th ann. ed. (New York: Harper and Row, Publishers, 1962), p. 884.

36. Walter White, *A Man Called White* (1948; reprint ed., New York: Arno Press and The New York Times, 1969), pp. 29–38.

37. 347 U.S. 483 (1954).

38. Richard Kluger, *Simple Justice: The History of Brown v. Board of Education and Black America's Struggle for Equality* (New York: Alfred A. Knopf, 1976).

39. Carnegie Commission on Higher Education, *Between Two Worlds: A Profile of Negro Higher Education* (New York: McGraw-Hill Book Co., 1971), p. 192.

40. Orley Ashenfelter and Michael K. Taussig, "Discrimination and Income Differentials: Comment," *American Economic Review* 61 (September 1971): 746–55; Finis Welch, "Labor Market Discrimination: An Interpretation of Income Differences in the Rural South," *Journal of Political Economy* 75 (June 1967): 225–40; James Gwartney, "Changes in the Non-White/White Income Ratio—1939–67," *American Economic Review* 60 (December 1970): 872–83.

41. Richard Bardolph, ed., *The Civil Rights Record: Black Americans and the Law, 1849–1970* (New York: Thomas Y. Crowell Co., 1970), pp. 473–91.

42. CPR, *Educational Attainment,* Table 1, pp. 9–16; 1960 Census of Population, *Characteristics of the Population, Vol. 1, Pt. 1, Sec. D, U.S. Summary* (Washington, D.C.: Government Printing Office, 1964), Table 174, pp. 419–21.

43. U.S. Office of Education, *Equality of Educational Opportunity,* by James S. Coleman (Washington, D.C.: Government Printing Office, 1966), p. 21.

44. Ibid., p. 22.

45. Ibid., p. 21.

46. Patricia Cayo Sexton, *Education and Income: Inequalities of Opportunity in Our Public Schools* (New York: Viking Press, 1961), pp. 16–7.

47. Christopher Jencks et al., *Inequality: A Reassessment of the Effect*

of Family and Schooling in America (New York: Basic Books, 1972), p. 100.

48. Robert P. Althauser and Sydney S. Spivack, *The Unequal Elites* (New York: John Wiley and Sons, 1975.)

49. Carnegie Commission on Higher Education, *Between Two Worlds,* pp. 285–315; *The College Blue Book, Vol. 1,* 12th ed. (Los Angeles: College Planning Program, LTC, 1968). The *College Blue Book* was used to supplement *Between Two Worlds* because the latter did not include accreditation information on the matched white colleges.

50. R. Descloitres, *The Foreign Worker: Adaptation To Industrial Work and Urban Life* (Paris: Organization of Economic Co-operation and Development, 1967), p. 35.

51. Ibid., p. 34.

52. Bernard Keyser, *Manpower Movements and Labor Markets* (Paris: Organization of Economic Co-operation and Development, 1971), pp. 167–8.

53. Portugal is the only developing country for which detail by occupation and education could be found. The difficulties of obtaining international statistics to reflect comparable conditions are well known. The information in this section comes from a dozen sources and, as yet, is not complete for all the countries discussed and about every issue. Uniform informational statistics for later or entirely comparable years were not possible to obtain. One investigator describes the problem as follows:

> The application of the principle of free movement of persons, introduced by the Treaty of Rome, as well as special provisions governing relations between various states with regard to migration are further obstacles [toward building] . . . up a true picture of migratory movements in Western Europe. . . . Controls . . . by emigration countries do not always provide a means of making the necessary check. . . . Some . . . are . . . conducted in a rather irregular manner. Indeed, emigrants frequently cross their country's frontiers not as "workers," but as "tourists." Finally, in some extreme and special cases the clandestine nature of the population . . . makes any counting impossible. (R. Descloitres, *Foreign Worker,* p. 19)

54. Stephen Castles and Godula Kosack, *Immigrant Workers and Class Structure in Western Europe* (New York: Published for the Institute for Race Relations by Oxford University Press, 1973), p. 82.

55. Ibid., p. 115.

56. Arnold M. Rose, *Migrants in Europe: Problem of Acceptance and Adjustment* (Minneapolis: University of Minnesota, 1969), pp. 97, 138.

57. Castles and Kosack, *Immigrant Workers,* p. 114.

Chapter 4: Uncle Sam As Employer

1. W. M. Kiplinger, *Washington is Like That* (New York: Harper and Bros., 1942), p. 148.

2. Ibid., p. 134.

3. Joseph P. Lash, *Eleanor and Franklin* (New York: W. W. Norton and Co., 1971), p. 528.

4. "The Roosevelt Record," *Crisis* 47 (October 1940): 311.

5. *Washington Post,* 14 September 1940.

6. Lash, *Eleanor,* p. 528.

7. U.S. Congress, Senate, Senator Neely offering an amendment to H.R. 960, 26 September 1940, *Congressional Record* 86: 12641.

8. Ibid.

9. U.S. President "Amending Certain Provisions of the Civil Service Rules," Executive Order 8587, 7 November 1940, *3 Code of Federal Regulations, 1938–43 Compilation* (Washington, D.C.: Government Printing Office, 1968), pp. 824–30.

The Civil Service Commission was created by the Civil Service Act of 1883. It acts as the personnel agent for the executive branch of the federal government, with responsibility for job classification, pay scales, training, personnel files, and, since 1961, for the collection and dissemination of statistical data and its analysis by racial groups. Since 1961, the CSC has been charged with some responsibility for Equal Employment Opportunity activities.

Except for personnel who may be employed without reference to the competitive requirements of the classified Civil Service, all of the following groups of employees come under the rules of the CSC: *Professional* (P), 10 grades requiring specialized skills and presuppose the Bachelors degree or more; *Sub-professional* (SP), 8 grades involving work of a semi-professional nature; *Clerical, Administrative and Fiscal* (CAF), 17 grades, the lowest of which involve routine skills like typing, filing, sorting, or operating simple business machines, but at middle levels include stenographers, accounting clerks, and receptionists, and at the highest levels include supervisory, administrative, personnel, and budget specialists; *Crafts-Protective-Custodial* (CPC), 10 grades covering laborers, chauffeurs, janitors, and building guards; *Clerical and Mechanical* (CM), 4 grades covering those in menial clerical functions. The *General Schedule* pay system (GS) began in 1949 with eighteen grades; it is the largest and covers all of the salaried positions in the executive branch and the District of Columbia government. *Wage System* (WS) absorbed CPC workers in 1949; its employees are in trades, crafts, and labor occupations and the pay is set in accordance with prevailing wages in the localities where they work.

10. U.S. President, "Reaffirming Policy of Full Participation in the Defense Program by All Persons, Regardless of Race, Creed, Color or National Origin and Directing Certain Action in Furtherance of Said Policy," Executive Order 8802, 25 June 1941, *3 Code of Federal Regulations, 1938–43 Compilation* (Washington, D.C.: Government Printing Office, 1968), p. 957.

11. Kiplinger, *Washington,* p. 150.

12. Paul P. Van Riper, *History of the United States Civil Service Commission* (New York: Row, Peterson and Co., 1958), p. 369.

13. Ibid., p. 378.

14. William C. Bradbury, "Racial Discrimination in Federal Employment," n.d., unpublished study from the files of the President's Committee on Government Employment Policy available through the U.S. Department of Labor, Officer of the Solicitor, Washington, D.C., p. History–3. Bradbury does not cite agencies or persons by name. However, through a knowledgeable informant and extensive investigations, the agencies and in some cases the particular individuals Bradbury discusses have been identified.

15. Ibid., p. History–12.

16. U.S. Committee on Fair Employment Practice, Proceedings Before the Fair Employment Practice Committee in the Matter of the Complaint of Leslie S. Perry, February 19, 1942. Transcript from the files of the Committee in the National Archives, Washington, D.C., pp. 12–28.

17. Van Riper, *Civil Service Commission History,* pp. 375–6.

18. Bradbury, *Racial Discrimination,* p. History–5.

19. Ibid., p. III–8.

20. Ibid., p. III–11.

21. Ibid.

22. James Evans, former counselor to the secretary of the navy, interview on May 17, 1976.

23. Roi Ottley, *New World A-Coming: Inside Black America* (Boston: Houghton Mifflin Co., 1943), p. 255.

24. Ibid., p. 264.

25. Ibid.; Kiplinger, *Washington,* pp. 152–4.

26. Kiplinger, *Washington,* pp. 152–4.

27. James C. Harvey, *Black Civil Rights During the Johnson Administration* (Jackson: University and College Press of Mississippi, 1973), p. 64.

28. "The Negro Should Support Stevenson," *Crisis* 63 (October 1956): 466–7.

29. Ottley, *New World,* p. 267.

30. U.S. Committee on Fair Employment Practice, *The Wartime Employment of Negroes in the Federal Government,* 1945, p. 28.

31. The Federal Security Agency (FSA) also had a large percentage of blacks (16 percent) and of salaried personnel, partly because Howard University and Freedman's Hospital, both of which had virtually all black employees, were included in their statistics. Nevertheless, with other parts of the agency, the proportion of maintenance personnel was very high.

32. The pay and promotion schedule of the State Department was the same as other departments until 1946, when it developed a special schedule for the foreign service officers who served in professional capacities overseas.

33. U.S. Committee on Fair Employment Practice, *Wartime Employment,* p. 7.

34. Ibid., p. 46.

35. Over the years the Post Office System has maintained its own frequently changing pay and promotion schedule that remains roughly but not perfectly comparable to the General Schedule employees of the classified Civil Service.

36. "Postal Employees: Government Mail Service is Biggest U.S. Em-

ployer of Negroes with 42,000 on Its Payroll," *Ebony* 5 (November 1949): 17–8.

37. Ibid., p. 15.

38. *Washington Post,* 24 July 1975.

39. Samuel Krislov, *The Negro in Federal Employment: The Quest for Equal Opportunity* (Minneapolis: University of Minnesota Press, 1967), p. 135.

40. "Postal Employees," p. 17.

41. Blacks did not accept the social degradation of segregation passively, and when traditional forms of opposition were blocked, they used other means, like placing "out of order" signs on white restrooms (to force whites to use the same facilities) or convincing painters to paint over signs saying "colored" and "white." Efforts to fight social segregation were sometimes crudely stifled. A group of black secretaries entering a government lunchroom in 1945 found all the tables full except one partly occupied by white men. When they took the empty seats, their lunch trays were swept to the floor by one of the men, who insisted that no blacks were going to eat at his table. (James Evans, 14 July, 1976).

42. Bradbury, *Racial Discrimination,* p. History–22.

43. Ibid., p. V–3.

44. Ibid., pp. V–2–12–8; U.S. Committee on Fair Employment Practice, "The Employment of Negroes in the Federal Government," unpublished paper from the files of the committee in the National Archives, Washington, D.C.

45. U.S. Committee on Fair Employment Practice, *Wartime Employment,* p. 7.

46. Bradbury, *Racial Discrimination.,* p. IV–6n.

47. L. J. W. Hayes, *The Negro Government Worker* (Washington, D.C.: Graduate School, Howard University, 1941), p. 76.

48. Bradbury, *Racial Discrimination,* p. V–1–8.

49. Ibid., p. V–1–17.

50. Ibid.

51. "Search for Negro Talent: 'We Mean Business'," *Newsweek* 57 (24 April, 1961): 45.

52. Bradbury, *Racial Discrimination,* p. IV–3.

53. Ibid., p. III–19.

54. Ibid., III–19–21.

55. Ibid., p. III–20–1.

56. Ibid., p. IV–2–4.

57. U.S. Congress, Senate, Committee on Labor and Public Welfare, Subcommittee on Civil Rights, *Antidiscrimination in Employment,* Hearings on S. 692 held February 23–5, March 1–3, 1954, 83rd Cong. 2nd sess. 1954 (hereafter known as *The Antidiscrimination Hearings*), p. 204.

58. "Employment," *Crisis* 54 (September 1947): 275.

59. Thomas Richardson, "Negro Discrimination by Uncle Sam," *March of Labor* 1 (July 1949): 22.

60. U.S. President's Committee on Civil Rights, *To Secure These Rights* (Washington, D.C.: Government Printing Office, 1947), p. 58.

61. U.S. Civil Service Commission Fair Employment Board, *Informational Bulletin No. 5,* 8 June 1951, p. 1; idem, *Informational Bulletin No. 10,* 1 August 1954, p. 1.

62. U.S. Civil Service Commission, Fair Employment Board, *Informational Bulletin No. 5,* p. 2.

63. *The Anti-Discrimination Hearings,* p. 204.

64. "Rectification," *Crisis* 56 (July 1949): 24.

65. "Politics," *Crisis* 55 (June 1948): 181.

66. Van Riper, *Civil Service Commission History,* p. 448.

67. The McCarthy era is described in detail in Fred Cook, *Nightmare Decade: Life and Times of Senator Joe McCarthy* (New York: Random House, 1971), and Lately Thomas, *When Even Angels Wept: The Senator Joseph McCarthy Affair: A Story Without a Hero* (New York: William Morrow Co., 1973). It was a period when people in all walks of life were condemned as traitors in closed hearings at which neither they nor their counsel were present.

68. "Civil Rights," *Crisis* 55 (December 1948): 371.

69. Richardson, "Negro Discrimination", pp. 22–3.

70. James L. Sundquist, *Politics and Policy: The Eisenhower, Kennedy and Johnson Years* (Washington, D.C.: Brookings Institution, 1968), p. 224.

71. In 1948, Truman had issued Executive Order 9981, desegregating the armed forces.

72. Sundquist, *Politics and Policy,* p. 224.

73. *The Antidiscrimination Hearings,* pp. 150–1.

74. "Quite a Contrast," *CIO News,* 25 October 1954, p. 5.

75. U.S. President, "Establishing the President's Committee on Government Employment," Executive Order 10590, 18 January 1955, *3 Code of Federal Regulations, 1954–8 Compilation* (Washington, D.C.: Government Printing Office, 1961), pp. 237–8.

76. "The Negro Should Support", p. 467.

77. *The Antidiscrimination Hearings,* p. 405.

78. "Why the Negro Should Support the Republican Party," *Crisis* 63 (October 1956): 455.

79. Van Riper, *Civil Service Commission History,* p. 515.

80. U.S. President's Committee on Government Employment Policy, *Five City Survey of Negro American Employees of the Federal Government,* 1956.

81. Ibid.

82. Dwight D. Eisenhower, "Address at the University of Kentucky Colosseum in Lexington, October 1, 1956," in *Public Papers of the President Dwight D. Eisenhower, Containing the Public Messages, Speeches and Statements, January 1 to December 31, 1956* (Washington, D.C.: Government Printing Office, 1958), p. 844.

83. U.S. President's Committee on Government Employment Policy, "Summary of Facts on Progress Reports by Agencies, October 1959," report from the files of the committee available through the U.S. Department of Labor, Office of the Solicitor, Washington, D.C.

84. Richard Kluger, *Simple Justice: The History of Brown v. Board of Education and Black America's Struggle for Equality* (New York: Alfred A. Knopf, 1976), p. 665.

85. U.S. Commission on Civil Rights, *Twenty Years After Brown: The Shadows of the Past,* 1974, pp. 65–8.

86. U.S. Civil Service Commission, "Minority Group Study, 1963," n.d., Table 1, n.p., unpublished survey covering 1961–63 conducted by the Commission at the request of the President's Committee on Equal Employment Opportunity.

87. U.S. President's Committee on Government Employment Policy, *Five City Survey.*

88. Minnesota, Governor's Interracial Commission, *The Negro Worker in Minnesota,* 1945, p. 41.

89. "Postal Workers," pp. 17–18.

90. The Hatch Act was only intended to inhibit public employees from using their positions for partisan political ends and to protect them from being used. Except for a stricture against running for partisan political office, the Hatch Act imposed no restrictions on government employees' rights as citizens. 5 U.S.C. Sec. 7321 *et seq.* (1970).

91. John Macy, Chairman of the Civil Service Commission, to Stewart L. Udall, Secretary of the Interior, a letter dated 26 March 1965. From the files of the Civil Service Commission, Washington, D.C.

92. John Hope Franklin, *From Slavery to Freedom: A History of Negro Americans,* 4th ed. (New York: Alfred A. Knopf, 1974), p. 478.

93. Chuck Stone, *Black Political Power in America* (Indianapolis: Bobbs-Merrill Co., 1968), pp. 49–50.

94. U.S. Civil Service Commission, Office of Federal Equal Employment Opportunity, "EEO History," n.d., unpublished history of the role of the commission in the evaluation of the equal employment opportunity program in the federal government from 1961 to 1968, pp. 4, 8.

95. Ibid., p. 5.

96. Krislov, *The Negro,* pp. 36–9; U.S. President, "Establishing the President's Committee on Equal Employment Opportunity," Executive Order 10925, 6 March 1961, *3 Code of Federal Regulations, 1959–1963 Compilation* (Washington, D.C.: Government Printing Office, 1964), pp. 448–54.

97. U.S. Civil Service Commission, *Federal Personnel Manual, Bulletin No. 713–11, October 14, 1969.*

98. "Negro Talent," p. 45.

99. Ibid., pp. 45–6.

100. Ibid., p. 45.

101. Leadership Conference on Civil Rights, *Federally Supported Discrimination* (New York: Leadership Conference on Civil Rights, 1961), p. 6.

102. "Johnson Urges Congress to Act; Emphasizes Civil Rights," *Congressional Quarterly Weekly Report,* 29 November 1963, p. 2089.

103. 42 U.S.C. Sec. 2000e(b) (1970).

104. Robert C. Weaver, "Eleanor and L.B.J. and Black America," *Crisis* (June–July 1972): 190.

105. George Butler, Acting Director, Office of Voluntary Compliance,

U.S. Equal Employment Opportunity Commission, interviewed on 2 June 1976.

106. Substantially the same provision became part of the Act in 1972, when the Civil Service Commission was charged with responsibility for its enforcement. U.S. Commission on Civil Rights, *The Federal Civil Rights Enforcement Effort—1974: Vol. 5: To Eliminate Employment Discrimination,* 1975, p. 11; 42 U.S.C. Sec. 2000 e–16 (1974 supp.).

107. U.S. President, "Equal Employment Opportunity," Executive Order 11246, 24 September 1965, *3 Code of Federal Regulation, 1964–5 Compilation* (Washington, D.C.: Government Printing Office, 1967), pp. 339–48.

108. U.S. Civil Service Commission, Office of Federal Equal Employment Opportunity, "EEO History," pp. 10–20.

109. U.S. Commission on Civil Rights, *Enforcement Effort Vol. 5,* pp. 69–70.

110. Harvey, *Black Civil Rights,* pp. 58–9.

111. Allan Wolk, *The Presidency and Black Civil Rights: Eisenhower to Nixon* (Rutherford, N.J.: Fairleigh Dickinson University Press, 1971), p. 182.

112. Ibid., p. 186.

113. Samuel Yette, *The Choice,* quoted in Harvey, *Black Civil Rights,* p. 60.

114. Harvey, *Black Civil Rights,* p. 60.

115. Ibid.

116. U.S. Civil Service Commission, Office of Federal Equal Employment Opportunity, "EEO History," p. 8.

117. Lyndon Baines Johnson, "Voting Rights Speech to Congress, March 15, 1965," quoted in Harvey, *Black Civil Rights,* p. 32.

118. Wolk, *Presidency,* p. 233n.

119. Congressional Quarterly, *Civil Rights: Progress Report 1970* (Washington, D.C.: Congressional Quarterly, 1971), pp. 23–4.

120. Ibid., p. 20

121. Wolk, *Presidency,* p. 148n.

122. Congressional Quarterly, *Progress Report,* p. 22.

123. Butler, Interview.

124. U.S. Commission on Civil Rights, *Enforcement Effort Vol. 5,* p. 14.

125. Unpublished data from the U.S. Department of State.

126. Alvin Pre Jean, director of Equal Employment Opportunity, U.S. Postal Service, interviewed in August 1975.

127. Unpublished data of the U.S. Civil Service Commission; "Civil Service," *Black Enterprise,* April 1972, p. 22.

128. "Civil Service," p. 22.

129. Ibid., p. 19.

130. U.S. Commission on Civil Rights, *Enforcement Effort Vol. 5,* pp. 619.

131. U.S. Congress, House, Committee on Education and Labor, Subcommittee on Equal Opportunity, *Oversight Hearings on Federal Enforcement of Equal Employment Opportunity Laws, Pt. 1,* Hearings held 27

March, 19 and 25 June, and 8 July 1975, 94th Cong., 1st sess., 1975 (hereafter known as *The Oversight Hearings*), p. 269.

132. U.S. Commission on Civil Rights, *Enforcement Effort Vol. 5,* p. 65.
133. *The Oversight Hearings,* p. 270.
134. Ibid., p. 192.
135. Ibid., p. 270.

Chapter 5: But Not Next Door

1. Thomas Pettigrew, "Attitudes on Race and Housing: A Social Psychological View," in *Segregation in Residential Areas,* ed. by Amos Hawley and Vincent Rock (Washington, D.C.: National Academy of Sciences, 1972), p. 25.
2. Ibid., p. 25.
3. Angus Campbell, *White Attitudes Toward Black People* (Ann Arbor: Institute for Social Research, University of Michigan, 1971), p. 136; Pettigrew, "Attitudes," p. 25. The question was, "What about you? Are you in favor of desegregation, strict segregation, or something in between?"
4. The Civil Rights Act of 1968. 42 U.S.C. Sec. 3601 *et seq.* (1970).
5. Andrew Greeley and Paul B. Sheatsley, "Attitudes Toward Racial Integration," in *Social Problems and Public Policy, Inequality and Justice,* ed. by Lee Rainwater (Chicago: Aldine Publishing Co., 1974), p. 242.
6. Campbell, *White Attitudes,* p. 133.
7. Gunnar Myrdal, *An American Dilemma: The Negro Problem and American Democracy,* 20th ann. ed. (New York: Harper and Row, Publishers, 1962), pp. 60–1. Pettigrew, "Attitudes," p. 38. See Table 4, which clearly illustrates less resistance to formal and informal interracial contacts than to intimate contacts.
8. *Washington Star,* 18 July 1976, p. A–5.
9. Thomas Pettigrew, "Black and White Attitudes Toward Race and Housing," in T. F. Pettigrew, ed., *Racial Discrimination in the United States* (New York: Harper and Row, Publishers, 1975); see Table 2 on p. 102.
10. Gordon Allport, *The Nature of Prejudice,* abr. ed. (Cambridge, Mass.: Addison-Wesley, 1954), p. 259.
11. Pettigrew, "Black and White," footnote 2, p. 413.
12. Ibid., p. 124.
13. Allport, *Nature,* pp. 254–64, 440.
14. One 1966 survey showed that half of the whites surveyed thought that blacks were less moral, and forty-three percent doubted that blacks were hardworking and ambitious. Harrell Rodgers and Charles Bullock, *Law and Social Change: Civil Rights Laws and Their Consequences* (New York: McGraw-Hill Book Co., 1972), p. 151.
15. Pettigrew, "Attitudes," p. 48.
16. *Chicago Sun Times,* 4 March 1975.
17. *Long Island Press,* 7 April 1975; *Baltimore Sun,* 14 January 1975.
18. *Cleveland Press,* 4 February 1975.

19. *Hunterdon Review,* 25 December 1974.

20. *Amsterdam News,* 22 March 1975.

21. *New York Times,* 4 March 1962.

22. U.S. President, "Equal Opportunity in Housing," Executive Order 11063, 20 November 1963, *3 Code of Federal Regulations, 1959–1963 Compilation* (Washington, D.C.: Government Printing Office, 1964), pp. 652–6; James P. Chandler, "Fair Housing Laws: A Critique," *Hastings Law Journal* 24 (January 1973): 172.

23. Chandler, "Fair Housing," p. 172.

24. *New York Times,* 14 June 1963.

25. *New York Times,* 15 August 1963.

26. Benjamin Muse, *American Negro Revolution* (Bloomington: University of Indiana Press, 1968), p. 251, 253.

27. Frank A. Aukofer, *City With a Chance: A Case History of Civil Rights Revolution* (Milwaukee, Wisc.: Bruce Publishing Co., 1968), p. 80.

28. Lyndon B. Johnson, *The Vantage Point: Perspectives on the Presidency, 1963–69* (New York: Holt, Rinehart and Winston, 1971), p. 176.

29. Ibid.

30. Title VIII of the 1968 Civil Rights Act outlawed blockbusting and discrimination in sales, rentals, advertising, broker activities, and financing covering 80 percent of the nation's housing. Exemptions from Title VIII are: (1) single-family houses sold or rented without the assistance of real estate agents; (2) owner-occupied dwellings containing no more than four separate units; (3) noncommercial housing operated by religious groups; and (4) lodgings operated by private clubs. That same year, in *Jones v. Mayer Co.* (392 U.S. 409 [1968].) the Supreme Court prohibited racial discrimination in all housing transactions.

31. Johnson, *Vantage Point,* p. 178.

32. Seymour Sudman, Norman M. Bradburn, and Galen Gockel, "The Extent and Characteristics of Racially Integrated Housing in the United States," *Journal of Business* 42 (January 1969): 54, 55.

33. The index of dissimilarity is defined as:

$$D = (100) \; \tfrac{1}{2} \sum_{i=1}^{n} \left| \frac{N_i}{N} - \frac{W_i}{W} \right|$$

where i = city block, numbered in any serial order
N_i = number of black households in block i
N = total number of black households in the city
W_i = number of white households in block i
W = total number of white households in city

The index varies from 0 to 100. A "D" value of 100 indicates that no block in the city has both blacks and whites in it. A "D" value of 0 indicates identical distributions of the two populations among city blocks. See Annemette Sorensen, Karl E. Taeuber, and Leslie J. Hollingsworth, *Indexes of Racial Segregation for 109 Cities in the United States, 1940 to 1970* (Madison: Institute for Research on Poverty, University of Wisconsin-Madison, 1974), Table 1, pp. 7–9.

34. Derived from Sorensen, Taeuber, and Hollingsworth, *Indexes,* Table 1, pp. 7–9.

35. Not counting New York City (with 1,668,115 blacks in 1970), a total of 841,522 blacks lived in all of these cities together in 1970. The twenty-four cities were:

Berkeley, Calif.	Harrisburg, Pa.	Rochester, N.Y.
Cambridge, Mass.	Minneapolis, Minn.	Sacramento, Calif.
Camden, N.J.	New Bedford, Mass.	St. Paul, Minn.
Denver, Colo.	New Haven, Conn.	San Francisco, Calif.
East Orange, N.J.	Oakland, Calif.	Seattle, Wash.alif.
East St. Louis, Ill.	Portland, Ore.	Wilmington, Del.
Evanston, Ill.	Providence, R.I.	Yonkers, N.Y.
Flint, Mich.	San Diego, Calif.	

Derived from 1970 Census of Population, *Characteristics of the Population, Vol. 1, Pt. 1, Sec. 1, U.S. Summary,* Table 67, pp. 329–33, and Sorensen, Taeuber, and Hollingsworth, "Indexes," Table 1, pp. 7–9.

36. This movement is reflected in the "replacement index" which expresses the minimum percentage of the total population that would have to move to achieve total desegregation. Total desegregation has a R value of zero. That index rose from 19.6 in 1940 to 28.7 in 1970. The index is $R = \Sigma \; 2q_i \, (1\text{-}q_i)$ Di where q is the proportion of nonwhites in the total population. Thomas Van Valey, Wade C. Roof, and Jerome E. Wilcox, "Trends in Residential Segregation 1960–1970," paper given at the 1975 American Sociological Association Convention, 25–8 August 1975, p. 5.

37. 1970 Census of Population, *Vol. 1, Pt. 1, Sec. 1,* Table 67, pp. 324–33.

38. Van Valey, Roof, and Wilcox, "Trends," Table 1, n.p.

39. Albert Hermalin and Reynolds Farley, "The Potential for Residential Integration in Cities and Suburbs: Implications for the Busing Controversy," *American Sociological Review* 38 (October 1973): 602–3; see also John Kain and John Quigley, *Housing Markets and Racial Discrimination* (New York: Columbia University Press for the National Bureau of Economic Research, 1975), p. 58.

40. Hermalin and Farley, "Residential Integration," p. 608. A dissenting study, by Zelder, states that "a *minimum* [Zelder's emphasis] of 30 to 50 percent of racial patterns in housing can be attributed to differences in the economic status of households." (See Raymond Zelder, "Racial Segregation in Urban Housing Markets," *Journal of Regional Science* 10 [April 1970]: 94.) He estimates "market segregation coefficients" which standardize for income for four SMSA's in 1960. However, these coefficients are actually lower than the dissimilarity indexes by only 11 to 25 percent, so for the 4 SMSA's cited by Zelder, the 30 to 50 percent estimate would appear to be much too high. Another weakness of the Zelder approach is that his method does not predict what actually happened to racial concentrations in the 1960s. If income differentials account for such a large amount of racial separation, one would expect the index of dissimilarity to fall as black and white incomes grow more equal. Black median incomes relative to median white family income grew about 10 percentage points between 1960 and 1970 but, as we have seen, the index of dissimilarity for 136 SMSA's did not change.

41. Pettigrew, "Attitudes," p. 44.

42. Ibid., p. 44; Kain and Quigley, *Housing Markets,* p. 60.

43. Mahlon Straszheim, *An Econometric Analysis of the Urban Housing Market* (New York: Columbia University Press for the National Bureau of Economic Research, 1975), p. 140.

44. Dick Netzer, *Economics of the Property Tax* (Washington, D.C.: Brookings Institution, 1966), p. 118.

45. The basic work in this area is in Luigi Laurenti's *Property Values and Race* (Berkeley: University of California Press, 1960). Other studies of housing prices in racially changing neighborhoods include: W. M. Ladd, "Effect of Integration on Property Values," *American Economic Review* 52 (September 1962): 801–8; Erdman Palmore, "Integration and Property Values in Washington, D.C.," *Phylon* 27 (Spring 1966): 15–19; Erdman Palmore and John Howe, "Residential Integration and Property Values," *Social Problems* 10 (Summer 1962): 2–6; Rapkin and Grigsby, *The Demand for Housing in Racially Mixed Areas;* Frederick E. Schietinger, "Race and Residential Property Values in Chicago," *Land Economics* 30 (November 1954): 301–8; Joseph P. McKenna and Herbert D. Werner, "The Housing Market in Integrating Areas," *Annals of Regional Science* 4 (December 1970): 127–33; Donald Phares, "Racial Change and Housing Values: Transition in an Inner Suburb," *Social Science Quarterly* 52 (December 1971): 560–73; Allen Dobson, "Price Changes of Single Family Dwelling Units in Racially Changing Neighborhoods" (Ph.D. diss., Washington University, 1970); T. E. Billette, "Santa Fe: A Study of the Effects of Negro Invasion on Property Values," *American Journal of Economics and Sociology* 16 (January 1957): 151–62; David H. Karlep, "Racial Integration and Property Values in Chicago," Urban Economics Report #7 (Chicago: University of Chicago, 1968).

46. Henry S. Terrell, "Wealth Accumulation of Black and White Families: The Empirical Evidence," *Journal of Finance* 26 (May 1971): 367.

47. CPR, Series P–60, No. 100, *Household Money Income in 1974 and Selected Social and Economic Characteristics of Households,* Table 2, p. 4.

48. Some of the best recent work on this question includes: Kain and Quigley, *Housing Markets;* Straszheim, *An Econometric Analysis;* Thomas A. King and Peter Mieszkowski, "Racial Discrimination, Segregation and the Price of Housing," *Journal of Political Economy* 81 (May–June 1973): 590–606; Richard F. Muth, *Cities and Housing: The Spatial Pattern of Urban Residential Land Use* (Chicago: University of Chicago Press, 1969); Victoria Lapham, "Do Blacks Pay More for Housing?" *Journal of Political Economy* 79 (November–December 1971): 1244–57; Gordon Bonham, "Discrimination and Housing Quality," *Growth and Change: A Journal of Regional Development* 3 (October 1972): 26–34; and John F. Kain, "What Should Housing Policies Be?" *Journal of Finance* 29 (May 1974): 683–98.

49. U.S. Congress, Senate, Select Committee on Nutrition and Human Needs, *Nutrition and Health: Pt. 4, Nutrition and Sanitation,* Hearings held September 16, 1970, 91st Cong., 2nd sess., 1970. See especially the testimony of Harold B. Wise, pp. 959–89.

50. Leadership Council for Metropolitan Open Communities, *Guide to*

Practice Open Housing Law (Chicago, Ill.: Leadership Council for Metropolitan Open Communities, 1974), p. 8.

51. John Yinger, *An Analysis of Discrimination by Real Estate Brokers* (Madison: Institute for Research on Poverty, University of Wisconsin-Madison, 1975), p. 8.

52. William H. Brown, "Access to Housing: The Role of the Real Estate Industry," *Economic Geography* 48 (January 1972): 68.

53. Ibid., p. 69.

54. Jack Greenberg, *Race Relations and American Law* (New York: Columbia University Press, 1959), p. 276–9.

55. Clement Vose, *Caucasians Only: The Supreme Court, the NAACP, and the Restrictive Covenant Case* (Berkeley: University of California Press, 1959), pp. 125–6.

56. Ibid., pp. 160–7.

57. Ibid., p. 200.

58. 334 U.S. 1 (1948); *Barrows V. Jackson*, 346 U.S. 249 (1953); Greenberg, *Race Relations,* p. 42.

59. Ibid., p. 63.

60. Vose, *Caucasians Only,* pp. 7–10.

61. Ibid., p. 229

62. Ibid., p. 223.

63. Rose Helper, *Racial Policies and Practices of Real Estate Brokers* (Minneapolis: University of Minnesota Press, 1969), p. 201.

64. Ibid.

65. John H. Denton, *Apartheid American Style* (Berkeley, Calif.: Diablo Press, 1967), p. 47.

66. Ibid.

67. Ibid., p. 18.

68. Brown, "Access to Housing," p. 74.

69. Alan H. Schechter, "Impact of Open Housing Laws on Suburban Realtors," *Urban Affairs Quarterly* 8 (June 1973): 458–60.

70. This reference is to the series of discriminatory actions. The sentence in quotation marks is the conclusion of the last entry and the words of this writer. See Yinger, *An Analysis of Discrimination,* pp. 32–5.

71. Ibid., pp. 21–5.

72. U.S. Housing and Home Finance Agency, "The San Francisco Bay Area Residential Mortgage Market," by Paul F. Wendt and Daniel B. Rathbun. Housing Research Paper No. 20, 1952, p. 43.

73. U.S. Commission on Civil Rights, *1961 Report, Book 4: Housing* (Washington, D.C.: Government Printing Office, 1961), p. 30.

74. Albert Mayer, "Russell Woods: Change Without Conflict: A Case Study of Racial Transition in Detroit," in *Housing and Minority Groups,* ed. by Nathan Glazer and Davis McEntire (Berkeley: University of California Press, 1960), p. 208; Advance Mortgage Corporation, *Midwestern Minority Housing Markets: A Special Report* (n.p.: Advance Mortgage Corporation, 1962), p. 26.

75. U.S. Commission on Civil Rights, *Mortgage Money: Who Gets It?,* 1974, pp. 12–19.

76. Ibid., pp. 19–24.

77. Ibid., pp. 24–32.

78. The agencies are The Federal Home Loan Bank Board (FHLBB), Federal Deposit Insurance Corporation (FDIC), Federal Reserve Board (Fed), and the Comptroller of the Currency (COC).

79. Atlanta, Ga.; Buffalo, N.Y.; Chicago, Ill.; San Antonio, Tex.; San Diego, Calif.; Washington, D.C.; Baltimore, Md.; Galveston, Tex.; Jackson, Miss.; Jersey City, N.J.; Tampa, Fla.; Vallejo, Calif.; Bridgeport, Conn.; Cleveland, Ohio; Memphis, Tenn.; Montgomery, Ala.; Topeka, Kan.; and Tucson, Ariz.

80. U.S. Federal Home Loan Bank Board, *Fair Housing Information Survey*, 1975; U.S. Comptroller of the Currency, *Fair Housing Lending Practices Pilot Project*, 1975; U.S. Board of Governors of the Federal Reserve System, *Fair Housing Survey*, 1975.

81. Technical problems in the data do not affect the major findings. For a description of the problems, see the U.S. Comptroller of the Currency's and the U.S. Federal Home Loan Bank Board's reports, sections III and II respectively.

82. U.S. Comptroller of the Currency, *Fair Housing Lending Practices*, p. II–3.

83. Federal Home Mortgage Disclosure Act, PL 94–200.

84. One exception to the local nature of red-lining studies is a 1972 national survey conducted by the Equal Opportunity Office of the Department of Housing and Urban Development (HUD), in which 18 percent of the surveyed lenders admitted that they refused to make loans in areas of high minority concentration. (U.S. Commission on Civil Rights, *Mortgage Money*, p. 32.) This 18 percent is certainly a gross underestimate. The questionnaire informed the respondents that the information obtained would be used by HUD and the federal financial regulatory agencies to develop policy for implementing the federal fair housing laws. It then asked each institution, in effect, whether it was violating those laws when it asked, "Are there neighborhoods or other areas of high concentration of minority group members in which your institutions refuses to make loans for residential purposes?" Considering the possible consequences that a positive answer to the question might bring, and the ease of avoidance by simply answering "no," it is surprising that 18 and not 0 percent of the respondents answered "yes."

85. U.S. Congress, Senate, Committee on Banking, Housing, and Urban Affairs, *Home Mortgage Disclosure Act of 1975*, Hearings on S. 1281 held 5–8 May 1975, 94th Cong., 1st sess., 1975 (hereafter referred to as *The Proxmire Hearings*), p. 303.

86. Illinois, Governor's Commission on Mortgage Practices, *Home Ownership in Illinois: The Elusive Dream*, in *The Proxmire Hearings*, p. 1281.

87. Richard J. Devine, Winston O. Rennie, and N. Brenda Sims, *Where the Lender Looks First: A Case Study of Mortgage Disinvestment in Bronx County 1960–1970*, in *The Proxmire Hearings*, p. 1281.

88. Northwest Community Housing Association, *Mortgage Disinvestment in Northwest Philadelphia*, in *The Proxmire Hearings*, p. 1224.

89. Home Ownership Development Program, *Home Ownership*, p. 1549.

90. Center for New Corporate Priorities, *Where the Money Is: Mortgage Lending, Los Angeles County,* in *The Proxmire Hearings,* p. 1050.

91. James Vitarello, *Redlining: Mortgage Disinvestment in the District of Columbia,* in *The Proxmire Hearings,* pp. 980–1.

92. Coalition to End Neighborhood Deterioration, *Why do Neighborhoods Deteriorate? Redlining in Indianapolis,* in *The Proxmire Hearings,* pp. 372–8.

93. Fran Matarrese, testifying in *The Proxmire Hearings,* pp. 418–19.

94. Debra S. McKee, *The Housing Analysis in Oakley, Bond Hill, and Evanston (January 1960–April 1974) Financial Investment Patterns,* in *The Proxmire Hearings,* p. 237.

95. Northwest Community Housing Association, *Mortgage Disinvestment,* pp. 1204–5.

96. Gale Cincotta, testimony at *The Proxmire Hearings,* pp. 180, 184.

97. Ibid., p. 190.

98. McKee, *Housing Analysis,* p. 238.

99. Ibid.

100. Northwest Community Housing Association, *Mortgage Disinvestment,* p. 1224.

101. Grover J. Hanson, testimony at *The Proxmire Hearings,* pp. 820–1.

102. William A Beasman, testimony at *The Proxmire Hearings,* p. 961.

103. Home Ownership Development Program, *Home Ownership and the Baltimore Mortgage Market,* in *The Proxmire Hearings,* pp. 1477–1623.

104. Guichard Parris and Lester Brooks, *Blacks in the City: A History of the National Urban League* (Boston: Little, Brown and Co., 1971), p. 324.

105. Leonard S. Rubinowitz, *Low Income Housing: Suburban Strategies* (Cambridge, Mass.: Ballinger, 1974), p. 32.

106. Ibid., pp. 32–3.

107. Ibid., p. 34.

108. Eric J. Branfman, Benjamin I. Cohen, and David M. Trubek, "Measuring the Invisible Wall: Land Use Controls and the Residential Patterns of the Poor," *Yale Law Journal* 82 (January 1973): 484. The study used a statistical test which showed the influence of taxation (fiscal efforts), race, housing availability, and zoning authority fragmentation on income clustering (concentration of people with less than the median income). The analysis found no relationship between income clustering and the fiscal variables, but did find positive relationships between clustering and the other three variables. The authors concluded from this that fiscal motives were unimportant and that race and class exclusion probably were important in explaining exclusionary zoning.

109. Rubinowitz, *Low Income Housing,* p. 31; Branfman, Cohen, and Trubek, "Measuring the Invisible Wall," pp. 505–6; National Committee Against Discrimination in Housing and Urban Land Institute, *Fair Housing and Exclusionary Land Use* (Washington, D.C.: Urban Land Institute, 1974), p. 7.

110. National Committee Against Discrimination in Housing and Urban Land Institute, *Fair Housing,* p. 22; 425 F.2d 1037 (10th cir. 1970); similar cases have been decided also for the developers. See especially *Kennedy Park Homes Association vs. City of Lackawanna*, N.Y., 318 F. Supp. 669 (W.D.N.Y. 1970), aff'd. 436 F.2d 108 (2nd Cir. 1970), cert. denied 401 U.S. 1010 (1971), p. 23.

111. 1970 Census of Population, *Subject Reports PC (2)–2B, Mobility for States and the Nation,* Table 17, pp. 171–6.

112. Ibid.

113. U.S. Commission on Civil Rights, *Above Property Rights* (Washington, D.C.: Government Printing Office, 1972), pp. 21–2.

114. Leonard Blumberg and Michael Lalli, "Little Ghettoes: A Study of Negroes in the Suburbs," *Phylon* 27 (Summer 1966): 117–31.

115. 1970 Census of Housing, *Metropolitan Housing Characteristics, HC(2)–1, United States and Regions,* Tables D–3, D–14, pp. 1–56, 1–66.

116. Hermalin and Farley, "The Potential for Residential Integration," p. 602.

117. William J. Kruvant, "Black Homebuyers in Suburb and City: Recent Experience and Preferences of Black Veteran Homebuyers in the Washington, D.C. Metropolitan Area," unpublished, 1975.

118. U.S. Department of Housing and Urban Development, *1973 HUD Statistical Yearbook* (Washington, D.C.: Government Printing Office, 1975), Table 178, p. 154. The FHA mortgage insurance program was originally instituted to stimulate the construction industry during the Depression by making houses easier to buy and pay for, and by making loans safer for bankers to make. Improvement in the quality and quantity of housing became a goal only after the 1930s. See Henry J. Aaron, *Shelter and Subsidies: Who Benefits from Federal Housing Policies?* (Washington, D.C.: Brookings Institution, 1972), p. 77.

119. 12 U.S.C. Sec. 1701 *et seq.* (1970); Aaron, *Shelter and Subsidies,* p. 76.

120. Comparison with other nations shows how successful U.S. homeownership has been. (See Table 5–3.)

121. 1940 Census of Housing, *Vol. 2, General Characteristics: Pt. 1, U.S. Summary,* Table 1, p. 7; U.S. Bureau of the Census, *Annual Housing Survey, 1974, Pt. A* (Washington, D.C.: Government Printing Office, 1975), Table A–1, p. 1.

122. The home-buyer pays the insurance premium, and these premiums cover all costs of the program. Tax dollars are not involved.

123. Eunice Grier and George Grier, *Privately Developed Interracial Housing* (Berkeley: University of California Press, 1960), p. 122.

124. Chandler, "Fair Housing," p. 161.

125. Ibid.

126. Ibid.

127. Grier and Grier, *Privately Developed,* p. 124.

128. Chandler, "Fair Housing," p. 162.

128. U.S. Commission on Civil Rights, *Equal Opportunity in Suburbia,* 1974, p. 38.

129. Chandler, "Fair Housing," p. 163.

130. U.S. Commission on Civil Rights, *Home Ownership for Lower Income Families* (Washington, D.C.: Government Printing Office, 1971), p. 38.

131. United States Housing Act of 1937, 42 U.S.C. sec. 1401 *et seq.* (1970); U.S. Bureau of the Census, *Annual Housing Survey, Pt. A,* Table A–1, p. 1; U.S. Department of Housing and Urban Development, *1974 HUD Statistical Yearbook* (Washington, D.C.: Government Printing Office, 1976), Table 113, p. 103.

132. CPR, Series P–60, No. 96, *Household Money Income in 1973 and Selected Social and Economic Characteristics of Households,* Table B, p. 1.

133. U.S. Department of Housing and Urban Development, *1973 Yearbook,* Table 80, p. 72.

134. "Myths/Realities of Public Housing," *Journal of Housing* 30 (April 1973): 181–3.

135. United States Housing Act of 1937, 42 U.S.C. Sec. 1401, section 15, as amended.

136. Leonard Freedman, *Public Housing: The Politics of Poverty* (New York: Holt, Rinehart and Winston, 1969), p. 140; U.S. Department of Housing and Urban Development, *1973 Yearbook,* Table 80, p. 72.

137. "Myths/Realities," p. 185.

138. Ibid., p. 185; U.S. Department of Housing and Urban Development, *1974 Yearbook,* Table 69, p. 74.

139. U.S. Department of Housing and Urban Development, *1973 Yearbook,* Tables 92, 98, pp. 81, 85.

140. Under the subsidy formula, the tenant pays one-quarter of adjusted income in rent; HUD pays the remainder of the market rent or the difference between amortization at market interest rates for forty years and amortization at 1 percent, whichever is less. Aaron, *Shelter and Subsidies,* p. 137.

141. U.S. Department of Housing and Urban Development, *Selected Multifamily Status Reports Mortgage Insurance Programs by Name and Location of Each Project Cumulative as of December 31, 1974,* 1975, pp. 0001–53.

142. U.S. Department of Housing and Urban Development, *1974 Yearbook,* Table 50, p. 60.

143. U.S. Department of Housing and Urban Development, *Housing in the Seventies* (Washington, D.C.: Government Printing Office, 1973), p. 4–83.

144. Louis Harris and Associates, Inc., "A Study of Public Attitudes Toward Federal Government Assistance for Housing for Low Income and Moderate Income Families," conducted for the Department of Housing and Urban Development, 1973 (unpublished). This favorable rating by tenants is not new. A 1957 study asked former tenants how they felt about their experience in a project. Eighty-one percent said it was a "good" or "fairly good" place to live. U.S. Public Housing Administration, *Mobility and Motivations: Survey of Families Moving From Low-Rent Housing,* 1958, pp. 9–10.

145. Freedman, *Public Housing,* p. 138.

146. Ibid., pp. 138–9.

147. Frederick Aaron Lazin, "The Failure of Federal Enforcement of Civil Rights Regulations in Public Housing, 1963–1971: The Co-optation of a Federal Agency by Its Local Constituency," *Policy Sciences* 4 (September 1973): 264.

148. Freedman, *Public Housing,* p. 147.

149. Lazin, "The Failure of Federal Enforcement," p. 265.

150. Ibid., pp. 265–6.

151. Charles Dean, "Site Selection for Public Housing and the Expanded Equal Protection Concept," in *1974 Urban Law Annual,* ed. by Gary H. Feder (St. Louis, Mo.: School of Law, Washington University, 1974), p. 336.

152. Mario Cuomo, *Forest Hills Diary: The Crisis of Low-Income Housing* (New York: Random House, 1974), p. 23. The project was approved in December 1966 and so was not subject to the 1968 law banning most high-rise public housing construction (ibid., p. 12).

153. *New York Times,* 10 June 1975.

154. Timothy R. Graham, "The Benign Housing Quota: A Legitimate Weapon to Fight White Flight and Resulting Segregated Communities?" *Fordham Law Review* 42 (May 1974): 891.

155. Ibid., p. 892.

156. U.S. Department of Housing and Urban Development, *Housing in the Seventies,* p. 4–45. Families of low to moderate income (those with between $4,000 and $10,000 gross income make up 96 percent of the participants) can buy new or existing homes with mortgages of between $18,000 and (occasionally) $24,000. The subsidy is never more than the difference between the full payments for the house under market conditions of prevailing mortgage interest, and payments under the same mortgage and 1 percent interest. (U.S. Commission on Civil Rights, *Home Ownership,* pp. 5–6.)

157. U.S. Department of Housing and Urban Development, *1974 Yearbook,* Table 151, p. 155.

158. U.S. Department of Housing and Urban Development, *Housing in the Seventies,* p. 4–45.

159. U.S. Department of Housing and Urban Development, *1973 Yearbook,* Table 245, p. 239.

160. U.S. Commission on Civil Rights, *Home Ownership,* p. 7.

161. Ibid., pp. 84–5.

162. Ibid., p. ix.

163. Ibid., p. 87.

164. For the $1.3 billion in public housing, about $715 million was paid directly by HUD, and $613 million was in taxes foregone on local authority tax-exempt bonds. Section 235 subsidy was $287 million; Section 236 was $151 million; rent supplements were $114 million; Section 502 of the Farmers Home Administration was $45 million (U.S. Department of Housing and Urban Development, *Housing in the Seventies*, pp. 4–81, 4–47, 4–59, 4–90–1, 4–101 respectively). Below-Market Interest Rate Loan Program was $29 million in 1970; and VA and FHA were $140 million in 1966

(Aaron, *Shelter and Subsidies,* p. 162). These and all other dollar figures given in the analysis of subsidies are estimates.

165. Aaron, *Shelter and Subsidies,* p. 53–5.

166. Ibid., p. 55.

167. Based on tax rates for joint returns, 1975.

168. U.S. Department of Housing and Urban Development, *Housing in the Seventies,* p. 4–31.

169. In 1970, 53 percent of the white households making less than $5,000 per year were owners, compared with only 33 percent of the blacks. 1970 Census of Housing, *Metropolitan Housing Characteristics, HC(2)–1, U.S. and Regions,* Table A–3, A–13, pp. 1–5, 1–14.

170. 42 U.S.C. Sec. 3610 (1970).

171. U.S. Commission on Civil Rights, *The Federal Civil Rights Enforcement Effort—1974, Vol. II: To Provide For Fair Housing,* 1974, p. 6.

172. Ibid., p. 67.

173. Ibid., pp. 31, 36.

174. Ibid., pp. 52–3.

175. U.S. Commission on Civil Rights, *The Federal Civil Rights Enforcement Effort . . . A Reassessment,* 1973, p. 48.

176. Chandler, "Fair Housing," pp. 195, 199; U.S. Commission on Civil Rights, *The Federal Civil Rights Enforcement Effort—1974, Vol. II,* pp. 14, 225.

177. U.S. Commission on Civil Rights, *The Federal Civil Rights Enforcement Effort—1974, Vol. II,* p. 1116.

178. Ibid., p. 1143.

179. U.S. Congress, Senate, Committee on Banking, Housing and Urban Affairs, *Fair Lending Enforcement by the Four Federal Financial Regulatory Agencies,* Senate Report 94–930, 94th Cong., 2nd sess., 1976, p. 3.

180. Ibid.

181. U.S. Commission on Civil Rights, *The Federal Civil Rights Enforcement Effort—1974, Vol. II,* p. 36.

182. Chandler, "Fair Housing," p. 189.

183. Ibid., p. 190.

184. "Blockbusting," *Georgetown Law Journal* 59 (October 1970): 170.

185. Ibid., p. 179.

186. Ibid., pp. 179–80.

187. Ibid., p. 180.

188. Ibid.

189. Ibid., p. 176.

Chapter 6: Second-Class Medicine

1. Max Seham, *Blacks and American Medical Care* (Minneapolis: University of Minnesota Press, 1973), p. 7.

2. Clarence Mitchell, Testimony before the Subcommittee on Civil Rights of the House Committee on the Judiciary reported in *Title VI Enforcement* *in Medicare and Medicaid Programs,* Hearings held September 12, 17, 24, 1973, 93rd Cong., 1st sess., 1973 (hereafter known as *Title VI Hearings*), p. 70.

3. Washington Metropolitan Health Council, *Health and Hospital Survey of Metropolitan Washington* (Washington, D.C.: Council of Social Agencies of the District of Columbia and Vicinity, 1946), p. xiii–10.

4. Bonnie Bullough and Vern Bullough, *Poverty, Ethnic Identity and Health Care* (New York: Prentice-Hall, Appleton-Century-Crofts, 1972), p. 2.

5. U.S. Commission on Civil Rights, *Title VI . . . One year after: A Survey of Desegregation of Health and Welfare Services in the South,* 1966, p. 5.

6. Clarence Mitchell, testimony at *Title VI Hearings,* p. 74.

7. Marilyn G. Rose, testimony at *Title VI Hearings,* p. 61.

8. *Washington Star,* 16 April 1976.

9. Martin Luther King, Jr., quoted in Herbert M. Morais, *History of the Negro in Medicine* (Washington, D.C.: United Publishing Corp., 1970), p. 6.

10. *Washington Afro-American,* 29 May 1976.

11. National Academy of Sciences, Institute of Medicine, Panel on Health Services Research, *Infant Death: An Analysis by Maternal Risk and Health Care* (Washington, D.C.: National Academy of Sciences, 1973).

12. Ibid., p. 14.

13. NCHS, *Selected Vital and Health Statistics in Poverty and Nonpoverty Areas of 19 Large Cities, United States, 1969–71,* Vital and Health Statistics, Ser. 21, No. 26, 1975, p. 14.

14. NCHS, *Vital Statistics Rates in the United States, 1940–1960* (Washington, D.C.: Government Printing Office, 1968), Table 38, p. 206; idem, *Vital Statistics of the United States, 1971, Vol. 2, Mortality, Pt. A* (Washington, D.C.: Government Printing Office, 1975), Table 2–1, p. 2–3; unpublished data from National Center for Health Statistics.

15. Martha M. Eliot, "The Health of Our Negro Children," *National Negro Health News* 12 (July–September 1944): 6.

16. Elizabeth R. Ferguson, "Nurse Midwives Serve a Rural County," *Public Health Nursing* 38 (April 1943): 187–92.

17. NCHS, *A Study of Infant Mortality from Linked Records by Birth Weight, Period of Gestation and Other Variables, United States,* Vital and Health Statistics, Ser. 20, No. 12, 1972, pp. 4–5, 7, 12.

18. Ibid., p. 3. Low-birthweight babies usually refers to those weighing 2,500 grams (about five and a half pounds) or less.

19. "Final Natality Statistics, Advance Report," *Monthly Vital Statistics Report* 24 (13 February 1976): Table 16, p. 13.

20. National Academy of Sciences, *Infant Death;* David Mechanic, *Public Expectations and Health Care* (New York: Wiley-Interscience, 1972), p. 91.

21. NCHS, *Vital Statistics Rates,* Table 45, pp. 296–7; idem, *Vital Statistics, 1971, Vol. 2, Mortality,* Table 1–16, p. 1–72; unpublished data from the National Center for Health Statistics.

22. Ibid.

23. Hyman Goldstein, "Demographic Information in Maternal and Child Health" in *Maternal and Child Health Practices: Problems, Resources and Methods of Delivery,* ed. by Helen M. Wallace, Edwin M. Gold, and Edward F. Lis (Springfield, Ill.: Charles C. Thomas Publisher, 1973), p. 104.

24. Ibid.

25. NCHS, *Vital Statistics Rates,* Table 38, p. 206; idem, *Vital Statistics, 1971, Vol. 2, Mortality, Pt. A,* Table 2–1, p. 2–3; unpublished data from the National Center for Health Statistics.

26. NCHS, *Differentials in Health Characteristics by Color, United States, July 1965–June 1967,* Vital and Health Statistics, Ser. 10, No. 56, 1969, p. 1; Jeremiah Stamler et al., "Hypertension Screening of 1 Million Americans," *Journal of the American Medical Association* 235 (24 May 1976): 2300, 2304.

27. Ibid.

28. Maureen Henderson and Linda Cowan, "Morbidity and Mortality in American Blacks," paper presented at the W. E. B. Dubois Institute for the Study of the American Black, Atlanta University, Atlanta, Georgia, October 1974.

29. NCHS, *Selected Family Characteristics and Health Measures Reported in the Health Interview Survey,* Vital and Health Statistics, Ser. 3, No. 7, 1967, gave standardized morbidity ratios for measures of illness by family income that showed consistently higher ratios among blacks than whites for restricted activity and disability bed days (p. 23). A later study on the poverty and nonpoverty areas of nineteen large cities concluded that income alone does not explain "the wide race differential," and that "further research is needed to account for the persistence of the race differential in health status that is observed irrespective of the poverty status of area of residence." NCHS, *Selected Vital and Health Statistics.* See especially p. 22 and Tables 5, 6, 8, 10, 11, and 12, pp. 29, 30, 31, 33, and 34, which give standardized death rates, percent of low-weight live birth rates, percent of live births to mothers lacking prenatal care, infant mortality rates, fetal death ratios, and death rates for tuberculosis, 1969–71 average, in each of the cities by poverty status of the area and race.

30. Montague Cobb, *Medical Care and the Plight of the Negro* (New York: National Association for the Advancement of Colored People, 1947), p. 27.

31. "The Negro in Virginia," *National Negro Health News* 8 (April–June 1940): 38.

32. U.S. President's Committee on Civil Rights, *To Secure These Rights* (Washington, D.C.: Government Printing Office, 1947), p. 73.

33. E. R. Carney, "Hospital Care for Negroes," *National Negro Health News* 10 (January–March 1942): 44.

34. Cobb, *Medical Care,* p. 29; Michael M. Davis and Hugh H. Smythe, "Providing Adequate Health Service to Negroes," *Journal of Negro Education* 18 (Summer 1949): 311.

35. Davis and Smythe, "Providing Adequate Health," p. 311.

36. Carney, "Hospital Care," p. 44.

37. T. Carr McFall, "Needs for Hospital Facilities and Physicians in Thirteen Southern States," *Journal of the National Medical Association* 42 (July 1950): 236. In 1950 there were 90 hospital beds per 100,000 for nonwhites and 204 per 100,000 for whites in the states of Virginia, North Carolina, Georgia, and Mississippi.

38. Jack Greenberg, *Race Relations and the American Law* (New York: Columbia University Press, 1959), p. 88.

39. Ibid., p. 89.

40. Walter White, *How Far the Promised Land* (New York: Viking Press, 1955), pp. 158–60.

41. U.S. Commission on Civil Rights, *Title VI . . . One Year After,* p. 12.

42. Cobb, *Medical Care,* p. 30.

43. Carney, "Hospital Care," p. 44.

44. Ibid., pp. 44–5.

45. Cobb, *Medical Care,* pp. 21–2.

46. Ibid., pp. 20–1.

47. Ibid., p. 21.

48. Ibid., pp. 22–3.

49. Ibid., p. 23.

50. Ibid., p. 26.

51. Ibid.

52. Ibid.

53. There may have been something to their fears. In the mid-fifties, a careful investigation of the extent of medical care integration in fourteen major cities found that the six communities with the highest level of integration—of hospital facilities, training opportunities, and health care—were also the six communities with no black hospital. See Dietrich C. Reitzes, *Negroes and Medicine* (Cambridge: Harvard University Press for the Commonwealth Fund, 1958), p. 333.

54. Ibid., pp. 111–12.

55. Lloyd A. Ferguson, "What Has Been Accomplished in Chicago," in *Medicine in the Ghetto,* ed. by John C. Norman (New York: Meredith Corp., Appleton-Century-Crofts, 1969), p. 89.

56. Ibid., p. 91.

57. R. M. Powell, "What Has Happened in the Watts-Willowbrook Program," in *Medicine in the Ghetto,* ed. by John C. Norman (New York: Meredith Corp., Appleton-Century-Crofts, 1969), p. 75.

58. Ibid., p. 76.

59. Ibid., p. 77.

60. Ibid., p. 78.

61. Whitney Young, *To Be Equal* (New York: McGraw-Hill Book Co., 1964), p. 190.

62. S. 3230, 76th Cong., 1st sess. (1940).

63. 42 U.S.C. Sec. 291 *et seq.* (1970).

64. U.S. Commission on Civil Rights, *Equal Opportunity in Hospitals and Health Facilities: Civil Rights Under the Hill-Burton Program,* 1965, pp. 4–5.

65. Ibid., pp. 5–6.

66. Oscar R. Ewing, "The President's Health Program and the Negro," *Journal of Negro Education* 18 (Summer 1949): 442.

67. V. M. Hoge, "What the Hospital Act Means to Negroes," *National Negro Health News* 15 (April–June 1947): 2.

68. *Simkins v. Moses H. Cone Hospital,* 323 F.2d 959 (4th Cir., 1963), cert. den. 376 U.S. 938 (1964).

69. U.S. Commission on Civil Rights, *Equal Opportunity,* p. 8.

70. U.S. Commission on Civil Rights, *The Civil Rights Enforcement Effort—1974, Vol. 6, To Extend Federal Financial Assistance,* 1975, p. 165.

71. "Title VI of Civil Rights Act of 1964—Implementation and Impact," *George Washington Law Review* 36 (May 1968): 981.

72. U.S. Commission on Civil Rights, *Enforcement Effort: Vol. 6,* p. 141.

73. Ibid.

74. Ibid., p. 142.

75. Ibid., p. 127.

76. Ibid., p. 142.

77. U.S. Social Security Administration, Office of Research and Statistics, *Medicare: Health Insurance for the Aged, 1968, Section 3.1: Participating Hospitals* (Washington, D.C.: Government Printing Office, 1971), pp. xviii–xix.

78. Ibid., Tables 3.1–1, 3.1–6, pp. 3.1–2, 3.1–12, 3.1–13.

79. Richard G. Hatcher, "Does Gary, Indiana, Reflect the National Problem of Medicine in the Ghetto?" in *Medicine in the Ghetto,* ed. by John C. Norman (New York: Meredith Corp., Appleton-Century-Crofts, 1969), p. 24.

80. Reitzes, *Negroes,* p. 279.

81. Ibid., pp. 281–3.

82. Ibid., p. 105.

83. Packinghouse Workers Civic and Community Committee, District One, UPWA-CIO, Chicago, Ill., untitled report cited in Reitzes, *Negroes,* p. 107.

84. 42 U.S.C. Sec. 1395 *et seq.* (1970).

85. U.S. Congress, Joint Economic Committee, Subcommittee on Fiscal Policy, *Handbook of Public Income Transfer Programs: 1975: A Staff Study,* Studies in Public Welfare Paper No. 280 (Washington, D.C.: Government Printing Office, 1974), pp. 197, 206. Since 1972–73, Medicare coverage is also available to disability insurance (DI) beneficiaries and to chronic renal disease patients.

86. U.S. Social Security Administration Office of Research and Statistics, *Medicare: Health Insurance for the Aged and the Disabled, 1973: Sec. 2: Persons Enrolled in the Health Insurance Program* (Washington, D.C.: Government Printing Office, 1975), pp. 17–9.

87. Ibid., pp. 19–20.

88. *Social Security Bulletin,* "Annual Statistical Supplement, 1973," p. 31.

89. U.S. Congress, Joint Economic Committee, *Handbook,* pp. 197, 206.

90. Ibid., p. 199.

91. Ibid., Table 4, p. 202.

92. Ibid., p. 207.

93. Ibid., p. 206.

94. Only 1 percent of blacks on Medicaid received nursing home care in 1973 compared with 5 percent of whites. Unpublished data from the National Center for Health Statistics.

95. U.S. Social and Rehabilitation Service, Assistance Payments Administration, *Characteristics of State Medical Assistance Programs Under Title XIX of the Social Security Act* (Washington, D.C.: Government Printing Office, 1971); U.S. Congress, Senate, Special Committee on Aging, *The Multiple Hazards of Aging and Race: The Situation of Aged Blacks in the United States: A Working Paper* (Washington, D.C.: Government Printing Office, 1971), p. 23.

96. According to unpublished data from the National Center for Health Statistics, average Medicaid payments per black patient were $286 in 1973 but $511 per white patient.

97. National Urban League, *Health Care and the Negro Population* (New York: National Urban League, 1965), p. 8.

98. U.S. Social and Rehabilitation Service, Medical Service Administration, *Medicaid Services, State by State, December 1, 1974,* n.d.

99. U.S. Social and Rehabilitation Service, Assistance Payments Administration, *State Medical Assistance Programs.*

100. U.S. Social and Rehabilitation Service, Assistance Payments Administration, *Characteristics of State Plans for Aid to Families with Dependent Children under the Social Security Act, Title IV–A,* 1974 ed. (Washington, D.C.: Government Printing Office, nd.)

101. Barbara Paige, testimony in *Title VI Hearings,* p. 82.

102. Jim Grant, "S.C. Women Sterilized, Doctor Fined $5," *Southern Patriot* 33 (June–July 1975): 3.

103. Barbara Paige, testimony in *Title VI Hearings,* p. 86.

104. Anne D. Peters and Charles L. Chase, "Patterns of Health Care in Infancy in a Rural Southern County," *American Journal of Public Health* 57 (March 1967): 422.

105. U.S. Commission on Civil Rights, Alabama Committee, *The Tuskegee Study,* 1973.

106. Franz Ingelfinger, "The Poor," in *Experiments and Research with Humans, Value in Conflict,* published by the National Academy, 1975, quoted in William A. Duritz, "Ethics in Human Experimentation in Health Care Delivery" in the "Conference Papers" of the National Minority Conference on Human Experimentation Conference held in Reston, Virginia, January 1976, p. 5 (photocopied).

107. On a February 1976 trip to observe health services in Mississippi, one of the authors was told repeatedly of discriminatory practices, including limited hours for black patients and "paper physicals." In town after town, black patients described their physical exams from white doctors as consisting entirely of words on paper—no undressing, no touching, just a nurse writing down what the patient described, and the doctor writing down a prescription.

108. Ibid.

109. Clarence Mitchell, testimony in *Title VI Hearings,* p. 70.

110. Citizens' Board of Inquiry into Health Services for Americans, *Heal Yourself,* 2nd ed. rev. (Washington, D.C.: American Public Health Association, 1972), p. 4.

111. Montague Cobb, *Progress and Portents* (New York: National Association for the Advancement of Colored People, 1948), p. 30.

112. White, *How Far,* p. 151.

113. Cobb, *Progress,* p. 31.

114. Reitzes, *Negroes,* p. 22; Redding S. Sugg and George Hilton Jones, *The Southern Regional Education Board* (Baton Rouge: Louisiana State University Press, 1960), p. 12.

115. *Missouri ex. rel. Gaines v. Canada,* 305 U.S. 337 (1938); *Sipuel v. Board of Regents,* 332 U.S. 631 (1948).

116. Cobb, *Progress,* p. 31.

117. Sugg and Jones, *Southern,* pp. 45–6.

118. Association of American Medical Colleges, *Minority Student Opportunities in the United States, 1971–72* (Washington, D.C.: Association of American Medical Colleges, 1971); Seham, *Blacks,* p. 46; James L. Curtis, *Blacks, Medical Schools, and Society* (Ann Arbor: University of Michigan Press, 1971), Table 111, p. 34.

119. Cobb, *Medical Care,* pp. 14–16.

120. Ibid., p. 17.

121. Association of American Medical Colleges, Liaison Committee on Medical Education, "Need For a Critical Mass of Basic Scientists," a policy decision from the Liaison Committee's minutes of 28 March 1973, incorporated in the association's accreditation guidelines.

122. White, *How Far,* p. 159.

123. Montague Cobb, "A New Dawn in Medicine," *Ebony* 18 (September 1963): 168.

124. Anne E. Crowley, ed., *Medical Education in the United States, 1973–74* (Chicago: American Medical Association, 1975), Table 33, p. 54. These statistics exclude Puerto Rico and the Canal Zone.

125. Mabel Staupers, "The Negro Nurse Advances," *National Negro Health News* 10 (April–June 1942): 5.

126. Ibid.

127. Leonard A. Scheele, "The Health Status and Health Education of Negroes—A General Introductory Statement," *Journal of Negro Education* 18 (Summer 1949): 205.

128. *New York Times,* 28 September 1946.

129. Mabel Staupers, "Story of the National Association of Colored Graduate Nurses," *American Journal of Nursing* 51 (April 1951): 223.

130. White, *How Far,* p. 157.

131. Morais, *Negro in Medicine,* p. 134.

132. "Local and State Associations Admit Negro Doctors" and "St. Louis Medical Society Admits Negro Doctors," *National Negro Health News* 18 (April–June 1950): 22.

133. Morais, *Negro in Medicine,* p. 134.

134. Hatcher, "Gary, Indiana," p. 23.

135. Greenberg, *Race Relations,* p. 89.

136. Ibid.

137. *Medical Tribune,* 9 August 1963, p. 15.

138. *Medical Tribune,* 2 August 1963, p. 18.

139. George A. Silver, "The Hand of Esau: Reflections on Federalism and Child Health Services in the USA," paper presented at the Sun Valley Forum, Sun Valley, Idaho, August 1975 (mimeographed), p. 43n.

140. *Medical Tribune,* 2 August 1963, pp. 18–9.

141. Ibid.

142. Reitzes, *Negroes,* pp. 300–1.

143. Seham, *Blacks,* p. 78.

144. J. A. C. Lattimore, "Address of the Outgoing President," *Journal of the National Medical Association* 40 (November 1948): 235.

145. Staupers, *Story,* p. 222; Morais, *Negro in Medicine,* p. 128.

146. Morais, *Negro in Medicine,* p. 128.

147. "Wanted, a Hospital and the Right to Practice," *Southern Frontier* 1 (December 1940): 1.

148. "An Appeal to the A.M.A. in Behalf of Negro Physicians in the South," *Journal of the National Medical Association* 39 (September 1947): 216.

149. Lattimore, "Address," p. 235.

150. Charles H. Marshall, "The Southern Governors' Educational Plan," *Journal of the National Medical Association* 40 (1948): 122.

151. Montague Cobb, "Federal Aid to Medical Education," *Journal of the National Medical Association* 42 (March 1950): 87.

152. "The N.M.A. and Civil Rights," *Journal of the National Medical Association* 58 (March 1966): 130.

153. "What Hath God Wrought," *Journal of the National Medical Association* 60 (November 1968): 519.

154. *Medical Tribune,* 5 August 1963, p. 1.

155. Richard Bardolph, ed., *Civil Rights Record* (New York: Thomas Y. Crowell Co., 1970): pp. 507–8.

156. "Chicago Physicians Sue for Admissions to Hospital Staffs," *Journal of the National Medical Association* 53 (March 1961): 198–9.

157. "Community Imhotep Committees," *Journal of the National Medical Association* 53 (March 1961): 198.

158. "Eight Physicians Arrested at Atlanta Cafeteria Stand-in," *Journal of the National Medical Association* 53 (March 1961): 200.

159. Max Seham, "Discrimination Against Negroes in Hospitals," *New England Journal of Medicine* 271 (29 October, 1964): 941.

160. Cobb, "New Dawn," p. 169.

161. Seham, "Discrimination," p. 942.

162. "Gadsden (Ala.) Freedom Movement Protests New Hill-Burton Hospital Arrangement," *Journal of the National Medical Association* 56 (January 1964): 99.

163. *Medical Tribune,* 12 August 1963, p. 5.

164. *Medical Tribune,* 5 August 1963, p. 18.

165. Ibid.

166. "The National Medical Association's Contribution to the Selma-Montgomery March," *Journal of the National Medical Association* 57 (May 1965): 244.

167. "NMA Leadership in Mississippi," *Journal of the National Medical Association* 58 (1966): 293.

168. Lionel F. Swan, "From Protesting to Pioneering," *Journal of the National Medical Association* 60 (September 1968): 445.

169. Seham, *Blacks,* p. 90.

170. Ibid., p. 54.

171. "Some Black Position Statements," *Journal of the National Medical Association* 61 (January 1969): 82.

172. Seham, *Blacks,* pp. 55, 80.

173. Samuel F. Yette, *The Choice: The Issue of Black Survival in America* (New York: Berkeley Publishing Corp., Berkeley Medallion Book, 1972): 260.

174. Seham, *Blacks,* p. 81.

175. *South Philadelphia Chronicle,* 6 March 1975.

176. *Chicago Metro News,* 17 May 1975.

177. Robert B. Scott, "Health Care Priority and Sickle Cell Anemia," in *Ethnic Groups of America: Their Morbidity, Mortality and Behavior Disorders: Vol. 2, The Blacks,* ed. by Ailon Shiloh and Ida Cohen Selavan (Springfield, Ill.: C. C. Thomas Publishers, 1974), p. 121–2; U.S. Congress, Senate Committee on Labor and Public Welfare, Subcommittee on Health, *National Sickle Cell Anemia Prevention Act,* Hearings on S. 2676 held November 11–12, 1972, 92nd Cong., 1st sess., 1971, p. 15; idem, "Amendments to the National Sickle Cell Anemia Control Act," unpublished transcript from its July 15, 1975, hearings, p. 16 (mimeographed).

178. A. Philip Randolph Institute, *The Reluctant Guardians; A Survey of the Enforcement of Federal Civil Rights Laws,* report prepared for the U.S. Office of Economic Opportunity (New York: A. Philip Randolph Institute, 1969), pp. 13, 1–13.

179. Paul B. Cornely, testimony at *Title VI Hearings,* p. 102.

180. A. Philip Randolph Institute, *Reluctant,* p. 13.

181. U.S. Commission on Civil Rights, *Enforcement Effort: Vol. 6,* pp. 129–35, 140, and 153.

182. A. Philip Randolph Institute, *Reluctant,* p. 13.

183. U.S. Commission on Civil Rights, *Enforcement Effort: Vol. 6,* p. 155.

184. Ibid., pp. 158–60.

185. "Title VI of the Civil Rights Act of 1964," p. 990.

186. A. Philip Randolph Institute, *Reluctant,* p. 10.

187. U.S. Commission on Civil Rights, *Enforcement Effort: Vol. 6,* pp. 167–72.

188. Ibid., p. 189.

189. Louise Lucas, acting director of the Office of Civil Rights, U.S. Department of Health, Education and Welfare, interview in her office May 1976.

190. U.S. Commission on Civil Rights, *Enforcement Effort: Vol. 6,* pp. 202–3.

191. Ibid., pp. 116–17.

Chapter 7: Making Do

1. The minimum wage, not tied to previous work experience, is incorporated in the Fair Labor Standards Act. It is a part of the total security system because it placed a floor under hourly wages and the number of hours workers had to work at straight time, before compensation for overtime.

2. P.L. 379, 76th Cong., 53 Stat. 1360; P.L. 761, 83rd Cong., 68 Stat. 1052.

3. *Social Security Bulletin,* "Annual Statistical Supplement, 1973," Table 142, p. 157. Unemployment insurance beneficiaries rise and fall with the business cycle; minimum wage coverage has also increased substantially.

4. CPR, Series P–60, No. 102, *Characteristics of the Population Below the Poverty Level: 1974,* Table 1, pp. 13–5.

5. Ellen J. Perkins, Chief, Division of Program Statistics and Analysis, Bureau of Family Services, Welfare Administration, Department of Health Education, and Welfare, memorandum entitled, "Why Some Poor Do Not Receive Public Assistance," to Ben Okner, Council of Economic Advisors, 11 October 1965. From the files of the Department of Health, Education, and Welfare, Washington, D.C.

6. Blacks had over twice the unemployment rate of whites in 1966, so the fact of a higher rate of unemployment benefit receipt reflects a negative rather than a positive situation. Blacks fare badly under the unemployment insurance system when compared with whites in terms of benefits received.

7. The median is the midpoint of the income distribution; half of all American families have incomes higher than the median and the other half have lower incomes.

In noncensus years income data are collected every March by the Current Population Survey of the Bureau of the Census. This survey is currently a sample of 55,000 households in 461 areas of the country and is carefully designed to reflect the American population at large. The income counted in this survey is only money income and consists of: (1) money wages or salary; (2) net income from nonfarm self-employment; (3) net income from farm self-employment; (4) Social Security or railroad retirement benefits; (5) Supplemental Security income; (6) public assistance or welfare payments; (7) interest; (8) dividends, income from estates or trusts, or net rental income; (9) veterans' payments or unemployment and workmen's compensation; (10) private pensions or government employee pensions; (11) alimony or child support, regular contributions from persons not living in the household, and other periodic income. CPR, Series P–60, No. 101, *Money Income in 1974 of Families and Persons in the United States,* pp. 157–76.

8. From 1947 to 1967 this series is only available for whites and non-whites—which includes blacks together with other nonwhite races, like Chinese and Japanese Americans, who have substantially higher median incomes than black Americans. The general nonwhite median and also the ratio to whites are thus overstated, the latter usually by about 1 to 2 percentage points.

9. Census statistics do not provide a breakdown permitting isolation of labor from other income. Farm and nonfarm self-employment income is recorded in addition to wages and salaries. Such income is clearly both part labor and part capital (property) income. Since wages and salaries amounted to about $449 billion in 1969, and farm and nonfarm self-employment income was only about $53 billion, wages and salaries alone account for most of labor income and is used as a proxy here. 1970 Census of Population, *Subject Reports, PC(2)–8A, Sources and Structure of Family Income,* Tables 5, 7, pp. 161, 314.

10. BLS, "Autumn 1974 Urban Family Budgets and Comparative Indexes for Selected Urban Areas," News Release U.S.D.L. 75–190, 4 April 1975, Table A, p. 2.

11. Rich and poor pay the same percentage of earnings into the system up to a given earnings level; because of that the highly paid are taxed less heavily than those earning at or below the earnings ceiling, which was $15,300 in 1976. On the other hand, benefits are designed to favor those at the lower end of the earnings range more than at the upper end. Resulting benefit levels, nevertheless, are much higher for the well-paid professional than for the low-paid janitor.

The benefit formula for 1976 was: 119.89 percent of the first $110 of the average monthly wage plus 43.61 percent of the next $290 plus 40.75 percent of the next $150 plus 47.90 percent of the next $100 plus 26.64 percent of the next $100 plus 22.20 percent of the next $250 plus 20 percent of the next $100. *Your Social Security,* HEW Publication No. (SSA) 76–10035 (June 1976), pp. 15, 23; *Social Security Bulletin,* "Annual Statistical Supplement, 1974," p. 19.

12. This excluded farm workers, workers in nonprofit institutions, domestic servants, federal workers, state and local government workers, self-employed persons, ministers, members of the armed forces, and various smaller groups. *Social Security Bulletin,* "Annual Statistical Supplement, 1971," p. 13.

13. *Social Security Bulletin* 13 (August 1950): 21.

14. *Social Security Bulletin,* "Supplement, 1971," p. 13. By 1960 about 90 percent of all workers were covered.

15. *Social Security Bulletin* 14 (November 1951): 20.

16. *Social Security Bulletin* 14 (May 1951): 21.

17. U.S. Social Security Administration, Office of Research and Statistics, *Demographic and Economic Characteristics of the Aged, 1968 Social Security Survey,* by Lenore E. Bixby et al., Research Report No. 45 (Washington, D.C.: Government Printing Office, 1975), Table 2.14, p. 32. No later data were available beyond these from the Social Security Administration's 1968 survey of the characteristics and sources of income of aged OASDI beneficiaries.

18. Congressional Quarterly Service, *Congress and the Nation, 1945–1964* (Washington, D.C.: Congressional Quarterly Service, 1965), p. 1289.

19. Ibid., p. 1290.

20. Unpublished data from the U.S. Employment and Training Administration.

21. U.S. Unemployment Service, *Significant Provisions of State Unemployment Insurance Laws, January 6, 1975,* 1975, n.p.

22. BLS, *Employment and Wages of Workers Covered by State Unemployment Insurance Laws and Unemployment Compensation for Federal Employees,* First Quarter, 1972, Table A–1, p. 3, and unpublished data from BLS.

23. Congressional Quarterly Service, *Congress,* p. 1291.

24. BLS, *Handbook of Labor Statistics 1975—Reference Edition,* Bulletin 1865 (Washington, D.C.: Government Printing Office, 1975), Table 62, p. 152; also derived from the U.S. Manpower Administration, *Unemployment Insurance Statistics,* December 1969–December 1975, Table 32 of each issue.

25. Walter W. Kolodrubetz and Donald M. Landay, "Coverage and Vesting of Full-Time Employees Under Private Retirement Plans," *Social Security Bulletin* 36 (November 1973): 20.

26. A closely related concept is portability of pension contributions. If a plan has this feature, a worker who leaves the plan not only has a right to benefits but can actually take his and his employer's accumulated contributions along to his new job and deposit them in the new plan.

27. Kolodrubetz and Landay, "Coverage," Table 16, p. 35.

28. U.S. Congress, Senate, Committee on Labor and Public Welfare, Subcommittee on Labor, Preliminary Report of the Private Welfare and Pension Plan Study, 1971 (Pursuant to S. Res. 35, Section 4), 92nd Cong., 1st sess., 1971, p. 4 and Table 9, p. 15.

29. Ibid., Tables 7, 7A, pp. 13, 14.

30. Frank Cummings, "Reforming Private Pensions," *Annals of the American Academy of Political and Social Science* 415 (September 1974): 81–2.

31. U.S. Social Security Administration, *Demographic and Economic Characteristics,* p. 31.

32. Walter Kolodrubetz, "Private and Public Retirement Pensions: Findings from the 1968 Survey of the Aged," *Social Security Bulletin* 33 (September 1970), Table 4, p. 7.

33. Ibid.

34. This limited group is not necessarily representative of all the elderly, but the difference is significant enough to support the general conclusion that black recipients of private pensions get less than whites. Walter Kolodrubetz, "Private Retirement Benefits and Relationship to Earnings: Survey of New Beneficiaries," *Social Security Bulletin* 36 (May 1973), Table 17, p. 32.

35. Kolodrubetz and Landay, "Coverage," Table 7, p. 28. About the same small proportion of black and white women were covered—32 and 36 percent respectively. Men were more likely to be covered—43 percent of black men compared with 53 percent white.

36. BLS, *Handbook of Labor Statistics 1975—Reference Edition,* Bulletin 1865 (Washington, D.C.: Government Printing Office, 1975), Table 19, p. 72.

37. Joseph A. Pechman and Benjamin A. Okner, *Who Bears the Tax Burden?* (Washington, D.C.: Brookings Institution, 1974), pp. 48–51.

38. Lee Rainwater, *What Money Buys: Inequality and the Social Meaning of Income* (New York: Basic Books, 1974), p. 98.

39. The historical trend for income among the top 5 percent, by race, is available only for white families and all others, the latter being "nonwhite," referring to blacks and all other nonwhite races.

40. Derived from the 1960 Census of Population, *Subject Reports, PC(2)–1C, Nonwhite Population by Race,* Tables 14–18, pp. 25–9; 1970 Census of Population, *Subject Reports, PC(2)–8A, Sources and Structure of Family Income,* Table 5, p. 160.

41. James D. Smith and S. D. Franklin, "The Concentration of Personal Wealth, 1922–1969," *American Economic Review* 64 (May 1974): 162.

42. Henry S. Terrell, "Wealth Accumulation of Black and White Families: The Empirical Evidence," *Journal of Finance* 26 (May 1971), Table 2, p. 367.

43. Ibid. Wealth data are not nearly as complete or detailed as social scientists would like. As economist Lester Thurow observed, "Many researchers believe that Government officials deliberately do not collect wealth statistics often because they do not wish to know the inequalities they would reveal." Lester Thurow, "Tax Wealth, Not Income," *New York Times Magazine,* 11 April 1976, p. 32.

44. James D. Smith, "White Wealth and Black People: The Distribution of Wealth in Washington, D.C. in 1967," in *The Personal Distribution of Income and Wealth,* ed. by James D. Smith (New York: National Bureau of Economic Research, distributed by Columbia University Press, 1975), pp. 357–8.

These data were based on persons with a net worth of $1,000 or more, and were estimated by estate multiplier techniques. These used the estimates of persons who died in 1967 to determine the wealth of living people. Smith, *White Wealth,* pp. 333–45.

45. Ibid., p. 359.

46. Income derived from wealth can be estimated from Current Population Survey data. The Census Bureau collects the amount of income derived from different forms of wealth. These are interest, dividends, net rental income and income from estates, trusts, and net royalties. These incomes derive from stocks, bonds, and other holdings of debt instruments, real estate, and other property. Added together, all of these types of income are termed "property income" and reflect most income-producing wealth. The major omissions are business and farm equity, but while black families held 2 percent of all wealth, they held only about 1 percent of business and farm equities. This would tend to make comparisons on the basis of our "property income" concept conservative. Since equity in homes and motor vehicles do not produce money income, they do not enter this comparison.

47. Self-employment income is not included here, and there are undoubtedly a number of rich entrepreneurs whose large equities in their businesses and farms would qualify them as recipients of a large amount of property income if their return from equity could be separated from their return from labor. Unfortunately, this is not possible. However, the number of wealthy black entrepreneurs is minuscule and so the basic comparison is valid, even conservative. A rough estimate of about 2,000 can be derived from CPR, Series P–60, No. 101, *Money Income in 1974,* Table 50, pp. 97–9.

48. Terrell, "Wealth," p. 367.

49. *New York Times,* 17 March 1974.

50. Philip M. Stern, *The Rape of the Taxpayer* (New York: Random House, 1973), pp. 44–5.

51. Ibid., pp. 45–6.

52. CPR, Series P–60, No. 103, *Money Income and Poverty Status of Families and Persons in the United States, 1975 and 1974 Revisions (Advance Reports),* Table 16, p. 33. Figures are for nonfarm families. Farm families are allowed 85 percent of nonfarm money incomes because they are thought to produce much of their own food. Few families, especially black families, lived on farms in 1975.

53. CPR, Series P–60, No. 101, *Money Income in 1974,* Table 10, p. 20.

54. CPR, Series P–60, No. 105, *Consumer Income,* Table 11, p. 49. Another result of the use of an absolute standard is that as the economy grows the people left in poverty will have lower and lower incomes relative to the average. The gap between all others and the poor grows. In 1959 the poverty-line income for a nonfarm family of four was 55 percent of the national median. In 1974 it was only 39 percent. This means that those left in poverty became more and more destitute relative to all others. Ibid., Table 10, p. 20; CPR, Series P–60, No. 102, *Poverty Level: 1974,* Table A, p. 1.

55. "Welfare" is really four programs: Aid to Families with Dependent Children (AFDC); Aid to the Blind; Aid to the Permanently and Totally Disabled; and Old Age Assistance. (All of these programs are now combined and called Supplemental Security Income, or SSI.) AFDC is the largest, has generated the most controversy, and is the program implied in this chapter when "welfare" is mentioned.

56. Aid to Families with Dependent Children was known as Aid to Dependent Children until 1950.

57. U.S. Bureau of Public Assistance, *Public Assistance 1940,* Public Assistance Report No. 1, 1940, p. 32.

58. U.S. Bureau of Public Assistance, *Families Receiving Aid to Dependent Children, October 1942: Part 1, Race, Size, and Composition of Families and Reasons for Dependency,* by Agnes Leisy, Public Assistance Report No. 7, 1945, p. 25.

59. Ibid., pp. 31–2.

60. U.S. Bureau of Public Assistance, *Families Receiving Aid to Depend-*

ent Children, October 1942: Part 2, Family Income, Public Assistance Report No. 7, 1945, p. 16; Gordon W. Blackwell and Raymond F. Gould, *Future Citizens All* (Chicago: American Public Welfare Association, n.d.), p. 72; M. Elaine Burgess and Daniel O. Price, *An American Dependency Challenge* (Chicago: American Public Welfare Association, 1963), pp. 71–4; unpublished data from National Center for Social Statistics.

61. Unpublished data from the 1967 AFDC study, provided by the National Center for Social Statistics.

62. U.S. Bureau of Public Assistance, *Dependent Children, October 1942,* Table 15, p. 51.

63. Frances Fox Piven and Richard A. Cloward, *Regulating the Poor: The Functions of Public Welfare* (New York: Pantheon Books, 1971), p. 133.

64. Winifred Bell, *Aid to Dependent Children* (New York: Columbia University Press, 1965), p. 29.

65. Social Security Act of 1935, Section 401 as amended, 42 U.S.C. Sec. 601 (1970), makes it clear that the purpose of the program is "enabling each state to furnish financial assistance . . . as far as practicable under the conditions in such State, to needy children. . . ." The states were expected to fill in the details. See Gilbert Steiner, *Social Insecurity* (Chicago: Rand-McNally, 1966), p. 80.

66. Grace Abbott, *The Child and the State* (Chicago: University of Chicago Press, 1938), Vol. 2, p. 240.

67. Statistically, there is little relationship between unemployment and welfare. Unemployment data were lagged one year on the assumption that unemployment would show up in welfare later. The coefficient of correlation (r^2) was .06. Similar low correlations resulted from estimating the effect of the percentage change of unemployment rates on the rate of change in AFDC—first at the time, and second, lagging AFDC a year after the change in unemployment (.15 and .04 respectively).

68. Gunnar Myrdal, *An American Dilemma: The Negro Problem and Modern Democracy,* 20th ann. ed. (New York: Harper and Row, Publishers, 1962), p. 359.

69. Ibid.

70. Bell, *Aid to Dependent Children,* pp. 34–5.

71. U.S. Bureau of Public Assistance, *Dependent Children, October 1942,* Tables 2, 3, 4, pp. 44–5.

72. U.S. Bureau of Public Assistance, *Public Assistance, 1940,* p. 59.

73. Bell, *Aid to Dependent Children,* p. 53.

74. Ibid., p. 55.

75. U.S. Bureau of Public Assistance, *Aid to Dependent Children in a Post-War Year, Characteristics of Families Receiving ADC, 1948,* Public Assistance Report No. 17, 1950, p. 6.

76. Piven and Cloward, *Regulating,* Source Table 4, n.p.

77. "Title VI of Civil Rights Act of 1964—Implementation and Impact," *George Washington University Law Review* 36 (May 1968): 971.

Throughout the South in the forties, only one school of social work was open to blacks, and that was the all-black Atlanta University. By the end of the decade, three schools of social work in state universities—Oklahoma, Kentucky, and Virginia—opened their doors to a few black students. In social work just as in medicine and nursing, those southern states that would not admit black students to their own programs made arrangements to pay for the education of black professionals outside the region. However, in social work the support was much more meager: by 1950 only 349 black southerners had been assisted in their pursuit of professional social work training, and the region had four times as many white as black social workers in proportion to their respective populations. North Carolina, Board of Public Welfare, *The Employment of Negroes in Public Welfare in Eleven Southern States, 1939–49,* by John R. Larkin, Information Bulletin No. 17, 1951, pp. 101–3.

78. Illinois, Interracial Commission, *Special Report on Employment Opportunity in Illinois,* 1948, p. 64.

79. Myrdal, *American Dilemma,* pp. 359–60.

80. Bell, *Aid to Dependent Children,* p. 42.

81. Piven and Cloward, *Regulating,* p. 134.

82. Ibid., pp. 212–13.

83. U.S. Bureau of the Census, *Statistical Abstract of the United States, 1973* (Washington, D.C.: Government Printing Office, 1973), Table 498, p. 308.

84. Ibid.

85. U.S. Bureau of Public Welfare, *Characteristics of Families Receiving Aid to Dependent Children, November 1953,* 1955, Table 8, p. 19; U.S. Welfare Administration, Bureau of Family Services, *Characteristics of Families Receiving Aid to Families with Dependent Children,* November–December 1961, Table 3, n.p.

86. U.S. Welfare Administration, Bureau of Family Services, *Study of Recipients of Aid to Families with Dependent Children, November–December 1961:* National Cross-Tabulations, 1965, Table 2, n.p.

87. Bell, *Aid to Dependent Children,* p. 68.

88. Ibid., pp. 87–92.

89. U.S. National Center for Social Statistics, *Findings of the 1969 AFDC Study: Data by Census Division and Selected States: Part 1, Demographic and Program Characteristics,* NCSS Report AFDC-3(69), 1970, Table 2, n.p.

90. U.S. National Center for Social Statistics, *Findings of the 1971 AFDC Study: Part 3, National Cross-Tabulations,* NCSS Report AFDC-3(71), 1973, Table 65.

91. Guichard Parris and Lester Brooks, *Blacks in the City: A History of the National Urban League* (Boston: Little, Brown and Co., 1971), pp. 375–6.

92. Keesing's Research Report, *Race Relations in the U.S.A., 1954–1968* (New York: Charles Scribner's Sons, 1970), p. 102.

93. The secretary of HEW ruled that states could no longer deny assistance to a child because a home was "unsuitable" while the child went on living in the home. Either alternative arrangements were to be made for the child, or the home made "suitable."

94. Lawrence N. Bailis, *Bread or Justice: Grassroots Organizing in the Welfare Rights Movement* (Lexington, Mass.: D.C. Heath and Co., Lexington Books, 1974), pp. 7–8.

95. Ibid., p. 11. See also Nick Kotz and Mary Lynn Kotz, *A Passion for Equality* (New York: W.W. Norton and Co., 1978).

96. 42 U.S.C. Sec. 602 (a) (8) (A) (1970).

97. 42 U.S.C. Sec. 602(a) (23) (1970).

98. P.L. 90–248 Sec. 203(b), 81 Stat. 883 (1967)

99. Federal funds for this purpose were first provided under the Economic Opportunity Act of 1964.

100. Public Assistance Statistics (June 1973), Table 7, n.p.

101. *Whitfield v. Oliver,* 399 F. Supp. 348, 352–3 (N.D. Ala., 1975).

102. Ibid., p. 353.

103. Ibid., p. 354.

104. Alvin L. Schorr and Carl Wagner, "Cash and Food Programs in Virginia," a study prepared by the Social Development Corporation for the U.S. Senate Select Committee on Nutrition and Human Needs, September 1969 (photocopied), pp. 21, 23.

105. Ibid., pp. 23, 49.

106. U.S. Commission on Civil Rights, *Children in Need: A Study of a Federally Assisted Program of Aid to Needy Families with Children in Cleveland and Cuyahoga County, Ohio,* Urban Studies Report: Cleveland No. 1, pp. 40–5, 48.

107. Robert E. Anderson, "Welfare in Mississippi: Tradition vs. Title VI," *New South* 22 (Spring 1967): 65–72.

108. "Title VI," p. 970.

109. Lester M. Salamon, "The Stakes in the Rural South: Family Assistance," *New Republic* 164 (20 February 1971): 17–8.

110. U.S. National Center for Social Statistics, *Findings of the 1967 AFDC Study: Data by State and Census: Pt. 1, Demographic and Program Characteristics,* NCSS Report AFDC–3(67), 1970, Table 2, n.p.; idem, 1969 AFDC Study, Table 2, n.p.; idem, *Findings of the 1971 AFDC Study; Part 1, Demographic and Program Characteristics,* NCSS Report AFDC–1(71), 1971, Table 2, n.p.; idem, *Findings of the 1973 AFDC Study: Pt. 1, Demographic and Program Characteristics* NCSS Report AFDC–1(73), 1974, Table 7, p. 22.

111. Restrictions were imposed to limit the ability of legal services lawyers to handle class-action suits and take action against government agencies on behalf of the poor.

Index

Page numbers in boldface type refer to tables or figures.

About the Authors

DOROTHY K. NEWMAN directed the research and writing of this book. She took a Ph.D. in sociology at Yale and has pursued a distinguished career in the U.S. Department of Labor, She also served as research director for the National Urban League Research Department and senior associate at the Washington Center for Metropolitan Studies. She is the author and co-author of numerous books, monographs, and reports; and her articles have appeared extensively in labor and economics journals. She is currently a lecturer and consultant in the areas of energy, housing, employment, and consumer affairs.

NANCY J. AMIDEI is deputy assistant secretary for legislation (welfare) in the U.S. Department of Health, Education and Welfare. She was educated at Loyola University and the University of Michigan, where she received her master's degree in social welfare policy and administration. In the past, she has served as professional staff member and acting staff director for the U.S. Senate Select Committee on Nutrition and Human Needs and has been a freelance consultant in the areas of health and welfare. She is the author of numerous articles on child health-care and nutrition and has traveled extensively throughout the world, studying the welfare systems and health programs of other countries.

BARBARA L. CARTER is associate provost for academic affairs at the University of the District of Columbia and holds an appointment as associate professor of sociology. She is an active member of the American Sociological Association and has done extensive reasearch on the experiences of women in prison. Her articles have appeared in *Society* and *The Annals,* and one,"Reform School Families," has been reprinted in two books: *The Nacirema* and *Sociological Realities II: A Guide to the Study of Society.* Ms. Carter received her doctorate in sociology from Brandeis University in 1972.

DAWN DAY is currently writing a book on racial discrimination in adoption agencies and is involved in a study of household energy consumption. She holds a doctorate degree in sociology from the University of Michigan. She has been a lecturer at the University of Maryland and served as associate professor of sociology at Brooklyn College. A contributor to various journals, among them *Social Work, Review of Radical Political Economics,* and *Contemporary Sociology,* Ms. Day is the author of *The Negro and Discrimination in Employment* and co-author (with Dorothy Newman) of *The American Energy Consumer.*

WILLIAM JAY KRUVANT holds a doctorate in economics from American University. He has lectured at American University and Trinity College, and worked as a research assistant for the Washington Center for Metropolitan Studies. A member of the American Economic Association and the American Sociological Association, Mr. Kruvant has contributed essays to two previous books, *The American Energy Consumer* and *Workers' Management and Workers' Wages in Yugoslavia.* He is currently employed by the U.S. General Accounting Office and engaged in work on the economics of energy.

JACK S. RUSSELL's field of expertise is employment. He is at present project manager for federal civil rights enforcement for the U.S. Commission on Civil Rights and is active in reviewing federal employment policies and legislation. Formerly he served as director of a federal employment training program and as a research associate at Associate Control Research and Analysis in Washington. His essay "Temporary Employment, Ideal Work Life" appeared in the book *The Work Place.* Mr. Russell holds a Ph.D. in public administration and urban studies from the Union Graduate School of Antioch College.